Organisation and Work Beyond 2000

Contributions to Management Science

H. Dyckhoff/U. Finke
Cutting and Packing in Production and Distribution
1992. ISBN 3-7908-0630-7

R. Flavell (Ed.)
Modelling Reality and Personal Modelling
1993. ISBN 3-7908-0682-X

M. Hofmann/M. List (Eds.)
Psychoanalysis and Management
1994. ISBN 3-7908-0795-8

R.L. D'Ecclesia/S.A. Zenios (Eds.)
Operations Research Models in Quantitative Finance
1994. ISBN 3-7908-0803-2

M.S. Catalani/G.F. Clerico
Decision Making Structures
1996. ISBN 3-7908-0895-4

M. Bertocchi/E. Cavalli/S. Komlósi (Eds.)
Modelling Techniques for Financial Markets and Bank Management
1996. ISBN 3-7908-0928-4

H. Herbst
Business Rule-Oriented Conceptual Modeling
1997. ISBN 3-7908-1004-5

C. Zopounidis (Ed.)
New Operational Approaches for Financial Modelling
1997. ISBN 3-7908-1043-6

K. Zwerina
Discrete Choice Experiments in Marketing
1997. ISBN 3-7908-1045-2

G. Marseguerra
Corporate Financial Decisions and Market Value
1998. ISBN 3-7908-1047-9

WHU Koblenz – Otto Beisheim Graduate School of Management (Ed.)
Structure and Dynamics of the German Mittelstand
1999. ISBN 3-7908-1165-3

A. Scholl
Balancing and Sequencing of Assembly Lines
1999. ISBN 3-7908-1180-7

E. Canestrelli (Ed.)
Current Topics in Quantitative Finance
1999. ISBN 3-7908-1231-5

W. Bühler/H. Hax/R. Schmidt (Eds.)
Empirical Research on the German Capital Market
1999. ISBN 3-7908-1193-9

M. Bonilla/T. Casasus/R. Sala (Eds.)
Financial Modelling
2000. ISBN 3-7908-2282-X

S. Sulzmaier
Consumer-Oriented Business Design
2001. ISBN 3-7908-1366-4

C. Zopounidis (Ed.)
New Trends in Banking Management
2002. ISBN 3-7908-1488-1

U. Dorndorf
Project Scheduling with Time Windows
2002. ISBN 3-7908-1516-0

Birger Rapp
Paul Jackson
Editors

Organisation and Work Beyond 2000

With 31 Figures
and 30 Tables

Physica-Verlag
A Springer-Verlag Company

Series Editors
Werner A. Müller
Martina Bihn

Editors

Professor Birger Rapp
Linköping University
Campus Valla
581 83 Linköping
Sweden
birger@rapp.se

Paul Jackson
Anvil Cottage
Pooles Lane
Charlbury
Oxfordshire, OX7 3RT
United Kingdom
paul.jackson@ipf.co.uk

ISSN 1431-1941
ISBN 3-7908-1528-4 Physica-Verlag Heidelberg New York

Bibliographic information published by Die Deutsche Bibliothek
Die Deutsche Bibliothek lists this publication in the Deutsche Nationalbibliografie; detailed bibliographic data is available in the Internet at <http://dnb.ddb.de>.

Physica-Verlag Heidelberg New York
a member of BertelsmannSpringer Science+Business Media GmbH

http://www.springer.de

Softcover design: Erich Kirchner, Heidelberg

SPIN 10890041 88/3130-5 4 3 2 1 0 – Printed on acid-free paper

Preface

The fifth International Telework Workshop was held in Stockholm in the fall of 2000. The conference was attended by almost 100 participants from all continents of the world. It therefore covered a broad range of subjects relating to Telework. Its success was in some part due to the work of the program committee composed of Birger Rapp (General Chairman), Maarten Botterman, Geoff Dick, Gil Gordon, Ursula Huws, Paul Jackson, Peter Johnston, Patricia L. Mokhtarian, Victor de Pous, Lars Qvotrup, Wendy Spinks and Reima Suomi.

After the conference we decided to write a book on the theme "Organization and the future after 2000". Many of the participants as well as others were invited to contribute a chapter of about ten pages. The resulting book of almost 400 pages therefore provides a comprehensive overview of ongoing research in the field of Telework. Birger Rapp and Paul Jackson edited the book.

The intended audience for this book spans disciplinary and professional boundaries. It primarily relates to the disciplines of Business and Management Studies, Information Management, E-commerce and E-business. In a broader sense, it relates to Sociology, Media Studies and Economics.

If you would like to get in touch with us about any of the ideas in this book, please contact birger@rapp.se or paul@pauljackson.org

Paul Jackson, Uxbridge, UK October 2002

Birger Rapp, Linköping, Sweden

Acknowledgements

In putting this book together, we are deeply grateful to a number of people and organizations. "The Swedish Council for Work Life Research" (RALF), "The Swedish Transport and Communications Research Board" (KFB) and the "Swedish Business Development Agency" (NUTEK) all generously supported the workshop and the compilation of this book. These organizations have now merged to form a new organization "The Swedish Agency for Innovation Systems" (VINNOVA). Furthermore we should like to thank the program committee for their work on the workshop and John Nolan and Peter Johnston of the European Commission DGXIII who gave it exposure and credibility.

We should also like to thank Werner A. Mueller at Springer-Verlag GmbH & Co. KG for publishing this book. Finally, we should like to thank Åsa Ericson at Economic Information Systems for her impressive work in preparing this book for publication.

Contents

Introduction

Paul Jackson and Birger Rapp

The crossing of thresholds is often laden with symbolism and portent. When Julius Caesar led his army across the Rubicon in 49 BC, the act marked a declaration of war – a military breach of a recognised territorial border. More than two millennia later, the event is preserved for posterity as a figure of speech. The 1st of January 2000, of course, represented a more recent (and peaceful) traversal, as well as an item of discursive rumination.

And as organisations arrived in the year 2000, there was also a battle to be joined – the post-industrial struggle in which the rules of engagement had been fashioned, at least in part, by advanced information and communications technologies (ICTs). Of course, this 'battle' had been raging for some time, but the year 2000 seemed more clearly than ever to demark the new world from the terrain of earlier industrial landscapes.

We now therefore find ourselves in a world of 'givens'. We are in a new millennium. The Y2K bug (in as much as the little critter existed at all) has bitten (or pinched) and gone. eCommerce, despite the over-hyping of the Dot.Coms, has a firm foothold in both business and consumer markets.

Accepting these givens, this book looks ahead at how our organisations and methods of work are shaping up for the years beyond 2000. It looks at the issues and challenges that lie in store – both practically and intellectually – and draws upon ideas and experiences from across the world to inform us of how we can best move on.

The book is split in to two main parts, each with a number of sections. The first part, *Organisation: Design and Strategy*, looks at the new organising context for work. In the opening section, *Factors Mediating the Use of ICTs,* the 5 chapters focus on variables that influence the design and take up of work innovations involving the new technologies. Particular attention is given to the social, cultural and psychological processes that mediate the use of new methods of work and which, in turn, shape the outcomes of ICT change projects.

The second section of Part One, *Design Issues in Virtual Working,* points to the need for rigorous analyses of change contexts when introducing new methods of work. Several of the 5 chapters respond to the call for more intellectually robust models with which to understand and cope with emerging ('virtual') organisational forms. They also highlight the requirement for new implementation methodologies, more suited to the demands of contemporary change.

Part Two of the book, *Work: Processes and Cases*, looks at some of the outcomes of recent work innovations, and the issues they raise for individuals, organisations and society as a whole. In the first section here, *Work, Flexibility and Life-Style Choices*, 4 chapters draw out some of the complexities underlying contemporary developments in work. They explore the attributes exhibited by different types of flexible working, and look at the intricate interrelationships between modes of working (such as mobile working and home-working), as well as between work and life in general. The following section, *Communication Dynamics and Consequences,* looks in particular at the consequences such developments have for communications and social interaction. In addition, the 5 chapters go into detail on the issues these arrangements create for individuals' careers, and the means by which their work is monitored and controlled.

The final section in Part Two provides further perspectives on telework developments around the world. 8 chapters are presented, which draw out the variety of initiatives, experiences and issues raised by new work initiatives. In drawing the book to a close, the chapters reminding us that while many developments, and the issues they raise, are often similar the world over; cultural, institutional and economic differences (among others) also produce a range of outcomes, despite use of the same technologies and work concepts.

If a battle is to be joined, to continue the earlier metaphor, it requires action on many fronts. It demands that managers and change agents are conversant with the new technologies and the opportunities they provide for rethinking organisational strategy and structure, as well as the design of work. But there is also the implementation front, which requires an awareness of how new ways of working can be rolled out in a sustainable and effective way. This demands not only an appreciation of factors that shape the application of new technologies and work concepts (factors that will vary between organisational and national contexts), but also an awareness of methods and tools that can be applied to realign people and processes consistent with the new ideas.

Underpinning this is an intellectual front: an engagement with theories that help us to understand and analyse the new organisational structures and work configurations. Organisations and managers that are not in the vanguard of both theory and practice may find the years beyond 2000 strewn with more threats than opportunities. A start on all these fronts can be made with the chapters that follow.

Part one

Organisation:

Design and Strategy

Factors Mediating the Use of ICTs

The opening section of the book concerns those factors that influence the design and take up of work innovations involving information and communications technologies (ICTs). Of particular interest are the social, cultural and psychological processes that mediate the adoption of new methods of work and which have a crucial bearing on the outcomes of ICT initiatives – particularly in terms of their business success and user acceptance. The chapters that follow show that because of often deep-seated differences between countries and enterprises, careful attention to both national and organisational contexts is essential if changes are to be effectively introduced.

We begin with a chapter by Akio Kunii, which examines the relationship between organisational culture and the introduction of ICTs. Drawing on Japanese data, Kunii points out the mutual shaping of organisational culture and technology-related change. Not only does the application of ICTs have consequences for culture, the cultural context within which it is introduced will itself influence potential outcomes. As such, Kunii suggests, different cultural settings will lead to different outcomes, even where similar technologies and change concepts are introduced.

Alf Westelius and Linda Askenäs in Chapter 2 examine the different roles that ICTs can and should play in regional development. In a similar way to Kunii, they point out that this is far from a matter that can simply be determined by the technology; rather, it relies on the actions of a range of actors, who can influence the diffusion and use of ICTs. Indeed, they note that there are five different roles the application of ICTs may take: as a 'bureaucrat', 'manipulator', 'consultant', 'administrative assistant' or as the 'dismissed'. By ensuring that ICTs adopts an appropriate role, say Westelius and Askenäs, the technologies can be most effectively applied to regional issues.

Despite many calls over the years for greater attention to social and psychological factors when designing and implementing technology related change, there is still a lamentable lack of awareness of the issues involved. This theme is picked up in Chapter 3 by Pekka Huuhtanen, which focuses on the psychosocial aspects of telework introduction. The chapter draws particular attention to issues of health and safety, and reminds us how our understanding of flexible working must go hand-in-hand with an appreciation of the human side of developments in employment practices.

For Shiri Ahuja in Chapter 4, the focus of attention is the redesign of work processes to take advantage of ICTs. The more routine processes in organisations, she notes, might be conceived of in terms of assembly-line working – where efficiency is the key to work design. However, such approaches tend to downplay the social needs that people bring to work. For Ahuja then, the redesign of work requires a systematic attempt to integrate new technologies not only with business strategies but also with the social and cultural structures of organisations. Drawing from experiences of Indian businesses, the chapter illustrates a phased process whereby these different elements can be understood and jointly optimised.

Finally in this section, Chiyoko Shimozaki examines the relationship between teleworking and Japanese Human Resources Management (HRM) systems. The traditional collectivist approach to HRM, says Shimozaki, while deeply embedded within Japanese culture, presents a number of barriers to the adoption of teleworking. More recent developments, which have led to greater 'individualisation' in the management of human resources, opens up new possibilities for developments such as telework. The chapter reminds us once again that only by attention to cultural structures and management systems can the ground be laid for the introduction of new technologies, particularly those that come with radical ideas about the redesign of work.

1 Corporate Culture and the Introduction of Information Technology

Akio Kunii

Institute for International Policy Studies, Japan

Introduction

It has been twenty years since Alvin Toffler wrote *The Third Wave*, predicting the advent of an 'information age' which we are now witnessing. Society has finally come to accept the transformations wrought by innovations in information technology (IT); this has even been dubbed the 'Third Revolution,' following the agricultural and industrial revolutions.

The proliferation of IT will be more than just a phenomenon that is reflected in changes to current business practices – such as transactions via e-commerce or change in employment structures due to telecommuting – and added convenience in the home. The proliferation of IT is thought to have the potential to reform established educational, financial and political systems as well as current administrative and security structures. It is perceived as a technology which has the potential to overhaul the very foundations of the current social system.

Society has become engrossed with claims that the IT revolution will initiate organisational change, through notions such as non-hierarchical organisational structures via the introduction of e-mail, and the expansion of telework via the introduction of video teleconference systems. On the other hand, there are cases where the introduction of e-mail, for example, has resulted in inefficiency and faced resistance from middle management. Even within corporations where telecommuting systems have been implemented, it is difficult to claim that there is a significant correlation between the adoption of a high quality communications system and the success rate of telecommuting.

Organisations and information-processing

The purpose of an organisation can be considered from both a quantitative and qualitative perspective. Galbraith's (1973) quantitative view considers an organisation to be an information-processing network. Weick (1979), on the other hand, had a qualitative and more definition-oriented perspective, claiming that the objective of an organisation is to eliminate equivocality. Depending on which of these definitions is used, the quality of information sought by a corporation will vary. Information with low uncertainty is dealing with a relatively well defined issue, the solution of which lies in data collection (this is the basic information gathering). On the other hand, when dealing with information which is ambiguous and that can have several different interpretations – that is information with a high level of equivocality – it is difficult to reach a clear definition of the issue. In the latter high equivocality scenario, information gathering would be through the exchange of views to identify and elucidate any ambiguities and to clarify the issue through consensus. (Wakabayashi (1994))

In order to minimise uncertainty or to reduce equivocality, an organisation will try to change its current structure to one where the issues are well understood, extensive discussion is not required and information gathering is a matter of routine data gathering. In a situation where uncertainty is reduced, an organisation needs to implement a consolidated system in order to reduce equivocality. Thus, the scramble between organisations to promote the use of office automation (OA) systems when computers first appeared on the market, can be interpreted as their attempt to reduce both uncertainty and equivocality, hence becoming more reliable.

The traditional OA system, however, did not have functions that minimised equivocality. Daft *et al* (1986) referred to the functional characteristics that minimise equivocality as *media rich*, as having the following key components:

1. The ability for instant feedback;
2. The capacity of the media to transmit multiple cues such as body language;
3. The use of natural language rather than numbers to convey subtleties; and
4. The personal focus of the media.

If these characteristics were to be applied to a communications media, they would be implemented as a two-way telecommunication media with the capacity to exchange multiple information. A communications media with this kind of capability is similar to a multi-media service. For instance, video teleconference systems and videophones are media-rich. Even a basic e-mail system has a certain amount of media-richness. If this is the case, the introduction of IT within an organisation is no more than an attempt by the company to minimise its equivocality; and can be considered to be closely linked to the 'meaning' of an organisation as an information-processing network. The need to analyse the relationship between the definition of an organisation (or what is should be) and the introduction of IT in that organisation can now be realised.

Methodology

The reasons underlying an organisation's decision to introduce IT and the corporate culture of that organisation, and the correlation with the impact of IT were analysed using a survey conducted with some of Japan's major corporations.

The following hypotheses were assumed:

H1: The purpose of IT implementation will depend on the corporate culture of the subject organisation.

H2: The purpose for which IT will be used will determine the IT functions selected by an organisation.

H3: The effectiveness of an organisation's IT implementation depends on the IT functions that are chosen.

H4: The impact brought on by the introduction of IT will have an influence on the corporate culture.

H5: Factors which expedite or hinder the introduction of IT are specified by the corporate culture.

The data analysed for this report was obtained from two surveys issued to major corporations in Japan. The research outline was as follows:

- Survey 1

  Date: February 1996

  Method: questionnaires mailed to targeted corporations

  Corporations: 1200 randomly selected major companies

  Participants: staff from the Corporate Planning or Information Planning Divisions of the targeted corporations

  Results: valid responses from 384 corporations (32 % response rate)

- Survey 2

  Date: September 1999

  Method, Corporations and Participants: same as Survey 1

  Results: valid responses from 238 corporations (20 % response rate)

Introduction of IT

Corporate culture of Japanese corporations

The data collected in Survey 1 in 1996 – when the majority of corporations surveyed had not fully introduced IT – revealed that the major Japanese corporations had distinctive corporate cultures. The survey included 38 questions about an organisation's structure. Each question had a five-point scale and the answers were based on the participant's assessment of their company.

Responses to questions such as 'expedited knowledge of sales and net cost information is needed' (76.8 %), and 'rapid changes are seen in industry/market environment' (64.8 %) scored high marks. The low responses to questions such as 'organisation often hires new employees throughout the year' (9.6 %), 'wide differences in performance-based pay' (16.1 %) and 'customer and market information shared throughout the organisation' (18 %) reflected the lack of progress in restructuring tasks in 1996.

An analysis of each of the 38 organisational characteristics was conducted, extracting 10 significant factors ((1)Corporate Effort, (2)Collaboration, (3)Performance, (4)Conservativeness, (5)Management Speed, (6)Differentiation, (7)Top-Down Management, (8)Third-Party Focus, (9)Market-Oriented and (10)Unconventional). The selection criteria was based on the formula: eigen value > = 1. Each corporation can be defined using these 10 factors derived through this analysis.

Purpose of IT introduction

Similarly, on the basis of the data obtained from Survey 1 (1996), 18 questions regarding the purposes for which IT will be used were developed with scores based on a four-point scale.

The high response to questions such as 'accumulated/shared information' (87 %) and 'increased job processing speed/efficiency' (81.3 %) show that many corporations aimed to increase efficiency within existing tasks. Further, the lower score of responses to questions on the 'expansion of sales and operational profit' (37.2 %) and 'new operation/market entry' (36.7 %), for example, show that direct operational benefits were not expected from the introduction of IT in 1996. Thus, 4 significant factors ((1)Customer Service, (2)Shared Information/ Information Exchange, (3)Operational Results and (4)Task Efficiency) describing the objectives of IT introduction were extracted on the basis of the same selection criteria: eigen value > = 1.

Relationship between corporate culture and objectives of IT implementation

The analysis of the correlation between the 10 factors describing corporate culture and the 4 factors describing the objectives of IT implementation based on hypothesis H1, show that an organisation which makes a conscious effort is likely to introduce IT in order to provide better customer service, and an organisation that appreciates performance is likely to introduce IT in order to improve their efficiency and operational results.

Relationship between objectives of IT implementation and selected IT functions

Five significant criteria ((1)Data Collection, (2)Communications, (3)Data Supply, (4)Visual and (5)Mobility) for IT use were identified (eigen value>=1) based on an analysis of the data obtained from Survey 1 (1996). The correlation between the four main reasons for IT usage and the five IT functions that were selected based on the H2 hypothesis can be identified through the following observations:

1. A corporation aiming for better customer service is likely to introduce data collection, data supply and mobility IT functions;
2. A corporation with the objective of better sharing and exchange of information is likely to introduce a communications function; and
3. A corporation aiming for better operational results is likely to introduce data supply and visual IT functions.

Impact of introducing IT

The impact of introducing IT (as understood by subject corporations at the time of Survey 1 in 1996) was analysed. Analysis was drawn from the answers to 21 questions regarding the introduction of IT.

The views on changes in communications on questions such as ‘increased speed of internal communications’ (34.1 %) and ‘changes in internal communications flow’ (31 %) were high overall. Changes in the actual form of tasks and organisational structures, however, were insignificant in 1996. This is reflected in the low score of responses to ‘decreased number of meetings’ (2.3 %) and ‘decreased number of middle management’ (3.6 %), for example.

Relationship between the selected IT functions and the impact of introducing IT

The correlation between the five selected IT functions and the effect of IT Introduction on the basis of the H3 hypothesis are shown as follows:

Corporations that had introduced data collection functions improved their data collection and expedited the decision-making process. Corporations that had introduced communications functions noticed changes to the flow of internal communication, in particular quicker communication, as well as both quantitative and qualitative improvements in internal communications. In many cases, for organisations which had selected data supply and visual functions the introduction of IT had been effective, but the effectiveness on those corporations that had selected mobility functions could not be discerned.

Cause and effect of introducing IT

The correlation between each factor derived from Survey 1 in 1996 was analysed and is mentioned below. The subject factors were the culture of an organisation, the objective of IT implementation, selected IT functions and the impact of IT introduction. The cause and effect and the interplay between the various factors were analysed and can be seen in Figure 1.

The experiences of introducing IT by the respective business sectors (plotted in Figure 1) were analysed and the following three common patterns of IT introduction were identified:

1. When an organisation which places great importance on effort implements IT data collection, IT data supply and IT mobility functions in order to improve its customer service, increased capability in data collection, quantitative and qualitative improvement in the flow of internal communications and increased customer satisfaction could be observed.
2. When a organisation which emphases co-operation implements IT with communications functions in order to create an environment for sharing and exchanging of information, changes in the flow of internal communications, in particular, quicker communications and an improvement in the quantitative and qualitative nature of internal communications could be observed.
3. When an organisation which values results and management effectiveness implements IT data supply and visual IT functions in order to improve operational results, increased sales and operational profits, changes in management philosophy and a quantitative and qualitative improvement in internal communications could be observed.

Based on the findings of Survey 1, one aspect of the cause and effect of a corporation's IT introduction process could be clarified. The impact of introducing IT on a corporation, however, especially on its corporate culture, could not be fully determined. This can be attributed to the fact that in 1996 (when the process of introducing IT was not yet fully developed and the characteristics of IT introduction were undefined), it was difficult to identify clearly what effect introducing IT would have. Another dilemma was differentiating between the corporate culture before and after the introduction of IT. To try and determine so many factors on the basis of just one survey was insufficient and thus inconclusive.

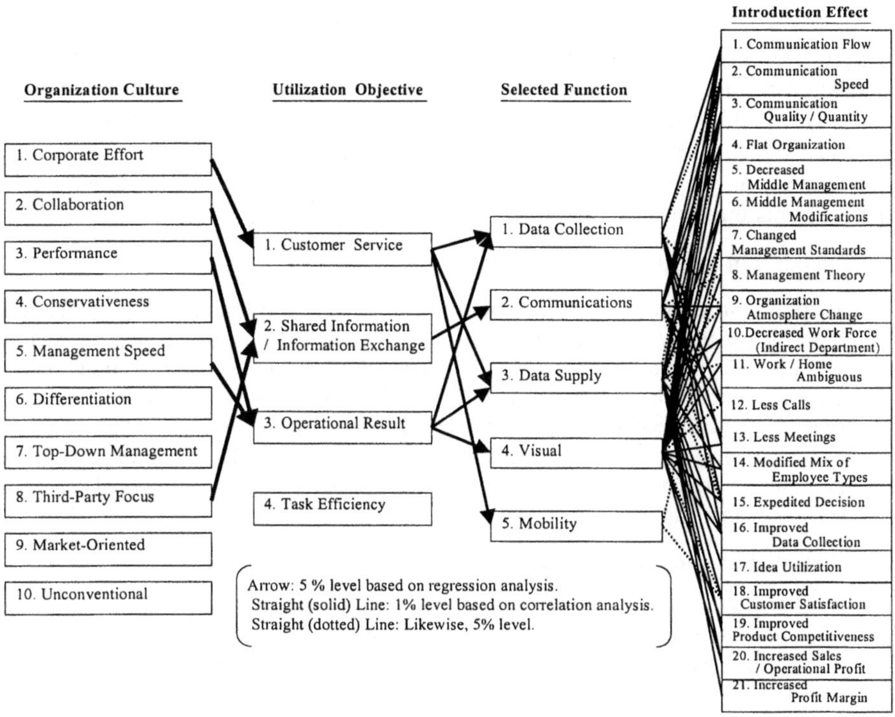

Figure 1. Correlation Between Various IT Introduction Elements and Their "Cause and Effect" Structure

Impact of introducing IT

Using the data obtained through Survey 2 (conducted in 1999); an attempt to clarify the impact of the introduction of IT on the corporate culture of an organisation will be made. The focus is on the differences in the corporate culture of Japanese corporations between 1996 and 1999 and discuss these trends and their correlation with the introduction of IT. A comparative analysis of the other factors will not be discussed.

Changes in traditional Japanese management

Factors such as promotion by seniority, lifetime employment, a system of uniform pay (as opposed to performance-based pay), *nemawashi* (typical of Japanese management, in which pre-briefing sessions are used to build consensus, making executive level meetings virtually redundant) and hierarchical division of labour are often identified as the characteristics of traditional Japanese management. Comparing Survey 1 and Survey 2, it is notable that the following changes took place in this three-year period:

1. Changes in traditional Japanese-style management.

   There was a reduction in the number of corporations with traditional rigid Japanese-style management. This can be seen by the differing responses to queries such as 'promotion by seniority is the norm' (1996=60.3 %: 1999=45.1 %) and 'tradition and precedent important ' (1996=39.1 %: 1999=32.9 %). In contrast, responses to queries such as 'large differential in performance-based pay' (1996=16.4 %: 1999= 26.7 %) and 'top management is innovative; not conservative' (1996=38.1 % : 1999= 51.5 %),' indicate the growing number of corporations moving away from traditional Japanese-style corporate culture.

2. Removal of internal barriers

   In the past, Japanese corporations were notorious for their lack of internal communication and for being very hierarchical organisations. The change in responses to questions such as 'active communications' (1996=19.6 % :1999= 28.8 %) and 'frequent inter-departmental collaborations' (1996=21.9 %: 1999= 34.3 %) were revealing. An increasing number of organisations have clearly incorporated non-traditional characteristics and are striving for a pro-active collaboration.

Although the change in Japan's traditional management style in a mere three years, from 1996 to 1999, is obvious, the cause of these changes may have been as a result of the recession in Japan during these years. Nor should the influence of globalisation be overlooked. Thus, it is difficult to assert that these changes were brought about solely through the introduction of IT.

Status of IT introduction in Japan

In this section, the scope that the impact of introducing IT has (or does not have) is examined, through verification of the H4 hypothesis. The analysis will be based primarily on data obtained from Survey 2.

In Survey 2, the status of corporate IT introduction were divided into the following eight categories:

(a) WebPages access via Internet browsers such as Netscape Navigator and Internet Explorer;

(b) E-mail communications via the Internet and inter-PC communications;

(c) Web page launch/introduction via Internet server (server either owned or rented);

(d) Usage of internal database, message board, e-mail communications via GroupWare (for example, Lotus Notes);

(e) Business database such as 'Nikkei News Telecom;'

(f) Video teleconferencing equipment installed in a conference room;

(g) Desktop PC video teleconferencing;

(h) Mobile devices such as laptop, personal digital assistant (PDA) and i-Mode mobile phones.

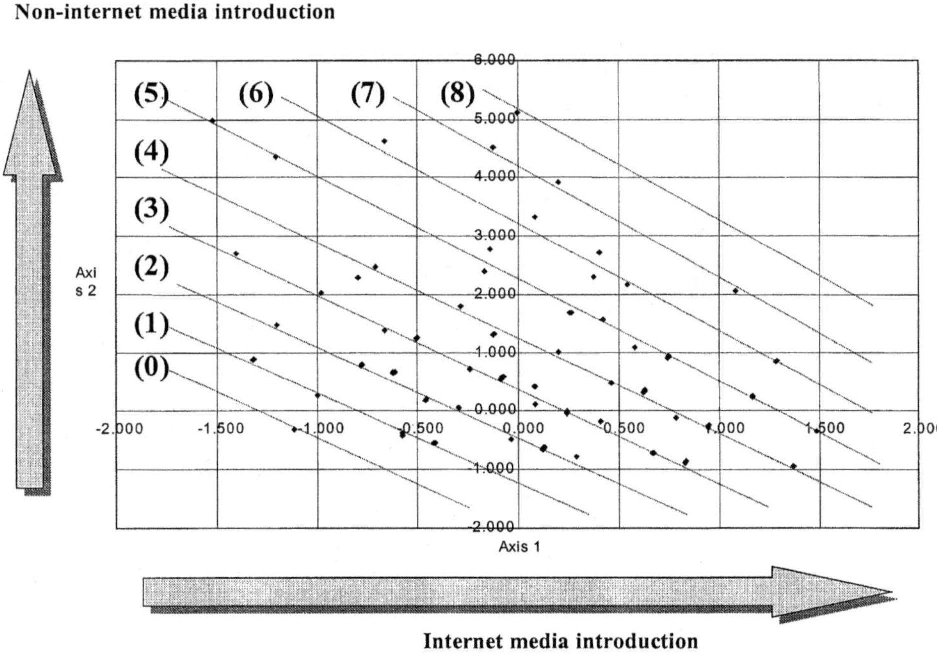

Figure 2. Plot Chart of Corporate IT Introduction Status and Defining its Meaning

IT such as WebPages (77.7 %), GroupWare (76 %), E-Mails (71 %) and the Internet browser (62.9 %) depict the expansive and rapid introduction between 1996 and 1997 in the corporations.

The status of each corporation's IT introduction can be seen in figure 2 (quantification type III has been used to plot these statistics on a two-dimensional chart). In this plot chart, the horizontal axis represents the status of Internet media introduction and the vertical axis represents the status of Non-Internet media introduction.

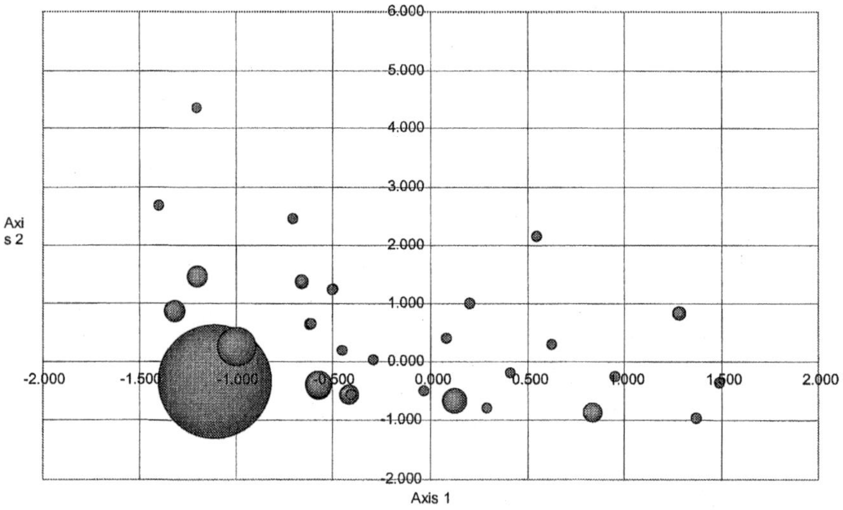

Figure 3. Satus of Corporate IT Introduction (1995)

The more a corporation introduces Internet media (browsers, e-mail), the further it is plotted to the right (in the direction of the horizontal axis). Similarly, the more a corporation introduces Non-Internet media (video teleconference systems), the further it is plotted toward the top (in the direction of the vertical axis). It can also be seen that corporations which have a similar proportion of Internet and non-Internet introduced media (IT) are plotted virtually on the same line. Obviously, the larger the number of introduced media; the further toward the top-right section of the chart the corporations will be plotted.

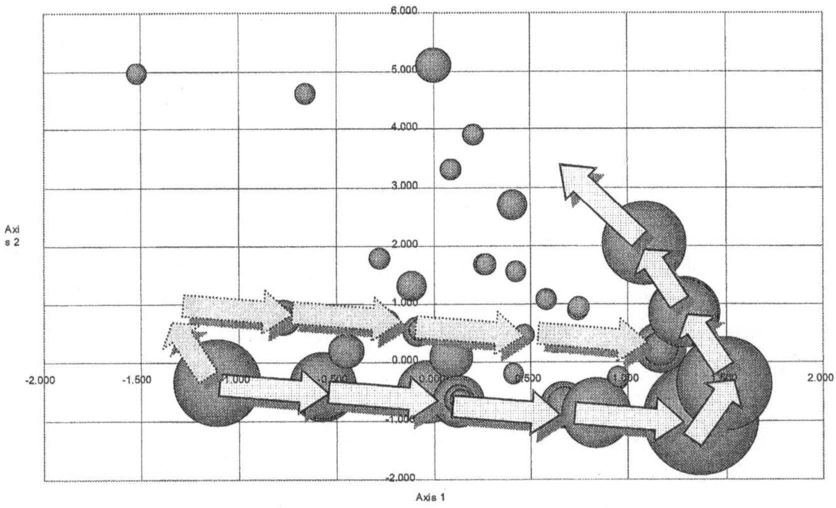

Figure 4. Status of Cortorative IT Introduction (1999) and Primary IT Introduction Pattern

On the basis of Figure 2, the status of IT introduction in 1995 (Figure 3) and 1999 (Figure 4) has been plotted. From these figures, it is notable that the majority of the corporations surveyed had not yet introduced any IT in 1995, and by 1999, the majority of corporations had introduced a number of Its -- primarily the Internet media. Figure 4 shows that the common pattern in the introduction of IT has been to introduce the Internet media first then to introduce non-Internet media at a later date, although there have been some reversals of this pattern.

Correlation between IT introduction and changes in corporate culture

In order to analyse the status of IT introduction and, especially, its impact on corporate culture, corporations will be classified in terms of their progress in introducing IT. By performing a cluster analysis based on the status of IT introduction in 1997 – the half way point in the survey period between the two dates – the corporations could be classified into three groups:

Group A: Corporations making progress in IT via Internet media (55 %)

Group B: Corporations not making significant progress in IT (15 %)

Group C: Corporations with absolutely no progress in IT (19 %)

A cross-analysis of the above corporate classifications with the corporate culture in Survey 2 (1999) showed that there was a strong correlation between the two, especially with the staff behaviour.

Group A corporations tended to have an open environment, where, for example, the ideas of younger employees were valued, specialists highly evaluated, with many distinctive employees and lead management executives were innovative and not conservative.

A factor analysis of corporations that responded to both the 1996 and 1999 surveys was also conducted, in order to ascertain the changes in corporate culture. While 10 factors of corporate culture were extracted in the 1996 survey (eigen value > = 1), 11 factors were extracted from this analysis under the same conditions (eigen value > = 1). When looking only at Factors 1 and 2, the following corporate cultures are not mutually exclusive:

Judging by these contributory characteristics, Factor 1 combines corporate effort and co-operation seen in the 1996 Survey and Factor 2 represents a conservative scenario.

Figure 5 shows the results of the survey with respect to these two factors, and the relationship of these two factors with the classification based on the status of IT introduction in 1997 (Group A and Non-Group A).

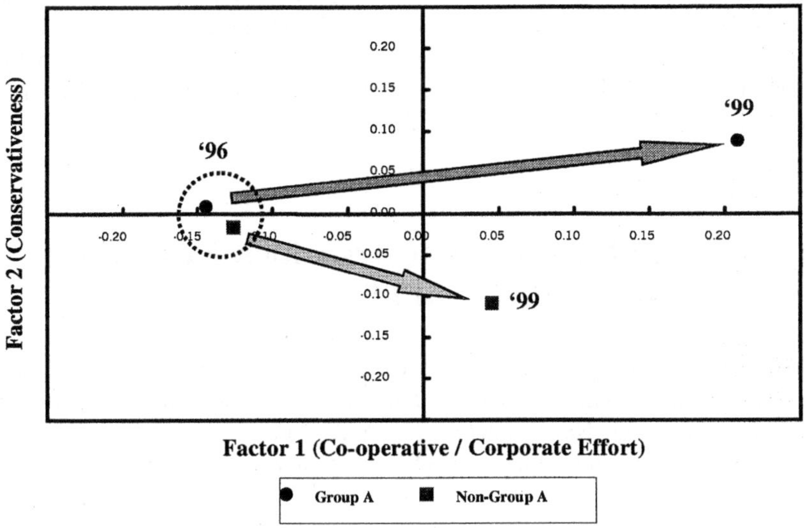

Figure 5. Relations Between Corporate Class Based on Status of IT Introduction and Changes in Corporate Culture

In 1996, the factor loading of Group A corporations that had made progress in IT were -0.14/0.01, respectively, and the scores for Non-Group A corporations which were not making progress in IT was -0.13/-0.02; reflecting virtually the same corporate culture. When the difference in the status of IT introduction became apparent in 1999, however, the scores were 0.21/0.09 and 0.04/-0.11, respectively, with a significant increase in Factor 1 of Group A corporations (corporate effort/co-operation).

In other words, these results suggest that the more a corporation makes progress in the introduction of IT, the more likely it is to gain a corporate culture with corporate reform and co-operation. It should be kept in mind, however, that the introduction of IT per se will not bring about corporate reform: as can be seen by the slight increase in conservativeness in the corporations in Group A by 1999.

These findings support hypotheses H1 (that the purpose of IT implementation is specified on the basis of the distinctive corporate culture within the subject organisation) and H2 (that the purpose of IT implementation specifies the IT functions selected for introduction by an organisation).

Similarly, a certain level of correlation can be seen in both hypotheses H3 (that the impact experienced by an organisation depends on the type of IT function the organisation chooses to introduce) and H4 (that the impact brought on by the introduction of IT will influence the corporate culture) -- although the insufficient statistics made a definite conclusion difficult.

Corporate Culture and Factors which Expedite or Hinder the Introduction of IT

Corporations generally modify their own corporate cultures by introducing necessary IT, albeit with the most suitable objectives for their corporate cultures always kept in mind. Nevertheless, an examination of the factors that actually expedite or hinder the introduction of IT is necessary.

Expediting factors in introducing IT

Fourteen questions regarding expediting factors in introducing IT (based on a four-point scale) were presented to survey participants.

Many corporations noted human resource qualities such as strong leadership at the top (87.8 %), employee IT awareness and training (83.1 %) as factors which contribute to expedite the introduction of IT. Progressive employment conditions however, for example, flexible employment conditions (17.2 %), were not recognised as an expediting factor by corporations in 1996. According to the analysis of the correlation between the 10 factors of corporate culture and expediting factors in introducing IT, the following are interrelated expediting factors: advanced-user leadership, OA leader training and performance in corporations with high corporate effort; a computer per employee and mandatory use of IT in corporations with high co-operation; and top leadership and reassessment of management and task process in corporations with quick decision-making management.

Hindrances to introducing IT

Survey participants were asked 14 questions about factors which may hinder the introduction of IT (based on a four-point scale). While the cost of introduction (58.9 %) and the cost of communications (58.1 %) were the most frequently identified hindrances, employee computer literacy (55.2 %) was also identified as a drawback. According to the analysis of the correlation between the 10 factors in corporate culture and the inhibiting factors in introducing IT, two distinct differences were observed: a lack of shared information and incompatibility with current communications style were identified as factors hindering the introduction of IT in very conservative corporations; while a lack of shared information was actually seen to be counterproductive in corporations which have a good record of co-operation.

Relationship between organisation culture and expediting/hindering factors in introducing IT

Based on these findings, a clear relationship between the expediting or hindering factors of introducing IT and the corporate culture of a corporation was identified.

The following correlation were identified:

- In corporations with a positive and proactive culture, such as those which valued corporate effort, communications and quick decisive management, the introduction of IT was promoted by the top management or through employee leadership, and in some cases, this was accompanied by a change in the way the job was structured. In the corporations surveyed, no drastic inhibiting factors were observed.
- In corporations with a conservative corporate culture, the incompatibility of concepts such as the mutual exchange of information and communications via IT with the traditional corporate customs and environment are an inhibiting factor to the introduction of IT. Definitive expediting factors, however, could not be found in the subject corporations.

Thus, hypothesis H5 (that the expediting and inhibiting factors of introducing IT are specified by the corporate culture) has been, to some extent, validated.

Classification of Japanese Corporations Based on the Way they Introduce I.T.

The major Japanese corporations have been classified into the following four categories depending on the way they introduce IT.

1. Advanced Corporation – corporations which have not only introduced e-mail systems, but are also actively introducing various other IT capabilities, acquiring quick decisive management and has a good track record with proven results.
2. Intermediate Corporation I – corporations which are moving toward introducing Internet WWW servers, browsers and business PC communications. These corporations tend to have a high level of corporate effort.

3. Intermediate Corporation II – corporations working primarily toward introducing internal e-mail systems. These corporations tend to display a high level of collaboration.
4. Stagnant Corporation – conservative corporations that do not even have e-mail capabilities, or are incapable of utilising such capabilities effectively.

Unique corporate culture – 'Top-Down Management'

It should be noted that both the Advanced and Stagnant Corporations – which are at two opposing environmental extremes – displayed hierarchical (top-down) management tendencies.

As top leadership and task reform are considered to be significant expediting factors in the introduction of IT, an innovative organisation's re-structuring process (via the introduction of IT) was probably implemented because of orders from the top. In contrast, a corporation with a conservative corporate culture can be expected to be a traditional organisation revolving around the top management but with an environment which lacks the sharing of information and media which is out-of-date and incompatible with current communications practices.

This is representative of communications often seen in bureaucratic corporations (as defined by Weber (1947)) which have, for example, job descriptions that are excessively-detailed and divided with a hierarchical system. This is the reason behind the invariably unsuccessful attempts to introduce IT to governmental organisations. In short, examples of both 'good top-down' and 'bad top-down' management styles are factors which influence the introduction of IT.

IT and organisations as information-processing systems

As mentioned above, organisations are can be considered to be information-processing systems in their own right. There are both quantitative (reduction of uncertainty) and qualitative (reduction in equivocality factors) aspects to an organisation's information-processing activities. The four types of corporate classification derived from the analysis of the IT introduction processes can be plotted (as seen in figure 6).

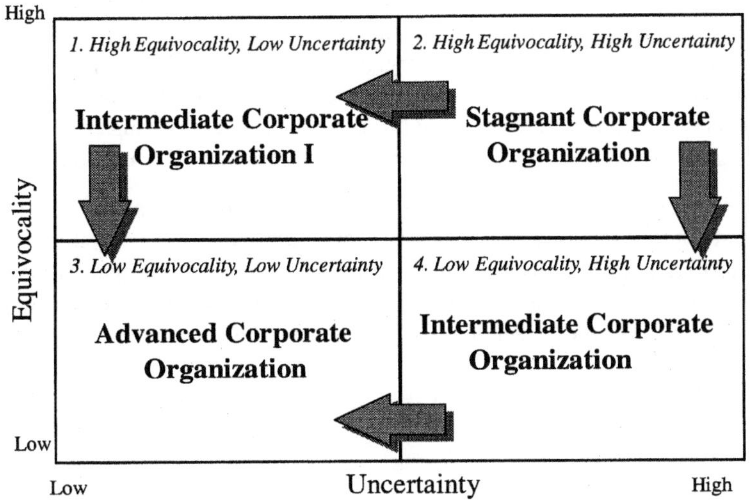

Figure 6. Organisational Information Processing Activity and Classification of IT-Introduced Corporations

In order to reach the status of an Advanced Corporation (plotted in quadrant III of Figure 6) surpassing the Stagnant Corporation (quadrant I), the Intermediate Corporation I (quadrant II) and the Intermediate Corporation II (quadrant IV) stages, an organisation needs to break away from very conservative corporate cultures with management by 'top-down' communications. There is a real need for these corporations to create an environment of information sharing. If this is not done, it will be virtually impossible for them to achieve significant results – much less organisational and corporate reforms – even if e-mail systems and the Internet are introduced.

Conclusions

In this chapter the validity of the claim that the IT Revolution will initiate organisational change has been examined. The potential impact (and the degree of that impact) that the IT Revolution might have on the organisational structure (as well as the possibility of no impact) through a sample of the major Japanese corporations was discussed.

This chapter also demonstrated, through the analysis of a series of case studies, that the corporate culture of an organisation is not only a determining factor in the introduction of IT but is also determined by the introduction of IT. Furthermore, the corporate culture, together with its distinctive expediting/hindering factors, has a significant impact on the corporate structure when IT is introduced.

The myth of the IT revolution – the belief that IT proliferation *per se* will immediately change the existing corporate and social systems – cannot be determined conclusively. What can be said, however, is that those organisations and societies with the potential for change are more likely to introduce IT with a tendency to be more receptive to the impact of the new technology.

References

Daft, R. L. and Lengel, R. H. (1986) 'Organisational Information Requirements, Media Richness and Structural Design', *Management Science*, 32, 5.

Galbraith, J. K. (1973) *Designing Complex Organisations*, Reading, Mass.,: Addison-Wesley.

Wakabayashi, N. (1994) 'The Role of Mediated Communication in the Change of Organisation Recognition', *Socio-Information and Information Environment*, Tokyo: University of Tokyo Press.

Weber, M. (1947) 'The types of authority and imperative coordination', trans. A.M. Henderson and Talcott Parsons in *The Theory of Social Economic Organisation*, New York: Free Press.

Weick, K. E. (1979) The Social Psychology of Organizing, Reading, Mass.,: Addison-Wesley.

2 Five Roles Of IT: Implications for Regional Development

Alf Westelius and Linda Askenäs

Linköping University, Sweden

Introduction

Ten years ago, technology (including IT) was viewed with suspicion by many in Sweden. Today the general sentiment is one of a strong belief in the power inherent in IT – IT will transform society and be a prerequisite for economic survival of enterprises and individuals. Less then a year ago, small IT companies were expected to expand and stand for the largest growth. Almi Företagspartner, a state-owned organisation that supports new business ventures, found that: "It is still only the IT companies which interest the venture capitalists" (Kuylenstierna, 2000).

But IT is not only for IT companies. Despite the recent downturn for IT-companies, there is still a belief that all companies need to invest in IT and be well versed in its use. In one newspaper they say that only 30% of the small and medium-sized enterprises (SMEs) are to be looked at as computerised and they conclude that: "The IT-train drives at high speed. It's important for the SMEs to catch up with it." (Arbetet, 2000). Another statement of similar nature is: "It's clear that those SMEs that do not get a quick and safe connection to the Internet risk being left behind." (Eliasson, 2000) Others talk of differences between countries and claim that without a forceful investment in a broadband capacity network, Sweden will fall behind as a nation (Ringman and Trägårdh, 2000).

The articles in the Swedish press tell us about an IT-train that all organisations need to board. Otherwise they will find themselves left helplessly behind. The articles in the Swedish press tell us about an IT-train that all organisations need to board. Otherwise they will find themselves left helplessly behind. Laitila *et al* (1999) and Benner (2000) find that this type of strong and one-sided debate is a rather Scandinavian phenomenon. The popular press articles also express an almost complete belief in that the use of IT will lift all regions that are wise enough to invest in IT-capabilities, and successful examples receive publicity. In the region on the Swedish south coast around Ronneby and Karlskrona, a Soft Centre and Telecom City was founded some ten years ago. Now it is a well functioning growth centre for IT related organisations.

> "We should never have been established here without the politicians' clear vision and investment in higher education and buildings tailored to suit IT companies, says Europolitan's press secretary Johan Holmgren" (Klein, 2000)

The rhetoric metaphor of the IT-train, which only makes a few tours around the country, indicates a view based on technology determinism – that the technology by itself will create the development of the regions. The voices brought forward by mass media seem to want to make the technology the only actor of importance for further development. By doing so, they further the IT adoption in Sweden, but they are also building an opinion that is highly simplified and may make investors and companies rush into the new way of doing business without understanding the difficulties of adopting a new technology.

In times where a new technology is entering the stage, there has to be an openness to changes, but that is not the same as running ahistorically into the future. By this, we are not trying to say that technology is unimportant, but that it is not the only actor and it has to be able to interact with other actors. It can not by itself drive a development. This interaction between actors, who the actors are, and what role the technology can play is discussed in this chapter. The aim is to theoretically analyse the technology's possibility to become a useful actor in the development of different regions.

Technology's Role in the Development

This chapter analyses Swedish IT infrastructure development: the rhetoric, the application and the possible effects. It focuses the capabilities ascribed to IT by people, and the interaction between these conceptions and the organisation of regional development.

The computerised information system is often viewed as an object, a technical construction, which is to be used by people. Neither the information system nor IT as such takes an active part in the processes studied. In this chapter, we take a social constructionist stance (Berger & Luckman 1966). People talk of information systems and of IT as if they were intentional beings. Based on that observation, we explore the way IT is presented and perceived by its proponents, opponents, users and other people.

Translation of technology

When large technical systems, such as the railroads, the telephone and electricity, found their way into the everyday life of humanity, the road was not straight and easy to travel. They all intruded into social life, and people gradually changed their way of acting when they started to use the technology. There has to be interaction between people and technology in order for useful applications to evolve. But for this interaction to take place there needs to be some attraction; the new technology will need to be thought to add value in some way to the life people lead or could lead. The railroads, the telephone and electricity all have made successful journeys in society; people have gradually developed worthwhile applications of them. The present day applications are, however, not directly those intended or envisaged by the initial inventors and developers.

The technology examples above all tell us that there is no simple straight line from when the first idea of a new technology arises in the inventor's head, to a totally integrated large system. Latour (1992) uses the word *translation* to denote a process of developing, involving technology's capacity, human knowledge and the capital investment. At times, each new investment may involve a large degree of exploration, and thus substantial translation. The people involved learn, and the capacity of the technology may be extended. At other points in time, investments copy each other and little translation takes place. The history of the technology forms through a large number of translations, some misguided, some successful. People's propensity to be attentive to and to understand the interplay of technology, investments and knowledge derived are critical in making the history successful. The technology is an important actor but it has to interact with the humans and available investments. Humans are bound by their history but they also need their historically derived pre-understanding to be able to understand how to translate the technology to fit people's everyday life without requiring excessive investment.

Technology as actor

As soon as someone makes a decision about something, the person is bound to it, and others will evaluate him or her based in part on their knowledge of the individual's decision (and previous decisions). The conceptions formed on the basis of the decision become a manuscript that the person is obliged to follow; the person no longer has the same freedom as she had before the decision. If she somehow does not want to follow the manuscript, she has to interact with the people who have a role in the script. We can say that the person is bound to the manuscript and has delegated her freedom of action to it (Latour, 1996).

If the use of technology is included, the delegation becomes even more rigorous. The developers, whose mission it is to adapt or design a technology that will work in an organisation, have some power over the manuscript of the technology. But as soon as they have made one decision, it will affect all subsequent decisions. They would also need to listen to other actors' wishes and understanding of how the technology should be constructed and functions within the organisation. Many different actors shape the manuscript of the technology, so there will never be only one or a few ideas in it. The users then become bound to the way the technology is built and have to interact with it in accordance with the existing manuscript.

The interesting part here is that when the technology is in use, it becomes one of the actors in the developing process of the organisation as well as in the region. A change in the structure will be based on the existing structure, of which the technology is a part and an actor in forming the structure. Other authors building on actor network theory have viewed information systems and IT as actors interacting with other technological and social elements of the network. For example, Hanseth and Braa (1998) provide a description of how the information system acted as change agent or enemy to those who wanted change in the organisation. Our exploration goes further, based on a more developed concept of roles that IT can play. Askenäs (2000) and Askenäs and Westelius (2000) investigate a structuration process in an organisation and find evidence of technology being experienced as an actor in this process by people in the organisation. In that organisation, the technology (an ERP system[1]) was found to act either as a manipulator, a bureaucrat, an administrative assistant, a consultant or was dismissed. We will here argue that these roles can be fruitful in analysing the role of IT in regional development. However, it is important not to forget that the technology does not have a role by itself; the role forms in the interaction with other actors and in their conceptions of the process. Because of the roles they ascribe to technology, they behave as if technology acted the role they ascribe to it.

Five roles for technology

The five roles that applications of IT may be allowed to take in an organisation or in relation to individuals according to Askenäs (2000) and Askenäs and Westelius (2000) – Bureaucrat, Manipulator, Administrative Assistant, Consultant and Dismissed – are described below. These roles need not be uniform across the organisation, the region or society. They may co-exist and be specific to the relations with an individual or a group of people. We suggest that the way IT is used is influenced by the perceived fit between the existing structure and the IT functionality on the one hand, and the user's perception of how IT is trying to influence the user's work on the other hand.

---

[1] Enterprise Resource Planning system: an information system designed to handle all or most of the administrative tasks in a company, such as materials requirement planning, marketing and sales administration, accounting, payroll and maintenance administration.

Bureaucrat

A bureaucrat is an official who adheres strictly to the rules and principles laid down for him, rather than making individual considerations. Given the role of a bureaucrat, IT maintains the structure in the organisation. It makes certain that the enactment of structure conforms to the existing rules. This may at times seem inflexible. However, unlike the manipulator, the structure it enforces is one accepted by its users.

Manipulator

A manipulator is someone who controls, directs or influences others in a way that is not entirely of their choosing. IT may be given the role of a manipulator if it is allowed to change or conserve work processes in ways not intended or wished by its users. If someone, with or without external pressure, feels bound to using an IT application, it may take the Manipulator role.

Consultant

A consultant is someone contracted to perform specific, nontrivial tasks, and to advise. The consultant is neither responsible for, nor in command of, the work the organisation performs. IT acting as a consultant provides the user with options and with solutions tailored to the situation. The use of IT follows the user's wishes and leaves the user in control. For this to happen, the user will have to understand the advice provided and be in a position to exercise the freedom of choice.

Administrative Assistant

An administrative assistant is someone who takes care of less complicated tasks in an orderly way. Given the role of an administrative assistant, IT is not used to the same extent as those acting as manipulators or bureaucrats. It administers and simplifies record keeping and dissemination of data, but does not affect (or indeed reflect) the processes and structures of the organisation in any fundamental way. The user takes a more active role and IT is put to limited use only.

Dismissed

The dismissed is someone who temporarily has been dismissed from work, but may be reinstated at some later point in time. It is not used at all by some or all intended users. IT that is dismissed becomes redundant. There may be many reasons for this but, to keep dismissing the system, the user will need good reasons or have a strong bargaining position. Buying and installing IT systems is costly, and the Dismissed system provides no return on the investment in it.

Regional Considerations

In media, we are constantly bombarded by the message 'Without knowledge of IT, you are out'. On a societal level, the politicians seem to believe the message, at least as far as provision of technology is concerned. IT should permeate society; everyone should have broadband access to the Internet and a personal computer at home. The Swedish government has subsidised private acquisition of personal computers. On an individual level, there are indications that people believe in the message too. Today, more than 80% of white-collar workers and close to 60% of blue-collar workers have a computer at home. For blue-collar workers, that is a fourfold increase over the past five years. (www.lo.se, 2000). Close to 70% of the white-collar workers and more than 40% of the blue-collar workers can connect to the Internet from home (although not at a broadband rate).

State supported net construction with broadband capacity to all regions is decided and largely completed, and the connection of individual work places and homes at high communication rates (although typically not broadband) is underway. Most voices heard in the media are positive towards the effort involved in putting Swedes on-line, but few discuss the actual value of it, and a deeper discussion of how it will help develop the Swedish economy is difficult to find (cf. Laitila et al. 1999, and Benner 2000). However, exceptions exist (Jacobson and Stock (1997) and Strömberg (1999)). It is difficult to be against IT investment, and especially broadband investment, today. The necessity of IT in tomorrow's society is a truth that does not seem to need any proof. It would be almost impossible to picture a municipal politician with a "No to broadband connection" platform and trying to get elected on a promise of saving the municipality from becoming "connected". In this way the IT wave is stronger than the railroad wave of a hundred years ago. Then there were politicians who boasted of having saved their village from getting a railroad. In the minds of Swedes, broadband is a road to the future – or at least there is a conviction that a work place or a home without broadband is a safe ticket to economic decline and social deprivation. Is this how we should socially construct the relationship between IT and the development of regions and enterprises? To give the technology and those who know and can handle the technology all the credit for the development? Does it not make people feel powerless, or the opposite, that they have power if they can only control the technology. The risk is that both ways technology is given the role of a negative manipulator.

The high Internet connection rate (and the wish to increase it even further) has made it possible for governmental agencies to move more of their mass communication and their forms to the WWW. Here, IT has served mainly as an administrative assistant. It has not made much difference to the actual communication between governmental agencies and citizens, only to the choice of medium for the communication.

Broadband as consultant? The IT versed physician can utilise international databases in his daily tasks. The local hospital can relay digital X-ray photos to expert radiologists for instant feedback. The helpdesk can be out-sourced, or at least out-located, while retaining full computer connectivity with company databases. For broadband to act as consultant, the user (or developer) must need to be able to envisage new and alternative applications, and to be able to implement and improve them. This requires knowledge of the technological capabilities as well as organisational knowledge and a deep understanding of work processes. But once the step has been taken, the new application could come to serve as the standard operating procedure and the users may stop to reflect over it. This is when the physician has become dependent on the international databases for keeping updated as well as for obtaining more trivial data; when digital x-ray transfer is the norm; when the helpdesk has been located in Söderhamn or the company switchboard on Möja. Then IT may at first turn into a bureaucrat: this is the way we work – the old way of working is no longer acceptable. Later on, if no one cares to keep sufficiently updated with the technical development and questioning the established procedures, IT may turn into a manipulator, making further development difficult or impossible, or an administrative assistant, becoming bypassed to an ever greater extent. Sometime in the future it may even be dismissed and circumvented altogether, if it gets sufficiently out of step with the development and there is no-one with sufficient knowledge to envisage and achieve the transformation into new and useful applications.

IT and SMEs

When it comes to SMEs and IT, there are two distinctly different groups. One group sells IT as a product. The other group mainly uses IT. The first group creates the basic characteristics of the technology and affects how it is possible for other actors to use the technology. This group derives competitive advantage from being able to translate new technology to the existing structure or develop new ways of using the technology. They need to interact with many different actors and understand how the technology is used and may be used in the future. Settings like those in Silicon Valley may be suitable for these enterprises.

The other group, some of which are customers of a proportion of companies from the first group, has a completely different relationship to the technology. Here, the technology is used as a tool for their business, not as the product they sell. Studies have shown that only a minority of such enterprises can make full use of the technology (Teller, 1994). Some do not use it at all, and others only make limited use of it. The obstacle is a lack of knowledge both of the existing technology as such and of how to use it (Iacovou et al, 1995 and Nordenstam, 1996). It seems as though this group somehow choose to dismiss the technology. This may be because the technology characteristics do not suit the role the actors of the enterprises want to give it. It could also be the case that, despite the popular clichés, the technology is not absolutely necessary for survival. To profit from IT, these companies may need a bureaucrat or a manipulator to help them get an effective structure in their support processes.

With that role, the technology could be able to translate knowledge to the enterprises. Small enterprises are more dependent on their region and often have more difficulty in keeping large contact networks, which could help them gain the knowledge of the possibilities of the technology and how it can be used (Iacovou et al, 1995 and Nordenstam, 1996). Those trying to promote regional development could then help these SMEs build a network of contacts and give them knowledge of how to use the technology. In this work, it may help to replace the standard cliché of IT as the silver bullet with a richer picture of possible roles of IT in the development process. Presenting IT as being able to take the roles of manipulator, bureaucrat, consultant, administrative assistant or of being dismissed could aid in identifying the importance – or lack of importance – of IT in the development of different enterprises.

IT in regional development

Giddens (1984) points to the history and the specific combination of resources and events that have led up to the routines and ways of thinking, working and acting that characterise each region: "I take the notion of regionalization to be a very significant one for social theory. It has always been a main concern of the writings of geographers, but I want to regard it as less of a purely spatial concept than they ordinarily do. The situated nature of social interaction can usefully be examined in relation to the different locales through which the daily activities of individuals are co-ordinated. Locales are not just places but *settings* of interaction [.]" (p. xxv)

It is not altogether easy to find ways in which IT will help underprivileged regions develop or stop degrading. Solutions that are found, such as the re-localisation of help-desks or switchboards, then tend to be paraded as exemplary and generally applicable. But are they really? Out-locating to Möja in the Stockholm archipelago may suit that region, but does that mean that it would work just as well to move to Pajala in northernmost Sweden? The Stockholm archipelago and the West Coast around Gothenburg have their appeal as places to live, and are at the same time close to major cities. Neither area is densely populated or has excellent physical communications, but could attract some competent people who would prefer living there and perform jobs that only need virtual communication. Gnosjö has its entrepreneurial climate and social networks, Linköping its university and community of IT companies. Umeå has its university and is the centre of an area where job opportunities are not too abundant, and could thereby provide a fairly competent workforce at lower salaries than overheated growth poles, while also being able to attract regional subsidies from Swedish as well as EU sources. They each have their traits and combination of resources. Different solutions would then probably be needed to find competitive alternatives for each area, rather than trying to copy existing examples unquestioningly. Ronneby/Karlskrona has, as mentioned above, developed IT competence over the past ten years, and are now in a rather good position once the IT wave has hit. But are they globally competitive or just ahead of their more immediate surroundings? Now, Kalmar, Söderhamn, and other places try to copy the Ronneby/Karlskrona recipe, but ten years have passed since the recipe was written. Does it still fit and will it fit them?

The technology is the society made durable (Latour, 1996). Durable it may be, but as shown above, if we treat technology as fixed and stop looking for ways to adjust to it and exploit it in changing settings, we will probably award it a negative manipulator role. Likewise, we cannot treat IT as a complete and final structure that needs no further development, and that is ready to use in different regions. The regional settings are built up by all actors who interact and shape a meaning around the existing structure (Giddens, 1984). How the technology affects the regional settings will be due to the history of the region, different actors' views of the technology and the characteristics of the technology. And would it really be meaningful to copy a recipe from one region to another, even if it were possible? The development of one region is always relative to the development of other regions, and to gain competitive advantage there has to be some unique setting which makes the product cheaper or different to others (Porter, 1985). Thus, there is no fixed causal relationship between the use of IT and regional development. The general and generic rhetoric claiming that there is, may make a region or actors in a region jump on a train, not actually knowing what train it is or whether it will go in a direction suitable to the regional settings.

The competitive advantage of a region will be based on how the actors in the region interact with each other and are able to translate the technology and the regional settings into a fruitful competitive environment. IT as manipulator can help implement preconceived changes, but for the technology to be able to shape or enable translations to new settings it has to act more or less as a consultant. It needs to make different solutions possible and not hinder the development of the region. But to act as a consultant demands that the actors interacting with it have good knowledge of both the technology and the structure in which it is used (Askenäs, 2000). Once a transformation has been achieved, other roles of the technology, such as the bureaucrat or the administrator, may suit better.

Concluding Discussion

In this chapter we have discussed IT as an actor in the structuration of regions. We have argued that the way in which the issue is treated in the rhetoric of public debate is all too simplified and may push the technology in a direction that we neither want nor even expect. Without more reflection on the role the technology has and how integrated it is and will be in our development, we may find ourselves in the hands of a manipulator – IT acting as a manipulator on its own, or maybe even worse, humans invisibly using the technology to manipulate others. We have seen it happen in an organisation to people so used with the technology and so unaware of how it works that at last it took control. We have seen large technical systems in the past find their ways into people's everyday life and become integrated in the development of society. The question now, is how IT shall be able to act in our society. What role or roles do we want it to act? And when and how do we want it to act which role – because, as we have seen, it is possible for IT to make a positive as well as a negative contribution to a development process depending on how appropriate the particular role is at that point in time in that process.

IT can not be an actor alone. To be able to act, it has to interact with other actors in our society and especially with the actors in its immediate surroundings. Therefore, we do not believe in a cure-all recipe for all forward-looking regions to follow. Instead, the question has to be "What can IT do for the actors in the region and in what role will IT best suit these actors?". Initiating interaction between different actors can be necessary to get positive effects for the development. History has shown that new technology is not always used in the way it was imagined at the start. What the region can do is to ensure a good base for the translation to take place, facilitating contact between different actors, both those viewing technology as an infrastructure and those viewing it as a product. The actors need to get to know each other, building and supporting networks between human actors. The actors will also need to develop knowledge of the technology, through education and through interaction with others, to help the interaction between technology and humans develop fruitfully. These activities are already in place in many regions, but do we in a deeper sense know how these translations are performed and under which circumstances they take place? We argue that viewing IT as an actor in the development process will make it easier to understand this complexity, and advocate the use of the different roles – manipulator, administrative assistant, bureaucrat, consultant and dismissed – as an analytic tool to help us understand the effects that IT has on SMEs.

References

Arbetet, (2000) 'Fram för mer IT', (Swedish. Translation of title: Go ahead with more IT) *Arbetet*, 2000-06-13.

Askenäs, L. (2000) 'Enterprise Systems - The technology's active and passive role in an organisation', In Swedish: *Affärssystemet – en studie om teknikens aktiva and passiva roll i en organisation*, lic.-avh. No. 808, Linköping: IDA-EIS, Linköping University and Institute of Technology.

Askenäs, L. and Westelius, A. (2000) 'Five roles of an information system: a social constructionist approach to analysing the usage of ERP', *Proceedings in the twenty-first International Conference on Information Systems*, Dec. 10-13, Brisbane, Australia.

Benner, M. (2000) 'UNDER STRECKET Länder bemöter IT-utvecklingen på olika sätt', (Swedish. Translation of title: Countries show different attitudes to the IT development) *Svenska Dagbladet*, 2000-05-04.

Berger, P. and Luckmann, T. (1966) '*The Social Construction of Reality – A Treatise in the Sociology of Knowledge*', London : reprint 1991 by Penguin Books.

Eliasson, P. O. (2000) 'Företagen har mest att tjäna på bredband', (Swedish. Translation of title: It is the companies that will benefit the most from broadband access) *Göteborgs-Posten*, 2000-05-06

Giddens, A. (1984) '*The constitution of society: outline of the theory of structuration*', Cambridge: Polity Press.

Hanseth, O. and Braa, K. (1998) 'Technology as traitor: Emergent SAP Infrastructure in a Global Organization', *Proceedings of the nineteenth International Conference on Information Systems*, Dec. 13-16, Helsinki, Finland.

Iacovou, C., Benbasat, I. and Dexter, A. (1995) 'Electronic Data Interchange and Small Organizations: Adoption and Impact of Technology', *MIS Quarterly*, Vol. 19, Dec., pp. 465-485.

Klein, H. (2000) 'Den nya ekonomin – gammal i Blekinge', (Swedish. Translation of title: The new economy: old in Blekinge) *Aftonbladet*, 2000-05-29.

Kuylenstierna, A. (2000) 'ALMIBAROMETERN Snabba kast i småföretagsvärlden', (Swedish. Translation of title: Quick turns in the small business community) *Svenska Dagbladet*, 2000-06-20.

Latour, B. (1992) '*Teknik är samhället som gjorts hållbart*', (Swedish) Translation by E. Wennerholm, Göteborg: Nerenius & Santérus förlag (Title of original: Technology is society made durable. In A Sociology of Monsters: essays on Power, Law, J. (Ed.) Routledge, London.)

Latour, B. (1996) '*Kan vetenskapssociologi lära organisationsteori någonting?*' (Swedish. Translation of title: Has sociology of science anything to teach organisational theory) Translation by E. Wennerholm, in Latour, B., Artefaktens återkomst – ett möte mellan organisationsteori och tingens sociologi, Göteborg: Nerenius & Santérus förlag.

Laitila, T., Von Hall, G., Lindahl, B., Augustsson, T., Rosin, B. E., Lundin T., Henriksson, K. and Mårtensson, M. (1999) 'Avspänd debatt i världen om bredband' (Swedish. Translation of title: Relaxed debate in the world concerning broadband access), *Svenska Dagbladet*, 1999-10-09.

Nordenstam, T. (1996) 'Småföretag och spridning av informationsteknik - Erfarenheter och föreställningar', (Swedish. Translation of title: Small enterprises and the dissemination of technology: experience and views) *IT för vem?*, No. 3, Handelshögskolan i Umeå in co-operation with Telia AB.

Porter, M. E. (1985) '*Competitive Advantage*', New York: The Free Press.

Ringman, M. and Trägårdh, M. (2000) 'Sverige spricker. Framtiden hänger på en tråd av fiber', (Swedish. Translation of title: Sweden cracks. The future is dangling on a fibre glass thread) *Aftonbladet* 2000-03-06.

Strömberg, M. (1999) 'Konsten att tvinga fram ett teknikskifte', (Swedish. Translation of title: The art of forcing a technology shift) *Aftonbladet*, 1999-06-21.

Teller, T. (1994) 'Fulfilling IT Needs in Small Businesses; A Recursive learning Model', *International Small Business Journal*, Vol. 14, No. 4, pp. 25-44.

www.lo.se, The Swedish labour organisation homepage, accessed 2000-07-14.

3 Psychosocial Issues of Telework: Challenges for Research and Development

Pekka Huuhtanen

Department of Psychology, Finnish Institute of Occupational Health

Introduction

Telework in the context of flexible work organizations

The accelerated speed of development in information and communication technologies (ICT) gives a good basis for new ways of working without limitations of time and place. However, the growth of teleworking has not satisfied optimistic expectations. A proper understanding of telework is needed not only as a technological phenomenon, but also in terms of associated economic, cultural and social issues. Telework should be placed into the context of change in business strategies, organizational culture and new management and leadership strategies.

This chapter attempts to address relevant study needs in relation to psychosocial aspects of teleworking in the future. Even if the forms of teleworking and technological tools have changed, the preconditions for good working conditions and individual workers' well-being have remained basically the same. Since the beginning of the 1980s, numerous reports on telework have been published. Many publications describing equipment, work stations and working conditions refer to EU directives and practical guidelines. Especially long-term follow-up studies with representative samples are lacking. As regards the social and psychological perspectives, it is important to ask which old study questions and concepts are still relevant, and which questions will be relevant in future.

In this chapter, telework is seen as one way to increase flexibility in work life, both from the organizational and individual perspective. Distance working is one form of flexible work practice. The literature on flexibility in organizations makes a distinction between quantitative (numerical) and qualitative (functional) flexibility, and between internal and external flexibility. Companies usually use different forms of flexibility in combination. The fragmentation of the companies into smaller independent decentralized units, subcontracting, outsourcing, and developing a flexible organization, (e.g. using multi-skilled teams), together with flexible working hours have both a positive and a negative impact on health and safety.

The relationship between flexible employment strategies, working conditions and health and well-being was analysed in seven European Union member states in 1998-1999. Qualitative case studies both in the service sector and in industry, and the opinions of labour market parties gave a basis for some interesting conclusions (Goudswaard & de Nanteuil 2000).

In most cases, flexible employment strategies have a clear impact on working conditions, generally worsening them. There are, however, differences between cases and countries. In some cases the relationship between flexibility and working conditions is reversed: flexibility policies are implemented in response to adverse working conditions. Most cases demonstrate a lack of control over working time, which is even worse for workers with a weak employment status. The study revealed a positive relationship between functional flexibility (multi-skilling and teamwork) and the improvement of working conditions. Furthermore, an increasing gap between job demands and job control was found. The intensification of work is growing in all countries. The differences found between cases can, for a major part, be understood by looking at government regulation and the labour relations system at the national level.

The direct impacts of flexibility on occupational safety and health have hardly been assessed. However, there are indications of health and safety problems linked to flexible employment policies, particularly to the intensification of work and time pressure, to lack of control over working time, and job insecurity. Almost all cases show evidence of increasing gender and/or age segmentation. (Goudswaard and de Nantieuil 2000).

Research has shown that functionally flexible workplaces are more likely than traditional ones to use various working time arrangements (e.g., flexitime, sabbaticals, adjusted periods, time banking (Antila & Ylöstalo 1999). There was a clear difference between flexible and traditional workplaces as to how common individually tailored working times were. Sectors with increased competition, especially in labour-intense service sectors, have begun to use different forms of working time arrangements primarily as a means to cut costs. In the service sectors with less or no significant change in competition, different working times have been applied mainly to increase the employees' options (Antila & Ylöstalo 1999).

Productive workplaces that increased their staff during the first half of the 1990s have several typical characteristics: extensive co-operation with others, the use of information technology, and readiness to develop work organizations. Consequently, it can be hypothesized that productive and innovative work places are more active than others to use teleworking as one tool to develop the work methods and the organization.

Position of teleworkers on the Finnish labour market

Finland has been in the forefront in taking advantage of mobile information and communication technologies and telework. The proportion of internet connections per 1000 inhabitants is second highest after the USA. According to the ECaTT survey in 1999, the proportion of teleworkers in Finland was highest in Europe, 16.8% of the workforce.

The preconditions for and the impacts of telework can be evaluated at personal, company and national levels in various labour market situations. Pekkola (1997) classifies national labour markets into two groups: regulated and less regulated labour legislation; employer's personnel strategy into high skills and high autonomy, vs. low skills and low autonomy, and personal labour market into high skill self-management vs. low skill strict formal control. On the basis of the labour market position and work life quality data collected in the mid-1990s, Pekkola concluded that the labour market position of teleworkers in Finland was systematically better than that of other employees in general; they felt a lesser threat of lay-offs, dismissals and transfers than other employees. Teleworkers belong more often to the labour market core group and are subjected to a personnel policy with qualitative flexibility features (Pekkola 1997).

These findings are in accordance with the results of the Quality of Working Life Survey: The largest group doing teleworking were upper white-collar employees with a high level of education (Lehto & Sutela 1999). Data was collected by personal face-to-face interviews, the sample consisting of 3,800 wage and salary earners, 2,979 persons in data. In autumn 1997, 66% of all wage earners were information technology users in Finland, women more extensively than men.

Teleworking had increased almost five-fold during the 1990s, with nearly 10% doing telework at least occasionally. About 4% regarded themselves as teleworkers, men twice as often as women. More than one in three (35%) employees said they were interested in teleworking. The age group of 25 to 44-year-olds included the largest number of those who said that they did teleworking. Interest in teleworking was the greatest among respondents under 25 years of age (47%, 14% in the age group of 55 to 64-year-olds, Lehto & Sutela 1999).

Key Psychosocial Issues in Teleworking: Summary of a European Study

An important question regarding the quality of the knowledge-base created by earlier research on work content and working conditions in telework arises: Do we already have valid and reliable knowledge about the much discussed issues like stress, overwork, musculoskeletal disorders, workaholism, isolation, and the balance between work and private life in different forms of teleworking? In the following chapters, a short summary is presented of a European study on the social implications of telework in all 15 EU member states in 1995-1996 (Huuhtanen 1997).

It was obvious from the beginning that marked differences exist at the societal, organizational and workplace level regarding expectations, types and impact of telework arrangements. Telework was seen as one form of work organization, not as a distinct category of work. Consequently in telework, as in any other type of work, the psychosocial environment, health consequences and stress levels will differ, depending on the job content and demands of the work, one crucial dimension being whether the tasks performed are low-skilled or high-skilled. Another key dimension, based on strong evidence from psychological stress research, is autonomy and control over the work content and work rhythms. It was concluded that in most cases, stress in telework is connected more to the type of work and work organization than to the actual place of work.

Many national reports stressed that the most important factor, as regards eliminating obstacles in moving toward a wider use of telework, is organizational culture. The motives for telework and ways of organizing it are keenly dependent on the management and leadership culture, company personnel policy, and motives for telework. These in turn have impacts on how preparation and training for telework is planned, and how telework arrangements and agreements on company level, if there are any, are organized.

In principle, telework gives room for independence and autonomy, and offers possibilities for concentrated work and possibilities for organizing work and timing on the basis of personal criteria. Significant increases in productivity have been reported in case studies – for example, in insurance companies.

The individual's freedom of regulating the work rhythm may, however, lead to overload, and in the most extreme cases involves being 'on-call' 24 hours a day. Long working hours can have adverse health consequences, especially in a badly designed workplace or where the tasks are repetitive. Another stress factor connected with timing can be difficulty in foreseeing the amount and timing of future tasks. 'Workaholic' behaviour may be an additional risk if external control does not exist, or if the teleworker is not able to control his/her own working styles.

In the case of the employee teleworker, the responsibility for carrying out the risk assessment of any workplace usually rests with the employer. Self-employed teleworkers are responsible for this themselves. The likelihood of a poorly designed work environment and insufficient ergonomic quality of VDUs may be higher in the homes of teleworkers than in typical office environments.

The time patterns in telework vary from occasional overload situations to full-time teleworking where physical and social isolation may be one of the biggest problems. A concern has been repeatedly expressed that the physical isolation of teleworkers can lead to the risk of their being marginalized from the workplace and colleagues, at the same time as the importance of teamwork is being emphasized. On the other hand, modern information and communication technologies offer totally new potential for support, training and guidance in problem situations.

Flexibility in telework gives teleworkers the opportunity to fit the work to their life and family situations and career phases. It offers great work opportunities for people who might not otherwise be employed for reasons of disability or family duties. This can, however, also create problems of its own in terms of the distinction between work and social and family life. In this connection, the gender dimension is important. Female workers still bear the main responsibility for housekeeping and caring for children and other family members, such as elderly parents, also in the Nordic countries.

On the basis of cross-sectional data it is not possible to analyse cause-effect relationships and the impact of selection of teleworkers, e.g. on the basis of personal characteristics and family patterns.

Challenges for Future Research on Telework

In order to plan future research, a critical evaluation is needed regarding the depth of understanding new forms of telework (covering different types of mobile telework, e-work, call-centre work, virtual teams), relevance of concepts used, quality of research methods and study paradigms.

Study populations and types of teleworking

Problems in making comparisons and generalizations on the basis of existing study literature have been addressed by many writers (see, for example, Hone *et al.* 1998; Valenduc & Vendramin 1998). The majority of published empirical work is based on small samples and with few controls of extraneous variables. Even more so, problems arise in drawing useful conclusions from previous studies due to different definitions and operationalisations of the core concept of teleworking. Many researchers have defined groups of teleworkers in contrast to those who are not teleworkers. Definitions differ according to the criteria (in relation to time, place, use of different technological tools at work) that distinguish an individual as a teleworker or the work as telework.

Hone et al. (1998) argue that, as the alternative approach in psychological studies of telework, there should be a move away from such definitions (as two separate groups of workers), and instead recognize teleworking as one facet of modern work life. A growing number of individuals are teleworking to a greater or lesser extent as a natural part of their job. Today it is misleading to study telework along any single parameter or dimension, but rather in relation to changing working practices in general. The key elements are working away from the traditional workplace, and using information and communication technology away from the traditional workplace. Other features like contractual arrangements (e.g. distinction between workers' status vs. self-employed) also apply to other forms of work. Rather than being used to differentiate teleworkers from non-teleworkers, these features should represent the dimensions of working along which individuals can be placed.

The use of ICT, mostly portable electronic tools, varies according to the complexity of the use, ranging from a telephone to e-mail and networked portable computers and mobile phones. It is a mistake to adopt arbitrary technological cut-offs in choosing who to include in study groups. What has been suggested is analysis of the complex relationship between work characteristics, health and other outcomes, and the time spent in various locations, rather than simply using the time spent away from the traditional office as a cut-off point between teleworkers and others. Arbitrary cut-off points may exclude people from the study population for whom telework has a significant impact on life-style and health, despite taking up a relatively small proportion of their total working time.

Significance of time

The rationale behind a longitudinal study design is to be able to analyse human and social processes in relation to time. In the field of occupational stress, temporal and causal relations between stressors, stress reactions and coping have been analysed. The stress process consists of a complex set of temporal relations between a perceived situation, choice of the response, and the effectiveness of the resulting responses. In appraisal of the situation and choice of the responses, predictability and controllability of the occurrence of the anticipated stressor are of crucial importance. Also individual coping activities have different time patterns.

Unfortunately, the design and analyses of stress investigations have been far from optimal. More specific assumptions about time lags and time course are needed regarding telework applications both from individual and organizational perspectives. The length of the necessary follow-up period and the intervals between measurements depend on the impact and exposure factors under study. Problems on the usability of computer applications, and unsatisfactory working postures and environment can be seen rather soon. However, the impact of telework and other flexible forms of work organization, on skills and organizational culture can be analysed only after a long period of time, generally over many years.

The three phases of change, 'de-freezing', 'moving', 'refreezing', originally adopted from Lewin, have proved to give one useful frame of reference for studies of organizational and individual change (Huuhtanen 1997). In continuous changes, however, refreezing is unlikely to happen at any point of time. In addition, traditional ways of analysing the empirical data of longitudinal studies are based on group level statistical analyses. On the individual level, however, changes are not unidirectional in time. There are winners and losers in change processes.

The adoption of a flexible form of work has very different implications depending on the person's life-cycle stage. At the beginning of one's career, the downsides of working at home may be confined to a reduction in the social context offered by a typical workplace. For elderly workers, the motivation and benefits of telework might be quite different.

More research is needed on the issue of social construction of time, (e.g. negotiations between family members). Most of the occupational safety and health (OSH) research has taken as its starting point workplace and individual workers, with only limited attention being paid to the accrued impact which it may have on the family.

Improvement of study design and methodology

Changing work life, with flexible work arrangements, fragmentary work contracts and an unstable work environment, has raised new challenges for study designs and methodology. Work and non-work exposure to physical, social and mental factors are difficult to differentiate, and analysis of the combinations of several different factors is needed.

With fragmentary work contracts and an unstable work environment, traditional follow-up studies with large samples of workers are not possible. The regular monitoring of the work environment and health becomes discontinuous, if not impossible. Company-based data may become less important than individual-based data. International mobility makes follow-up studies even more demanding.

New methods must be developed in order to monitor the work environment and to follow, register, and assess the workers' health and exposure. There might be a growing need for personal monitoring in addition to environmental monitoring. Personal monitoring should cover only work performance, not the teleworkers behaviour in a larger social context. Research is also needed for making summaries of personal occupational histories and occupational exposures (Rantanen 1999). All in all, new strategies for the compilation of information are needed, like quick field surveys with modern ICT. Internet-based real-time monitoring systems are under development.

The share of teleworkers is still quite small in the whole working population, as seen in the Finnish study example in the previous chapters. In order to control for numerous background and confounding variables in the analysis, researchers should concentrate on studying samples of workers performing the same job for the same organization. Hone *et al.* (1998) suggest that further research could then test whether the results, the relationships between different telework characteristics and the outcomes regarding health and safety, can be extrapolated to other types of teleworking. Sophisticated statistical analysis can be used to test complex relationships as soon as enough data is available.

In addition to the problems with the definition of telework and study design, the reported studies have difficulties in showing whether the psychosocial and health problems and outcomes are specifically related to teleworking. Often listed study variables such as isolation, privacy, control of work, and social support are of course not unique to teleworking, but apply equally to all forms of work. Work exposure is difficult to differentiate from non-work exposure, and analysis of combinations of several different types of factors is needed. In most studies, no satisfactory solutions have been found for analysing multicausality, and for controlling the impact of third variables as potential confounders of the stressor-strain relationship.

The research on teleworking as a new form of work offers one platform to test existing psychological theories of work and well-being in the post-industrial society. In this respect, interesting theoretical questions are, e.g. the changing meaning of presence, absence, privacy, the erosion of normal working time, and the significance of the work community. More understanding is needed on issues like telemanagement, and how trust and emotional bonds are created and maintained in virtual, electronic communities between teleworkers and others.

Application of Results, Prevention and Control of new Risks

Rigorous research on psychological aspects of telework is still limited. The implementation of new forms of work organization should be analysed as a technological, organizational, social and individual change process, linked with many actors at different levels. This means that longitudinal multidisciplinary research and development together with efforts from companies are needed for analysing the impact of the time factor both in short-term and long-term work.

Experiences of the development of remote work in expert organizations in Finland have revealed that organizations proceed slowly and informally when applying telework (Hanhike et al. 1998). Concrete models are lacking and it has been difficult to show the influence of telework on business activities. The focus has been more on individual teleworkers than on groups and organizations.

When implementing new technologies at work, the following trends have been demonstrated since the late 1970s (Huuhtanen 1997). In the first 'adaptation' phase, technical tools were taken more or less as given. The role of psychologists and personnel consultants was to select and train individuals to fit this technology. The next step ('moulding') was to mould and modify equipment and human-computer dialogue to fit the cognitive and health demands of human beings. Special attention was paid to the user-friendliness of computers, (e.g. by developing user interfaces). Finally, the third 'evolutionary' strategy might adopt as the frame of reference the entire entity of organizational, technological and individual goals. In terms of developmental gains in the long run, both organizational effectiveness and human well-being and skills development are enhanced.

Too often, telework arrangements have been technology-driven. Office work has been reduced to a simple flow of information and, in the design of new ways of working, the social aspects of work have been overlooked too often. In analysing the slow increase of home offices, Brown and Duguid stress the importance of social help systems:

> "a curious paradox is that information technology, by ignoring the role played invisibly by the social system, is keeping people out of the home and in conventional office, and not the other way around" (Brown & Duguid 2000, p. 79).

A successful design of new work systems with new technologies draws on the social resources.

Innovative solutions are needed also regarding the application of occupational safety and health (OSH) research results. A major challenge is to reconcile the flexibility of work arrangements and modern work tools with the worker's security, not only at work but in the social and family context. Work will continue to spill relentlessly over into private and family life. Reciprocal spill-over complicates the task of researchers and risk monitoring, given the various types of families in the information society (see also Standen *et al.* 1999).

Regarding the development and implementation of new information and communication technologies, research is also needed on the demands of the visual and auditory sensory system in the design of new technologies, cognitive ergonomics, and the organization and management of information work (Rantanen 1999). New exposure factors emerge, for example in human-human interaction between service workers and clients. Confounding factors are different in different environments and cultures. This is a very important question when discussing and studying telework from the international perspective.

The role of the OSH research is to increase knowledge and understanding of the changes at work and well-being and their relationship, and to provide a scientific basis for actions, prevention and control of new risks. Attention to health and safety risks of the applied material, equipment and work environment should start in the stage of purchase, consulting teleworkers. Systemic control is suggested with health and safety surveillance directed toward internal rules and routines of the companies. These, like the other options presented, should be fitted with cultural characteristics and different inspection and guidance roles of labour inspectors in different countries.

The accessibility of workplaces is a key issue, particularly in the case of tele-homeworking. In most countries, citizens have a right to the inviolability of their home. Therefore two problems arise: first, how can employers be responsible for complying with occupational health and safety regulations if they cannot access the workplace? Secondly, the same applies to control bodies if they cannot enter private homes. For most cases, in practice, however, accessibility is not a major problem, because the teleworker has interest in good and safe working conditions. Permission to enter the home is unlikely to be withheld, because a teleworker's own well-being is at stake.

Dissemination of specific health and safety information is needed with guidance and training on how to proceed with respect to relevant issues (e.g. health surveillance, how to organize work patterns and working times, selection of teleworkers, re-training, risk assessment of the home work station, data security, safety of third parties, burden of proof in case of occupational accidents). Support is important especially for small and medium-sized enterprises, for mobile teleworkers and for self-employed teleworkers. Finally, more systematic evaluation of the measures and supportive roles taken by OSH and HRD experts is needed.

In developing new forms of work organizations using modern information and communication technologies, many of the critical social and psychological challenges listed in this chapter have been thus glossed over. Abandoning the strict technological determinism paradigm has given room for a more encompassing frame of reference in the implementation of new technologies.

In sum, the basic argument in this chapter is that the decisions on work organization and the division of tasks between computers and people are made in connection with the system design process. Success in implementing telework is based more on social than on technical innovations. To shift the attitudes toward telework in a more positive direction, for example, among middle managers and supervisors, the creative experimentation of new work organization and supervision should be encouraged. A multidisciplinary approach is needed in research and development. Telework or e-work, if these concepts are relevant at all any more, should not be seen as an end, but as one option for individuals and organizations in the information society.

References

Antila J., Ylöstalo P. (1999) *Functional Flexibility and Workplace Success in Finland*, Labour Policy Studies Nr 20, Helsinki: Ministry of Labour.

Brown J. S. and Duguid P. (2000) *The Social Life of Information*, Boston: Harvard Business School Press.

ECaTT - Electronic Commerce and Telework Trends (1999) *Benchmarking Progress on New Ways of Working and New Forms of Business across Europe.* Http://www.ecatt.com. Empirica, Bonn.

Goudswaard A., de Nanteuil M. (2000) *Flexible Employment Policies and Working Conditions.* European Foundation of Living and Working Conditions. Consolidated Report, Dublin.

Hanhike T., Immonen J., Kanerva L. and Luukinen A. (1998) *Etätö muutoksen välineenä* (Telework for Managing Structural changes). ESF Publications 29/98. Ministry of Labour, Edita, Helsinki. (in Finnish with an English summary).

Hone K., Kerrin M. and Cox T.: CORDiT 'A Multidimensional Model for Evaluating the Psychological Impact of Teleworking' *European Psychologist*, Vol. 3, No 3, September 1998, 227-237.

Huuhtanen P. (1997 a) *The health and safety issues for teleworkers in the European Union*, Consolidated report, European Foundation for the Improvement of Living and Working Conditions, Working Paper No: WP/97/29/EN.

Huuhtanen, P. (1997 b) Towards a multi-level model in longitudinal studies on computerization in offices. *Int. J Human-Comp Interaction*; 9 (4), 383-405.

Huuhtanen P. (2000) 'Safety and health implications of telework. Changing World of Work', *Electronic Magazine of European Agency for Safety and Health at Work*, http://agency.osha.eu.int/publications/magazine/, February 2000.

Korte E. and Wynne R. (1997) 'Telework. Penetration, Potential and Practice in Europe', Amsterdam: IOS Press.

Lehto A.-M. and Sutela H. (1999) 'Efficient, more efficient, exhausted. Findings of Finnish Quality of Work Life Surveys 1977-1997', Statistics Finland, Labour Market 1999:8, Helsinki.

Pekkola J.: 'Telework and Labour Market', paper presented at *Telework 97; Good practice for the future*, 4th European Assembly on Telework and New Ways of Working, Sept 24-26 1997, Stockholm, Sweden.

Rantanen J. (1999) 'Research challenges arising from changes in worklife', *Scand J Work Environ Health*; 25 (6, special issue): 473-483.

Standen, P., Daniels K. and Lamond D. (1999) 'The Home as a Workplace: Work-Family Interaction and Psychological Well-being in Telework', J Occup, *Health Psychology*, Vol. 4, No. 4, 368-381.

Valenduc G. and Vendramin P. (1998) 'A Social Approach to Flexibility in Distance Working', paper presented in International Seminar: *Building for a New Millennium; Telework and Tomorrow's Organization*, Turku, Finland, September 4-8.

4 Teleworking: Redesign Strategies for Organisations

Shiri Ahuja

Institute for Integrated Learning in Management, Lodhi Institutional Area
New Delhi, India

Introduction

Today organisations in the developed world are putting their money into computer networks and other technologies that can boost efficiency and effectiveness, not just that of the organisations but also of the employees in their personal lives. With the new motto of 'working anywhere, anytime' privacy is being coupled with productivity, hierarchy is being replaced with teamwork, and status with mobility. But this organisational embrace of technology and the resulting computer mediated communication has human ramifications. Changing how we work is linked closely to our attitudes and habits. Hence it is imperative that we consider its development in the light of a broader backdrop.

India is being looked at by all countries in search of an IT-savvy work-force, which is available in India. The Indian software professionals, as well as the other labour segments are attractive to other countries due to various reasons:

- A large pool of English speaking labour.
- Skilled professionals at costs cheaper than international standards.
- India's geographical location within a different time zone.

The Indian government has also been quick in responding to the attention India lately started getting as a result of it's IT potential. India set up a task force in May 1998 to assess the potential of this sector and design ways so as to gain maximum benefits from the boom. The task force has concentrated on working out strategies to make 'IT available for all'. The outcome of this effort is the Information Technology Act 2000, which has made India one of the first countries to pass dedicated legislation for E-Commerce (Bagchi 2000: 11). All these efforts have definitely encouraged the growth of an IT industry in India in a short time, but have not yet succeeded in merging this industry in the form of an efficiency building tool for the already existing conventional industries.

In the conventional Indian industries, the use of IT has now started as a stray tool to solve some existing problems within the organisations. A conventional organisation, in the process of looking for small solutions usually chooses from IT 'objects'. The objects chosen as independent solutions are not able to work as building blocks of a complete system. They remain to function as tiny programme pieces that automate bits of business functions, like displaying a list. At a later stage these objects are not – or cannot be – upgraded further to build up a complete system. In a survey done by the Indian Market Research Bureau on E-Commerce, only 20% of organisations where CIOs were surveyed said that they were trying to use E-Commerce at least to some extent. 80% of the industry is in the process of gearing up for the show. Banks want to wait and watch while sectors like IT and courier/ travel/ transport are the forerunners (Indian Market Research Bureau 2000). These organisations which are incorporating certain components of E-Commerce without a long term vision are most likely to end up with IT 'objects' that may be difficult to fit into future redesigning plans.

Early web commerce initiatives in India were primarily driven by the large global and rapidly increasing local Internet user community and were therefore heavily focussing on Business to Consumer (B2C) commerce. As more and more businesses take to integrating their suppliers, vendors and partners into the value chain, the majority of future work, predicted by International Data Corporation to be in access of 70%, is forecasted to be in the area of Business to Business (B2B) commerce. International Data Corporation (IDC), a leading market research firm, predicts this shift to be in excess of 70% in favour of B2B commerce over the next few years. But there is hardly any firm planning forward to incorporate Business to Employee (B2E) interactions. While call centres are being established by so many companies for faster reach to customers, employees still come to the office to attend these calls and follow the conventional 9 to 5 routine. Thus there seems to be a studied silence over the transferring of IT benefits to employees in the form of new work flows and flexible processes.

Corporate teleworking in India is in its evolutionary stages. For a transitory period, a great deal of exploration is needed, and both organisations and individuals must make experiments. Each new way of using remote locations as a workplace will create new exposures and require new methods of management approach. The role of an office is changing, and today's question concerns which functions are best undertaken in which location. The office is a place for interaction, the home for reflective work or a base for the peripatetic (Kinsman 1987). There is, therefore, a spectrum of home or remotely possible tasks, which require study of work flows in Indian organisations in order to assess their suitability for teleworking.

An organisation is a combination of various processes, which may be simple or complex, routine or non-routine, repetitive or non repetitive. An in-depth study of these processes is a pre requisite for the introduction and success of a radically different work practice like teleworking. In this process, the human as well as techno-professional factors play an important role. As the redesigning of Indian organisations for teleworking is in its very initial stages, this chapter concentrates on reengineering the routine process at an early step.

The Conveyor Processes

This section will take a look at the routine work flows in Indian organisations by comparing and contrasting them with an assembly line.

Step 1: The work process in an organisation needs to be performed by people with different specialised skills, but while so many people contribute to the final result the end customer is mostly left to suffer for the delays caused during the process, which he fails to identify till the end. While an assembly line makes it feasible to locate even the very first part of the product at anytime during the process, the same does not happen while different stages of a work process are being performed by different people in an organisation.

Step 2: Ideally the completion time of a process in an organisation should be predetermined. Once a chassis in an assembly line is loaded, there is a predefined duration for taking off the completed automobile. But most work processes in organisations have excessive human intervention, thus leading to inability in predefining completion time.

Step 3: Once a machine part enters the conveyor belt, it can easily be located along with the stage of production. But once a job enters the organisation's system for processing, it is near impossible to keep a continuous track of developments without extra efforts.

Step 4: Whenever a step in the work process requires approval of a few people, need for pushing and chasing by the customer concerned is taken for granted. In contrast to this, in an assembly line a conveyor belt brings a job and takes it for further work/ processing on completion of a certain stage. Such a predetermined arrangement for movement of work in the process can eliminate the need for a worker to search for pending work, or push it further after making his contribution.

Step 5: In an assembly line, if one tries to hang on to the job one can't because warning lights and bells would go off, triggering corrective action by the line supervisor. But if one person in the service chain does not process a customer service request, the system fails to detect it till the irate customer calls up.

Step 6 : An assembly line worker never needs to search around for instructions to work or parts to be integrated. But organisational work processes are rarely accompanied by support information required to take the decision, which can save great amounts of time presently being consumed in work processes.

With increasing B2C reach, the volumes of Indian businesses are scaling up rapidly. This is simultaneously leading to increased work loads for employees. But the corporate consideration has yet failed to focus on the use of technology to obviate the presence of employees while increasing their productivity. It is so because the work processes are in contrast to the efficiency of an assembly line system as mentioned above. The typical characteristics of organisations' work processes necessitate the presence of all members involved in the chain, thus setting a breeding ground for stagnant practices.

Redesigning Organisations

Information and communication technologies have added completely new dimensions to businesses. Whether the need is to web enable a business or reach customers through the web, the challenges go far beyond the 'automation only' needs of the past. Businesses need to be strategised to telework. The solutions need to focus on matching employee needs with organisations' needs and create a synergy rather than simply streamline procedures. Innovative ICT solutions need to wrap robust architectures with compelling interactions and interfaces. In the remaining part of this chapter the methodology for conceptualising, developing and delivering architectures suitable to teleworking will be discussed.

At the highest level, the solution development lifecycle for teleworking may be divided into four partially overlapping phases:

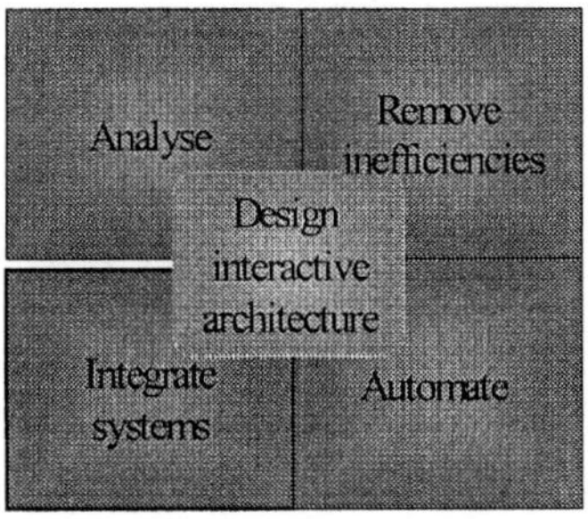

i. Elimination of inefficiencies

ii. Automation

iii. System integration

iv. Design of interactive architecture.

Only after delivery and implementation does the architecture enter the fifth phase: Manage. In order to redesign structures, thus making them e-work friendly, organisations need to execute these phases in a continuity.

i) Elimination of Inefficiencies

Elimination of inefficiencies require a few progressive steps. It has to begin with the broader understanding of the business environment and the rules under which the organisation operates. This exercise begins with listing and mapping out all the work processes in the business. These processes may range from raw material purchase to new product development, salary disbursement to e-recruitment and post retirement benefits, handling interest rates to digging new sources of finance. Theoretically, it is possible to optimise all these processes. But the company has to start with identifying those few that are most critical to the business. Out of these the prime candidates for removing inefficiencies will be the ones which are critical to the efficiency of present operations. For example, inflow and outflow of goods is important for a marketing organisation but with B2C commerce, removing inefficiencies or rather optimising the process of marketing plan approvals is more critical than the purchase process. Process criticality will thus depend on the macro environment and the crucial micro factors in business.

Once the decision on important processes for optimisation has been taken, the area of optimisation has to be decided. There are six areas in which any given workflow can be optimised: (Kobielus 1997)

- Speed
- Cost
- Accuracy
- Quality
- Customer satisfaction
- Flexibility.

This decision on area of optimisation will eventually decide the type of teleworking structure that suits best to a business process. An ideal situation would be where the optimisation areas are prioritised while determining teleworking solutions, because all solutions cater to different areas in different degrees.

After the removal of inefficiencies leading to optimisation of process, these processes should now be subjected to automation. As they get automated, work flows will become shorter and will require lesser human intervention and interaction.

ii) Automation

Most processes in the organisation have a definite beginning and end. They involve information that is used to arrive at a decision based on certain rules and the information decision moves from one person to another, calling for specific action by each. Thus a requirement for stationary gets generated in one department, goes to the stores/ purchase / maintenance department where it is subjected to certain processes and finally takes the same route back in the form of actual stationary. As the volume of such transactions increases, the chances of documents getting misplaced or being set aside for later action also increase. Thus, the heavier the traffic, the larger the need for the customer to chase up the process. An alternative to this chasing up can be creating automatic routing of documents to the concerned people for action. Automation would also require certain steps to be followed:

- Defining the information necessary to arrive at a decision.
- Identifying the chain of people for whom the action is required.
- Putting in a system that will automatically organise and route this information through to those people.

In the process of automation, the workflow will undergo a change, thus leaving some previous links redundant. This automation should also cater for possible delays in the completion of the process. Suppose someone in the workflow delays action, there has to be a mechanism to alert that person as well as his supervisor.

This can be done by identifying time limits for each action and defining who is to be intimated in case of default. Incorporating alternate actions in case of delay will make the process even stronger. While routine processes can have an image based or form based workflow, a framework for achieving this end can be designed even for less routine processes.

In this way, once the businesses have reengineered from hierarchical and functional organisation to process orientation, systems based strategies for incorporating teleworking in a phased manner can be adopted.

iii) System Integration

After automating the processes, designing structures on the basis of systems concepts would suit Indian organisations very well. Because of various socio-cultural, political and economic reasons, the employees in all organisations here have some attitudes ingrained very deeply in their work psyche. Slowly developing the new structure, deriving from the developmental phases of the networking systems concepts will give enough time, practice and the right environment so that the employees can unlearn old attitudes and relearn & adapt to the new ones, thus developing effective characteristics to become international members of teleworking organisations (Ahuja and Pandey 1999)

Evolutionary Stage I: Single User Single Tasking

This stage would be analogous with the systems of the early 1960s, which had one processor and in particular one common system clock. Thus a machine could do one task for one user at a time. The present Indian work ways represent this relationship, where a majority of the labour force works for a single company at a time. While information and communication technologies may be used to remain physically away from the job, the employees working for a single company may not be able to take complete benefit of freedom of time as they would be in a 'permanent' or 'full time' employment. On the other hand, companies in this stage of teleworking will have optimised their processes, thus leading to some degree of redundancy of employees. These mutually conflicting interests of the employers and employees will prepare the ground for the more advanced stage of teleworking.

The biggest pay back of this evolutionary stage will come when the company maps it's teleworking efforts to a key aspect of its business strategy. For most companies that will mean focusing on one or more of the four following areas:

- Innovation
- Responsiveness
- Productivity

- Competency

The success at this stage will further depend on choosing the right IT tools with distant vision and far reaching plans.

Evolutionary Stage II: Single User Multi Tasking

Once the need for access to many different units when climbing up and down the various levels has been pruned and the technology embedded in such a manner as to be used as a tool in every process, the first stage has been fully attained. Now the companies need to incorporate an understanding of human behaviour into technology. This will lead to three quantifiable results:

- The realisation of the excess in terms of human resources in the company.
- An urge among employees to utilise their idle time which increases as a result of making a habit of technology.
- The setting of a strong ground for knowledge management.

Once the networking systems are recreated, cutting down the interaction time of each unit, the effective time spent by a person for a single organisation will be drastically reduced, leaving enough work time to be devoted to other services in the same organisation, or the same service in another company. The same employee who was working for 8 hours a day in the first stage could now be hired for 3 hours for the given job responsibilities. To organisations it will give the benefit of reduced pay cheques due to reduced working time, to employees it will give the freedom to offer their services to another client simultaneously.

As this stage takes away the 'full time job' attitude and replaces it with 'contracts' more and more employees will willingly adapt to this new development; as it will provide the opportunity to expand skills and a personal network while one earns more for the same time devoted on work each day. Moreover, survival in the world of work would demand competent skills and uninterrupted as well as reliable human efficiencies for multiple contracts, thus constantly improving the quality of work in organizations.

The success at this stage will typically depend more on a company's cultural preparedness than on the virtues of any one technology. Cultural preparedness will have to incorporate a well thought out plan to change all human habits at work which impede efficiency and effectiveness of the work flows. The key would be to explicitly design technology to offset human barriers. For example, if employees were asked to keep their resumes up to date all the time, there are chances that they'd let that slip on their 'To Do' lists. But, if the price of parallel entry to a new project was that an employee had to submit an updated resume, that would probably be done at all times. The immediate reward will more than compensate for the effort required.

Similarly, interaction and process time would be lesser and lesser if all employees save important information or documents to a database ensuring that everyone was made aware of what was saved and where. This can be ensured if the system made some simple demands for key words, categories etc. before saving a document.

iv) Designing Interactive Architectures

By the culmination of Stage II, teleworking through IT would have transformed from a tactical initiative to a strategic one and traditional system integration services will no longer deliver the desired impact. This stage will thus be identified by the felt need for leveraging IT implementation. Thus the architectures created at this stage will have to be a mix of system integration, business strategy, internet technology and creative design skills to deliver a teleworking solution.

The initial stage (Evolutionary Stage I) for teleworking in Indian organisations has arrived and is heavily focusing on profits through B2C commerce. As more and more businesses move towards optimising their processes including supplies, vendor and partners the second stage would evolve simultaneously with result of the focus on B2B commerce. *Ad hoc* technology implementations will have given way to well understood and planned systems, not as solutions to business problems, but as advancements. The design of interactive architectures would see an integrated focus on B2C, B2B and B2E – all three interacting to build up the most effective organisational teleworking architectures. In such architectures, teleworking would not be a conscious decision but a part of the organisational culture stemming from customer demands and a reduced cycle time facilitated by increased efficiencies of employees as empowered members of an organisation.

References

Ahuja, S. and Pandey, A.D. (1999) 'Strategies for Managing Human Resources in Indian Teleworking: A Systems Based Approach', *in Value Creation- The Challenge of Human Resource in the New Millennium*, New Delhi : Tata McGraw Hill.

Bagchi, P. (2000) 'Make Law in Haste, Repent at Leisure', in *Business Standard*, May 25, New Delhi, p.11.

Indian Market Research Bureau (2000) *A Survey of E Commerce in India*, www.imrbint.com\ec990615survey.htm

Kinsman, F. (1987) *The Telecommuters*, Chichester: John Wiley.

Kobielus James G. (1997) *Workflow Strategies*, Comdex.

5 Telework and Japanese Human Resources Management System

Chiyoko Shimozaki

Kobe University of Commerce

Introduction

The number of teleworkers in Japan has been a little over 1 million in 2000. However, it is much smaller than the number of teleworkers in Europe and the U.S. What is the obstacle to increasing teleworkers in Japanese society? We can find out the most important issue in Japanese Human Resources Management System (JHRMS). The old-JHRMS had a lot of contradictory aspects for telework, for example, an attitude assessment, an unspecified job assignment, their preference of face to face communication, collectivism and so on.

However, the old-JHRMS is being restructured into two entirely different JHRM systems that have different paradigms and consist of opposite elements. One is HRMS based on 'Individualizing' ('Individualizing' HRMS), which tries to replace all elements of the old-JHRMS; the other is HRMS based on 'Sharing' ('Sharing' HRMS), which keeps most elements of the old-JHRMS, except the Seniority System.

I will infer that with regard to the introduction of telework, companies with 'Individualizing' HRMS will be easier, but companies with 'Sharing' HRMS will be more difficult. This is one hypothesis to be verified in this chapter. I have confirmed this hypothesis by the following research that analysed this data, and was collected from the 'Telework Company' and 'Non-Telework Company' by our questionnaire survey.

The Old-Japanese Human Resources Management System

In Japan, most elements of the old-Japanese Human Resources Management system have been constructed with the Japanese economic growth following the Second World War. It has been said that this old-JHRMS is unique to Japan, compared with HRM in the United States, European nations and other countries in Asia.

As shown in Figure 1, this old-JHRMS consists of three elements, which are customs or institutions; these are Life-time Employment, the Japanese Seniority System and Company-based Trade Unions. Why and how have these elements been constructed? In this section, I will explain the old-JHRMS through an organizational behaviour approach.

Three psychological compatibilities with the old-JHRMS

I will extract the psychological relationships between employees and the old-JHRMS by using an Organizational Behaviour approach, which will explain for us how the old-JHRMS fits with Japanese psychological factors. In this analysis, I will show three compatible relations in this section. It is important to note that this relationship has generated a driving force for Japanese company growth.

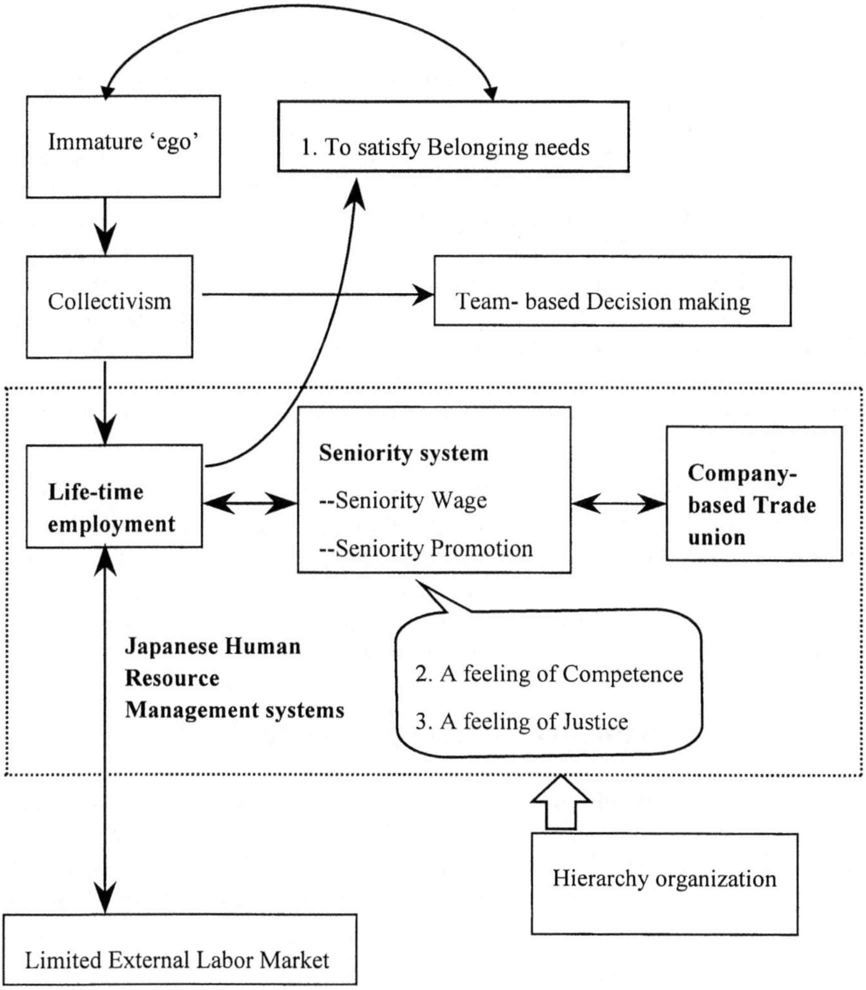

Figure 1. The old Japanese Human Resources Management System

The first compatibility – immature 'ego'

At first, Japanese employees seek to keep a sense of belonging to their company. It means that the Japanese have strong belonging needs to wish to commit to any one group or organization. This is not only for most of the employees but also for most of the employers, who regard it as a matter of course to keep their job in one company until retirement. As a result, Life-time Employment has been constructed. Yet Life-time Employment has also been making growing companies keep low labour costs.

Why do the Japanese crave a sense of belonging to their organization? Some famous clinical psychologists insist that 'ego' never matures completely in most of the Japanese (Doi 1975, Kawai 1976, Minami 1983). This characteristic leads to the wish for a sense of belonging and to the hesitation in decision making by oneself. I suppose that these psychological characteristics turn to the typical tendency of the Japanese strongly committing to a specific group. By Hofstede's cultural dimension, Japan is classified as 'Collectivism' (Hofstede 1991). This Collectivism has the same meaning as the strong commitment to a specific organization in Japan. These psychological backgrounds have been functioning so as to reinforce Life-time Employment.

This means that the Life-time Employment is suited to Japanese psychological characteristics. This is the first psychological compatibility with the old-JHRMS. Life-time Employment could provide Japanese employees not only financial stability, but also substantial 'psychological stability'. However, on account of Life-time Employment, the labour market in Japan has not been built in such a way that it covers every occupation and every function.

The second compatibility – a feeling of 'justice'

In general, it is difficult to motivate employees so as to work hard under employment security. However, the old-JHRMS includes a sub-system that can cultivate their morale. That is within the Japanese Seniority System. This Seniority System consists of a Seniority Wage System and Seniority Promotion System.

Under the Seniority Wage System, soon after students have graduated from their university, they are employed as recruits in most companies. They are almost the same age, with perhaps 1 or 2 years difference. The main part of the wage for each employee is determined by the length of his or her service. Their wages are raised on the same day every year, almost at the same ratio. In this way, employees in a Japanese company are able to obtain a feeling of justice – that is a feeling of equity. They never feel inequity, even though employees of the same age may be engaged in different jobs at the same wage. The Japanese do not regard equity via a ratio of outcome to input as justice, rather equality, necessity and equity by seniority (Deutsch 1975, Shimozaki 2000).

This is the second psychological compatibility with the old-JHRMS. In Japan, the main part of a wage has not been decided by job role or performance, but instead by the length of service. It is a feeling of justice for the Japanese. It is also noteworthy that the Japanese wage has not been decided by job role or performance since the Second World War.

The third compatibility – improving 'competence'

Under the other Seniority Promotion System, some excellent personnel are selected among the same seniority group and promoted to higher positions, faster than other colleagues. In general, the other employees are also promoted to upper positions sooner or later, depending on length of their service. It seems that the difference is only in the speed of promotion and the importance of each position.

The most powerful motivational factor in a human being is to improve 'competence' (White 1959). A feeling of 'competence' needs 'recognition' by the others, which is also regarded as the strongest needs of a human being (Fukuyama 1992). Promotion can give people a stronger feeling of 'competence' or 'recognition' in Japan than in any other country. Therefore, it is said that promotion is the strongest motivator to make people work hard in Japan.

Therefore, the Seniority Promotion System brings out the third psychological compatibility with the Japanese. People can satisfy their growth needs by improving 'competence' and acquiring 'recognition' through their promotion. Moreover, they are competing with each other in order to gain promotion into a good position as fast as possible. This competition for good positions has facilitated the growth of organization (Iwata 1977). This is one reason why high economic growth has been achieved in Japan.

Functional disorder in the old-JHRMS

However, the current economic environment does not allow us to keep the old Japanese Human Resources Management System, the reason being that most of the Japanese companies are no longer able to pay their seniority wages and to prepare positions for promotion. It can safely be said that we cannot maintain a Japanese Seniority System. Yet this Seniority System has been the incentive system to employees under the Life-time Employment system. If incentives in the old-JHRMS disappear, it could prevent the companies from keeping Life-time Employment. Because the old-JHRMS has been functioning as a system, the dysfunction of a subsystem will affect the whole. Then, the fact that Japanese Seniority Systems cannot function well will lead to a functional disorder of the old-JHRMS itself.

We have to reform the old-JHRMS. However, the JHRMS in a company is not operating by itself – rather, it is co-operating with employees as an internal environmental factor and with a socio-economic system as an external environment. Therefore, if JHRMS will be transformed into another new system, as a matter of course, internal and external environments will also require reform.

To transform these systems into new systems as a whole would be extremely difficult and take a long time. Is it easier to change the psychological nature and behaviour of the Japanese into another pattern? It would take dozens of years (or perhaps even a century), not several years. We cannot wait so long, and restructuring has already gradually begun.

Consequently, the next question concerns which patterns the old-JHRMS will be evolving into. In this chapter, I present two different Scenarios of a new HRMS, which are HRMS based on 'Individualizing' and HRMS based on 'Sharing'. Before explaining these two Scenarios, let me explain how difficult it is to adapt telework to a Japanese company under the old-JHRMS.

The old-JHRMS and telework

Under the old-JHRMS, it is very difficult for a Japanese company to introduce telework as a new way of working. The reason seems to be that JHRMS is related closely to Japanese culture. Job assignment and job assessment are serious obstacles for a teleworker working under the old-JHRMS. Most managers do not know how to manage and evaluate a subordinate who is working as a teleworker. The essence of this problem rests on the ambiguity of job description, which helps the company activate Life-time Employment. In Japanese organizations, there is no specific job assignment for each employee. His or her job is only decided vaguely. When a job needs to be performed occasionally by someone, a manager assigns an appropriate subordinate to the job. A manager needs to understand the situation of his subordinate, and to do so, they and their subordinates must be staying nearby in the same room, and he must continually look over them. Consequently, both employees and management in Japanese organizations prefer a face-to-face relationship. A manager can give a subordinate the command of what and when something is required. This tendency is inconsistent with the conditions of telecommunication in telework.

HRMS based on 'Individualizing'

One of the new JHRMS is HRMS based on the concept of 'Individualizing' that is replacing all elements of the old-JHRMS. It is on the assumption that the Japanese personal 'ego' can mature perfectly and the Japanese labour market can be free and open for all employees.

In this JHRMS, it is predicted that employment will turn from life-time to short-term except core-personnel. Moreover, it is assumed that the Japanese no longer want to keep belonging to a specific organization after the ego has matured.

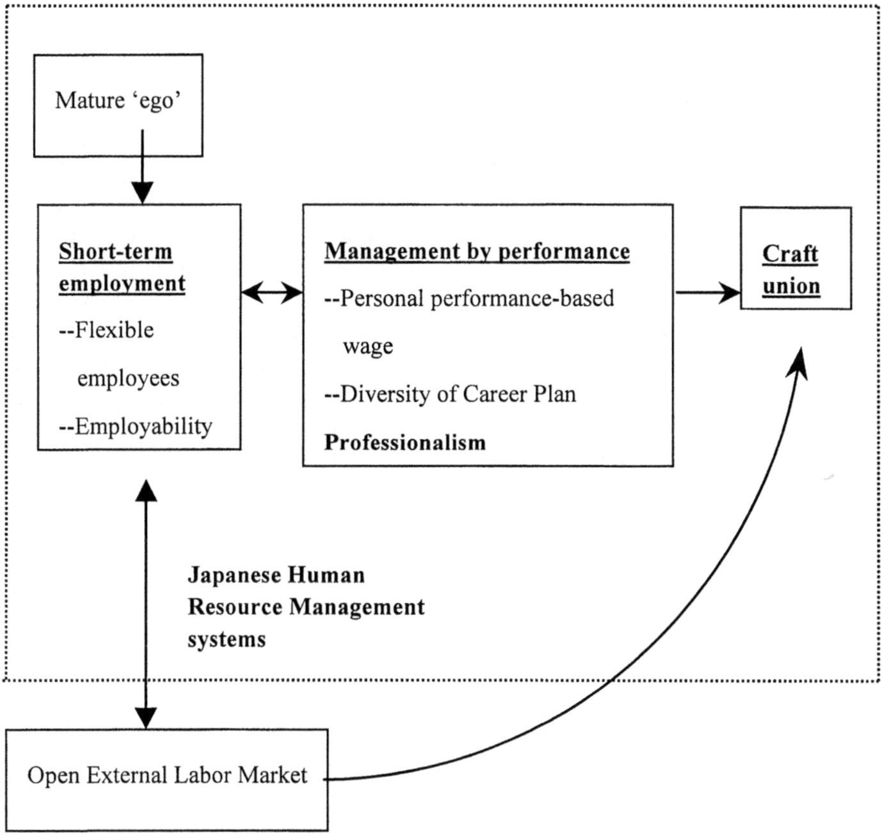

Figure 2. HRMS based on 'Individualising'

However, the true reason for reform is because the Japanese Seniority System cannot be maintained, largely because the System leads to labour costs increasing and company profits decreasing. Before a reform of Life-time Employment, the Japanese Seniority System has to be modified into new institutions. It is changing into the direction of management by performance, and is hoped that the wages and promotion for each employee would be decided by the assessment of performance or competence, and not be relevant to seniority or family.

Employees with high performance, professional skills or high competency are regarded as core-personnel who will engage in core-management or the core-operations of their business. The non-core-management or non-core-operations are performed by non-core-personnel (part-time workers or contingent-workers).

These labour costs must be treated as a variable cost that does not necessarily increase every year, because they are employed only when needed. Moreover, they are employees with a contract of a given limited period.

In this case, I can point out a contradiction between the Japanese mentality and 'Individualizing' HRMS. This HRMS is constructed on the assumption that (1) the Japanese personal 'ego' matures perfectly, (2) employees are motivated to work by wage incentives, and (3) the equity among employees is recognized by their outcome to the input (Shimozaki 2000). However, these assumptions are inconsistent with the three psychological compatibilities in the old-JHRMS. As a result, 'Individualizing' HRMS and Japanese psychological needs would be badly mismatched. Moreover, this HRMS is based on the assumption that social systems can be similary restructured. For example, that free and open labour markets can function easily, that the social security system which is linked to big companies can be completely enriched, and so on.

Since these assumptions are unrealistic, I propose that 'Individualizing' HRMS will be accepted only by a limited number of companies.

HRMS based on 'Sharing'

The other new JHRMS is HRMS based on the concept of 'Sharing'. This JHRMS includes the reform of the Japanese Seniority System and the retention of other elements with a certain level of modification. However, if the Seniority System is destroyed, the problems of what motivates employees and how employees have a feeling of justice will occur. This is the most serious problem in 'Sharing' HRMS, because the promotion as a motivator cannot be given to all employees. We have to discover a new incentive for employees.

'Sharing' HRMS consists of three sub-systems, which are 'Employment Sharing', 'Wage Sharing' and 'Position Sharing'.

The first 'Employment Sharing' means job security for people who want to work. Under 'Sharing' HRMS, employees are not dismissed easily and these companies are required to secure their jobs, even if employment should be cut off. It is held here that Japanese Life-time Employment has unconsciously been aimed at 'Employment Sharing'. Still more, there are other 'Employment Sharing' institutions, which are 'work-sharing', 'job-sharing', 're-employment after retirement', 'loan into an affiliated company' and so on. This 'Employment Sharing' can give employees psychological stability, because it helps employees to have a sense of belonging.

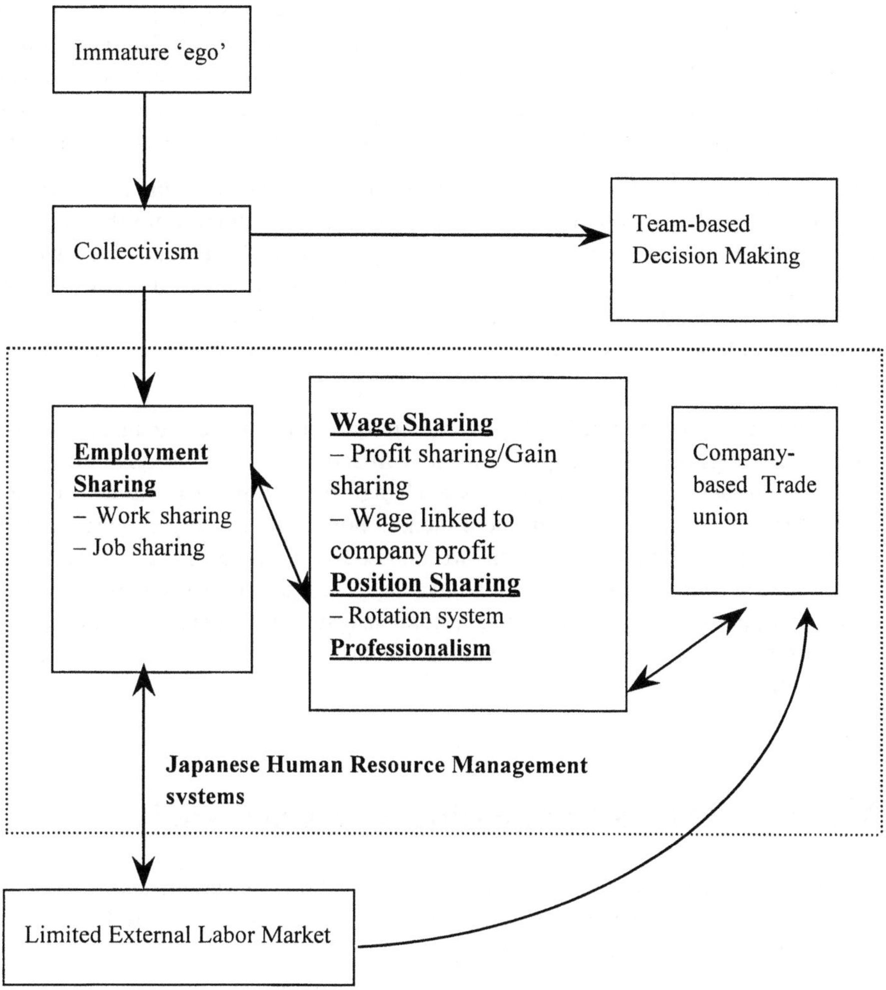

Figure 3. HRMS based on 'Sharing'

Also under 'Employment Sharing', our wages must be flexible or variable. If our wage would be inelastic, most companies could not avoid dismissing employees in order to maintain their going-concern under frequent recessions. If our wages would be flexible, companies could keep their employment only on the condition that salary is variable. Then, wages need to be connected to the company performance, not to personnel performance. As a result, our wage is decided by the way of sharing among employees, stockholders and the company itself. This can be explained as 'Wage Sharing'. Other institutions of 'Wage Sharing' consist of 'stock option', 'employee ownership', 'wage or a bonus based on company performance', 'profit sharing', 'gain sharing' and so on. I understand the Japanese Seniority Wage System as 'Wage Sharing' among the ages and the same seniority.

The third element is 'Position Sharing'. Most business organizations are structured as a hierarchy. The employees believe that they can be climbing up the ladder of promotion. They have never imagined stepping down the ladder. This way of thinking brings an inflexibility of organization. In order to avoid this inflexibility, organizations should be flat. In the flat organization, there is no promotion, because hierarchy does not exist. Therefore employees cannot hope to get their position.

However, 'position rotation' is also needed in order to activate organization. Even though an employee is in a position, he will have to leave his position after a specific number of years. Employees exchange these limited positions amongst each other. The most serious problem then, is how to motivate personnel without promotion. To resolve this problem, we must develop some new rewards instead of promotion. The new rewards would be 'recognition' of personnel skills, profession, competency or outcome. A company must give employees the reward of 'recognition', which can provide a feeling of competence, in place of promotion.

Which HRMS is Compatible with Telework?

From the above observation, I have set up the following hypothesis. In order to test this hypothesis, I have performed my questionnaire research and this data has been analysed statistically.

Hypothesis

> The company which adopts 'Individualizing' HRMS has a tendency to introduce telework as a new way of work. On the other hand, the company which adopts 'Sharing' HRMS has more difficulty in introducing telework.

Procedure

We have verified the above hypothesis by analysing results of the questionnaires about HRMS. In May 2000, these questionnaires have been sent to 30 companies that are introducing or have introduced telework. We have received the answers from 14 companies (47%). These companies are scattered all over Japan. We label these companies as a 'Telework Company'.

Moreover, we have collected the answers of the questionnaires from 13 companies that have taken part in a study group of Japanese Human Resources Management in Hyogo in April 2000. These companies are located only in Hyogo prefecture. Since these companies do not introduce telework, we label these companies as a 'Non-Telework Company'.

Conclusion

Results are shown in Figure 4. Noting my conclusion first, I can mention that these research results support the above hypothesis. It is clear that, the scores of 'Individualizing' HRMS are higher than that of 'Sharing' HRMS in the Telework companies. On the other hand, the Non-Telework companies are higher in the scores of 'Sharing' HRMS than in that of 'Individualizing' HRMS. Furthermore this data has been verified by a Mann-Whitney test. Then this hypothesis has been confirmed.

Moreover, we can find another interesting result. According to an Industrial classification, only 4 of 14 Telework companies are classified as part of secondary industry; the other 10 companies are classified as part of tertiary industry. Since two out of four companies are assembling IT products in the secondary industry, two companies may be classified within the tertiary industry. On the other hand, only three of Non-Telework companies, are classified into the tertiary industry, and the other 10 companies are classified into the secondary industry.

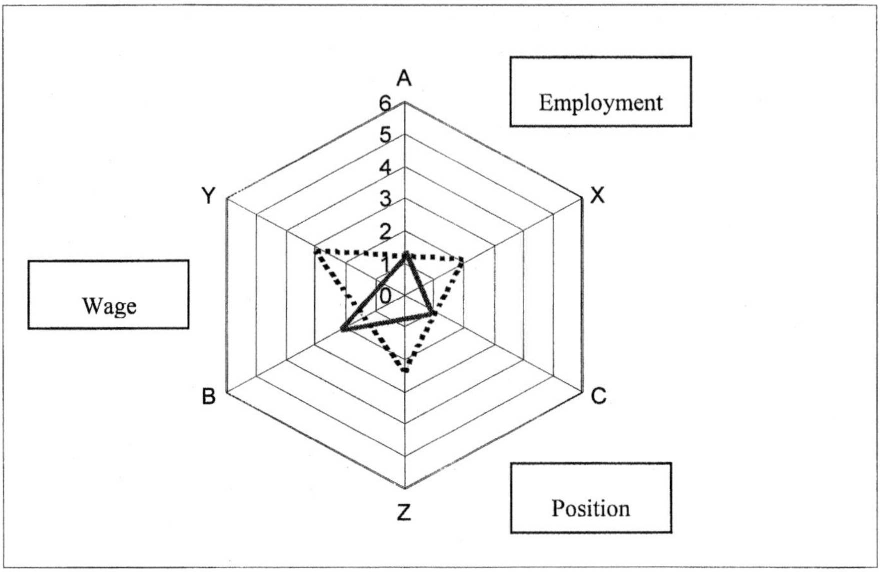

Figure 4. Scores of 'Sharing' and 'Individualizing' (Telework Company).

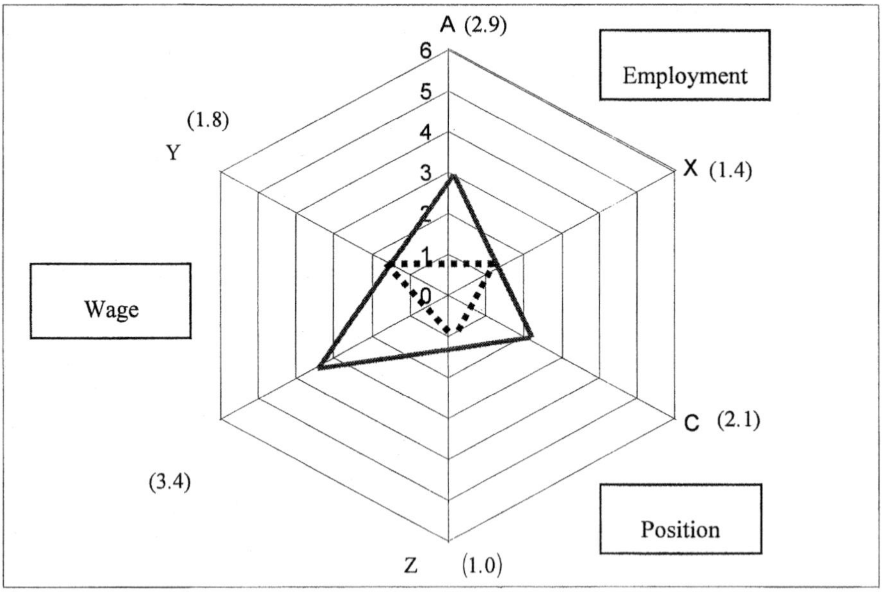

Figure 5. Scores of 'Sharing' and 'Individualizing' (Non-Telework Company).

From this data, I may be able to conclude that telework must be the new way of working in the post-industrial society, because the companies in the tertiary industry are reforming their HRMS into 'Individualizing' HRMS. This tendency would help them introduce Telework. In this way, the pattern of HRMS has a clear interrelation to telework.

What are the reasons for these differences between a 'Telework company' and a 'Non-telework company'? I can assert that these differences are based on a difference of industrial structure, that is, secondary or tertiary industry. The needs from the industrial structure regulate which pattern of HRMS will be adopted. In the secondary industry, it is necessary for employees to stay and work at the same time at the same place for mass-production. Under these conditions, the old JHRMS regarded as 'Sharing' HRMS was developed in Japan. Yet companies in a tertiary industry are dealing with knowledge and information. They are not regulated by operating machinery, but have flexibility in where and when to work. It is possible to introduce in these companies the other HRMS. That is, the 'Individualizing' HRMS.

However, at this point, we have a serious problem, namely incompatibility with 'Individualizing' HRMS and the Japanese mentality. Under 'Individualizing' HRMS, most Japanese are not able to get psychological stability and a feeling of justice. Only within limited companies will it be better and easy to introduce 'Individualizing' HRMS. Is this HRMS able to come into wider use? Some authors make points of the problems brought by 'Individualizing' HRMS (Mitra, Gupta and Douglas 1995, Pfeffer 1998). From these criticisms, a Japanese company must be careful in introducing 'Individualizing' HRMS. We should not make a mistake in which direction is to be taken.

References

(* Japanese)

Adams, J. S. (1965) 'Inequity in Social Exchange', in L. Berkowitz (ed.) *Advanced in Experimental Social Psychology*, 2: 267-299.

Deci, E. L. (1975) *Intrinsic Motivation*, Plenum Press.

Deutsch, M. (1975) 'Equity, Equality, and Need: What Direction Which Value Will Be Used as the Bases of Distributive Justice?', The Journal of Social Issues, 31.3: 137-149

Doi, T. (1977) *The Anatomy of Dependence*, Kodansha International.

Economic Planning Agency (1998) 'Rethinking of Japanese Human Resources Management', (http://www.epg.go.jp/98/f/19980415f-ank-1.html)*

Fukuyama, F. (1992) *The End of History*, The Free Press.

Fukuyama, F. (1995) *Trust*, The Free Press.

Hofstede, G. (1991) *Culture and Organization: Software of the Mind*, McGraw-Hill.

Iwata, R. (1977) *Principles Structuring Japanese Management System*, BUNSHINDOU*.

Kawai, H. (1976) *Psychological Disease in Japanese Maternal society*, CHUOUKOURON*.

Labour Administration, Inc. (1944) *Directions of Human Resources Management in 21'th Century*, ROSEIJIHO Separated volume*.

Luthans, F. (1997) *Organizational Behavior 8th ed*, McGraw-Hill.

Maslow, A. H. (1954) *Motivation and Personality*, Harper & Row.

Maslow, A. H. (1971) *The Farther Reaches of Human Nature*, The Viking Press.

Minami, H. (1983) *Japanese 'ego'*, IWANAMI*.

Mitra, A., Gupta, N. and Douglas, J. Jr., G. (1995) 'The Case of the Invisible Merit Raise: How People See Their Pay Raises', Compensation and Benefits Review, May-June, 71-76.

Morsh, J. M. and Lorsch, J. W. (1970) 'Beyond Theory Y', Harvard Business Review, May-June: 37-44.

Ota, H. (1994) *Japanese Company and Individuals*, HAKUTOSHOBO*.

Pfeffer, J. (1998) *The Human Equation*, Harvard Business School Press.

Shimozaki, C. (1991) *Organizational Behavior in Contemporary Company*, HAKUTOSHOBO*.

Shimozaki, C. (2000) 'Japanese Human Resources Management Based on 'Sharing'', SHODAIRONSHU, 51, 5*.

Spinks, W. A. (1998) *Telework Century*, The Japan Institute of Labour*.

White, R. W. (1963) *Ego and Reality in Psychoanalytic Theory*, International University Press.

Design Issues in Virtual Organising

In the second section of Part One, we address the matter of design. In their various ways, the chapters point to the need for a systematic analysis of the contexts within which change is to be introduced, and for a more intellectually rigorous appreciation of the dynamics of virtual structures. Not only are new theoretical frameworks called for to make sense of organisational change, the authors also point to the need for new models and tools to support the implementation of change. Taken together, the chapters that follow thus provide new ways of understanding the array of changes affecting organisations; but they also show how this knowledge can be combined to produce methodologies for bringing about sustainable and successful change itself.

According to Ali Yakhelf, in Chapter 6, 'we have always been virtual'. As he points out, virtuality can be (and has been) understood in many different ways – ways that have characterised organisations and their products for some time. Yakhelf suggests that virtuality can be thought of in terms of detachment from the 'here' and 'now'. Given changes to the temporal and spatial constitution of work, the boundaries between the here and now have gradually blurred – a process that started with such developments as writing but was subsequently heightened by innovations in ICTs. Yakhelf is particularly concerned to show us how this has impacted upon organisational relations, especially between the 'self' and 'others'. In so doing, he provides us with a deeper theoretical grasp of many contemporary changes in organisational design, and most significantly, those we discuss under the label 'virtual'.

In Chapter 7 by Reima Suomi, we look at the acceptance of teleworking and virtual organisation. According to Suomi, attitudes towards such ICT related developments vary depending on the perspective adopted. He explains this using five approaches: transaction cost theory, agency theory, resource-based theory, process thinking and organisational learning. By producing a more rounded analysis of virtual work innovations, Suomi shows us how we are better placed to design effective work solutions, as well as convince decision-makers as to the merits of particular ICT innovations.

Transaction cost theory makes another appearance in the next chapter, by Andrew Gaudes. The author uses a range of frameworks – most notably psychological contract theory – to provide an integrative conceptualisation of virtual organising processes. For Gaudes, the key challenge here is to provide a more sophisticated way of understanding the exchanges that characterise relationships and flows in virtual structures. The chapter shows that only by drawing together economic and psychosocial dimensions (among others), can we arrive at rigorous models for making sense of – as well as managing – the contexts of virtual organisations.

In Chapter 9, by Diana Limburg, we examine the design and implementation of telework. Drawing on case study work in the Netherlands, Limburg develops a framework that reflects the need for situated design and learning. Her starting point is that telework introduction involves alteration to the social routines that have been built up in a given work context; as such, it is necessary for those involved to 'un-learn' old modes of behaviour, as well as to learn new routines consistent with the envisaged change. Limburg shows how learning mechanisms can thus bridge the design and development phases of change. While this may be more incremental than re-engineering type methods, the chapter suggests that such approaches are likely to be more effective in bringing about desired changes.

The final chapter in this section, and of Part One of the book as a whole, is by Pedro Almeida and Óscar Mealha. It focuses on the need for a robust conceptualisation of teleworking environments, such that communications and interface issues can be better understood and addressed. The authors develop a model of the telework environment and go on to discuss the issues that govern its implementation. Like Limburg, Almeida and Mealha remind us that to design effective innovations, we first need a systematic examination, and accurate representation, of the contexts within which new technologies and new ways of organising are being employed.

6 We Have Always Been Virtual

Ali Yakhlef

School of Business, Stockholm University, Sweden

Introduction

The expression 'virtual corporation' was mostly popularised by Davidow and Malone (1992) and Byrne *et al* in *Business Week* (1993, Feb 8th). A virtual corporation is characterised as an edge-less and porous structure, with continuously shifting interfaces among a company, suppliers, customers, regulators, etc. Its design is constantly reforming according to customer needs. Virtual products and services are defined in terms of information and knowledge. To some theorists, information technology (IT) is a determining factor (Byrne et al 1993). Others (i.e. Davidow and Malone 1992; Hedberg et al 1994) simply emphasise its role as a facilitator. According to the former view, the virtualisation of organisation opens up new modes of interactions and relationships—all of which are attendant upon the advent of information technologies (customer databases, simulations, e-mails, videoconferencing, Internet, Intranet, Extranet, virtual reality, etc) (Byrne et al 1993; Franke 2000). Central to most such considerations is the idea of time-space compression, or the erosion of time-space constraints. Removing time-space co-ordinates enables firms to save time and costs. Because unrelated suppliers are involved in the sharing of resources, information and knowledge in a virtual setting, there has been a renewed interest in the role of *trust* as an alternative control or co-ordination mechanism, as a substitute for contract, price or authority (Arrow 1974; Handy 1990; Bradach and Eccles 1989; Hedberg et al 1998; Franke 2000). The underlying assumption is that management is unable to exert direct control within virtual contexts. "Virtuality... [means] without a place as its home. Virtuality requires trust to make it work." (Handy 1995: 44).

Despite the much-hyped concept of virtuality - virtual book-shops, virtual universities, virtual shopping malls, virtual offices, virtual factory, virtual workers, virtual communities, etc - there is no consensus on what the notion of 'virtuality' stands for. For instance, Hale and Whitlam (1997) lament that 'virtual organization is the name given to any organization which is continually evolving, redefining and reinventing itself for practical business purposes' (Ibid. 3). The description of such form of organising does not necessarily inherit its features from the notion of virtuality; it could have been called adaptive, flexible, agile, etc, leaving unanswered such questions as how can technology, knowledge and trust be conceptually related to a theory of virtual organisation. Furthermore, it is assumed that virtual entities are claimed to involve a brand new mode of being. For instance, Davidow and Malone (1992) point out that virtual products and services are "so remarkable, so distinct from anything that came before that they deserve a special name. In this book they are referred to as *virtual products*" (pp.3-4). But how unlike their precedents are these products? What is new about the current wave towards virtualisation? What makes an organisation virtual?

Aim of the Chapter

The aim of this chapter is to explore the features of virtuality, to argue that virtual entities are not new (for we have always been virtual) and to describe the modes of virtualisation. The assumption is that virtuality is the very process of humanity's *becoming other*, the process through which humanity creates itself (Deleuze 1968/1994; Lévy 1998). It is a movement from the real, or the actual towards the virtual. Although information and communication technologies (as a different intellectual technology and media of communication) seem to lie at the heart of the on-going virtualising wave, imagination, memory, knowledge, institutions and religion are the vectors of virtualisation that have enabled humans to leave this 'here' and this 'now' long before the appearance of computerisation and digital networks (Lévy 1998).

The next section (Section 2) is devoted to an exploration of the features of virtuality, attempting to tie together the various theoretical threads into a coherent conceptual tapestry, drawing on Deleuze (1984: 208) and Lévy (1998). Section 3 looks into three main modes of virtualisation - writing (conventional and electronic) for the virtualising of objects and on-going (cognitive) processes, social artefacts (i.e. institutions) for the virtualising of social relations, and technological artefacts (i.e. tools, machines, cybernetic devices) for the virtualising of human action. The first mode relates to the symbolic, the second to the social, relational and the third to the practical being. The chapter concludes with some implications for our understanding of the notion of virtual entities, virtuality, virtualisation and its modes.

The Features of Virtuality

An organisation is traditionally conceived of as a bounded space to which employees go to in order to work. As a workplace, it can be regarded as a gathering, geographical place, in which each employee occupies a personal/physical space and a position during a certain amount of hours everyday. Organisational members are defined as such in terms of their proximity (or physically being there) performing a number of well-determined tasks for which they are rewarded. However, when an organisation is virtualised, the link between its members and their workplace is loosened. Proximity loses its meaning as a defining feature of organisational membership. The link between employees and their organisation can, for instance, be established through electronic communication networks. Virtualisation involves a process whereby employees' being 'there' at a certain place and time is transformed into other technical possibilities, problems and solutions (Lévy 1998). Hence, people's bodies break loose from the constraints of space and time; they are thus deterritorialised and detemporalised, taking on a nomadic mode of being. In some sense, virtualisation is not a way of being, but rather a dynamic process of becoming (Lévy 1998).

Virtualisation involves a detachment from the 'here' and 'now', for the virtual is often literally speaking 'not here'. Once virtualised, the corporation cannot occupy a specific location, it migrates from a physical space to new spaces where synchronisation replaces spatial unity, and interconnections substitute for temporal unity (Lévy 1998). Within virtual settings, geography becomes contingent, since the geographical position of things and humans is not pertinent to the same degree as before. Over and above deterritorialisation and detemporalisation, virtualisation involves inside-outside displacement, a transition from interior to exterior, and from exterior to interior. It leads to an interplay between the public and the private, subjective and objective, personal and shared, etc. For instance, the traditional worker had his office, the virtual worker, however, shares a number of resources (software and infrastructure) with other workers in order to co-ordinate their work with that of others. Whereas the traditional worker travels from the private space (home) to the office (public space), a telecommuter turns their private space (home) into a public space (office). Clear boundaries give way to blurred divisions, calling into question those very distinctions. Virtualisation, thus, involves a mode that questions categorisation based on inclusion, exclusion and excluded middles, since these blend and fade into each other. Resources can be ours and theirs at the same time. From the viewpoint of the relation between the individual and others, virtualisation involves an attempt at embracing or sharing the perspective of the others, thereby seeking to reduce conflicts and discrepancies, and to blur the boundaries between the self and other.

The virtualisation of an entity involves a shift away from given solutions (such as defined structures, boundaries, identities, routines, practices, determined work hours, etc) to new, but different problems. In the case of the virtualisation of the corporation, this "consists primarily in transforming spatio-temporal co-ordinates of work into a continuously renewed problem rather than a stable solution. Although problematic, the process of virtualisation is pregnant with possibilities, freedom and flexibility (in operating). The organisation's centre of gravity is no longer a group of buildings, workstations and schedules, but a process of co-ordination" (Lévy 1998: 27). This transformation of reality into a continuous problematic, by making existing distinctions fluid, and by increasing the degree of freedom and also of the risk involved, is according to Lévy (ibid.), "one of the principal vectors in the creation of reality", for virtualisation opens up realms, new spaces for interactions and new velocities.

When a person, community, act or piece of information is virtualised, there arises the need for creating a communicative medium for social interactions in which these can be reconfigured in novel ways. These media, or systems for reinventing new relations, recording, sharing and transmitting information and knowledge have evolved from oral means, through writing, audio-visual to the latest digital networks. These are arenas for people to interact, exchange and share values, ideas and resources. By means of communications and telepresence entities can be simultaneously 'here' and 'there'. In this context, the inside, personal and the outside, public permeate and blend. Telepresence devices do not only represent entities, but they also double them, by making them 'here' and 'there', personal and public, at one and the same time.

In sum, virtualisation involves a shift from a given solution to a (different) problem (Lévy 1998), where identities, their structures, boundaries and functions fade into one another. It is an escape from the 'here' and 'now' to becoming other. It deterritorialises and detemporalises them, subjecting them to various inside-outside transformations and displacements. Written messages on papers, in audio-visual or network media are devices that allow us to transcend face-to-face modes of interaction and communication; they enable us to leave this 'here' and 'now'. In this sense, they constitute a bonding object that holds virtual interactants linked up, enabling them to share a set of common values and cognitive grids. Hence writing (in all its forms) is one of the most pertinent virtualising devices. The sharing of ideas, values and culture leads to a 'common' mind, a set of comparable ways of thinking, defining themselves, producing artefacts and relating to one other. Writing then precipitates the exchange of cognitive processes, thereby virtualising knowledge. Technological artefacts (such as a hammer, the wheel, machines) substitute for and extend bodily functions. They virtualise human action. Finally, social artefacts, rituals, contracts, trust, institutions, etc, reduce the necessity for people to interact and negotiate their relations every time they enter into a social/economic transaction.

The Vectors Towards Virtualisation

Virtualisation is a process by which human beings evolve and create their world through three processes: *writing*, *technology* and *institutions*. Whereas technology (such as a bicycle, an answering machine), virtualises human action and intention, writing virtualises a 'here and now' and sets it free from the chuckles of time and space, and institutions virtualise social relationships which may be potentially replete with conflicts, hence doing away with physical proximity, friction and even violence. Lévy's (1998) refers to the symbolic, relation/social and practical being as the *trivium* of being.

The Virtualisation of the 'Here' and 'Now' through *Writing*

Goody (1977) observes that 'A face-to-face group has no great need of writing'. Even in traditional organisations, writing has been an engine in the process of its virtualisation. One of the properties of language is *displacement*, which refers to the ability to refer to objects and events that are remote in time and place from the act of utterance itself (Lyons 1977: 80). Hence, the virtualisation of a corporation is not a new phenomenon, but rather, a process that is attendant upon the advent of writing and the keeping of written documents and records. Weber (1947: 330-2) has already pointed out the complicity of the rise of large bureaucracies with writing; noting that in bureaucratic organisations the conduct of official business was performed on the basis of written documents. For, 'in earlier systems of administration, official business is transacted in personal encounter and by oral communication, not on the basis of impersonal documents' (Bendix 1960: 420, quoted in Goody 1977: 15).

Goody (1977), Ong (1982), Havelock (1978), Eisenstein (1979), and Benedikt (1991) have explored the effects of the shift from an oral to a literate society. Predominantly, oral communication relies on *indexical* features, or situational and operational frames of reference that remain close to real-life, human activity (Ong 1982). This contrasts with writing abstracts from the human experience, virtualising personal ideas and cognitive processes. In his seminal thesis, Goody (1977.) contends that in exchanging ideas with a large community, and by making ideas available in written material, critical thinking and speculation was fostered in classical Greece. Written information is a more stable account of events, beliefs and experiences, which allows scrutinising, alteration and omission (Foley 1997: 418). Goody (1977) suggests that comparing written data and different texts has led 'to an attitude of scepticism and critical inquiry, culminating in the Greek philosophy of Plato and Aristotle. Moreover, writing, according to Goody, has also resulted in another cognitive skill – namely logical, rational reasoning. Explaining different views aims at reconciling contradictions and differences among members of a society, since in a text the specific social configuration (such as the sex, class or caste of the speaker or the addressee) is not taken for granted by individuals. Because it is virtualised, impersonal and objectivated, individuals tend to be more critical and to view information in a more rational way. It has also increased the potentialities of storing information, enabling cumulative knowledge to develop since 'a wider range of 'thought' was made available to the reading public' (Goody 1997: 37). By enabling access to a wide range of views, reviews, comments and comments on comments over distances and over a much larger time span, writing has led to the growth of public knowledge and increased rationality, giving rise to a scientific mind.

The Emergence of the Electronic Text

Messages could only travel where their container could be transported - scratched clay tablets, bark shards, smoke, personal couriers, papyri, sheets of paper, etc. Speed of message delivery increased with the advent of the telegraph, telephone, radio, television and recently computers. The reach (the number of people that a message can reach) and richness (the amount of information encoded in a message) are constrained by the container or the carrier in which messages are incorporated. Hand-written book scribes were slow and expensive to disseminate. The invention of the printing press led to a massive increase in books and the invention of steam-powered press led, in its turn, to their mass production (Goldman 1998). Although the proliferation of new means of transportation (railroads, boats, cars, trucks, and airplanes) enabled paper-written messages (books, letters) to diffuse fairly easily, these still suffer from the cost of their container and of their physical transportation. The move from physical transportation of information to electronic transmission along wires is a step towards solving the problem of resistance, cost and delay. Hence the on-going electronic textualisation of all walks of social life could be seen as a further stage in the project already initiated by literacy in the 15th century, with the invention of the movable type and the steam-empowered press in the 19th centuries. As touched upon above, the electronic text is emerging as the new bonding object of the virtual world (Lévy 1998). This bonding object insures the sharing of, and access to, from a distance, resources, ideas and information, enabling coordination of actions, producing new forms of relations and interactions. The advent of this mediation is giving rise to an 'electronic text through which organizational events, objects, transactions, functions, activities, and know-how could be enacted or observed' (Zuboff 1988: 179).

One of the aspects in which electronic writing detracts from conventional writing is its reliance on *hypertext*. Hypertext is a language that is able to connect fairly quickly to other documents, texts or other media. Another feature is the degree of interactivity it offers its users. In this hypertext, anyone with a computer can become author, editor and publisher. Being an asynchronous, interactive communication medium, electronic writing accentuates the movement towards virtualisation - namely, deterritorialisation, detemporalisation, displacement and blurring of inside-outside elements, sharing of resources, and so on. Computer mediation goes beyond 'discrete activities or procedures to a more comprehensive textualisation of work content' (Zuboff 1988: 178). The electronic text is not discrete, but comprehensive and systematic (Zuboff 1988: 179-185) in the sense that, unlike memos or reports, access to the text allows access to all aspects of the organisation, providing a view of administrative, management, productive, expert systems, personnel data bases, markets, sales, etc. Second, unlike writing, the programmed logic underlying it implies that procedures of how to solve problems and make decisions can be codified and incorporated into an information system. Hence, knowledge of an expert can, to some extent, be extracted and built into the design of the system, automating aspects of the production or managerial processes. Third, the electronic text exists independently of space and time. Fourth, it does not have a specific author, being constantly produced by a variety of people. Besides, authorship is not confined to humans, since a raft of microprocessors, scanners and electronic agents are actively participating in shaping and reshaping the text (Gatarski 2001). What cognitive, social and practical effects will the rising digital code bring about? This will shed some light on the often-assumed link between virtual corporation and knowledge, virtual corporation and trust, and finally the relation between human action and machine-controlled, virtualised 'action'.

Cognitive Effects of the Electronic Text

Over and above blurring the distinction between writer and author, the electronic text also makes fuzzy the distinction between individual and collective performance. For it is as much an individualising as it is a collectivising device. That is to say, although the overall body of the text, and the mode of thinking underlying it are collective, each individual input could be isolated and assessed on its own merit. By the same token, the distinction between the action of animate and inanimate is fused and merged (Gatarski 2001), but the input of each of them could be traced back to its origin and identified, even the most sophisticated virus perpetrators can be identified. The electronic text creates a symbolic universe, some sort of intelligence that is both collective and individual. It is also animated and inhabited by both humans and machines, and is at the same time personal and public, delocalised and detemporalised -all of which are features of virtualisation.

Analogous to the effects of conventional writing, the electronic text can be a window for creating new meanings, new ideas, insights and knowledge. When meaning is detached from the context in which it arises, a new playfulness becomes possible (Zuboff 1988: 180). As events, processes and practices are objectified, they fall victim to scrutiny, examination, evaluation, calculation, and even greater comparison and tabulation than paper-based texts. Such cognitive practices may lead to innovation and creativity. Zuboff (1988: 181) draws on Havelock (1978) to discuss the role extra-mental devices (such as the electronic text), which relieve the human mind from the burden of memorising, play in enhancing human cognition and in accelerating the growth of knowledge: 'The human mind became capable of creating and manipulating theoretic, logical, ideational statements' (Havelock 1978; cited in Zuboff 1988: 181). These findings are much in line with those of Goody (1977) and his followers, such as Havelock, on which Zuboff draws. Most such research tends to suggest that when knowledge is liberated from its source, and is set free from the grip of time and space, it can be appropriated and carried beyond the moment. This seems to be a condition not only for its growth but also for the development of new knowledge and innovation.

The Growth of Knowledge

Today it is widely held that information and knowledge are the sources of wealth production. But hasn't knowledge always been the mainspring in the creation of economic value? True enough; but what is new, maintains Lévy (1998), is our relationship to it, which we have experienced since the Second World War, and to a greater extent since the seventies. Until that time, a person could utilise the skills learned during their youth throughout their career. Furthermore, the stock of knowledge learned can be transmitted to children or apprentices nearly unchanged. This pattern today is disrupted, for people are required to adopt new skills several times during their lives. Even within a given trade, knowledge has a short life span. The design of basic skills has become problematic in a given field. New technologies and new socio-economic configurations accelerate and redefine this change process. In this way, individuals are transformed from implementers of knowledge and skills to continuous learners and producers - a condition of constant learning.

The Virtualisation of Social Relations Through Institutions

Alluding to the stability of social relations Ferguson (1986: 19) writes: 'The mighty engine which we suppose to have formed society only tends to set its members at variance or to continue their intercourse after the bonds of affection are broken' (Ferguson 1986: 19). Institutions virtualise individuals' immediate impulses, instincts, desires, (violent) conflicts, etc. Institutions, such as culture, laws, rules, contracts, agreements, trust virtualise conflicting social interactions and settles differences between people. What a contract does, for instance, is define a relation independently of the emotional changes of those bound by it. It seeks to reduce circumstantial changes in the relations of forces holding among people (Lévy 1998). It does not stipulate all the possible details, but rather a small number of these are explicitly mentioned in its written/verbal form. How do institutions virtualise –make contingent – social relationships and interactions?

Institutions are the building blocks of any social order. Berger and Luckmann (1966: 53) trace the origins of institutionalism to the *habitualisation* of human activity. Habitualised actions become carried as routines, almost at the level of the unconscious. There is no need to define each situation anew in all its minute details; and the pattern of habitualised actions can be extended to other, similarly perceived situations. While routinised actions are delegated to habitualisation, the human mind can focus more on what is not habitualised, that is, what is new and innovative. Further, institutions have a history, which frames them and controls them. Predetermined patterns, which are developed historically, will serve as guidelines and control mechanisms for future patterns of behaviour. In a way, they could be seen as in-advance control modes of human conduct. When we say that a segment of social activities has been institutionalised, we mean that it is subsumed under social control (Berger and Luckmann 1966), creating institutionally defined situations for actors to behave and interact. The more conduct is institutionalised, the more predictable and thus the more controlled it becomes. In this regard, institutions render interactions among individuals predictable. In an institutionally defined situation, each actor appropriates the other's role, taking it as a model for his/her role-playing (Berger and Luckmann 1966: 56). The boundaries between the other and self are transcended. Actors are, to some degree, able to predict each other's move. Since their expectation from one another is reciprocal, both actors save time and spare the efforts of predicting all possible alternatives the other's behaviour can take. Institutions constitute a background for actors, which stabilises their actions and interactions. Within an institutionalised context, each partner's action neither comes as a surprise to the other, nor is it a source of danger (Berger and Luckmann 1966).

Because institutions outlive the social context in which they strike roots, and because they develop into a reality that exists over and above their members, precede them and antedate them, they are experienced as *objective*, confronting their members as facts. The objective feature of institutions, their experienced facticity insures their continuation and their transmission from one generation to the other and from one context to another. An institutionalised world is a human product; but because it is objectivated, and because it acquires a life of its own, it acts back on the producer in the form of various constraints that lead to an internalisation process. It is in this sense that institutions require *legitimation* (Berger and Luckmann 1966), that is to say, ways of explaining and justifying the 'wherefores' and 'therefores' of their existence. This process involves the elaboration of theories, which gradually develop into a body of (consensual) knowledge. In order for this body of knowledge to persist and evolve, it has to be objectivated into a sign system, a form of explicitly articulated (not necessarily written) language, whose aim it is to convince members and make them see their interests in those of others, so as to reach a consensus, a social contract. Depending on the complexity of institutions, these could be tacitly shared (in myths), or practised (in rituals) or more or less explicitly articulated in oral or written stories, law books, codes of behaviour, contracts, or bonds of trust. Again writing plays a key role not only in the virtualisation of the 'here' and 'now', but also in the virtualisation of social relations and interactions. For example, Foley (1997) stresses the point that through writing, the relation between ruler and ruled became impersonal, formal and standardised, thereby leading to abstract rules listed in a code. This depersonalised, formal, abstract system of governance assigns less importance to face-to-face intercourse among employees, since clear-cut rules are used to mediate among them, and instructions prescribing the tasks and duties assigned to them. Such formal rules, formal standard procedures and instructions are devices for virtualising, detemporalising, delocalising and making impersonal the skills for conducting business and administrative routines, as\well as co-ordinating activities among members of a community. Thus, through written or tacit institutional forms, certain patterns of behaviour and relationships are prescribed and promoted. Once shared and accepted, they could be de-localised and detemporalised. Standardised titles of ownership, shares and other rights, which initially involve two parties can be transported to other realms, sold and exchanged among an indefinite number of people.

Trust as a Virtualising Device

As noted above, institutions may involve explicitly and formally written contracts, or tacit codes of behaviours, ritualised patterns of practices developed through shared values and meanings. In institutionally defined settings, where members interpret the situation in similar ways, interactions can take place through mutual adjustment. Trust is an outcome of the sharing of values and views, which are accentuated in the flows of information and knowledge among members of a community. Hence, as O'Hara-Devereaux and Johansen (O'Hara-Devereaux and Johansen 1994) suggest, "Trust is the glue of the global workspace-and technology doesn't do much to create relationships" (pp. 243-244). Trust is nourished through intense patterns of communication – through the development of a common language. Trust, as an institution, is subject to a habitualisation process through which it develops; it is constructionist, rather than spontaneist: that is, it is a relationship that does not form on the spur of the moment, but rather develops over time.

Virtualisation assumes, then, a process of sharing ideas and views that leads to the transcendence of on-going (thought) processes and the standardisation of codes of behaviour and institutions for settling eventual disputes and for insuring the smooth unfolding of social relations and interactions. Institutions substitute socially thick, confrontational, real-time relations and exchanges for contracts, agreements, trust, rituals, mutual understanding, etc.

As noted in the previous section, when an entity, an event or a process is virtualised it implies an escape from the present and the specific context in which it is situated, leading to its deterritorialisation and detemporalisation, the blurring of its boundaries, the inside-outside displacement and the sharing of resources and the adherence to standards and institutions.

The Virtualisation of Human Action Through Technology

Technology is concerned with displacing a bodily function into a tool, a machine or a cybernetic device. In this connection too, the process of virtualisation has been in operation for centuries. Hence, the invention of the wheel could be seen as the problematisation of walking – due to the frailty of human organs, to its shortcoming as a means of locomotion – and its displacement into an external artefact. There is a process of exchange: on the one hand, humans externalise part of their bodily function, and they have to learn (internalise) the necessary skills to efficiently use the artefacts. On the other hand, once the bodily function is displaced into a tool it becomes public, and could be used in different places and at different times – it is detached from any one physical or cognitive subject and from any specific temporal reference: it is virtualised. The technological history of weaponry affords an evident example of the process of virtualisation of human action (and the skills underlying it) (Zuboff 1988: 182-83). In his study of the transformations that have taken place at Beretta - the Italian small arms manufacturer - over the course of half a millennium, Jaikumer (1988) identified six different epochs. During the firm's first three hundred years, guns were made by hand, by master gun makers who tentatively designed and made guns without plans, using gigs, champs and files. Apprentices observed and learned from their masters by watching closely and imitating. Every gun was unique, for no two guns can be identical in all their parts. The advent of the so-called scientific engineering at the end of the eighteenth century introduced the use of tools in the production process, such as metal lathes. This marks the beginning of the virtualisation of gun-making. For, now apprentices are taught to be proficient in the use of tools, rather than the production process itself. Jaikumer (1988) says that the 'process took on a life of its own, enabling process improvements to be made independently of product constraints'. This meant the impoverishment in the worker's skills, for the making of a gun has become reliant on interchangeable, tool-centred skills and workers. The Industrial Revolution transformed once more the production of guns. By bringing with it the need for mass production it led to the mechanisation of work and product specialisation. Beretta reduced its product range from a wide range of models to just three. The third epoch began with the introduction of Taylor's Scientific Management Principles, which shifted the focus away from machine tools to labour, seeking to render it efficient, specialised and interchangeable. Under this regime, traditional work responsibility was broken down and assigned to specially trained workers. Virtualisation implies that craftwork has shifted from the domain of the craftsman to that of the engineer and the manager. In the late 1950s, *Statistical Process Control* made an appearance, altering once more the nature of work at Beretta. By this time, machines had taken over the actual performance and workers were reduced to the role of quality controllers, detecting and solving problems. In the 1970s, numerical control machines based on computers and microprocessors were introduced. These machines had turned the manipulation of physical products into purely abstract information processing operations. Gradually, Beretta began to evolve into an information-based manufactory, where much of the skills required to manufacture guns are stored in computers. However, computer operators were required to learn new (tacit) skills instead.

This transformation requires a new type of craftsmanship, new kinds of skills and a new stripe of workers; this time these are called 'knowledge workers'. Needless to stress the point that virtualisation through technology does not only displace the skills of the workers, but also forces them to learn and internalise new skills. The story of Beretta provides an example of the virtualisation of a set of human actions, their segmentation and breaking down into manipulable parts, their mechanisation and inscription in a written, digital code. In this instance, action has been displaced from the body of the worker into a tool, a machine, a digital code. It is deterritorialised and detemporalised. It is subjected to the play of inside/outside exchange and the sharing of information and resources. Personal skills have been objectivated and made public and shared; and new skills are internalised by workers, since these have now found themselves involved in the abstract processing of information and symbolic manipulations. What is noticeable in this connection is the point that mental and physical activities have fallen prey to the grips of the technology of writing, leading to the convergence of action, technology and writing. More than any previous form of writing, computerisation of the productive and administrative processes in organisation 'takes over for a certain amount of human activity' (Zuboff 1988: 181) - activities that can be performed with 'lights out', with minimum human intervention, and practically controlled from anywhere in the world. The outcome of the textualisation of human skills implies a shift away from an engagement with the world, from using tools, moving and transforming concrete material towards manipulating figures, images and words on a screen. Writing and technology are intrinsically bound up with each other. Their joint impact on the growth and spread of knowledge is obvious. Human action and machine processes are fusing into a hybrid, human-machine 'action'. Most likely, this merger is due to the incremental de-materialisation of a number of the artefacts invented to virtualise action. For, just like in the fate of the container of information that has gradually been miniaturised and subsequently reduced to digits, some artefacts (not all) that are meant to substitute for human action will also be reduced to a digital code. Recent trends in information technologies are enhancing the possibility of writing to combine data symbolised in more than one format, combining text, audio, video and graphics, mediated via hand-based telephones, air-based, wireless, modem-based PCs, or satellite transmissions. Such media are set to further make the time-space significance more contingent, increasing the degree of freedom and flexibility. The use of voice, wireless communication is the epitome of virtuality since they attempt to reconstruct virtually real settings.

Concluding Remarks

Writing, institutions and technology are some of the age-old modalities by which immediate presence, experience, knowledge, action and social relations are made independent of any particular time and space, and of any particular social actor. Through repeated exchanges and mediated interactions, the three processes create shared uses and generate various forms of knowledge. The distinction among writing, institutions and technology is blurred. For instance, human action can be virtualised through tools, machines or digital coding (which is a form of writing).

Likewise, the virtualisation of social relationships involves formally written contracts, informal, unwritten, handshake contracts, or just trust and mutual understanding - which develop through habitualisation and the sharing of consensual knowledge. The on-going electronic textualisation of organisational (and social) aspects is leading to a widespread codification and diffusion of ideas, practices and information, creating a repository of knowledge. Individuals are implicated in different ways in consuming, producing, commenting up, criticising, refining this repository of knowledge. Everybody can be seen as an editor, writer and reader of this fluxing text. However, the authorship of this text is collective but also individuating.

Within the suggested framework, the various features of virtualisation – deterritorialisation, detemporalisation, the blurring of boundaries, the sharing of resources and ideas, the growth and spread of knowledge, trust, etc – can be conceptually integrated to form the beginning of a theory of virtuality. One of the implications of such a conceptualisation is that virtuality is not new and that it is based as much on institutions and writing and codification as it is on technology. The overemphasis on technology as a central virtualising vector may produce an unbalanced view, since it tends to overlook the role that virtualisation has played and is still playing in the evolution of human beings.

References

Arrow, K. (1972) 'Gift and Exchanges', *Philosophy and Public Affairs*, 1, 4, pp 343-362.

Bradach, J. L. and Eccles, R. G. (1989) 'Price, Authority and Trust: from Ideal Types to Plural Forms', *Annual Review of Sociology,* 15, pp 97- 118.

Byrne, J. A., Brandt, R. and Port, O. (1993) 'The virtual corporation', *Business Week,* Feb 8, pp 98-102.

Deleuze, G. (1968/1994) *Difference & Repetition*, trans by P Patton, London: The Athlone Press.

Eisenstein, E. (1979) *The Printing Press as an Agent of Change.* Cambridge: Cambridge University Press.

Ferguson, A. (1986) *An Essay on the History of Civil Society,* Edinburgh.

Franke, U. (2000) 'The Knowledge-Based View (KBV) of the Virtual Web, the Virtual Corporation, and the Net-Broker', in *Knowledge Management and Virtual Organization,* ed. Malhotra, Y, Idea Group Publishing.

Gatarski, R. (2001) 'Relationships with Artificial News Aggregators', *Working Papers* (2001), School of Business, Stockholm University.

Goldman S. L., Nagel R. N. and Preiss K. (1995) *Agile Competitors and Virtual Organizations: Strategies for Enriching the Customer.* Van Nostrand Reinhold.

Goody, J. (ed.) (1968) *Literacy in Traditional Societies,* Cambridge: Cambridge University Press.

Goody, J. (1977) *The Domestication of the Savage Mind,* Cambridge: Cambridge University Press.

Hale, R. and Whitlam, P. (1997) *Towards the Virtual Organization*, McGraw-Hill International (UK) Limited.

Handy, C. (1995) 'Trust and the virtual organization', *Harvard Business Review*, 73, 3 (May-June 1995). 40-50.

Hedberg B., Dahlgren, J. H. and Olve, N.-G. 1994. *Imaginära Organisationer*, Malmö: Liber-Hermods.

Lakoff, R. (1987) *Women, Fire and Dangerous Things*, Chicago: University Press.

Lévy, P. (1998) *Becoming Virtual: Reality in the Digital Age*, New York: Plenum Press.

Lyons, J. (1977) *Semantics I & II,* Cambridge: University Press.

O'Hara-Devereaux, M., and Johansen, B., (1994) *Global Work: Bridging Distance, Culture, and Time*, San Francisco: Jossey-Bass, 1994.

Ong, W. (1982) *Orality and Literacy,* London and New York: Methuen.

Venkatraman, N. J. and Henderson, C. (1998) 'Real strategies for virtual organizing' *Sloan Management Review*, Cambridge, Fall 1998.

Weber, M. (1946) *The Theory of Social and Economic Organization*, London: Free Press.

Zuboff, S. (1988) *In the Age of the Smart Machine: The Future of Work and Power,* Heinemann Professional Publishing.

Autobiographical Note

Ali Yakhlef received his PhD in organisation theory from the School of Business, Stockholm University, Sweden. He is working as a senior lecturer in management at the same university. His main research areas include emerging forms of organising, organisational knowledge, the impact of information technology on core business, IT-based entrepreneurship, and market communications. His recent publications include 'IT Outsourcing and the Construction of Accountable Worlds' in *Organization,* 1998; 'The Internet as an Opportunity to Rethink the Role of the Intermediary' (2000), Special Issue of *Consumption, Market & Culture*, Vol. 3, No. 2, 'Does the Internet Complement or Compete with Banks' Brick-and-Mortar Branches?', *International Journal of Retail and Distribution Management*, (forthcoming); 'The Intranet and the Management of *Making and Using Skills'*, *Journal of Knowledge Management*, Vol. 1, 2002 (forthcoming). His E-mail address: AYA@fek.sus.se

7 Different Conceptual Approaches to Virtual Organization

Reima Suomi

Turku School of Economics and Business Administration, Finland

Introduction

A central topic in the research on telework of the author has been that of management resistance to the issue (Suomi-Pekkola 1998). I have tried to find reasons for this resistance through many directions: from hostile organizational cultures towards telework (Suomi-Pekkola 1999), from the non-cooperative relationship between employees and their managers (Suomi 1999), and even from the limited mind-sets of managers (Suomi *et al* 1998). In this chapter this mission is continued: this time the issues of missing social innovation and standardization are taken up.

Thereafter, we will point the 'finger of blame' to the research and consultant community. Perhaps there is something wrong or missing within the frameworks researchers and the academic community offer for practicians within telework. Maybe the theories and frameworks used show telework in a negative light. For this reason, we study five typical approaches to organizational life usually found in management literature, and discuss their relation to telework. Our research question is as follows:

Which issues in popular management approaches favour and inhibit telework application in organizations?

We take up the following popular management approaches:

1. transaction cost approach
2. agency theory
3. resource-based theory
4. process thinking
5. organizational learning

The selection of these approaches is of course random and subjective. We believe, however, that each of the selected approaches:

- has an established position in the thinking patterns of managers and researchers
- has multiple areas of application
- is established on sound scientific research
- possesses normative implications practical in telework management.

In the conclusions of the chapter we close the circle: is telework not becoming popular perhaps as a result of too much or too little standardization in management thinking? Are managers maybe not innovative enough, especially as it comes to social innovation, because of this? Our asnswer to the question remains open: current management literature is so rich that depending on the desired viewpoint, one can find topics that either support or reject telework, depending on the needs of the interpreter.

Telework, Standardization and Social Innovation

Despite the vivid academic discussion around it, telework has remained a marginal phenomenon in the labour market. The reasons are many and intertwined. Here we conduct a short discussion on two topics that are critical to the adoption of any innovation: standardization and social innovation.

It has been known for a long time that innovation and standardization are central topics in the diffusion of any innovation (Vervest 1987, King & al 1994). The concepts are closely connected to each other: both are feasible characteristics of action in any organization, but have a delicate relationship. Too much standardization makes innovation impossible, but without standardization innovations do not survive in the long run. We define the following short value chain of innovation and standardization:

Technical innovation

$\Rightarrow$ Technical standard

$\Rightarrow$ Social innovation

$\Rightarrow$ Organizational standard

The technical innovations for telework are mainly there. We have the needed technical infrastructure, and in most cases telework fits in with the regulatory frames offered by work legislation, if only a willingness to interpret so exists. Even technical standards exist to some extent: for example the needed telecommunication facilities and access methods for databases and other organizational data stores are there. Web-browser-based solutions seem to emerge as the winners in the "standard war". However, too many standards still fight for the interest of the telework society. What we are missing is the social innovation of telework, and without it we cannot see telework becoming an organizational standard. Arnbrak (1988) nicely made this clear in his classic article, how even a good technical solution like the mobile phone needs social acceptance in order to become generally accepted. In the Nordic countries, an atmosphere making this possible existed in the case of mobile phones. Social innovation can be defined as the shared operationalized pinion of a group in accepting or rejecting something. What is missing in the case of telework is accepting the social innovation.

Some reasons for missing the social innovation in the area of telework follow:

- Big companies are resisting innovativeness
- Missing organizational slack
- Telework arrangements discussed with individuals, not in groups
- Risk aversion of short-run focus of management

Telework is advancing to some extent with small companies (see for example Regerinskansliet 1998), but bigger companies have difficulties in adapting to it. This is well in line with the mainstream innovation literature. Innovation is not likely to flourish in big, bureaucratic organizations with long traditions, but in small businesses (Grossi 1990, Jarratt 1999).

A disturbing factor in the innovation from telework is that of missing organizational slack. For any innovation to proceed, a certain amount of organizational slack is needed (Nohria– Ranjay 1997). Human resources are usually the scarcest resources in any company, and playing with them is too risky and costly. In human resources management, the needed organizational slack is missing, and thus there is no growing ground for innovation.

Innovation is to emerge in human interaction preferably in small multitalented groups (Ciborra 1993). Human resource management is usually a professional entity within a bigger organization, with its own traditions, organizations and a limited set of external contacts. Contracts of employment are worked out with individuals with little negotiating power. The needed social network for innovation in telework usually does not exist.

Innovations are by definition new things, and involve costs in the short run and risks (see Karlsson 1989). Changing working conditions always means a disturbance to routines, and decreased productivity in the short run. Organizations are usually focusing too much on short-term productivity and are not willing to make the needed investments in future productivity, especially with such risky arrangements as telework. Short-term orientation and missing risk-carrying capacity are inhibiting telework.

As managers should foster innovation in organizations in general, they should also be especially sensitive to innovations in telework, which seems to have many factors that inhibit innovation.

Different Approaches to Understand Telework

The transaction cost approach

A working relationship can be interpreted as a transaction, or a set of transactions, depending on the detail of needed investigation. It is loaded with costs, both for the employee and the employer. So a transaction cost analysis is possible in connection with telework.

The transaction cost approach (TCA) is founded upon the following assumptions (Williamson 1985, 41-42)

1. The transaction is the basic unit of analysis.
2. Any problem that can be posed directly or indirectly as a contracting problem is usefully investigated in transaction cost economizing terms.
3. Transaction cost economics are realized by assigning transactions (which differ in their attributes) to governance structures (which are the organizational frameworks within which the integrity of contractual relations are decided) in a discriminating way. Accordingly
    a. the defining attributes of transactions need to be identified
    b. the incentive and adaptive attributes of alternative governance structures need to be described.
4. Although marginal analysis is sometimes employed, implementing transaction cost economics mainly involves a comparative institutional assessment of discrete institutional alternatives of which classical market contracting is located at one extreme; centralized, hierarchical organization is located at the other; and mixed modes of firm and market organization are located in between.
5. Any attempt to deal seriously with the study of economic organization must come to terms with the combined ramifications of bounded rationality and the conjunction with a condition of asset specificity.

The basic distinction of TCA among different organizational forms is the distinction between markets and hierarchies (Coase 1937), which are forms of economic organizations. Given the division of labour, economic organizations control and coordinate human activities.

A market is an assemblage of persons which tries to arrange the exchange of property, where prices serve as both coordinating guides and incentives to producers in affecting what and how much they produce Ð as well as the amount they demand. At the equilibrium free-market price, the amounts produced equal the amounts demanded Ð without a central omniscient authority (Alchian-Allen 1977)

In a hierarchy (firm) market transactions are eliminated and in place of the market structure with exchange transactions we find the entrepreneur-coordinator, the authority who directs production. (Coase 1937)

The transactional approach stresses the characteristics of actors that make them or their working condition less than perfect:

- Bounded rationality
- Opportunism
- Information asymmetry
- Asset specificity

The concept of "opportunism" is particularly ruining telework acceptance. According to TCA, any transaction involves opportunism, the desire of taking ones own benefit instead of the shared, and maybe in total, bigger benefit. On the one hand, the approach is interested in the costs of organizing work, and not so much on its productivity and results. Even when the approach has a strong tradition and theoretical background, it is not widely known by managers, maybe because of its very difficult conceptual approach. On the other hand, the rich set of concepts offered by the approach can help in the understanding and analysing of teleworking relationships.

The agency theory

The agency theory can be regarded as a specific, more limited and worked out extension of the general discussion of governance structures, rooted in the transaction cost approach. Central concepts are those of a principal and an agent. "Agency relationship is a contract under which one or more persons engage another person to perform some service on their behalf which involves delegating some decision making authority to the agent." (Jensen – Mecklin 1976). Any working relationship can be included in this definition – the similarly between a working relationship and an agency relationship is carefully sorted out in Anderson (1985). This approach suits the teleworking environment especially well, where we tend to see goal incongruence and information asymmetrics, central topics for the agency theory. According to Eisenhardt (1989), the agency theory can be well used in situations involving goal conflicts, outcome uncertainty and unprogrammed and team-oriented tasks. All these characteristics are usual with telework.

An agency relationship causes agency costs. They can be divided to the following components (Jensen – Mecklin 1976):

- Monitoring costs, costs for the principal to follow up the actions of the agent
- Bonding costs, cost invested to maintain the agency relationship
- Residual loss, the difference between the agent's performance and the performance that would have been obtained by the principal doing the task himself.

The agency theory perspective puts a focus on the relationship between the worker and his manager, which is the critical part in any telework relationship. As the transaction cost approach, it rather defines the problem area and gives concepts to handle it, but gives few solutions or normative guidance. It tends to emphasize goal incongruence, and in doing so does not give a good mental starting point for introducing telework. However, it makes clear the truth in any relationship, that participants have different goals, and simultaneously forgets that through negotiation and articulation work, goals can be at least partly integrated.

Both the transaction and agency costs are suitable theories for the information society and research on information technology and relationships, since they put information on a central key position. Problems in relationships and economy exist because of missing information and capability to handle it. This is by no means in the classical microeconomics, where information is more or less a free commodity and without any value or attention.

With the transaction cost approach, the agency theory is deeply rooted in classical economics, and commands a complicated set of concepts. Whereas the transactions cost theory focuses on the exchange of any commodity, more naturally physical goods, the agency theory focuses clearly on the exchange of labour and decision making. So it focuses on the very heart of telework.

Taking into attention these strong sides of the agency theory, it is frustrating to see that there are not any (or at least many) research efforts to use the agency theory in the study of telework. One reason might be that it is considered as an economic theory, and so far researchers in the key economic areas have been insensitive to telework. Other researchers have been reluctant to use the agency theory because of its strong economic background, which we believe is just a part of the truth. As relationships and information exchange are put into a central place, we would argue that the agency theory is a management and information theory rather than an economic theory.

Resource-based theory

The resource-based theory is one of the current theories enjoying the wide acceptance by the scientific community. After a long period of market-oriented theories (for example Porter 1980, 1985, 1990) it turned attention to the internal issues of any organization, the assets and resources which are of permanent character to the organization, and with which one must live and of which one must take advantage – on the contrary to the ever changing external world and market.

Amit and Schoemaker (1993) define the importance of resources: "For managers the challenge is to identify, develop and deploy resources and capabilities in a way that profits the firm with a sustainable competitive advantage and, thereby, a superior return on capital."

Clearly we can define labour as a key resource for any organization. The resource-based theory should give us insights on how to master and foster this resource. One of the weaknesses of the resource-based theory is again the complexity of used concepts. The concepts of capabilities, resources and competences are far from settled (see for example Andrey-Ciborra 1996). Again, however, the conceptual richness of the theory is its strength. Important and interesting concepts from the viewpoint of telework include:

- Resource mobility and heterogeneity: Organizations command resources of different kinds and qualities. Resources can be very immobile. Clearly, the workforce fits well to this definition of resource.
- Social complexity (Barney 1991): resources may be imperfectly imitable because they are a very complex social phenomena, beyond the ability of firms to systemically manage and influence. This is the case in most human labour, but especially in information professions and in virtual and other non-traditional organizations, where telework is a common way of conducting work.
- Causal ambiguity (Barney 1991): causal ambiguity exists when the link between the resources controlled by a firm and a firm's sustained competitive advantage is not understood or understood only very imperfectly. It is easy to agree that this is the case between telework(ers) and the firms sustained competitive advantage.

Interesting too is the discussion on the strategic potential of resources. A capability has strategic potential if it is (Barney 1991):

Valuable

- takes advantage of opportunities in the environment and neutralizes risks

Rare

- demand is bigger than supply

Difficult to imitate

- difficult to get

Does not have strategically comparable substitutes.

Whether teleworkers have strategic potential in this sense would deserve a study of its own. As resources are heterogeneous, the situation clearly varies between different organizations.

A brilliant definition of operational and strategic management is made by Hinton and Kaye (1996). They define that operative management masters over existing resources. Strategic management makes definitions over the total amount of resources. In this way, operational telework management masters existing teleworkers, whereas strategic management in the area of telework decides over the amount of teleworkers.

The resource-based theory is very reality-oriented. It takes up many concepts of great importance for daily organizational live. Again, it is not very easy to understand and apply. The most important message for telework is that workers in general should not be seen as costs but as strategic assets and resources that demand constant management attention. Of the theories discussed so far, it is the richest because it places information processing and learning, and social complexity of daily organizational action, into a central place. Thus, it should we well armed to address the complicated reality of telework.

Process thinking

Process thinking has been a dominant management paradigm for over 15 years. The main idea was that instead of functions and functional areas management should focus on processes, that cross organizational boundaries, and are usually even inter-organizational. Process thinking and value-chain thinking are not far away from each other.

Processes were first natural to see in the process industry, but quite naturally they could also be found in the information professions. For the teleworker, implications of this kind of thinking are many. The positive factor for telework might be that working is understood as a chain of activities, which are guided by the computer, and can thus be performed anywhere, even at a distance through telework. This kind of thinking totally ignores the social complexity of work, and the need for articulation work, which is a key concept in any complicated organizational setting (Schmidt – Bannon 1992). The teleworker is degraded to a part of a machinery, with no need for social contact. Just this has been seen as a key fear by teleworkers: they do not want to be away from the office because of the fear of losing their social contacts.

Process thinking has very much to do with quality and efficiency of processes. Measuring them is important. This might well address the fear of many managers: the output of teleworkers can not be measured, neither in quality or quantity.

Though many would like to introduce telework, very often the muscles to perform that are missing. Introducing a telework program is often considered risky and painful, and research has shown that telework is often performed on an ad-hoc basis, not as a centrally planned and controlled activity (Luukinen & al 1996). Cowherd, Douglas M. ; Luchs, Robert H. (1988), among others, stress out that business process re-engineering is a total effort by organization, where several issues must be addressed. When performing business process re-engineering, one easily finds a natural place to introduce telework simultaneously. Top management is usually very motivated and positive towards business process re-engineering, and binding telework to business process re-engineering to telework makes it possible to extend this good-will even to telework.

One of the established sayings in business process re-engineering is that there is no gain without pain. This should apply too to telework. In order to arrive at the jointly decided goals, all stakeholders in the telework arrangement should be ready to carry some inconveniences. For example, managers should understand that they are going to lose some of their direct control over employees, and teleworkers should accept that they lose some of their "social visibility" in their organization, and that the working conditions might not perfectly match those of their main office. Too often telework initiatives are abandoned when even a minimal amount of "pain" emerges.

Process thinking emerges from engineering sciences. Study of working relationships is more a social activity. No wonder these two disciplines have met too seldom. As even our short discussion shows, telework research and practice could gain a lot from the ideas of business process re-engineering. What one must vary is the "mechanizing" tendency of process thinking: humans and teleworkers should not be seen as parts of a big machinery.

Organizational learning

Whereas the resource-based theory could be interpreted as a kind of static view of an organization, the organizational learning perspective stresses the constant change of organizational environment, which organizations can master only through constant learning. Every organization must be learning at least to some extent, but a "real" learning organization is defined as (Garvin 1993): "A learning organization is an organization skilled at creating, acquiring, and transferring knowledge and modifying its behaviour to reflect new knowledge and insights. Another definition emphasises the 'learning to learn' (Senge 1990): "Learning organizations are places where people continually expand their capacity to create the results they truly desire, where new and expansive patterns of thinking are nurtured, where collective aspiration is set free, and where people are continually learning on how to learn together".

In a way, organizational learning is a science itself: its task is to interpret and understand the world (Daft-Huber 1987): "The reduction of equivocality is the central problem to be resolved during organizational learning, and is the essence of organizational learning."

Organizational learning can be approached from two perspectives (Daft-Huber 1987):

- The systems-structural perspective
  - focuses on the acquisition and distribution of information that is required for an organization to learn about its environment
- The interpretative perspective
  - focuses on
    - understanding organizational members' individual interpretations of the environment
    - understanding the alignment and interaction of organizational members' environmental interpretations

Romme and Dillen (1997) differentiate between four different conceptual backgrounds through which organizational learning can be studied. All these seem to be relevant point of views for telework too:

- contingency theory
- psychology
- information theory
- system dynamics

Central concepts for organizational learning are those of single- and double-loop learning (Agryris-Schön 1978). Single loop learning involves processes in which errors are tracked down and corrected *within the existing set of rules and norms.* Double loop learning involves in addition changes to the fundamental rules and norms underlying action and behaviour. To interpret this in a telework environment, double loop learning begins when telework is introduced, and when performing it, mainly the mode of single-loop learning is active.

The organizational learning perspective opens up new avenues for telework, as for any new and risky undertaking of a company. If no immediate operative or even strategic benefits emerge, the gained knowledge makes the effort worthwhile anyway. To look at the other side of the coin, the organizational learning perspective is more academic, and not so popular with practitioners. This might be because of the loose touch of the approach with concrete results of actions, at least in the short run. A manager wanting to see immediate results and concrete profit-making action can not do much with the learning organization approach on the short run. Organizational learning might be seen as an 'academic nonsense' thing, and if we anchor telework strongly with it, we might throw out the baby with the bath water.

Approach	**Primary unit of analysis**	**Issues highlighted**	**Issues hidden**	**Strenghts**
Organizational learning	Learning in and through telework	Diffusion of innovations Individual and org. learning Knowledge formulation	Competitive advantage	Used in several disciplines Dynamic view of an organization
Transaction cost approach	Costs of organizing telework	Transactional view Participant shortcomings	Results gained Productivity of work	Strong theory background A good conceptual set
Agency theory	The employee-employer relationship	Different goals	Co-operation	A good conceptual set
Resource-based approach	Resources used and saved by telework	Competitive advantage Cumulating resources Workers as a valuable resource	Outputs, results	Fresh Discusses reality
Process analysis	Work processes their implementation into IS	Streamlining processes Saving time and money Measuring output	System integration Social complexity	Effectiveness Quality issues of high importance

Table 1 Different approaches to understand telework

Conclusions

Which issues in popular management approaches favour and inhibit telework application in organizations? For all the approaches, we can see both negative and positive sides, if we think of telework. Using all of the approaches discussed above, we can find both factors that support the introduction of telework and that inhibit it. In Exhibit 1 we summarize our findings about the different approaches.

The author would like to continue with the exploitation of transaction cost approach, agency theory and resource-based approach. These are deeply rooted in science and academia, whereas organizational learning and process thinking are more practically-oriented issues, the latter perhaps less so. Central to this is to have a theory that provides order and gives concepts that understand telework as a social phenomenon – that puts information into a central position.

Telework is not socially accepted in many organizations. Managers as well as actual and potential teleworkers do have fears and doubts about it. Surely one reason for this is that there is no dominant management theory that would have the authority to say that telework is good. Yet there are many management truths that are jointly accepted by managers (see Astley, 1985), as for example that of top management support, that is critical for all information system undertakings. Proponents of telework have to work out current theories and theoretical frameworks, and show through and with their authority that telework is good for organizations. Even our short analysis showed that there is a lot of potential in the management theories for that. Maybe, then, even in the near future, we might witness a day where socially accepted standard management norms towards telework are advancing and supporting it.

References

Agryris, C. and Schön, D. (1978) *Organizational learning*, London: Addison-Wesley.

Alchian, A. A. and Allen, W. R. (1977) *Exchange and Production: Competition, Coordination and Control*, Wadsworth Publishing.

Amit, R. and Schoemaker, P. J. H. (1993) 'Strategic assets and organizational rent', *Strategic Management Journal* Vol. 14, 33-46.

Anderson, E. (1985) 'The salesperson as outside agent or employee: the transaction cost analysis', *Marketing Science* No. 3, 234-254.

Andreu, R. and Ciborra, C. (1996) 'Organizational learning and core capabilities development: the role of IT', *Journal of Strategic Information Systems* Vol. 5, 111-127.

Arnbrak, J. (1988) 'Trans-Border Communications Networks: Technology-Driven or Social Innovation?' *European Management Journal* 4/88, 330-337.

Astley, G. W. (1985) 'Administrative Science as Socially Constructed Truth', *Administrative Science Quarterly*, 30 (1985): 497-513.

Barney, J. (1991) 'Firm resources and sustained competitive advantage', *Journal of Management*, Vol. 17 No. 1.

Ciborra, C. (1993) *Teams, markets and systems: business innovation and information technology*, Cambridge: University Press.

Coase, R. H. (1937) 'The nature of the firm', *Economica*, No 3, 1937, 386-405.

Cowherd, D. M. and Luchs, R. H. (1988) 'Linking Organization Structures and Processes to Business Strategy', *Long Range Planning* October/88, 47-53.

Daft, R-L. and Huber, G. P. (1987) 'How organizations learn? A communication framework', *Research in the Sociology of Organizations*, Vol. 5, 1-36.

Eisenhardt, K. (1989) 'Agency theory, an assessment and review', *Academy of Management Review* Vol. 14 No. 1, 57-74.

Garvin, D. A. (1993) 'Building a learning organization', *Harvard Business Review* Vol. 71, 78-91.

Grossi, G. (1990) 'Promoting Innovation in a Big Business', *Long Range Planning* 1/90, 41-52.

Hinton, C. M. and Kaye, G. R. (1996) 'The Hidden Investments in Information Technology: The Role of Organizational Context and System Dependency', *International Journal or Information Management*, Vol. 16 No. 6, 413-427.

Huarng, A. S. (1995) 'System development effectiveness: An agency theory perspective', *Information & Management* 28 (1995), 283-291.

Jarratt, A. (1999) 'Managing diversity and innovation in a complex organization', *International Journal of Technology Management*, Vol. 17 Nos ½, 5-15.

Jensen, M. and Mechling, W. H. (1976) 'Theory of the Firm: Managerial Behavior, Agency Costs and Ownership Structure', *Journal of Financial Economics*, 305-360.

Karlsson, C. (1989) 'High Rates of Innovation: The Japanese Culture Shock to Europe', *European Management Journal* 1/89, 31-39.

King, J. L., Gurbaxani, V., Kraemer, K. L., McFarlan, W. F., Raman, S., Yap, C.S. (1994) 'Institutional Factors in Information Technology Innovation', *Information Systems Research* Vol. 5, No. 2, 139-169.

Luukinen, A. (editor), Pekkola, J., Heikkilä, A., Zamindar, M. (1996) 'Directions of Telework in Finland', Report by the *Finnish Experience with Telework Project*, Ministry of Labour.

Nohria, N., Ranjay, G. (1997) 'What is the Optimum Amount of Organizational Slack? A Study of the Relationship between Slack and Innovation in Multinational Firms', *European Management Journal* Vol. 15 No. 6, 603-611.

Porter, M. (1985) *Competitive Advantage*, The Free Press.

Porter, M. (1980) *Competitive Strategy*, The Free Press.

Porter, M. E. (1990) 'The Competitive Advantage of Nations', *Harvard Business Review* March April/90, 73-93.

Regeringskansliet (1998) *The Swedish Government Commission on Telework – Summary*, September 1998.

Romme, G. and Dillen, R. (1997) 'Mapping the landscape of organizational learning', *European Management Journal* Vol. 15 No. 1, 68-78.

Senge, P. M. (1990) *The Fifth Discipline, the Art and Practice of the Learning Organization*, London: Doubleday Currency.

Schmidt, K. and Bannon, L. (1992) 'Taking CSCW Seriously: Supporting Articulation Work', *Computer Supported Cooperative Work (CSCW)* 1/1992, 7-40.

Suomi, R. and Pekkola, J. (1999) 'Adjusting telework to different organizational cultures', in Jackson, P.J. (1999) (editor) *Virtual Working: social and organisational dynamics*, London: Routledge, 121-130.

Suomi, R. and Pekkola, J. (1998) 'Inhibitors and motivators for telework: some Finnish experiences', *European Journal of Information Systems* Vol. 7, 221-231.

Suomi, R. (1999) 'Management's and Worker's attitudes towards Telework: Seeking Self-Interest', in proceedings of the Fourth International Telework Workshop, *Telework Strategies for the New Workforce*, Tokyo 31.8-3.9.1999, 29-39.

Suomi, R., Luukinen, A. and Pekkola. J. (1998) 'Telework - The Critical Management Dimension', in Jackson, P.J. and Van der Wielen, J.M. (eds) *New International Perspectives on Telework: From Telecommuting to the Virtual Organisation*, London: Routledge, 329-226.

Vervest. P. (1987) *Innovation in electronic mail*, North-Holland.

Williamson, O. E. (1985) *The Economic Institutions of Capitalism. Firms, Markets, Relational Constructing*, The Free Press.

8 Virtual Organisations: Exchange and Context

Andrew J. Gaudes

I.H. Asper School of Business
University of Manitoba, Canada

Virtual organisations have been cast into various forms by researchers in attempts to explain and predict their structure. Researchers have used metaphorical terms such as 'clusters' (Goldman et al 1995); 'alliances' (Boudreau et al 1998); and 'hybrids' (Wassenaar 1999). However, those that have described virtual organisations as analogous to a fluid (Crandall and Wallace 1997; Grabowski and Roberts 1998; and Mowshowitz 1997) may be the most accurate. Like a fluid, a virtual organisation can take on many different forms, limited only by its scope. 'A virtually organised company can have centralised or decentralised control structures, centralised or decentralised units, and centralised or decentralised functions' (Mowshowitz 1997: 36). These findings suggest that a more fundamental task of studying the virtual organisation at the 'molecular' or transaction level is required. Like an amorphous fluid, the virtual organisation has macro properties, which are based upon its molecular, or micro composition.

The objective of this chapter is to examine, from a conceptual standpoint, the nature of a virtual organisation. This chapter will provide explanation of the virtual organising phenomenon at the 'molecular' or 'micro' level. The intent here is to identify the content of a virtual organisation so that it may lead to measurement, and ultimately the explanation and prediction of outcomes from the design and application of various types of virtual organisations. The approach applied is intuitive and deductive, integrating literature on virtual organisations with exchange literature spanning macro/micro and economic/social boundaries. The initial focus of discussion is on the relationships formed within virtual organisations, applying transaction cost theory and leader member exchange theory. The exchange is then viewed through the evaluative lens of psychological contract literature, drawing conclusions on the factors that are most salient in ascertaining the context in which virtual organisation exchange relationships form.

Integrating or drawing from several theories is certainly not new. Virtual organisation research has referred to psychological contract literature in the past (Cooper 1999; Johnson 1998; Perin 1998). Also, there has been integrative research with the psychological contract literature and leader-member exchange theory (Balser and Stern 1999). Still, in spite of the integrative attempts made involving any of the virtual organisation, macro/micro–economic/social exchange, and psychological contract literature, there has not been any integrative work that seeks explanation towards a system perspective. Guest (1998) has proved to be a strong advocate for further research of this genre, looking for research that applies a 'more imaginative use of social exchange theory' (662) that will shift study back to the market-driven organisation. Within the context of psychological contracts: 'there may be scope for some integration of social exchange and transaction cost economics to explore the interaction between transactional and relational contracts' (662).

The Virtual Organisation

In the mid-1980s, organisational theorists began to dismiss bureaucratic structures as stagnant behemoths, unable to adapt to international competition and demographic pressures (Ashkenas *et al* 1995, Fukuyama 1999, Fulk and DeSanctis 1995). Nohria and Eccles (1992) argued that this was a result of the 'changing character of industrial economies' (290). They cited economic globalisation, a mobile and heterogeneous work force, shorter product research and development times as well as product lifespan as causes for these changes. Some twenty years earlier, Burns and Stalker (1961) had presented a discussion regarding 'organic' organisation. Today, their contribution is considered seminal toward network-like alternatives for bureaucratic structures in conditions of uncertainty and ambiguity (Nohria and Eccles 1992; Travica 1998). However, the ability to implement these organic organisations was delayed until the efficient merging of computerisation and telecommunications in the 1980s facilitated such amorphous and permeable structures (Roberts and Grabowski 1999). The resulting network-like alternative, known as virtual organisation, is largely derived from the application of information technology and can provide organisations with greater interaction, agility, and flexibility (Byrne 1993; Metes et al 1998; Palmer 1998).

For all the cited benefits of applying a virtual organisation model (see Byrne, 1993; Davidow and Malone, 1992 and Handy, 1995), a shortcoming with the concept in much of the literature has been the inference of structure, which implies a static form. Recognising a virtual organisation, instead, as a process of virtual *organising* is a more appropriate approach to framing discussion in this area. It changes the concept from an organisational form into a dynamic method of organisational management or strategy. Venkatraman and Henderson (1998) also 'reject a virtual organisation as a distinct structure (like functional, divisional, or matrix). Instead, [they] treat virtualness as a strategic characteristic applicable to every organisation' (34). Recognising virtual organising as a method of organisational management allows us to move more comfortably into a discussion focused on the management of multiple dyadic relationships that are formed between agents within a virtually organised exchange.

A key important criterion in understanding a virtual organisation is to recognise that they are, first, organisations. This means that, as in traditional organisational relationships, they are comprised of two or more entities (individuals, groups, corporations) that are interdependent (having some form of influence or control upon each other) and are working cooperatively towards a common goal or objective (DeSanctis et al 1999). Coase (1937) explained that the reason organisations exist is because sometimes the cost of managing economic exchanges across markets is greater than managing economic exchanges within the boundaries of the organisation. Virtual organisations subscribe to the same rationale. A key departure from Coase is that, in comparison, a virtual organisation can have characteristics, which are more akin to a market rather than a hierarchy (i.e. a large number of buyers and sellers), but it is still under the rubric of controlling the cost of managing.

Exchange in the Virtual Organisation

In transaction cost theory (TCT), determining governance of an economic transaction is the focus. Whether the transaction is more efficiently governed in a market form or a hierarchical form is dependent upon their potential to mitigate exchange problems created by bounded rationality and opportunism (Barney and Hesterly 1999). In a virtual organisation formed between two economic agents, their transaction begins with the agreement they construct in order to work together. By introducing a virtual organisation there is an amelioration of both market-related exchange problems identified by Williamson (1981), and hierarchical issues, which are discussed by Ouchi (1980). In other words, virtual organisations are formed because first, market governance of an economic transaction does not solve exchange problems created by bounded rationality and opportunism, and second, it is deemed less costly than hierarchical governance.

Although transaction cost theory can be applied to both individuals and firms (Barney and Hesterly 1999), the analysis remains largely economic in content with limited recognition of social relationships. This suppresses full explanation for the human or 'relational' characteristics of an exchange, thus remaining mostly applicable to macro perspectives, which occur at an organisation-wide level of analysis, rather than at the individual. This has been an ongoing criticism of transaction cost theory for some time (Barney and Hesterly 1999; Granovetter 1985). Homans (1958) is recognised as the first to conceptually include social interaction between at least two individuals as an exchange of goods, both material and non-material (Jacobs 1970). There have also been numerous studies and theories that recognise the exchange as extending beyond the economic (Adams 1963; Kahneman and Tversky 1979; Rousseau 1995). In light of this it is possible to argue that a virtual organisation may initially be driven by economic influences, however the exchange between members of a virtual organisation will ultimately be comprised of both economic and social factors.

Graen and Scandura's (1987) work provides a good link between the organisation-wide and economic-focused transaction cost theory and study that is more individual and relational. They apply a theory that provides explanation for the development and effects of dyadic relationships. Using Leader Member Exchange (LMX) theory, Graen and Scandura argue that analysis at the dyadic level allows examination beyond the individual, and also breaks large groups into numerous paired variations. LMX views organisations as systems comprised of agents and dyadic relationships with interdependent behaviour patterns that formulate mutually shared outcome instrumentalities, conceptions of environments, cause maps, and values (Scandura, Graen and Novak 1986). Relational attributes associated with a dyadic relationship include values such as trust, respect, loyalty, liking, intimacy, support, openness, and honesty (Graen and Scandura 1987: 184) and are measurable by applying the LMX 7–item measure developed by Graen and his associates.

The importance in recognising LMX theory here is that it reinforces study seeking a unified system of explanation for macro-organising based upon paired relationships (Graen and Scandura 1987; Graen and Uhl-Bein 1995; and House and Aditya 1997 provide reviews of LMX studies). This supports the argument that individual relationships can determine macro-organisational form. Graen and Scandura (1987) mention that 'any focal actor can share a large number of different dyads' (202) and they conceptualise this as a 'dyadic network' in which there may exist dyads where the focal actor is not actually a member. With this view of organisational form; 'drawing a boundary around the limits of the network is problematic' (Graen and Scandura 1987: 202), thereby maintaining a process-oriented appearance. House and Aditya mention that LMX Theory 'has the potential to be a theory of systems of dyadic relationships' (430) if given further theoretical development. Graen and Scandura (1987) concur, stating that research is needed on other types of dyadic relationships, other than direct reporting, to determine their effects on various organisational systems.

Context in the Virtual Organisation

Although exchange theories help us appreciate the economic and social characteristics involved in virtual organisation exchange relationships, we are unable to evaluate that which comprises the context where the exchange occurs and relationships form. Literature on the psychological contract aids us in determining the dimensions which encompass 'the deal' between agents. The psychological contract has made its presence in a broad range of research, providing explanation for variance in outcomes such as absenteeism (Nicholson and Johns 1985), exit and loyalty (Turnley and Feldman 1999), innovation (Herriot and Pemberton 1997), job satisfaction (Cavanaugh and Noe 1999), intention to quit (Larwood *et al* 1998), organisational commitment (Scandura and Lankau 1997; Van Dyne and Ang 1998), and performance (Stiles et al 1997).

The psychological contract is a concept that was first introduced by Argyris (1960), and subsequently defined by Levinson *et al* (1962) as the sum of mutual expectations between the organisation and the employee (Anderson and Schalk 1998). The concept brings forward expectations within an agreement that may not be explicit or written (such as flexibility, future employability, career development) so that they may be considered in conjunction with the expectations that are explicit or written (such as salary, benefits, job description). A fundamental shift occurred in the psychological contract when Rousseau (1990) moved the concept from a bilateral relationship to a unilateral assessment. She described it as an individual's assessment of their work relationship, based upon their perceptions of obligations of the employee to the employer and the employer to the employee (Anderson and Schalk 1998). The rationale for shifting the concept to solely the view of the employee is due to the problems of agency. An organisation cannot be solely recognised as an individual, and an agent representing the organisation in a relationship cannot be solely recognised as the organisation. Rousseau and McLean Parks (1993) assign two different types of psychological contracts, the transactional contract and the relational contract. These two types are placed at the ends of a 'contract continuum' with an individual's psychological contract positioned somewhere on the continuum. The transactional, on one end, represents that which is explicit and agreed, while the relational on the other end, emphasises the social exchange and interdependence (Guest 1998).

Two major criteria, which have been used to assess psychological contracts, are *content* and *dimension* (Rousseau and Tijoriwala 1998; Guest 1998; Anderson and Schalk 1998). Content refers to identifiable items within the work arrangement, such as job security, professional development, and flextime. Clearly, the variety of content-related items contained within a psychological contract could be endless and ever changing, which presents a weakness in this form of analysis (Anderson and Schalk 1998). Also, content has been found to be less generalisable across groups than the dimensions of a contract (McLean Parks *et al* 1998). The general consensus by researchers on psychological contract content is that it is an indicator of change in the items contained within 'the deal' over time (Anderson and Schalk 1998; Cavanaugh and Noe 1999; Guest 1998; Hall and Moss 1998; Sparrow and Cooper 1998).

Dimensions, on the other hand, provide an overall description of the environment in which psychological contracts are present, based on established attributes placed upon Rousseau's transactional-relational contract continuum. For this reason, it is argued that assessing the dimensions of a psychological contract provides a better method of measurement, transcending the fickleness of changing trends and values placed upon a myriad of contract items. It is the dimension component of psychological contract literature that is relevant to the analysis of virtual organisations. Much like content within contracts, the methods of virtual organising and the means in which they are supported will continue to vary, resulting in limited generalisability across groups and time periods, particularly when referring to enabling information technology and mediated forms of communicating. However, assessing the dimensions in which virtual organising methods are applied can generate a context that can be assessed and compared across different virtual organisations. Rousseau and McLean Parks (1993) offer five different dimensions that can be placed upon the contract continuum: stability, scope, tangibility, focus, and timeframe (Anderson and Schalk 1998).

'*Stability* is the degree to which the psychological contract is limited in terms of its ability to evolve and change without an implied renegotiation of the terms' (McLean Parks et al 1998: 706). For example, if the work arrangement is regularly in a state of flux, changing or evolving without any renegotiation of the arrangements, then it is deemed to have low stability. Arrangements that are low in stability would be considered high in relational quality. A virtual organisation may be deemed high or low in stability. Determination of this would be dependent upon an individual's perception of the level of flexibility and predictability of activities in their work.

'*Scope* is the extent to which the boundary between one's employment relationship and other aspects of one's life is seen as permeable' (McLean Parks et al 1998: 707). This dimension examines the boundary between an individual's work and personal life. If a contract has wide scope, then there is a high degree of crossover of work into one's personal life, consuming personal time. This would be considered an arrangement that is high in relational quality. Conversely, if the work arrangement was narrow in scope, then the boundaries between work and personal life would be clear and rarely crossed. These arrangements are considered more transactional in nature. Virtual organisation's are more likely to have a wider scope than traditional work arrangements.

'*Tangibility* is the degree to which the employee perceives the terms of the contract as unambiguously defined and explicitly specified, and clearly observable to third parties' (McLean Parks et al 1998: 708). This refers to the level of explicitness of the terms of the work arrangement. A contract where the exchange is without any subjective interpretation or ambiguity is considered high in tangibility and would also be deemed high in transactional quality. Work arrangements where there is little formal definition of activities or where quantifying an individual's work is problematic would be considered high in relational qualities. Virtual organisations are likely to be found having both.

'*Focus* is the relative emphasis of the psychological contract on socio-emotional versus economic concerns' (Mclean Parks et al 1998: 711). This refers to the emphasis placed upon socio-emotional, or interpersonal, attributes within a work relationship. A high socio-emotional contract would have items such as growth, status, and loyalty. However, they may also involve work arrangements where caring and empathy are intrinsic to the job, such as nursing and childcare. Work involving high socio-emotional or interpersonal attributes is also deemed high in relational quality. Examples of virtual organising are likely to be found with either focus (high in transactional or high in relational qualities).

McLean Parks *et al* (1998) broke the dimension of timeframe into two separate components. The argument here was that the impact of timeframes can be attributable not only to the expected length of the contract, but also to the degree of certainty when the contract will terminate. Therefore, *timeframe* includes (1) the *duration* of the timeframe, which is 'the extent to which the employee perceives the relationship to be short- or long-term' (Mclean Parks et al 1998: 712). Timeframe also includes (2) the *precision* of the timeframe, which is 'the extent to which the employee perceives the duration of the relationship to be finite (defined) or indefinite (undefined)' (Mclean Parks *et al* 1998: 712). This results in having four variations of transactional/relational composition when considering work arrangements. For example, an individual with a specific length of employment and specified date of termination has an arrangement that is high in transactional quality. On the other end of the continuum, an individual that has no set length to their work arrangement and no set date of termination would be high in relational quality. Somewhere in the middle resides work arrangements such as those which have set objectives for length, such as termination upon successful completion of a project, but are unclear as to exactly when the project may be completed. Again, virtual organisations are likely to be found existing in all variations.

McLean Parks *et al* (1998) introduce three more dimensions (particularism, multiple agency, and volition) to Rousseau and McLean Parks' (1993) initial five. The context in which they assign these new dimensions is one that integrates literature on psychological contracts with contingent work arrangements in order to highlight the differences that occur in various alternative work arrangements. Seven of the ten contingent work arrangements as defined by McLean Parks *et al* have characteristics that are similar to virtual organising activities (networked, in-house temps, leased workers, temp firm workers, subcontracted workers, consultants, independent contractors). As such, including their dimensions here is appropriate.

'*Particularism* is the degree to which the employee perceives the resources exchanged within the contract as unique and non-substitutable' (McLean Parks et al 1998: 714). This dimension is based upon the substitutability of the individual in a work arrangement. A high level of particularism presents a perception of high human asset specificity (Williamson 1981), where an individual is difficult to substitute or replace. Particularism also draws attention to the earlier discussion on the scarcity of resources and the superior bargaining position gained (Jacobs 1970). Work arrangements that contain a high level of particularism would display a high relational quality. Work arrangements where there is very little particularism, that is, many individuals could do the same job, are high in transactional quality. Virtual organising strategies are likely to emphasise high levels of particularism, assembling agents together based upon competencies that contain little redundancy or overlap.

McLean Parks *et al* (1998) argue that much of the research in psychological contracts assumes a single employer relationship. However, the frequency of working for one organisation and consulting for another is now commonplace. The earlier literature on psychological contract dimensions did not recognise this and for this reason McLean *et al* include *multiple agency* as a dimension of the psychological contract. 'A multiple agency relationship exists when an act by an employee simultaneously fulfils obligations to two or more entities, with full knowledge and sanction from each' (718). This specifically refers to the level of openness and simultaneity of actions taken by the individual. Multiple agency has high relevance to the dyadic form of virtual organising argued here in this chapter. Although the dyadic form of virtual organising is comprised of individual dyads, there is a great potential for an individual's work arrangements to involve multiple agency. Arrangements that entail multiple agency are high in relational quality, while arrangements that involve a single employer are high in transactional.

The last dimension presented here is *volition*. McLean Parks *et al* (1998) place volition as a moderator to the psychological contract. They believe that an individual's perception as to their level of volunteerism upon entering a work arrangement impacts upon their attitudes and performance. They define volition as 'the degree to which employees believe they had choice in the selection of the nature of the employment relationship, including but not limited to, the degree to which they had input or control into the terms of the contract or formation of the deal' (720). Individuals that had little volition in their work arrangements possess a high transactional quality in their work contract. Individuals that believe they had a high level of volition in their work arrangements have a high relational quality. Virtual organising strategies that are optional for entering agents will have higher relational qualities than those that are more coercive.

By assessing the dimensions of a virtually organised relationship on the transactional/relational contract continuum, it is possible to generate an aggregated value that factors all the dimensions and places the relationship somewhere along the contract continuum. This now allows researchers to consider varying virtual organising relationships based upon generalisable information.

Conclusion

The literature reviewed in this chapter forms the basis for the following characterisation of a virtual organisation: A virtual organisation is a process initiated by agents seeking to reduce the problems of opportunism and bounded rationality present in market-related exchanges, and the structural weight of bureaucracy in hierarchy-related exchanges. Virtual organisation relationships may initially be driven by economic influences, but will soon develop social values such as trust, loyalty, liking, intimacy, support, openness and honesty. These attributes are present at the dyadic level of exchange, and can have an impact on the overall characteristics of the dyadic network formed. Virtually organised relationships can possess a wide array of exchange methods encompassing a myriad of competencies and instrumentalities. This characteristic makes virtual organisations difficult to compare across groups and time. Alternatively, the context in which all virtual organisations exist can be determined by examining their dimensions (stability, scope, tangibility, focus, timeframe, particularism, multiple agency and volition). This way, virtual organisations can then be described in a manner which enables comparison across groups and time. These dimensions may also lead to explaining variance in performance and attitudinal outcome within and between virtual organising relationships.

The objective of this chapter has been to discuss the nature of a virtual organisation; to provide explanation of the virtual organisation phenomenon at the 'molecular' or 'micro' level and to prepare a method of evaluating the context in which exchange occurs in a virtual organisation. Literature on exchange and the psychological contract allow us to better describe a virtual organisation relationship. This review of literature from several research areas provides an opportunity to form a framework that presents linkages between them and the method of how they may be applied towards explaining and predicting performance and attitudinal outcomes of individuals in virtual organisations. Virtual organisations are creating new methods of working and managing. It may take several more years before the general public is fully comfortable in relationship exchanges that are limited to a telepresence. Perhaps a satisfactory comfort level may never be achieved. But with the increasing ubiquity of computer-mediated technology, the raised level of transparency as an interface between individuals, and today's youth being immersed in the medium at infancy, the overall comfort level is bound to be elevated. Albeit at the possible expense of other social norms.

References

Adams, J.S. (1963) 'Toward an understanding of inequity', *Journal of Abnormal and Social Psychology,* 67: 422–436.

Anderson, N. and Schalk, R. (1998) 'The psychological contract in retrospect and prospect', *Journal of Organizational Behavior*, 19: 637–647.

Argyris, C. (1960) *Understanding Organizational Behaviour*, London: Tavistock Publications.

Ashkenas, R., Ulrich, D., Jick, T. and Kerr, S. (1995) *The boundaryless organization: Breaking the chains of organizational structure.* San Francisco, CA: Jossey Bass Publishers.

Balser, D. B. and Stern, R.N. (1999) 'Resistance and cooperation: A response to conflict over job performance', *Human Relations*, 52, 8: 1029–1053.

Barney, J. B. and Hesterly, W. (1999) 'Organizational economics: Understanding the relationship between organizations and economic analysis', in S.R. Clegg and C. Hardy (eds.) *Studying Organization: Theory and Method* (109–141), London: SAGE Publications.

Boudreau, M., Loch, K. D., Robey, D. and Straud, D. (1998) 'Going global: Using information technology to advance the competitiveness of the virtual transnational organization', *The Academy of Management Executive*, 4: 120–128.

Burns, T. and Stalker, G.M. (1961) *The Management of Innovation*, London: Tavistock.

Byrne, J. A. (1993) 'The virtual corporation: The company of the future will be the ultimate in adaptability', *Business Week*, February 8: 98–103.

Cavanaugh, M. A. and Noe, R. A. (1999) 'Antecedents and consequences of relational components of the new psychological contract', *Journal of Organizational Behavior*, 20: 323–340.

Coase, R. H. (1937) 'The nature of the firm', *Econometrica,* 4: 386–405.

Cooper, C. (1999) 'The changing psychological contract at work', *European Business Journal*, 11, 3: 115–118.

Crandall, F. N. and Wallace, M. J. (1997) 'Inside the virtual workplace: Forging a new deal for work and rewards', *Compensation and Benefits Review*, 29, 1: 27–36.

Davidow, W. H. and Malone, M. S. (1992) 'Virtual corporation', *Forbes*, Dec. 7: 102–107.

DeSanctis, G., Staudenmayer, N. and Wong, S. (1999) 'Interdependence in virtual organizations', in Cooper, C. L. and Rousseau, D. M. (eds.) *Trends in Organizational Behavior Volume 6: The virtual organization* (81-104), Chichester: John Wiley and Sons.

Fukuyama, F. (1999) *The great disruption: Human nature and the reconstitution of social order*, New York: The Free Press.

Fulk, J. and DeSanctis, G. (1995) 'Electronic communication and changing organizational forms', *Organization Science*, 6, 4: 337–349.

Goldman, S., Nagel, R. and Preiss, K. (1995) *Agile competitors and virtual organizations: Strategies for enriching the customer*, New York: Van Nostrand Reinhold.

Guest, D. E. (1998) 'Is the psychological contract worth taking seriously?' *Journal of Organizational Behavior*, 19: 649–664.

Grabowski, M. and Roberts, K.H. (1998) 'Risk mitigation in virtual organizations', *Journal of Computer-Mediated Communication*, [online] http://www.ascusc.org/jcmc/vol3/issue4/grabowski.html.

Graen, G. B. and Scandura, T. A. (1987) 'Toward a psychology of dyadic organizing', *Research in Organizational Behavior*, 9: 175–208.

Graen, G. B. and Uhl-Bien, M. (1995) 'Relationship-based approach to leadership: Development of leader-member exchange (LMX) theory of leadership over 25 years: Applying a multi-level multi-domain perspective', *Leadership Quarterly*, 6: 219–247.

Granovetter, M. (1985) 'Economic action and social structure: The problem of embeddedness', *American Journal of Sociology*, 91.

Hall, D. T. and Moss, J. E. (1998) 'The new protean career contract: Helping organizations and employees adapt', *Organizational Dynamics*, 26, 3: 22–37.

Handy, C. (1995) 'Trust and the virtual organization', *Harvard Business Review*, 73, 3: 40–50.

Herriot, P. and Pemberton, C. (1997) 'Facilitating new deals', *Human Resource Management Journal*, 7, 1: 45–56.

Homans, G. C. (1958) Social behavior as exchange, *American Journal of Sociology*, 63: 597–606.

House, R. J. and Aditya, R. N. (1997) 'The social scientific study of leadership: Quo vadis?' *Journal of Management*, 23: 409–473.

Jacobs, T. O. (1970) *Leadership and exchange in formal organizations*. Alexandria, VA: Human Resources Research Organization.

Johnson, S. A. (1998) 'Teleworking service management: Issues for an integrated framework', in Jackson, P. J. and van der Wielen, J.M. (eds.) *Teleworking: International Perspectives* (185–206). London: Routledge Publishing.

Kahneman, D. and Tversky, A. (1979) 'Prospect Theory: An analysis of decision under risk', *Econometrica*, 47: 263–291.

Larwood, L., Wright, T. A., Desrochers, S. and Dahir, V. (1998) 'Extending latent role and psychological contract theories to predict intent to turnover and politics in business organizations', *Group and Organization Management*, 23, 2: 100–123.

Levinson, H., Price, C. R., Munden, K. J., Mandl, H. J. and Solley, C. M. (1962) *Men, management and mental health*, Cambridge, MA: Harvard University Press.

McLean Parks, J., Kidder, D. L. and Gallagher, D.G. (1998) 'Fitting square pegs into round holes: mapping the domain of contingent work arrangements onto the psychological contract', *Journal of Organizational Behavior*, 19: 697–730.

Metes, G., Gundry, J. and Bradish, P. (1998) *Agile networking: Competing through the Internet and intranets*, Upper Saddle River, NJ: Prentice Hall.

Mowshowitz, A. (1997) 'Virtual organization', *Communications of the ACM*, 9, Sep: 30–37.

Nicholson, N. and Johns, G. (1985) 'The absence of culture and the psychological contract – who's in control of absence?' *Academy of Management Review*, 10, 3: 397–408.

Nohria, N. and Eccles, R. G. (1992) 'Face-to-face: Making network organizations work', in Nohria, N. and Eccles, R.G. (eds.) *Networks and Organizations. Structure, form, and action* (288-308), Boston: Harvard Business School Press.

Ouchi, W. G. (1980) 'Markets, bureaucracies, and clans', *Administrative Science Quarterly*, 25: 129–141.

Palmer, J.W. (1998) 'The use of information technology in virtual organizations', in Igbaria, M. and Tan, M. (eds.) *The virtual workplace* (71–85), Hershey: Idea Group Publishing.

Perin, C. (1998) 'Work, space and time on the threshold of a new century', in Jackson, P. J. and van der Wielen, J. M. (eds.) *Teleworking: International Perspectives* (40–55). London: Routledge Publishing.

Roberts, K. H. and Grabowski, M. (1999) 'Organizations, technology and structuring', in Clegg, S. R., Hardy, C. H. and Nord, W. R. (eds.) *Managing Organizations: Current issues* (159–173), Thousand Oaks: SAGE Publications.

Rousseau, D. M. (1990) 'New hire perspectives of their own and their employer's obligations: A study of psychological contracts', *Journal of Organizational Behaviour*, 11: 389–400.

Rousseau, D. M. (1995) *Psychological contracts in organizations*, Thousand Oaks: SAGE Publications.

Rousseau, D. M. and McLean Parks, J. (1993) 'The contracts of individuals and organizations', *Research in Organizational Behavior*, 15: 1–43.

Rousseau, D. M. and Tijoriwala, S. A. (1998) 'Assessing psychological contracts: Issues, alternatives and measures', *Journal of Organizational Behavior*, 19: 679–695.

Scandura, T. A. and Lankau, M. J. (1997) 'Relationships of gender, family responsibility and flexible work hours to organizational commitment and job satisfaction', *Journal of Organizational Behavior*, 18, 4: 377–391.

Scandura, T. A., Graen, G. B. and Novak, M. A. (1986) 'When managers decide not to decide autocratically: An investigation of leader-member exchange and decision influence', *Journal of Applied Psychology*, 71: 579–584.

Sparrow, P. and Cooper, C. L. (1998) 'New organizational forms: The strategic relevance of future psychological contract scenarios', *Canadian Journal of Administrative Sciences*, 15, 4: 356–371.

Stiles, P., Gratton, L., Truss, C., Hope-Hailey, V. and McGovern, P. (1997) 'Performance management and the psychological contract', *Human Resource Management Journal*, 7, 1: 57–66.

Travica, B. (1998) 'Information aspects of new organizational designs: Exploring the non-traditional organization', *Journal of the American Society for Information Science,* November: 1224–1244.

Turnley, W. H. and Feldman, D. C. (1999) 'The impact of psychological contract violations on exit, voice, loyalty, and neglect', *Human relations*, 52, 7: 895–922.

Van Dyne, L. and Ang, S. (1998) 'Organizational citizenship behavior of contingent workers in Singapore', *Academy of Management Journal*, 41, 6: 692-703.

Venkatraman, N. and Henderson, John C. (1998) 'Real strategies for virtual organizing', *Sloan Management Review*, 40, 1: 33–48.

Wassenaar, A. (1999) 'Understanding and designing virtual organization form', *virtual-organization.net,* [online] http://www.virtual–organization.net.

Williamson, O. E. (1981) 'The economics of organization: The transaction cost approach', *The American Journal of Sociology*, 87, 3: 548–577.

9 Learning to Telework: Self-reflection and Learning in the Process of Introducing Telework in an Organisation

Diana O. Limburg

University of Twente, the Netherlands

Introduction

This chapter results from our research on how to make telework work in an organisation. Not to promote telework in general, but to support management and workers with the process of introducing telework. This requires insight, both in the 'essence' of telework – what does it do with an organisation and its workers – and in the process leading from the old 'traditional' way of working towards people actually teleworking.

In this chapter we will go deeper into an important aspect of this process, namely learning. We found learning to be important for two reasons. First, learning is considered to be an important aspect of organisational innovation, because existing routines are to be replaced by new routines. This can both be seen on individual and an organisational level (e.g. Dodgson 1993). The second, more direct motive for paying closer attention to learning was our choice for 'situated design' as a basis for constructing a method to support management and workers in the process of introducing telework. Situated design (Greenbaum and Kyng 1991) argues that people need to actually experience a new situation to be able to find out what they have to change in their work routines, what are good aspects of a (proposed) design, what needs to be changed in the design to improve it. Offering working prototypes or mock-ups can, for example, do this. When introducing telework, a pilot can serve as a working prototype, provided that it is seen as such by all parties involved. In our research we aim at filling in the concept of situated design specifically for telework, both with content (what aspects of organisation and work are involved and how) and with activities for actors (the process: who needs to do what). During our case studies it became clear that for explaining how situated design works, and what role the pilot and the final design play, learning was a good term to use. So we started to apply the term 'learning', both at an individual and at a group level. In this chapter we will elaborate upon this intuitive choice of terms.

We will start with a short explanation of our understanding of telework. This is essential, because this is what the people and the organisation will learn about. It also supports the idea that learning is needed to actually implement telework. Next we will go deeper into learning as a part of organisational change in general, and situated design specifically. We will describe how the learning process can be guided, and illustrated with case material. Finally some conclusions will be drawn.

The Impact of Telework on the Organisation

We see telework as a change in the temporal-spatial structure of an organisation. Employees are allowed, forced or encouraged to work (part-time) at another location than the traditional office, usually supported by modern information and communication technology (ICT). The temporal-spatial structure of an organisation has evolved over time, and is important for the work routines and social contacts in an organisation (e.g. Giddens 1985). For example, offices provide desks with computers to do the routine work, but also a context for social interaction, as colleagues also come to the same office, to do related work. For this purpose of interaction, colleagues from the same department are usually located near each other. If not, even within one office interaction often is. To see telework as just transporting information instead of people is therefore at least incomplete, as it only refers to the office as a place for (routine) activities, and not to the social interaction.

Becker and Steele (1995) explain about the silent messages an office can have. This means that changing the use of the office space, or the place where work is done, will inherently remove references to the old identity, history and values, which implies that things that were obvious before have to be re-invented. Having employees working at home consequently not only simply defines the place where they are working (location), but can also be a statement of trust, of flexibility, and so forth. Here we see a close relation between organisational culture, values and beliefs and the place and time were work is done. Again this indicates that introducing telework can have a major impact. Old routines will become obsolete and new routines will have to be developed, which brings us to learning.

To achieve a 'teleworking design' that fits the situation, several aspects of technology, organisation and work can be influenced. In other words: a design can be made, consisting of several building blocks, which together constitute a new organisational form that can be categorised as 'telework'. The specific situation indicates what building blocks are available, what building blocks are useful, and how the building blocks should be shaped. Like in a jigsaw puzzle, the shape of one piece is dependent on that of other pieces. For example: whether an organisation can implement the rule that e-mail has to be checked every hour, depends on the network conditions.

Situated Design and Learning

In the previous section it has become clear that introducing telework influences both (tacit) work routines that have evolved over time, and the context for social interaction. Creating new work routines will take time and effort. The context for social interaction will change drastically, resulting either in less communication, or the use of other contexts (e.g. technology). These can be seen as learning new social routines. An important task for the manager of the process of introducing telework will therefore be to guide the learning of new routines and un-learning of old routines. How can this best be done? Section 2 has provided two ingredients: knowledge on the aspects that are involved when introducing telework and knowledge on design options that are available to create the new situation. Insight into the process leading from the old to the new situation is also needed, as we do not believe that 'implementing the design' instantaneously creates a new situation (see for example Muller and Kuhn, 1993).

Situated design and evolutionary prototyping

As a basis for our model for the process of introducing telework we chose the 'situated design' approach (e.g. Greenbaum and Kyng 1991). This choice is based on the same arguments we mentioned in the start of this section, and more: introducing telework involves many aspects of the organisation, social as well as technical. Therefore the final new situation, and more important the way employees and managers will cope with the changes, can hardly be estimated. Greenbaum and Kyng summarise their approach in the following points (p. 15):

- The design process needs to start with an understanding of the use situation (designers and users learn about each others' basic assumptions)
- When computer systems are introduced within an organisation they change the organisation, likewise computer systems[1] adapt as they are used. Therefore systems should be designed for ongoing change
- The design process is firmly rooted in experience, not just rules
- Users are competent practitioners

Greenbaum and Kyng recommend the use of reflective action, or a cooperative approach, to bridge the gap between a static design and real change. The employees and managers will not just comment upon paper designs and proposals, but a design (prototype) will actually be introduced in the daily work. The daily

---

[1] Greenbaum and Kyng refer to computer systems in their work, meaning mostly the technical side. We think their ideas are also applicable to socio-technical systems like telework, amongst other because they stress the links between IT and organization themselves.

life of the organisation will reveal problems and opportunities in the design. Employees and designers will reflect on these together. Based on this reflection the initial design can be adapted, and also the users can carry through changes in the way of doing their work. This approach resembles an evolutionary use of prototyping (Hardgrave et al. 1999). Figure 1 illustrates the basic idea of this process.

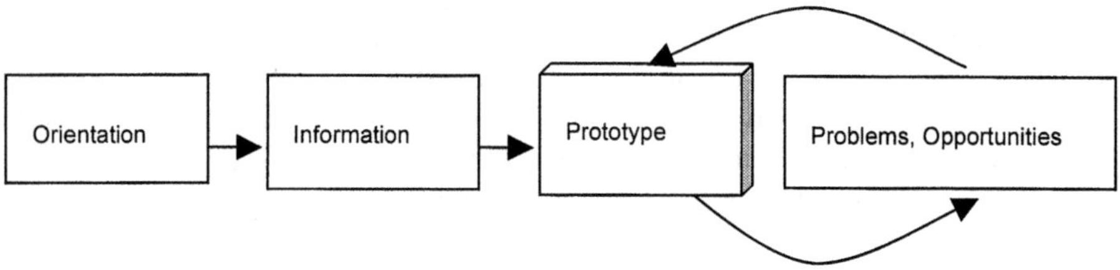

Figure 1. Evolutionary prototyping

First somewhere in the organisation the idea occurs that telework could be interesting. Before making this public an orientation takes place: could telework contribute to one or more organisational goals? Than information is gathered in the organisation, to find out what the current situation is, and what changes need to be made. Based on this information a prototype is introduced and used. During use, problems and opportunities occur, which can lead to actions to change the prototype. Thus, slowly the prototype evolves into a full-grown new situation.

In practice it became clear that this use of a prototype is too vague to be practical. Firstly it is usual to start a project with a pilot, a trial to decide whether telework is feasible and to learn about the specific situation of the organisation. How does a pilot fit evolutionary prototyping? Secondly, it is felt that at some point in time the design should be more or less final. Otherwise administrative tasks will become complicated, and other daily processes will remain unstable, which is unwanted both for external and internal customers. On the other hand, even after two years teleworking, people still make changes to their work routines, for example because someone's environment finally has become used to teleworking. So there should also still be room for changes in the final design, for specific individual cases and other developments in and around the organisation. We accumulated these insights into a new model for the introduction of telework, illustrated in Figure 2. The process described in this model starts with an orientation and information stage (that is not depicted), the same way as the crude first model did. Based on the information gathered in these stages, a pilot design is created, preferable as a joint effort of all parties involved, and based on the knowledge presented in section two of this chapter. This pilot design will than be introduced in a part of the organisation.

During the daily routines individuals will learn the new way of working, along the way experiencing aspects of the design that could be improved. Some improvements will be made immediately; others will have to wait to be incorporated in the final design. Not only the individual has to learn; the group will have to acquire new routines too. The yields of this phase will be higher if exchange of experiences will take place. Also the experiences should be documented for the final design, and for informing the future users of the final design. After a certain period of time (usually 4 to 6 months) all experiences will be collected, and put into use in the final design (as far as possible). Though the final design is 'final', still every new teleworker will have to learn this new way of working, and every new situation will bring about new experiences that might be incorporated into the design. It is also important to note that many difficulties in daily routines that are accepted in a pilot situation are not acceptable in a final design. The new teleworkers will be able to learn from the experienced teleworkers.

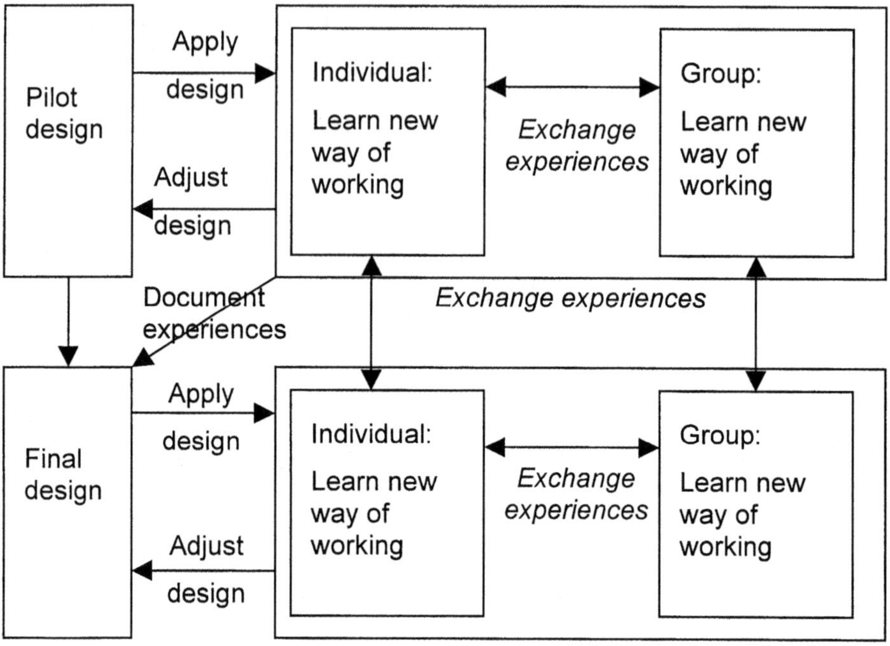

Figure 2. Learning during Pilot and final design

Learning and organisational change

Now we have introduced learning as a communication tool: to explain in the organisation what happens when the design is used and adjusted to the use situation. But what is learning? Dodgson states that there is rarely agreement as to what learning is, both within and between disciplines (Dodgson 1993: 376). Learning relates to both process and outcomes, it can be described as the ways firms build, supplement and organise knowledge and routines around their activities and within their cultures, and adapt and develop organisational efficiency by improving the use of the broad skills of their workforce (Dodgson 1993: 377). In the context of this chapter we refer to the second part of this definition: learning playing a role in improving the performance of an organisation. This can be done continuously (a learning organisation) and as a part of change process. Learning can take place at different levels. Usually single-loop learning and double-loop learning (or higher order learning) are distinguished (Argyris and Schön 1978). Single-loop learning involves making improvements within the existing set of principles, assumptions and paradigms. Double-loop learning means that new principles, assumptions, and paradigms are adopted. As became clear in section two, the introduction of telework requires such higher order organisational learning. But it also involves first-order learning, when new principles are tailored to the situation and to daily changes.

Learning builds a bridge between design (something that is made) and development (gradually incorporating the design in the daily routine). This idea is used by Robey *et al* (1995), by incorporating BPR in organisational learning (see figure 4). From an organisational learning perspective a design operates as an enabler (and disabler) of *learning*, change takes place incrementally, this in contrast with the starting point of BPR which is that change is radical.

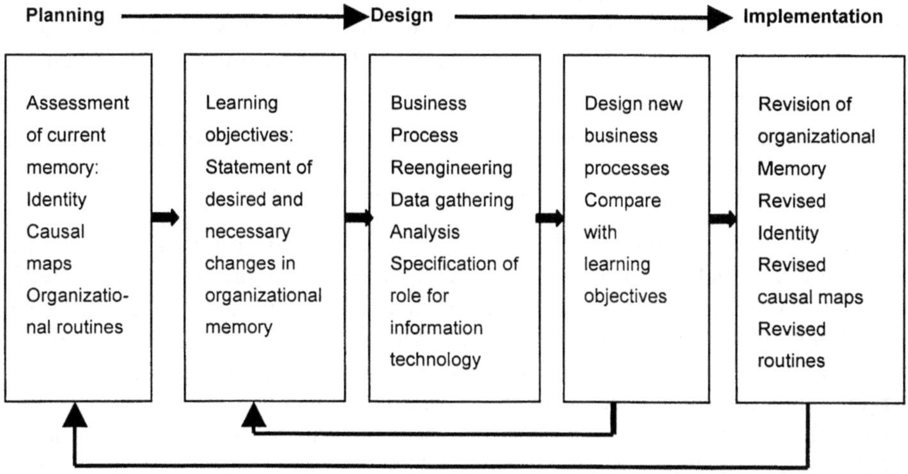

Figure 3. Business process reengineering as a component of the organizational learning process, in: Robey et al. 1995:36

The approach of Robey *et al*:

> ...conceives of business process reengineering as a component of the more general process of organisational learning. Organisational learning provides the rationale for change as well as insights into how such changes may be implemented; reengineering focuses on the tools for converting planned objectives into realised form.' (Robey et al.: 35).

This process starts with the assessment of the current memory, and establishing of objectives for change. This will provide a shared understanding of where the implementation process should lead. Based on the information from the first stage, a design is made. The design will subsequently provoke changes. It will be in the middle of changes, some parts being rather fixed, other parts changing while the organisational members are learning, changing their interpretive schemes. The first stage is a form of self-reflection, in organisational learning terms establishing the identity, the causal maps and organisational routines. The importance of this self-reflection is also stressed in the rules for situated design. Paying sufficient attention to agreeing on the (learning)goals of the change process and discussing the current situation helps to prevent a never ending, undirected evolution of the prototype.

After the design phase, during the process of implementation, another type of learning takes place. The newly designed processes must be accepted and shared as revisions to organisational memories. According to the ideas of situated design, in this phase the design itself can also change. This conforms with ideas behind structuration theory:

> ...human action can be seen on the one hand to constitute the institutional properties of social systems, yet on the other hand it can be seen to be constituted by institutional properties. (Orlikowsky and Robey 1991: 147).

In other words: on the one hand a design is created (routines, procedures, technology), which is released into the daily work, changing the social system. Exposed to this daily work, the design is changed as well, for example because something that is at first new will gradually become routine. This is also one of the principles of situated design as mentioned earlier: computer systems and organisation influence each other during use. For double-loop learning to take place, the design, and the change management should provoke and support double-loop learning, which occurs when members question underlying assumptions and norms, and modify their shared maps and theories in use. For the change process it is important to realise that the design is a pivot in the learning process, and therefore should be made with maximum learning value and also the communication during the process of making the design and implementing the design should be aimed at learning from the (experiences with) the design. In section two we concentrated on design aspects related to the content of telework, during the change process it should be stressed that the design is not the final answer, but a learning tool.

Ang *et al* (1997) adapted the model of Robey *et al* because they found that technical knowledge on how IT will impact business processes is necessary for change. In the situation of introducing telework this can be translated in the necessity of knowledge on the relation between time/space structures and the organisation. Therefore a model to support the introduction of telework should also incorporate this knowledge.

Recap

The similarities between approaches to organisational learning, situated design and the ideas of structuration theory are striking. Together they lead to the following conclusions:

- Introducing telework requires higher-order learning, because users have to modify their shared maps and theories in use; first-order learning is also necessary for modifying the design to the situation
- To change a situation towards telework three main steps are to be taken: self-reflection (consisting of identifying current situation and learning objectives), design and revision of memory (learning)
- The design should be made such that it stimulates learning, by provoking users to question underlying assumptions and norms
- Knowledge on telework is essential for the change process

The next section will describe and analyse the process of introducing telework at Compu-NL, based on these conclusions.

Experiences with Learning in Practice: The Case of Compu-NL

Background

Compu-NL is the Dutch branch of a large international organisation in the field of information processing systems, products and services. Over 4000 people are employed, and this number is rising. The teleworking project at Compu-NL mainly concerned sales-staff (approximately 2000 employees). Headquarters of sales are in Amsterdam, clients are based all over the Netherlands (and so are the employees). Desk sharing was introduced for sales-staff in 1992, employees also have had the possibility to work from home before, but this was not really incorporated in the work situation. In April 1997 renewed interest in telework occurred, due to an increasing pressure on housing costs. Management thought telework should be introduced for all sales-staff (voluntarily). Employees were very eager to be home-based, because they travel allot and traffic-jams bring about stress and are time-consuming. Partly based on the experience with the prior attempt to introduce teleworking, the project sponsor and project team thought the introduction of large-scale telework should be seen as an important organisational change, also needing a cultural change.

The first phase in introducing telework at Compu-NL has been described in an earlier paper (Limburg 1998). The pilot study showed that employees highly benefited from telework, but problems might occur with teamwork and management. At that moment the housing department took over the project, which than became integrated in a large-scale redesign of housing, aiming at better, more flexible (and more efficient) support of work. We will describe and analyse how the teleworking part of this project was structured. This description will be mainly based on the second pilot study that took place (125 participants), but if relevant also the follow up to the pilot will be described. At the end of June 2000 a total of 500 employees were teleworking, a further 1000 employees had limited facilities for working from home.

Design of the user support process

A multidisciplinary project team was formed, with representatives of the IT-department, Human Resources, Helpdesk, User-groups (three departments took part), Communication technology (phone, ISDN). The author was responsible for the support of the user groups in their transformation process. The project team first conducted a second, large-scale pilot study, from April till September 1999, in three departments, with approximately 125 participants. Knowledge on the content-side was used to develop surveys and for indicate possible problems with telework in meetings with user groups. This information concerning the content was both of a general nature, and also based on the prior experiences with the first pilot study. In the following sub-sections we will subsequently describe the phases in the learning process as described by Robey *et al.*

Self-reflection

The self-reflection stage in the change process consists of two parts: assessment of the current situation and identification of objectives.

Identification of objectives

It is important to realise that the project described was framed from two angles: firstly, the international bodies of Compu-International ordered flexible workplaces to be introduced, and also have provided guidelines for this. Flexible workplace fitted with a general tendency in the organisation towards more mobility (both mentally and physically). Secondly, the first pilot was inspired by the employees, who were very eager to work from home, for two main reasons: less travelling, and better working conditions. So two types of objectives already were established. The pilot was not seen as a basis for a go-no go decision, it was aimed at gathering more knowledge on how telework would work in practice at Compu-NL, to be able to further improve the design, and the user support process.

Goals of the pilot, and of introducing telework have been discussed in the project team. The project team saw it as its responsibility to identify all aspects necessary for successfully introducing telework at a large scale. But it also stressed the individual responsibilities of employees, management and several organisational functions to take appropriate measures.

The baseline survey (December 1998) was used to get an impression of the individual objectives of the participants; this was done by asking open questions. Supplementary, participants were also asked to explain why they participated in the pilot. The employees were also asked about expected drawbacks. The survey was executed when most of the design for the pilot was ready. This was done to be able to present this design to the participants, who than could get a better impression of what to expect. Because there was already much information from the earlier pilot, and from the representatives of the user departments this could be done. In the survey participants were also asked about their expectations by indicating to what extent they expected a decrease or increase in several aspects of their worklife (e.g. time spent privately, productivity, contacts with manager). This inventory was meant to get a more detailed and detached impression of expectations. Later real results could be compared to expectations. This information could than be used to better support new groups of users (how do expectations differ from real life). So this study was not really about setting goals, but neither was it just a part of assessing the current situation (though current expectations could be seen as part of the current mindset).

Members of departments were urged to discuss their expectations and their conditions collectively. Especially the conditions could be seen as part of the learning objectives, for example: we want to introduce teleworking in our department, but we do not want to loose teamwork. This brings us to the second aspect of self-reflection: assessment of the current situation.

Assessment of the current situation

The assessment of the current situation had two objectives: to be able in the future to see what has changed, and to identify explicitly what is considered important in the current situation. As was discussed in the second section, and also explained to the participants, introducing telework will alter the space-time structures in the organisation, which naturally helped the employees and managers to do their jobs. Because it also created problems, it is being changed. Much of the role of time-space structures is tacit. The assessment was only done at a local level, not for Compu-NL as a whole.

At the information meetings the departments were urged to discuss amongst each other what they considered to be important aspects of being a department (what binds us) and what was expected from the manager. From the earlier pilot it had become clear that in many departments the managers' idea of his/her role was different from the employees' expectations, especially concerning the preservation of teamwork. Some departments reported that these discussions were very illuminating. Other departments never had them. The project team only saw it as their responsibility to bring the option of such discussions to the attention of the departments, not to enforce them. Another tool in assessing the current situation was the baseline survey. Questions were asked about the personal situation, time spent working at home, working at clients' site and working at the Compu-NL office, time spent travelling, what activities are performed at what location, work situation (stress, motivation, importance of teamwork and informal communication), and communication means. The results of these questions were both used by the departments themselves, and by the project team to identify possible problems. Finally, one of the managers representing the users made a document with the most important social aspects of introducing telework for his own department. This document was found to be very helpful, and therefore also distributed among the user representatives.

Reflection

The link between goal setting (what do you want from the future situation) and expectations confirms our feeling that goal setting and assessment of the current situation are closely connected. People assess what is wrong with the current situation, and based on that assessment they form ideas about a better future. If employees had been satisfied with the old situation, they would never have considered teleworking to be interesting. One stage of learning, therefore, has more or less taken place at the beginning of it all: identifying the need to change the theories in use. This makes the learning objective rather straightforward: achieve a teleworking situation, in which departments still can function as a team. If it was only the higher management that wished to change, it would have been very difficult to communicate the learning objectives.

Effort spent on goal setting and assessing the current situation was highly dependent on the managers. In general, there was less time available than the project team wished. Departments that put more effort in this process learned a lot from it, but the other departments did not have much more problems. This might have been just luck: the departments that did their best did not come up with very big problems. Therefore handling the problems when they would come along, as the other departments did, worked more or less fine. Sometimes the more enthusiastic departments were even less satisfied, when they came up with problems and/or ideas and the project team did not react to those as they had expected. This might lead to the conclusion that if a general scan does not give the impression that big problems are to be expected, a more re-active, in stead of pro-active, approach should be recommended. This fits to some extent with situated design: let the real life come up with situations that call for a reaction, and than react if the situation is urgent enough.

Finally some remarks on the position of the pilot and the users in the pilot group. On the one hand, the pilot is a part of the process of identifying objectives and assessing the current situation for Compu-NL as a whole. On the other hand, for the users in the pilot group, it involved the actual implementation of telework, therefore they go all the way in the learning process. But they could be confronted with another design if after the pilot large changes have to be made to the design. This would mean that they had to go through another stage of learning.

The design

Much work on the design had been done in the first pilot: what equipment do people need at home (both ICT and furniture) for example how best to distribute equipment, tax-arrangements and software (for example for dialling in from home). Therefore, much feedback was available from use situations on the design aspects. Still, most of the effort of the project team concerned the design, including (administrative) procedures like how to handle a call to the helpdesk from someone working from home, should there be a special procedure, or should it be transparent. Optimising the design took more time than expected, delaying the start of people actually starting to telework (officially and fully equipped). Like in earlier cases, it became clear that accumulations of small problems with different aspects of the design, combined with wishes from different functions and user departments, result in a time-consuming design process.

Many of the rules and regulations were designed centrally, though departments were free to add their own. Agreements were to be made locally, the project team provided departments with ideas on what aspects of telework need agreements to be made (for example distribution of mail), but left it to the departments to fill this in. This makes this design aspect taking place on the borderline between the next stage, learning, and the design. In supporting departments some job design issues occurred, like who is responsible for changing the software on the laptops. The design may change after implementation in two ways: locally aspects are added and based on experience changes can be made to the central aspects.

A striking deficiency in the design was the lack of concrete action to support managers. From all evidence so far it was clear that the role of management was crucial, and possibly problematic. Therefore the Human Resource (HR) department was asked to participate in the project team. It took a long time before a representative of HR was actively involved; this was after this pilot period. Knowledge on the position of managers was communicated, but was not made concrete. In the final roll-out, after the pilot, HR will have a more distinct role. The representatives of the HR department think that introducing the telework design, especially concerning location, helps to enforce some changes that many people have wanted for some time. For example, managers have to change their style now, because they can no longer rely on visual control. For a long time, employees and managers have chosen to just ignore suggested changes. This change they cannot ignore, because the building changes, they do no longer get a fixed workplace. So now they have to learn to do it differently. This is an example of how a design can provoke learning. Again, if it is unclear to the employees what the learning objective of the change is, even such a provoking design will not be sufficient to achieve the desired situation.

Learning to telework: learning to work the new way

For the users in the pilot group the learning stage is during the pilot, for the other users it will be much later: after a (final) design has been made and has been implemented. We discussed that there is not a clear demarcation between this phase and the design. It is helpful to define the transition from design to learning with the actual implementation of the hardware and procedures. That moment was different for all users, and took place between March and May 1999. The official start of the pilot study was set at April 1999. As explained in the previous subsection, this was much later than planned, which explains the long period between the baseline survey and the implementation of the design. This period of relative silence for the user created a discontinuity in the learning process, which started with the information meeting and the survey. Because those also were much later than at first communicated with the participating departments, the delays caused irritation. One department even threatened to cancel its participation. First they had become convinced that introducing telework was important and urgent, now it seemed that their expectations were not considered important. It took much deliberation to keep this department on board.

During the pilot period a trainee had several conversations with representatives of user groups. During this conversations they articulated problems that occurred. Much of these problems were not directly related to the project itself, though they appeared to be more urgent because of teleworking. The trainee discussed the results of the conversations with members of the project team. Some problems were followed up; others were left as they were. This created another episode of irritation: the representatives of the user departments had used some of their precious time to make an inventory of problems. They felt that this was not appreciated fully by the project team. An important lesson from this is that the project team should not just gather information from the use situation for the final design, but should be prompt in giving feedback on what they intent to do with the experiences of users. Someone in the project team should have the task to keep the eyes of both groups open towards each other's worlds and agendas.

Departments were again urged to discuss their experiences with telework during their regular meetings. Some departments acted on this advise. The project-team especially stressed that it was important to talk about feelings, suggestions, irritations and needs, to prevent escalations. For example: if everybody acts as if it is normal to phone somebody at home at 11 PM, but you do not want to be disturbed then, it is better to talk about that.

Conclusion

The case shows that the steps derived from Robey *et al* play an important role in the change process. The first stage, assessment of the current situation, combined with identifying the learning objectives has taken place over a long period of time, during several stages of the project, and at different levels. We think the combination of a strong need from the employees, and a strong incentive from the international organisation formed the winning combination. It made the learning goals clear at different levels: the employees were eager to do their best, but also the higher level management was involved. Often either one of those parties is neutral or even negative. The assessment of the current situation was especially important at the local level: the level where routines had to change. For the project team information on the current situation was important for the design and for the communication process. Because of the changes (learning) at the local levels, more encompassing changes will gradually take place. Many of these changes have been in the pipeline for a long time, but never found a foothold. A combination of the learning goals and the compelling nature of the design formed this foothold. This confirms the status of the design as a pivot in the learning process and structuration theory. Because a telework design automatically does change the temporal-spatial structure of an organisation, people are forced to react. But, if they do not agree on the learning objectives, this could lead to fierce resistance and (innovative) measures to work around the detested design.

The final step is the process of learning the new way, supported and challenged by the design and the learning objectives. Again, some departments are very active in this, discussing problems, measures and changes; others just do their work. Because each can learn from the other this has not led to problems. The advise from Ang et al, that information concerning the content of change (telework) is important was confirmed as well. It helps to chart the current situation, to provide employees, managers and project team with ideas on what is possible (learning objectives, design options) and clarifying examples and anecdotes help to convince people that the change should be taken serious. During all stages of the change process, information from the collection of knowledge on telework is used, but also new information can be added to this collection.

In the case of Compu-NL there were several stages and loops in the complete process. There have been two pilots, and a workplace design coming from 'above'. At each moment in time, different groups are in different stages of the learning process. We think the second model we made is useful in understanding and communicating that the change takes place in different phases for different groups.

The whole process was managed with the ideas of situated design and learning at the background. The relevance of all stages was communicated to all parties involved, emphasising the relations between the stages. It was sometimes hard to explain to a user why a desired measure could not be taken, or to an expert why something was a problem to a user. With so many functions involved it is important that relation between the different participants is actively managed as well.

The case clearly shows the importance of learning for the process of introducing telework. In the learning process the telework design plays an important role, as a trigger of real changes, and as a way to fix a desired situation.

References

Ang, K.-T., Thong, J. Y.L. and Yap, C.-S. (1997) 'IT implementation through the lens of organisational learning: a case study of Insuror', in *Proceedings of the Eighteenth International Conference on Information Systems*, 1997: 331—348.

Argyris, C. and D. Schön (1978) *Organizational Learning: a Theory of Action Perspective*, Reading, Massachusetts: Addison-Wesley.

Becker, F. and Steele, F. (1995) *Workplace by Design; mapping the high-performance workscape*, San Francisco: Jossey-Bass Publishers.

Dodgson, M. (1993) 'Organizational Learning: A Review of Some Literatures', *Organization Studies*, 14, 3: 375—394.

Giddens, A. (1985) 'Time, Space and Regionalisation', in D. Gregory and J. Urry (eds), *Social relations and spatial structures*, New York: St. Martin's Press: 21—48.

Greenbaum, J. and Kyng, M. (1991) 'Introduction: Situated Design', in Greenbaum, J. and Kyng, M. (eds), *Design at Work: Co-operative Design of Computer Systems*, Hillsdale, New Jersey: Lawrence Earlbaum Ass.: 1—24.

Hardgrave, B. C., Wilson, R. L. and Eastman, K. (1999) 'Toward a Contingency Model for Selecting an Information System Prototyping Strategy', *Journal of Management Information Systems*, 16, 2: 113—136.

Limburg, D. O. (1998) 'Teleworking in a managerial context', in Suomi, R., Jackson, P., Hollmén, L. and Aspnäs, M. (eds.), *Teleworking environments, proceedings of the Third International Workshop on Telework*, September 1-4, Turku, Finland: 93—106.

Muller, M. and Kuhn, S. (1993) *Participatory Design; Special Issue of the Communications of the ACM*, Vol. 36, No.4: 29—37.

Orlikowski, W. and Robey, D. (1991) 'Information technology and structuring of organisations', *Information Systems Research*, 2, 2: 143—169.

Robey, D., Wishart, N.A. and Rodriguez-Diaz, A.G. (1995) 'Merging the metaphors for organizational improvement: business process reengineering as a component of organizational learning', *Accounting, Management & Information Technology*, 5, 1: 23—39.

10 Conceptualising a Telework Environment

Pedro Almeida, Óscar Mealha

Department of Communication and Art
Universidade de Aveiro, Portugal

Introduction

When writing about telework there is a natural tendency to promote the successful aspects, and in this way, positive experiences are usually referred to. However, in order to allow a sustained implementation of telework it is important to explore some of the causes of unsuccessful experiences. Resulting from these experiences, there are many disadvantages which have been associated with telework: social isolation, management problems and communication difficulties are some examples. Many of the disadvantages come from the inadaptation of teleworkers to the displaced office, the home office.

Isolating the organisational relations in an inter and intra environment is fundamental for understanding the viable expectations of teleworkers and to ensure operability success in a different interaction and management format which is in accordance with the institution's original mission and culture.

The telework is seen as 'a *vision of the future'*, rather than considering its practical merits as a technology-supported work innovation' (Jackson 1998: 3). This concept of '*vision of the future*' can deflect us from the real difficulties and concerns one must have in designing adequate environments for telework activities. Telematic services – as independent services – are developed to answer specific communications needs and to be adapted to different users (though no-one specifically); consequently, they are not for teleworkers in particular.

Teleworkers have specific and strong communication needs as they rely for their contact on the business of telematic services. Therefore, it is important to understand the real necessities of teleworkers, to know their profile, and to conceptualise a communication environment that fits their needs.

Some major technical constraints can arise from the lack of specific telework tools demanded by the teleworkers, or whoever implements telework, to search for the best combination of available telematic services.

> "It is presumed, for instance, that technologies will be appropriated and configured in ways that accord with the teleworking, rather than supporting alternative arrangements in general". (Jackson 1998: 3)

It is important to develop a working environment specific to teleworkers that answers not only the technical difficulties but also the broader telework-related problems.

Consequently, this chapter introduces an answer to the major question: 'what is the correct methodology to equate the appropriate system infrastructure and optimal human-computer communication scenario so as to support teleworkers and managers?'. The answer put forward is: a system that allows i) efficient participation of the teleworker in the fulfilment of tasks, ii) proximity to the distance office dynamics, iii) adaptability to different organisational scenarios, iv) multiple platforms for accessing the system.

Telework(ers) Problems

The most valuable resource of New Economy activities is based on manpower and knowledge. Therefore, it is important to focus our concerns on establishing the most appropriate conditions for workers to perform their tasks. To build an appropriate environment, teleworkers can be the first to give us the feedback to understand their needs. What are the needs of teleworkers?

Though the figures can change from country to country, some indicate that isolation is the major concern of teleworkers and that fast technological evolution inhibits the implementation of a telework plan (Sousa 1999: 96, H R Executive 1999, ECATT 1999: 53).

Teleworker isolation is a result of the lack of face-to-face communication resulting from the displacement of the worker. Consequently, major investment must be made to allow the same level of communication that existed in the enterprise, especially as 'a minimum primary requirement of telework is that it should have no negative bottom line impact. It is thus necessary for the teleworkers to be able to communicate with their co-workers and customers at least as effectively as they did before' (Nilles 1997).

Many experiences and examples demonstrate the importance telematic services can have for telework. Nevertheless, as in most software applications, they lack an integrated and uniform interface with other telematic services. The services are not specifically designed for telework and have problems communicating with other telematic services from other software houses.

Human-computer Interaction Problems

The referred incompatibility is not a specific problem of telework-oriented software; it is a wider concern, the poor convergence towards a user model, and the lack of flexibility and adaptability, because 'creative, interactive communication requires a plastic or mouldable medium that can be modelled' (Licklider 1968: 22).

The human-computer interface research teams have worked for several years to find the right working metaphor. Probably the most successful interface is the 'desktop metaphor' first demonstrated by Engelbart in 1968 (Myers 1998: 48) and gained the first major commercial success with the Apple Lisa in 1982 (see Byte 1983 for details). This Graphical User Interface (GUI) uses a collection of widgets (windows, icons, menus and pointing devices (WIMP)) to form an integrated workspace. The success of the desktop metaphor has contributed to the adoption of an integrated and uniform interface for operating systems, but applications that run on it still use different approaches. The user mainly uses applications; he therefore has to face the different interfaces. Limitations of human learning force us to achieve a convergence of interactive styles (Olsen 1998: 3).

From this, questions can be asked. Is the desktop metaphor applicable for a telework environment? How can different telematic and communication services be integrated? How will it work in a server centred environment?

The discussion on the interface type that should be adopted will appear later in this chapter. As for the integration of different telematic services, the description that follows tries to explain how it can be achieved.

The Proposal – an Integrated Approach for a Telework Environment

> Our computer or the screen is a window onto this vast network, this vast network of information and other people. (Maes 1997: 50)

This affirmation by Pattie Maes focuses an important concept – the Internet as the gateway to information and as a communications convergence tool. Though technology is not the key factor (Cano 1999), the Internet has brought an important impulse to telework situations by facilitating communications and allowing the contact between human resources and entrepreneurs in specific web sites (see, for example, Almeida 2000: 5, ETO 2000: 3). Therefore we believe that the telework environment should be implemented with on-line technology, be server centred and Internet oriented.

Why a server centred system?

A teleworker can perform his work in a variety of places: home, office, telecentre, car, public transport, etc. In order to constantly have (and in all those places) the information he needs to perform his work, a strategy of networking and virtualisation must be established. The teleworker can either carry a portable computer, for example a notebook packed with information, or he can rely on an Internet connection to a web server where he has all his data and updated information. The use of a web-based system allows the centralisation of information and resources in one place and improves the articulation with the other members of this network. As for technology barriers, these are breaking fast with the increasing possibility of Internet access virtually everywhere – for example, the upcoming UMTS protocol for mobile phones. Therefore, 'jobs that need access to this stored information are now portable' (Robertson 1999: 10)

How it is organised

The telework environment congregates in a uniformed and integrated metaphor a group of communication and management services to support telework activities as seen in Figure 1. It is believed that 'when added to the more comfortable teleworking environment, all of these technologies act to increase the effectiveness not only of individual teleworkers but of their fellow members as well' (Nilles 1997). We believe that the *comfortable environment* should be understood not only as the physical environment but also as the computer based communication environment. Built over a central structure that controls the system and establishes relations with communication technologies, it offers the user an integrated metaphor, transparent in what concerns technologies or protocols, as computer users are less specialised – largely as they are no longer only engineers or academics (Maes 1997: 50).

The virtual telework environment shall reflect the real communication and managing necessities of teleworkers and managers. Therefore, the environment must be mouldable and adaptable to users in terms of the communication services available and the interface to 'display' those services. Depending on the type of user, the system provides the set of tools more adapted to his needs.

The system is composed of a set of software agents, independent applications that are prepared to work together in a common front-end interface. The personalisation of the system, in a broader sense, consists of removing the access to some of the software agents and allowing access to other or to adapt some tasks to the user preferences. Though each software agent is an independent application it has the ability to establish relations with other agents, allowing the system to manage *task interdependencies* in a *common information space* (Carstensen 1999: 11).

Figure 1 exemplifies how the system could be configured for three different types of users: managers, teleworkers type B, and teleworkers type C.

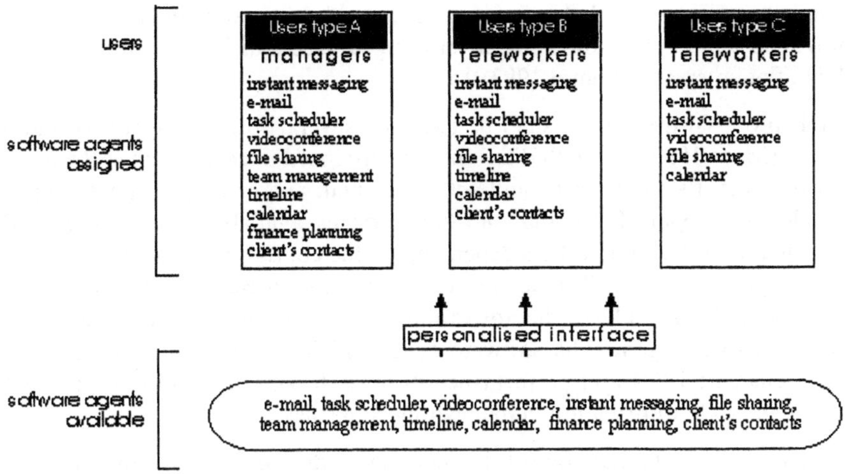

Figure 1. The personalisation of the system for specific users

As reflected in Figure 1, the system is intended to be group configured in order to adapt to each type of telework plan and consequent users. This configuration is allowed over a central and inner structure, which is defined and built, based on typical organisations.

The system's objectives are mainly: the work support, specially management and communication support. The specification of the system's characteristics must reflect the implications of the organisation's internal communications, the culture of the organisation (Huws 1999: 34) and eventually interdepartmental relations.

Technologically Mediated Methodology

The integration effort can also be understood and positioned in the theatrical perspective proposed by Brenda Laurel. In her work, she considers human-computer interaction to be a correct example of a theatrical set-up, where agents have an autonomous behaviour, interact with one another and besides an individual contribution for a major leisure goal also synchronise in achieving the global final message (Laurel 1993: 15).

In this proposal the system shall be based on several software agents or interface agents (Maes 1997: 49) with different tasks assigned to each. Each software agent will perform it's set of tasks and act as an input and/or output agent. The tasks include the support for communication services available for telework. Each agent will correlate with others depending on the configuration of the system for a specific group of users. The agents communicate with each other by a set of tags and keywords that allow the forwarding of any received information for the related software agent. The software agent will be personalised by tracking the user's characteristics and performance in order to automate some tasks, such as finding the right information, remembering some tasks.

But software agents that control the input and output of information are invisible to the user. Based on direct manipulation concepts (Shneiderman 1997: 44), the user has a *friendly* metaphor to interact with the system. Built on a multimedia interface it includes elements from the desktop interface: icons, menus, and windows. This environment shall also provide manual configuration options to adapt the system to user preferences.

To understand the way the system works, let us suppose that User A receives an e-mail message from User B. The e-mail software agent (SA) receives the message, extracts and reads the subject. By analysing the subject, it finds two keywords: *delay* and *salary*. The SA detects that the e-mail sender is a manager of one of the organisation's departments and sends the e-mail message automatically to the personnel department.

Another example of the services integration can be applied to team management. Two different tools of the system may communicate with each other in order to perform their objectives. In the case of team management, a tool such as instant messaging can be of great importance not only for the communication possibilities it allows but specially for the capacity to identify who's on-line, who's temporarily or permanently away. This information can be used by another agent in assisting the user to plan teamwork, for example, automatically rejecting the request to assign a task to a user that is away.

The manipulative agent

By explaining the system's structure, some Human-Computer Interaction concepts were introduced. It is important to make an analysis of some of the actual interface theories and position the proposed system related to recent research.

As for user interface, the system will adopt a hybrid solution of the two actual dominant researched concepts: direct manipulation and interface agents. We will call this hybrid solution a *manipulative agent.*

Shneiderman's ideas about direct manipulation (Shneiderman 1997: 44) assume importance for the advantages a graphical representation can have in, for example, visualisation of the project's timeline or the graphical representation of currently on-line team colleagues. The adoption of widgets such as icons organised by windows allows a fast and immediate interaction with the system. Direct manipulation interfaces can help users execute their tasks faster and better. Users can just drag messages, files or any other type of information directly to the icon of the recipient in the network representation area. The system should decide what communication protocol, service or technology to use, and the recipient's computer the best way to warn and show the received data. This example shows how an inexperienced user can send different type of information not needing to decide what service or protocol to use.

The system should adopt a GUI, with windows, icons, menus and pointing devices in a multimedia environment, which offers a higher number of resources and output capabilities. Though current common Internet access lines make it very difficult for a multimedia interface to be implemented with success, due to low bandwidth, up-coming technologies such as XSL, DSL and cable connections allow us to adopt more bandwidth demanding interfaces. The use of multimedia allows an exploration of more complex information levels in easy to use interfaces.

The system may provide *metawidgets*, interface elements that learn the user habits and decide on the interface output to use according to the analysed user profile (Blattner 1999: 126). For example, these *metawidgets* can be important elements for adapting the system to different type of users, providing a GUI for the majority of users complemented with voice recognition for disabled people.

Interface agents (Maes 1997: 49) play a complementary role by allowing the definition of a set of tasks to be performed autonomously, releasing the teleworker to perform other more important tasks. The agent can assist the user in situations, such as: reminder of activities, detector of low on-line presence of a teleworker, convergence of competences within an organisation, and finding the right information. Advanced functionality for interface agents must be adopted depending on the teleworkers necessities which are detected in the survey phase.

These advanced functionalities could be an automatic e-mail reply based on content analysis of the sender or a task calendar.

Figure 2 shows how different interface systems interact with each other in an on-line telework environment session.

Between the basic platform and the user, the system performs its activity structured in three layers:

1. The basic layer consists of the inner structure. Based on the interface agent's properties, a group of software agents with specific individual tasks control the input and output of data and establish communication with the other software agent's universes. The different software agents in the system dynamically connect and disconnect to other agents depending on the task requirements, information analysis or user characteristics;
2. The middle layer acts as the personalisation module for both the software agents in layer 1 and interface objects of layer 3. In this layer, we propose an integration and correlation of interface agents and direct manipulation objects in the so-called manipulative agent module. This module allows the user to personalise the system interface and software agent tasks. The module also allows the tracking and register of user activities and preferences to dynamically configure the software agents;
3. The surface layer acts as the contact/interface layer between the complexity of the system and the user, direct manipulation concepts play an important role in simplifying this process. In order to achieve this simplicity in use and a maximal adaptation to different user's characteristics, the surface layer must offer different options and input/output devices or interfaces as: speech recognition, pen devices, idiographic dynamic interface objects or multimedia.

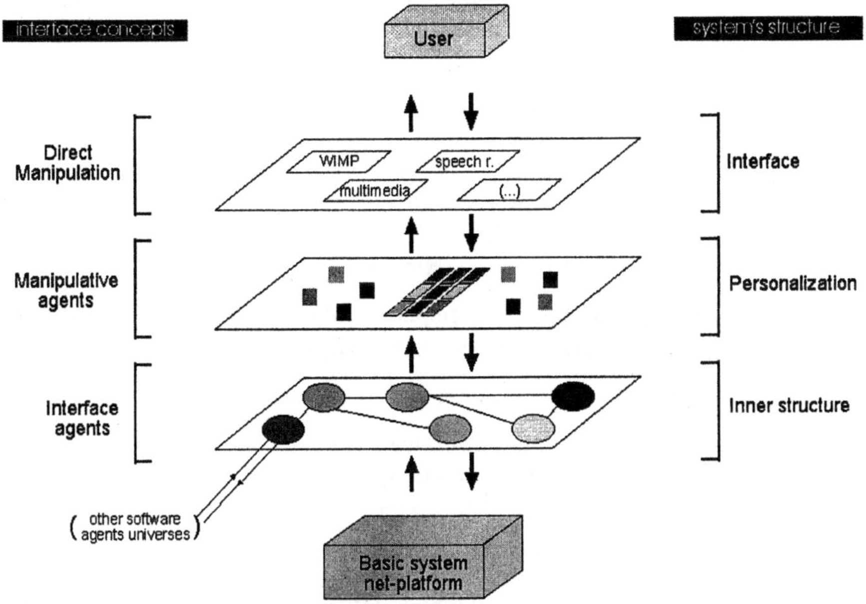

Figure 2. The structure of the telework environment

Tracking and Register Mechanisms

The interface agents are also important in the dynamic modification of front-end interface. Built with inner tracking mechanisms, the system registers the user activities. Interface agents designed to personalise the system will use this data. This personalisation includes:

- *Changes to front-end interface* – the reorganisation of the access metaphors to certain tasks will allow the highlight of the most used tasks. It will also choose between the most appropriate input and output strategy to adapt to the specific user;

- *Creation of a set of rules, based on the user preferences, to automate some tasks*: relevant information finding, tracking of competences, automatic e-mail reply and task warning, automatic selection of the communication service to use with most frequent contacts.

The tracking and registration of the environment usage will also be used to detect necessary changes to the inner structure of the system, a type of dynamic debugging tool. These mechanisms prove to be of great importance in systems improvement aiming the effectiveness of the interface in the five characteristics pointed by Shneiderman (Shneiderman 1998: 202), which also comply with the heuristics proposed by Jakob Nielsen (Nielsen 1990: 250):

- *Ease of learning* – optimised metaphors with easy to understand meanings. Direct manipulation has advantages in the use of the system;
- *High speed of usage* – fast response to user requests;
- *Low user error rate* – intuitive interface and solid software agents that perform the user requests with no errors or ambiguity;
- *User satisfaction* – an interface that complies with the first three characteristics referred will lead to user satisfaction;
- *User loyalty* –satisfied users will remain loyal in their use.

If actions are simple, reversibility is ensured, and retention is easy, then anxiety recedes, users feel in control, and satisfaction flows. (Shneiderman 1998: 202)

Implementation Phases

The conceptualisation and practical prototyping of the telework environment consists of four phases:

1. *Characterisation of the teleworkers and managers needs* - this phase achieves a characterisation of the specific needs of communication in a telework scenario. The opinions of teleworkers and managers concerning distance communication, the services used and their expectations towards an on-line integrated communication environment are of great importance. The adoption of IT must be understood as a social and political process, in which actors (the end users of IT) shape their needs (Jackson 1998: 3).

2. *Parameterisation of the telematic services organised into software agents to support the environment* - This phase aims to achieve a profile of the synchronous and asynchronous communication telematic services used in a telework context and to define which services and how to integrate according to the conclusions of Phase 1. The services and/or agents' characterisation

consists of understanding them bearing in mind, for example, the following communicational properties: i) position/role; ii) space/time intervention; iii) interaction levels; iv) modification, parameterisation and flexibility; v) relation with other services and/or agents; vi) associated usability metrics. Along with this characterisation of the services it is important to evaluate the impact of these telematic services in the organisational dynamic. This approach implies an understanding of the organisation's structure, namely the internal communication and the organisational culture or the 'socially defined collective behaviour' (Gupta 2000).

3. *Conceptualisation of the telework environment and it's intra and inter communication mechanisms* - According to Norman (Norman 1999: 38), the phase of underlying the conceptual model is the hardest part 'formulating an appropriate conceptual model and then assuring that everything else be consistent with it'. The correct understanding of the data allows a definition of the services to include it's correlation, the levels of information access and the implementation process using the *manipulative agent* interface concept.

4. *Prototyping, testing and evaluation* – This phase includes building a prototype of the proposed system and it's evaluation. Traditionally defined as usability evaluation (Shneiderman 1998: 127), this task is expected to obtain a whole set of methodologies and techniques that allow parameterisation of the usage level that the system offers as compared to performance expectations. This approach should allow measurement, in a qualitative and quantitative way, of the 'empathy level' that can be achieved between the user and the system. This task should allow the definition of system changes as well as directions to further research.

Future Research

The conceptualisation of this system must try to reflect some of the research done worldwide in the interface design fields (see (Myers 1998) for a brief research history). The focus must be on communication issues and telework related problems/needs.

One expected result is the establishment of a tested prototype with implemented modules. Continued research will require the complete development of this system and extensive testing to get the necessary feedback for an optimal definition of the telework environment.

References

Almeida, M. et al. (1999) 'Understanding the user, his role and participation in the development of telematic services', *CITIDEP*, Lisboa.

Almeida, P. and Mealha, Ó. (2000) 'Framework to understand and promote telework in Portugal', *Proceedings from The 5th International Telework Workshop - Telework 2000*, Sweden.

Cano V., Hatar C. and Zapatero A. (1999) 'Teleworking: conceptual and implementation problems', Queen Margaret University College, Edinburgh – Scotland in http://jimmy.qmced.ac.uk/usr/imres/fulltxt/txt_VC2.htm (17-01-2000).

Carstensen, P. H. and Schmidt, K. (1999) 'Computer Supported Cooperative Work: New Challenges to Systems Design, in *Handbook of Human Factors'*, Kenji Itoch, Tokyo.

ECATT Report (1999) 'Electronic Commerce and New Ways of Working Penetration, Practice and Future Developments in the USA" in '*Benchmarking Progress on New Ways of Working and New Forms of Business across Europe', project EP29299* by Emprica, in http://www.ecatt.com (19-01-2000).

ETO - European Telework Online (2000) 'A new market for work', European Congress *New jobs in the Information Society*, Luxembourg, 20-21 March 2000.

Gupta, Y. P., et al (2000) 'A Study on the Usage of Computer and Communication Technologies for Telecommuting', *IEEE Transactions on engineering Management*, vol. 47, n°1 pp 26-39, February 2000.

'Human Resource Executive Survey' (1999) in *Human Resource Executive Magazine*, in http://ercdpns.ercdataplus.com/hrexecutive (02-04-2000).

Huws, U., et al (1999) 'Teleworking and Globalisation*', Institute for Employment Studies*, Report 358, Brighton, UK.

Jackson, P. J. (ed.) et al (1998) 'Teleworking: International Perspectives, From Telecommuting to the Virtual Organization', New York: Routledge.

Laurel, B. (1993) 'Computers as Theatre', USA: *Addison-Wesley Publ. Company.*

Licklider, J. C. R, Taylor, Robert W. Henry (1968) 'The computer as a communication device', in *Science & Technology*, 21-31, April 1968.

Myers, B. A. (1998) 'A Brief History of Human Computer Interaction Technology' *ACM interactions.* Vol. 5, no. 2, March 1998. pp. 44-54.

Nielsen, J., and Molich, R. (1990) 'Heuristic evaluation of user interfaces', *Proc. ACM CHI'90 Conf.* (Seattle, WA, 1-5 April), 249-256

Nilles, J. (1997) 'Telework: enabling distributed organizations', in *Information Systems Management 124(4):7-14*, Fall 1997.

Norman, D. A. (1999) 'Affordance, conventions and Design*'*, The Nielson Norman Group in *Interactions*, May-June 1999 pp 38-43.

Olsen, D. R. Jr. (1998) 'Interacting in Chaos', Computer Science Dep., Brigham Young Univ., USA in http://icie.cs.byu.edu/papers/Interactinginchaos (22-03-2000).

Robertson, K. (1999) 'Work Transformation: Planning and Implementing the New Workplace', New York: HNB Publishing.

Shneiderman, B. (1998) 'Designing the user interface: strategies for effective human-computer interaction', 3rd edition - *Addison-Wesley.*

Shneiderman, B. and Maes, P. (1997) 'Direct Manipulation Vs Interface Agents in Interfaces', November 1997 *ACM – 1072-5520/97/1100.*

Sousa, M. J. (1999) 'Teletrabalho em Portugal – difusão e condicionantes', Lisboa: *FCA – editora de informática.*

Williams, G. (1983) 'The Lisa Computer System', *Byte: 33-35*, February 1983.

Part two

Work:

Processes and Cases

Work, Flexibility and Life-style Choices

We start Part Two with a section on flexibility and life style choices. The chapters that follow attempt in different ways to reveal the complexities that underlie contemporary developments in work flexibility. They show that despite superficial similarities, different flexible working arrangements can exhibit quite diverse characteristics, and well as complex interrelationships. Moreover, flexible-working initiatives can also produce quite dissimilar outcomes and experiences, often with asymmetrical benefits for the stakeholders involved.

The first chapter of Part Two is the first of two short reflection piece in the book. This one, by Patricia Mokhtarian, provides on overview of some of the issues that developments such as teleworking have openened up for individuals, and society as a whole.

In Chapter 12 by Beverly and Owen Leeds, we examine the assumption that teleworking schemes are axiomatically family friendly. Drawing upon empirical data, the chapter sets out to test where the balance of advantage lies in teleworking arrangements: between the individual worker on the one hand, or the employer/business on the other. The authors show that teleworking falls far short of a universal win-win. Indeed, it is much more likely, they say, that the benefits of flexibility will be realised on the side of capital (such as achieving cost reduction, and improved retention and recruitment), with the labour side often failing to realise putative teleworking benefits (greater control over work, improved childcare arrangements, better work-life balance, etc). Indeed, many teleworkers may experience the downside of flexibility, such as greater insecurity. The chapter reminds us that many claims about work innovations (particularly those made by Government and IT vendors) can be coloured with political interests and warrant careful analysis by researcher in order to test their empirical validity.

In the following chapter, by Karsten Gareis, we turn to the interrelationship between two emerging forms of work: home-based and mobile telework. The author points out that in the context of organisational change more generally, the relationship between on-site, mobile and home-based work is becoming much more dynamic. Drawing on data from across 10 EU countries, Gareis notes that it is increasingly rare to find pure forms of work arrangements (in other words, work that is office-based or home-based or mobile). Of course, depending on the organisation and the work involved, the balance between different work domains is likely to vary. In any case, these developments, says Gareis, have important implications for traffic flows, and in some respects may question established assumptions in transport models. This will be particularly important, he notes, for public policy makers as they seek to grapple with the changing nature of working patterns and its effect on travel behaviour and society more generally.

Chapter 14 pulls together a team of researchers from Iceland, Norway, Italy, Portugal and the UK. The chapter presents the outcomes of work on the relationship between teleworking and quality of life. In a similar way to the previous two chapters, the authors seek to draw out the complex dynamics that lie between new work developments and their social and psychological consequences. In this case an attempt is made to test and refine a model that examines the complex linkages and mediating factors between teleworking and quality of life. Given the scope and sophistication of the model – not to mention the attempts at its validation - the chapter provides us with a quite robust framework to take forward our understanding of the issues at hand. It reminds us that a range of factors will influence the experience of teleworking for the individual; and as with other new work innovations, we ought to refrain from simplistic deduction and generalisation until we have the frameworks and empirical support to talk knowledgeably about developments.

11 Reflections

Patricia L. Mokhtarian

In pondering this interesting collection of research studies, I am struck once again by the diversity of this phenomenon we call "telework". Students of this phenomenon are accustomed to encountering a wide variety of definitions, and the present set of chapters is no exception. The definitions used herein include:

- "employees who did work at home by formal agreement in lieu of, rather than in addition to, office based work for more than one day per week" (Leeds and Leeds);
- *home-based teleworkers:* "those who work from home (instead of commuting to a central workplace) for at least one full working day per week, use a personal computer in the course of their work, use telecommunications links (phone/fax/e-mail) to communicate with their colleagues/supervisor during work at home and are either in salaried employment or self-employed in which case their main working place is on the contractor's premises"; *mobile teleworkers:* "those who work at least 10 hours per week away from home and from main place of work, e.g. on business trips, in the field, or on customer's premises, and use online computer connections when doing so" (Gareis); and
- "work performed at a distance from the employer or client for whom the work is being performed, and where work is mediated by information and communications technologies" (Akselsen, *et al.*).

These choices illustrate some of the various components that a definition of telework might include:

- *employment status* – salaried, self-employed but contract worker with one or a small number of clients, or completely independently self-employed;
- whether or not the teleworking arrangement is *formal*;
- a threshold *frequency* or amount of interest, such as one day a week or more;
- whether or not the remote work *replaces* time in the regular workplace or *augments* it (as would be the case for overtime work at home, for a second job that is home-based, for some mobile work, and simply for the use of telecommunications in the ordinary course of office-based work – all of which could qualify as telework under some definitions including the third one above); and
- whether or not certain *technologies* must be used.

The purpose in drawing attention to this heterogeneity is not to analyse distinctions in depth, nor to suggest that one definition is better than others. It is, rather, to stress that the answers we obtain depend very much on the questions we ask, and framing the phenomenon of interest is central to framing the questions.

It is not just the precise forms of work being studied that can affect the answers, but the context in which those forms occur. For example, some of the findings of Leeds and Leeds are almost diametrically opposed to those of Akselsen, *et al.* The former study finds that teleworking can degrade quality of life, in the sense of being family-unfriendly, while the latter study finds that the overall effect of teleworking on quality of life appears to be positive even if small. In seeking to reconcile these two sets of results, we can point to several confounding factors. Both studies are based on small and unrepresentative samples (which does not, nevertheless, negate their usefulness for providing information about the phenomenon). Each study used different definitions of teleworking, with the latter study apparently including the full spectrum from overtime work at home to independent self-employment, so the results could be partly a consequence of distinct types of work arrangements appearing in different proportions in the two analyses.

Perhaps most important, however, is the fact that in the Leeds and Leeds study, teleworking appeared to be predominantly an involuntary arrangement imposed by the employer to save organisational costs, whereas in the Akselsen, *et al.* study, teleworking appeared to be predominantly a voluntary arrangement offered by the employer to benefit employees. It should not be surprising then, that when teleworking is voluntary it will not be chosen *unless* it is perceived to improve one's quality of life on net, whereas when it is involuntary for the employee, the negatives may well dominate. The lessons that I draw from these results are:

- We should not make the mistake of projecting results from a self-selected group of volunteer adopters to the entire population of potential adopters and expecting similar average outcomes.
- Neither should we throw out the baby with the bath water and conclude from the experiences of those required to telework against their will that the arrangement is unequivocally exploitative and a net disbenefit to the worker (although we should endeavor to expose and terminate such exploitation where it *does* occur, and proactively prevent it where possible).
- When teleworking *is* voluntary, many people whose jobs are well-suited and whose managers are willing will choose not to do it, because for them, the disadvantages such as those experienced by the workers in the Leeds and Leeds study (workaholism and interference with family life, among others) will outweigh the advantages.

Thus, forecasts of the adoption of teleworking should be realistic about its drawbacks as well as its benefits in order to properly assess its appeal. The

Akselsen, *et al.* study also illustrates that the impacts of teleworking – in their case, on productivity – may not be monotonic with the amount of time spent teleworking: more is not necessarily better.

If the first and third chapters in this section demonstrate that the impacts of teleworking on organisational dimensions such as productivity, and personal dimensions such as quality of life, depend on the definition and context in which teleworking occurs, the second chapter offers the same message with respect to impacts on societal dimensions such as transportation. Among other contributions, Gareis corroborates the findings of previous studies that teleworkers tend to have longer commutes than non-teleworkers, although it should be cautioned that other differences, such as in income, occupation, gender, and household composition, may partly account for the observed disparities. Taking the finding at face value, however, it does have implications for forecasting the demand for teleworking, and its transportation impacts. Is having a long commute an important motivation for teleworking? If so, are we overestimating the appeal of (voluntary) teleworking to those with shorter commutes when we focus purely on occupational suitability measures in analysing the potential for teleworking? Perhaps more importantly, is teleworking an *effect*, or a *cause*, of long commutes? I.e., in the latter case, does the ability to telework motivate employees to move farther away to higher-amenity residential locations?

The transportation impacts of teleworking can range from substitution (through reduction of commute travel) to no impact (when, e.g., teleworking is defined to include overtime work at home after a conventional commute) to generation of new travel (when, e.g., the increased efficiencies made possible by telecommunications result in spending time with more clients). The data presented by Gareis show that even "home-based" teleworkers are probably more mobile than non-teleworkers, and he comments that, absent stronger policy intervention than we have seen to date, the likely net impact for both home-based and mobile teleworkers is greater mobility.

As a social phenomenon, the diversity of teleworking is a strength. That diversity contributes to the flexibility of life-style choices that is the main theme of this section – it adds new options for a worker without (except in cases of involuntary telework) removing the existing ones. It is completely safe to say that teleworking is here to stay – that in fact, teleworking in some form(s) will become completely commonplace. As a topic of research, the diversity of teleworking is a challenge that is probably also here to stay. For the research community, it will continue to be imperative to construct a study with a well-formulated definition of teleworking, to communicate that definition clearly to the participants if appropriate, to precisely frame the research questions of interest and ensure that they can be answered with the data being collected, to be unambiguous when communicating results, and to be cautious when generalising beyond the immediate context.

12 Telework: Family Friendly or Employer Friendly?

Beverly Leeds[1] and Owen Leeds[2]

[1]Lancashire Business School, University of Central Lancashire, Preston

[2]Liverpool Hope University College, Hope Park, Liverpool

Introduction

For the past two decades telework has been given prominence by a number of authors (Tofler 1981; Wilkes, *et al.* 1994; Berry 1996), by information and communication industries (BT 1995) and by both the UK Government and the European Commission. Many organisations, such as Rank Xerox, Sainsbury's and BT, have launched telework as part of a range of flexible working practices. A number of authors have reported that some employers have recognised the value of telework and teleworking programmes they have implemented (Caudron 1992; Ford and McLaughlin 1995; Weiss 1994). Employees are also said to gain from this working arrangement and the image of telework portrayed by many authors (Baruch 2000; Burch 1991; Olsen and Primps 1984) has been one of a win-win situation in which both employer and employee benefit. It can be argued that the capacity for individuals to organise their own work time, workspace and work place provides workers with the ability to balance work and family life. Telework, therefore, is seen as one of a number of work/family initiatives popularly known as 'family friendly'. There have been numerous studies, reports and articles that extol the benefits of telework for both employee and employer (Caudron 1992; Ford and McLaughlin 1995; Weiss 1994). However, there have been few studies that examine telework as a specific family friendly form of work, or examine the benefits claimed for telework and whether these contribute to a successful work/life balance. This chapter examines telework as a family friendly form of work with reference to empirical data using as a case study an organisation well known for its teleworking practices. Furthermore, it examines the specific nature of the benefits that are claimed for telework and who gains from this working arrangement. It is not the intention of this chapter to deny that telework can offer benefits to families, but to refute the idea that these benefits are universal.

Family Friendly and Flexibility

Exponential growth in the implementation of information technology, and the decline of the male breadwinner (Crompton, *et al* 1996) has impacted on family/work issues. It has been stated (Kanter 1989) that our traditional assumptions concerning the separation of work and personal life are no longer viable. These cultural changes have implications for the individual and the family as well as organisations. It appears that organisations are increasingly responding to the pressure to create a family friendly workplace, but some have relabelled this as a 'work life balance' (Toynbee 2000). For some organisations these new working practices have been forced on them by legislation, for others it has been a repackaging and rebranding of existing flexible working practices into family friendly or work life balance employment policies.

In the literature there is no one clear definition of family friendly. Goldstein (1994), for example, describes a family friendly workplace as one where there are four or more policies or strategies that support employees with families. Whereas, Simkin and Hillage (1992) state that there are two primary areas of employer involvement in work family issues: the provision of child care benefits and the use of options which enhance workforce flexibility such as flexible working hours, voluntary shifts, part-time working, teleworking, job sharing and flexible holidays. Some authors view family friendly working practices as the introduction of flexibility by stealth and consequently the latest manifestation of the eternal battle between labour and capital (Edwards 1986). Others, by comparison view family friendly working practices as the catalyst that may change organisations and make them better places for all of us (Fletcher and Rappoport 1996). The UK Department of Education and Employment (DfEE) focuses on the employee when defining family-friendly practices as formal or informal terms and conditions that exceed the statutory minimum, designed to enable an employee to combine caring responsibilities with paid employment (Bevan *et al* 2000). However, it can be maintained that the flexible working arrangements introduced and extended by management have been as much *employer friendly* as *family friendly* (Simkin and Hillage 1992). Furthermore, the term 'family friendly' may be an oxymoron, as the flexibility offered by family friendly working practices often refers to atypical working hours implemented for the benefit of the company, not for the employees, and they are often linked with less secure forms of employment.

Types of Teleworkers

One of the problems with viewing telework as a family friendly option is that teleworkers are not an homogenous group (Huws *et al* 1990). Teleworkers have different working patterns and different types of work, hence, what may constitute a family friendly option for one type of teleworker may not for another. Most studies, distinguish between two distinct types of teleworkers; the home based teleworker and the mobile teleworker. Stanworth (1997) highlights the fact that mobile teleworkers who work from – but not always at – home, tend to be male, work full time and to be highly skilled. In contrast, the home-based teleworkers are found to be female, part time and undertaking lower skilled jobs. She further comments that many of these workers are low paid and have unpredictable workloads and work unsociable hours (Stanworth 1997). Statistics produced by the Institute for Employment Studies in the UK have also highlighted that females are more likely to work part time and at home (Huws *et al* 1999). Galpin and Sims (1999) also define two distinct groups of teleworkers but differentiate them as either knowledge worker or operative. They argue that the experiences of the two types are somewhat different. A flexible worker who can dictate terms to his or her employer is considerably different from that of a parent teleworking in order to combine work and family obligations (Galpin and Sims 1999). The widening division between the elite knowledge worker and operatives is also reflected in the literature surrounding core and periphery workforce (Atkinson 1989). Galpin and Sims (1999) refer to a certain type of operative known as *Cottage coders* producing *information widgets* who work at home for the company but are not always in full employment from the company. The distinction between the two types of teleworkers is important when examining the family friendly benefits.

Benefits of Telework

Hill *et al* (1996) note that because working in a virtual office provides more flexibility in where and when work is undertaken, it is assumed that it is advantageous to the individual and the family. For the employer, there can be access to a wider labour market, increases in productivity, reduction in overtime, cost savings on office space and an overall reduction in absenteeism. For the employee it is claimed that telework can break down segmented gender roles, increase employee control over working conditions, flexibility of working hours, assistance with childcare arrangements and can contribute to the balance of work and family life (Baruch 2000). Despite these assertions, there is very little empirical evidence that these advantages are realised in practice and directly benefit the family. Hill *et al* (1998) suggest that research has overestimated these benefits to the work life balance. Although it has been argued that telework is what employees need to balance work and home life (Jenson 1994) others argue that rather than provide a balance telework merely blurs the boundaries between the two. There are a number of authors that refer to this difficulty in separating work and home life. Hartman *et al* (1991) identify a negative relationship between family relationships and satisfaction with telework. Indeed a closer examination of the benefits claimed for the employee may actually represent benefits to the employer. Furthermore, many of the benefits for the employer may be disadvantageous to the employee and although telework may offer flexibility and benefits for both employees and employers, in the long run it may mostly benefit the employer (McQuarrie 1994). Employees may be under the illusion that telework provides a number of advantages and little or few disadvantages. Hence it is necessary to examine both employer and employee benefits to determine whether or not the work-family interface benefits.

Employee Benefits

Gender Bias

Fletcher and Rappoport (1996) maintain that the limited scope of many family friendly policies such as telework do not address the wider societal issues including the overemphasis on the role of work and the long-term gender stereotyping of male and female roles. They argue that because the driving factor for these policies is the increased take up of employment by females, then family friendly working policies paradoxically re-enforce the stereotype that childcare provision is exclusively a concern for the female worker. Whilst this perception remains, they argue, men will always be less likely to take up caring duties, as they fear for the negative impact that this may have on their careers. Moreover, Stanworth (1997) argues that working in the home reinforces the gender roles.

Flexible Working Hours and Control of Working Conditions

It is argued that one of the key organisational issues affecting teleworkers are the opportunities afforded by flexible working schedules. Verespej (1994) foresaw a pattern that would emerge worldwide where employers would allow workers to put together their own place-time combinations to support their diverse work, family, lifestyle, and financial needs. Although flexible working practices in the UK doubled between 1984 and 1994 (Economist 2000) it cannot be concluded that these all support work, family or lifestyle requirements. Neither can it be shown to be flexibility for all as DfEE research shows that women with higher qualifications and job levels are more likely to have access to flexible working hours than women with poor qualifications (Bevan *et al* 2000)

Control of Working Conditions

Huws *et al* (1990) maintain that the greater freedom from central control experienced by some professional teleworkers may be an illusion resulting from an alteration in the mechanism of control. They also claim that there is no real loss of control over the workforce as it is still the employer who controls the work and the payment and therefore the balance of power remains unaltered. McQuarrie (1994) supports this argument maintaining that it is clear that in most teleworking relationships power and control over work and work conditions still lie mainly in the hands of the employer, even though the work is being performed in the employee's home. She further highlights that the limited choices available to the teleworker support Braverman's (1974) argument that advances in technology serve to de-skill workers and put greater power in the hands of owners and managers.

Childcare

Another frequently cited benefit of telework is the ability of employees to care for their children while working at home. However, many authors (Christensen 1992; Riley 1994) argue that telework and dependent care cannot be combined effectively and hence this benefit may be difficult to realise in practice. For example, Galt (in Mirchandani 1999) found that home-based workers often worked late into the night after caring for children all day. Many teleworkers arrange for child care for children at home which negates the cost-saving *benefit* of being able to care for one's children while working (Risman and Tomaskovic-Devey 1989). McQuarrie (1994) also argues that telework provides a means for the organisation to escape responsibilities and commitments to its workers, as encouraging workers with children to telework may remove the pressure on an organisation to provide day-care services for working parents (Risman and Tomaskovic-Devey 1989). Furthermore Huws *et al* (1999) argue that given the marital status and age of teleworkers, the number who have childcare responsibilities is only slightly above average for the population. Therefore, it is difficult to use the current statistics to support an argument that teleworking results from a life-style choice to put family before work (Huws *et al* 1999).

Work Life Balance

McQuarrie (1994) highlights the difficulty of making a psychological division between home and work, when work is located in the home. This financial or psychological inability to create a home/work division may lead to the employee to become a workaholic, unable to separate herself from work when it is physically present in the home (McQuarrie 1994). Hill (1995:2) highlights the dangers of this by suggesting that '(g)iving a workaholic an electronic briefcase may in some ways be like giving an alcoholic a bottle of Gin' Although workaholism may be beneficial to the firm in the short term because of increased output, it is obviously detrimental to the individual's physical and mental well being as well as an intrusion on family life and in the long term it may also be damaging to the organisation.

Employer Benefits

Cost Saving

Expense reduction has been a major driver for the increase in mobile and home-based workers. By decreasing office space and providing individuals with suitable technology to work elsewhere, savings can be realised by an organisation within a short space of time (Hill *et al* 1998). McQuarrie (1994) argues that changing office-based workers into home-based teleworkers may be an example of a transfer, rather than a reduction, of costs. That is, the employee bears the costs previously covered by the employer. Thus the *'energy and space saved at the office is instead relocated to the employee's home'* (McQuarrie 1994: 81). The perceived benefits of teleworking rarely mention the possibility of the employer compensating the employee for home-based work by paying a portion of rent, mortgage, or utility costs. Stanworth (1997) has highlighted that teleworkers all share an increased vulnerability to cost cutting by employers and furthermore, those employees who combine work at office and home are having their rights to ownership of physical space eroded.

Improvements in Recruitment and Retention

The opportunity for remote working has been portrayed as a major advantage of telework and identified as a solution to shortfalls in labour (Poole 1989). Telework provides employers with access to a wider labour market, enabling them to attract and retain staff. However, as telework frees work from the constraints of time and place (Bailyn 1988) it may prove to be detrimental to both existing employees and potential recruits. It is possible for jobs to move to the lowest cost base away from existing employees, to labour markets elsewhere with the requisite language skills. McQuarrie (1994) reports that US firms have contracted with prison authorities to have inmate teleworkers, hence argueing that this exemplifies the severe imbalance of power between employer and employee in telework arrangements (McQuarrie 1994).

Productivity/Reduction in Overtime

It has been argued that work productivity increases because teleworkers may have more control over interruption and take less informal breaks and work (Olson 1988). However, this lack of regimentation coupled with the inability to create a home/work division can have disadvantages and may lead to increased working hours and eventually to *workaholism* (McQuarrie 1994). In a recent MORI poll in the UK many employees reported that they worked longer hours at home and one in three worked more than 48 hours a week (Dawe 1999). The reduction in commuting time is often cited as a source of increased productivity. However,

Gordon and Kelly (1986) and Nilles (1994) suggest that teleworkers give half of their saved commuting hours back as longer working hours. Thus the increased output may be generated by working longer hours and not from increased productivity. Mirchandani (1999) highlights that the primary source of increased productivity is the teleworker's own motivation.

Reduced Absenteeism

Steward (1997) has drawn attention to the fact that the ability to commute has defined fitness-to-work and that teleworking has redrawn the boundaries between the sick and the healthy worker. Pollert (1988) also maintains that in this form of work it is possible from the employer's perspective to expect workers to continue to work during illness. A recent survey by MORI for BT found that three out of four home based teleworkers said that they had rarely taken time off work because of sickness, and two out of three thought that their stress levels were lower working from home than in an office. (Dawe 1999)

The Company

The company used for the research was a large organisation with more than 20,000 employees, employing a variety of teleworkers involved in the sale, design, development and integration of IT systems and services. For this study, teleworkers, project managers, an HR manager and a senior director were used to investigate the issues raised. All teleworkers were employees who did work at home by formal agreement in lieu of, rather than in addition to, office based work for more than one day per week. The respondents ranged in age from 26 to 54; all but 4 were married; about half those interviewed were female; the majority of married women were in dual-income families. Teleworkers and managers were questioned through a semi-structured interview and were asked about the perceived benefits of telework. They were specifically asked to comment on productivity, morale, flexibility, the timing and location of work as well as work/life balance and family issues.

The New World

At the time the research was conducted, the company was undergoing a four-year property initiative known as *New World,* to reduce office costs. As part of the property strategy some offices have been closed, some relocated and others renovated or *New Worlded.* The project involved assessing employees' working patterns and identifying those jobs that did not require a permanent office desk. Home based jobs were defined as those jobs that enable an employee to work at or from a home base for 70% or more of the time, office based jobs being those that require an on-site presence for 70% of the work time and mobile jobs those that fall between these two categories. Only those jobs requiring an on-site presence were provided with a PAD, a Permanently Allocated Desk. Other employees classified as teleworkers were provided with suitable equipment that allowed them to be mobile or home based. Mobile workers with laptops can use a variety of 'rendezvous' points around the building that are fitted with network connections. These 'rendezvous' points include restaurant areas as well as meeting points. There are no offices but desks scattered across an open plan office with private meeting rooms.

Types of Teleworkers

A number of differences were identified between the mobile and home-based teleworkers. The mobile teleworker was found to be younger and male whereas the home based teleworker was found to be older and predominantly female (75% overall). All the mobile teleworkers interviewed worked full time whereas the hours worked by the home based teleworker ranged from 25 hours to full time. The majority of the mobile workers were project managers, consultants or technical specialists. In contrast, the home based workers tended to be system designers and programmers. Differences in pay could also be identified with those teleworkers based at home earning less pro rata than those who were mobile. Many of the home based, part time teleworkers have more in common with Galpin and Sims (1999) *cottage coders* than highly skilled knowledge workers. These part time employees cannot work for other employers, are hourly paid and paid only a 10% monthly retainer if no work is available. As employees they are not independent contractors yet the company has the flexibility of treating them as if they were. By treating the home based teleworkers as peripheral to the business and employing them on an hourly paid basis, rather than provide family friendly working practices the company has effectively introduced an insecure environment hostile to the family. Furthermore, the fact that the majority are female serves only to reinforce the gender stereotyping of family roles.

Perceived Benefits of Telework

Control of Working Conditions

The company teleworkers did not feel more in control of their work, and many felt that their working pattern was more rigid than that of some office based staff. In particular, the company's mobile teleworkers have very little control over their work and many of those interviewed were unhappy with the demands placed on them through mobile telework. It is argued that telework should operate within a framework of volunteerism (Mirchandani 1999), but for many of the company's mobile teleworkers this is not optional, but part of their job description. The flexibility of work is attached to the job description and hence contractual, thus the company believe the choice of being a mobile teleworker is voluntary as it is by agreement. Many of the employees from these *New Worlded* offices had previously worked as mobile workers but also had an office space. Now they have to provide a home environment that will allow them to work there for part of their working week. These mobile workers do not qualify for tax relief unless they spend at least 40% of their contractual hours working from their home address. Currently the company does not record who is a mobile teleworker. This will change as the company intends charging its business units for space occupied in offices, thus increasing the pressure on managers to move employees to being home or mobile teleworkers.

Flexible Working Hours

Although a number of teleworkers reported increased flexibility, some highlighted that this was not always possible due to the need to be available during office hours. The company allow teleworkers to work unsupervised but demand that they are available during normal office hours. Any teleworker who wishes to work outside these hours '*must seek managerial approval for any period between the hours of 9.00 a.m. to 5.00 p.m., Monday to Friday, during which they will be unavailable for work'*. (Company HR Documentation). Hence, the promise of flexible hours cannot be realised unless by prior agreement. Some teleworkers argued that teleworking gave them greater flexibility with regard to caring for sick children or being at home when children returned from school, however, this was confined to home based teleworkers.

Childcare

The company do not provide on-site childcare facilities arguing that to provide these would only benefit some of their workers and therefore offer other benefits instead. Although all home based teleworkers reported that childcare arrangements were easier than those for office based staff, it was still necessary to arrange childcare for children under 12. Thus many of the so-called savings are not realised for parents with younger children. The mobile teleworkers found little or no savings in childcare costs, as their work patterns were too irregular to allow less childcare to be used.

Work Life Balance

Many of the mobile teleworkers found the separation of work and home difficult, in particular the mobile teleworkers reported less satisfaction with opportunities to balance the family and work. Both types of teleworker reported working atypical hours out of necessity rather than choice and many also reported difficulties in *switching off*. Part time workers were often contacted on non-work days.

Therefore, rather than teleworkers having the freedom to enjoy an improved work-life balance, a situation of work being omnipresent has been created, where staff are effectively permanently on-call without being paid. Part time home based workers were under a great deal of pressure to work longer hours with the company arguing that there was a business need for increased hours - *'Being home based is not a problem, but part time is a problem. Development timescale's so short nowadays that we can't afford to use part time staff.'* (Company HR Director)

Cost Reduction

The property initiative has necessitated all home based and many mobile teleworkers having to provide offices at home. Home-based staff are reimbursed with the costs of additional telephone lines and provided with suitable IT equipment. Furniture is not provided and no payment is given for the use of space, heating, lighting or other running costs. The company argue that the tax allowance negotiated with the Inland Revenue in the mid '90s for home based workers and updated regularly provides teleworkers with the necessary reimbursement for heating, lighting etc. This tax allowance varies from £250 to £500 depending on whether they are full-time (over 21 hours) or part-time staff. Mobile teleworkers are not given this allowance unless they work more than 2 full days at home. By shifting the costs of space and associated overheads, the cost savings of teleworking are passed to the teleworker. Costs are also being passed onto the UK government through the tax allowances.

Improved Recruitment and Retention

The company recognises that there is potentially a global labour force and that technology allows access to it. Some of the company's UK home based teleworkers noted that some project work that they had bid for had been lost to another in-house unit in India. The teleworkers are therefore no longer only competing with external competitors but also internally against their own organisation. As a result, many of the home based workers have been forced to look for work elsewhere or be faced with working less than their contracted hours or even redundancy.

Increased Productivity and Reduced Sickness Absenteeism

Many of the teleworkers did not volunteer to work away from the office and even those that did admitted working long hours to justify their presence at home. Thus the productivity argument is difficult to prove as teleworkers may just ensure that output is improved through working additional hours. The company recognises that workaholism may occur in teleworkers but they have no procedures to deal with it and issue no warnings to staff to safeguard against it. Moreover, many of the managers argue that teleworkers are more productive because they are more conscientious. There was a certain expectation of improved productivity and there was evidence that teleworkers were expected to work when feeling ill – *'often what stops you coming into work is the journey, but if you can stay at home and maybe start a little later then often you can carry on'* (HR Manager).

Conclusions

In common with other telework studies many respondents commented favourably about reduced travelling, fewer distractions, more comfortable environment and most felt that they were more productive. However many acknowledged that this perceived increase in productivity may have been gained through longer working hours rather than less distractions or a more comfortable environment. In general more positive comments regarding telework came from the home based workers. All the mobile teleworkers made negative comments with regard to the work arrangement. Furthermore, many of the benefits claimed for the employer were disadvantageous to the employee and their family. It was clear that the teleworkers were vulnerable to cost cutting exercises by the organisation, particularly in the area of employment-related expenses that can be passed on to the employee. Overall the qualitative analysis undertaken failed to support the perception that telework contributes favourably to the work/life balance and is a family friendly working practice. The biggest failing is the claim that flexibility is provided to all and can assist with the work family balance. Telework does provide flexibility, but it is flexibility for a few – and mainly the employer. The benefits do exist but are not always available, nor as great, as some authors portray them. In particular, the benefits of childcare savings, the flexibility of hours and the control of work are not always fully realised. Others such as productivity and reduced absenteeism are seen to only benefit the employer. It can be shown that telework can be detrimental to the family through increased threat of job loss, workaholism, increased work costs, reinforcement of the gender bias, creation of a dual labour market and difficulties in home-work separation. It can be seen, therefore, why it has been suggested that flexible working policies, like teleworking, masquerading under the guise of Family Friendly working policies, are merely the latest manifestation in the age-old battle between capital and labour.

There is evidence that, if carefully implemented, flexible-working solutions can provide a number of benefits (Kossek and Ozeki 1998). However, it is difficult to envisage these benefits being realised if flexibility is one sided and not mutually beneficial. Indeed, Lewis and Taylor (1996) point out that flexible working develops most successfully when both employees and employers are willing to be flexible to meet both individual and business needs. The introduction of the concept of telework as a family friendly working practice has been a somewhat re-active response to economic business pressure. Flexibility is not the sole prerogative of the organisation it should also be available to the employee. It must be recognised that what is important is the flexibility to meet non-work demands not the flexibility of work itself. Bailyn *et al* (1997), for example, believe that only by relating work and personal issues through a long-term agenda can organisations reframe the conflict between work and the family into an opportunity for change. Successful implementation of family friendly policies would capture the synergy between individual and business goals giving rise to huge potential for continuous learning and improvement (Fletcher and Rapoport 1996). Nevertheless, there is still evidence of a lack of fit and compatibility between work and family (Acker 1998). As the HR Director notes, *'Teleworking today is definitely different. More flexible working to suit the business not the employees'.*

References

Acker, J. (1998) 'The future of gender and organisations: Connections and boundaries', *Gender Work and Organisations* 5, 4: October.

Atkinson, J. (1989) 'Four Stages of adjustment to the demographic downturn', *Personnel Management.* August.

Bailyn, L. (1988)'Freeing Work From The Constraints Of Location And Time', *New Technology, Work and Employment* 3, 2: Autumn.

Bailyn, L., Fletcher J. and Kolb, D. (1997) 'Unexpected connections: considering employees' personal lives can revitalise your business' *Sloan Management Review Summer*, 38, 4 : 11-20.

Baruch, Y. (2000) 'Teleworking: Benefits and pitfalls as perceived by professionals and managers.' *New Technology, Work and Employment*, 15, 1 34-49.

Berry, S. (1996) 'Teleworking Today', *Computing & Control Engineering Journal,* 7, 1: February.

Bevan, S., Dench, S., Tamkin, P. and Cummings, J. (2000) *Family-Friendly Employment: the Business Case*, London: DfEE Publications.

Braverman, H. (1974) *Labour and Monopoly Capital: The Degradation of Work in the Twentieth Century* London: Monthly Review Press.

BT, (1995) *Teleworking - A Glimpse of The Future*, Martlesham: BT.

Burch, S. (1991) *Teleworking: A Strategic Guide for Management,* Kogan Page.

Caudron, C. (1992), 'Working at home pays off', *Personnel Journal*, 7, I & II, 40-49.

Christensen, K. (1992) 'Managing invisible employees: How to meet the telecommuting challenge.' *Human Relations Today* 19 133-143.

Company Documentation (2000) *Flexible Working* Human Resources

Crompton,R., Gallie, D. and Purcell, K. (eds.) (1996) *Changing Forms of Employment. Organisations skills and gender*. London. Routledge.

Dawe, T. (1999) 'Taking work home' *The Times;* London; Nov 8.

Economist (2000) 'Family policy - Leave it to me', *The Economist* April 29, v355 i8168 pNA.

Edwards P. K. (1986) *Conflict at work: A materialist Analysis* Oxford: Basil Blackwell.

Fletcher, J. and Rappoport, R. (1996) 'Work-Family Issues as a Catalyst for Organisational Change' in Lewis, S. and Lewis, J. (eds.) *The Work Family Challenge –Rethinking Employment* London: Sage.

Ford, R. C. and McLaughlin, F. (1995), 'Questions and answers about telecommuting', *Business Horizons*, 38, 2:66-72.

Galpin, S. and Sims, D. (1999) 'Narrative and identity in flexible working and teleworking' in Jackson, P. (Ed.) *Virtual Working* London: Routledge.

Goldstein J., (1994) 'Institutional pressures and strategic responsiveness: employer involvement in work-family issues': *Academy of Management Journal* 37 2, 305-387.

Gordon, G. E. and Kelly, M. M. (1986), *Telecommuting: How to Make it Work for You and Your Company*, Englewood Cliffs, NJ: Prentice-Hall.

Hartman, R. I., Stoner, C. R., Arora, R. (1991). 'An investigation of selected variables affecting telecommuting productivity and satisfaction'. *Journal of Business and Psychology,* 6, 2: 207-225.

Hill, E. J., Hawkins, A. J., Miller, B. C (1996) 'Work and family in the virtual office Perceived influences of mobile telework', *Family Relations*, 34 293-301.

Hill, E. J., Miller, B. C., Weiner, S. P. and Colihan, J. (1998) 'Influences of the virtual office on aspects of work and work/life balance', *Personnel Psychology,* 51, 3: 667-684.

Hill, E. J., (1995)

Huws, U., Jagger, N. and O'Regan, S. (1999) *Teleworking and Globalisation* , Brighton: Institute for Employment Studies.

Huws,U., Korte, W.B. and Robinson, S., (1990) *Telework: Towards The Elusive Office,* Chichester: John Wiley.

Jensen, G. (1994) *Balancing work and family: Challenges and Solutions*, Logan, UT: Utah State University

Kanter, R.M. (1989) *When Giants Learn to Dance*. New York: Basic Books.

Kossek, E. E. and Ozeki,C. (1998) 'Bridging the work-family policy and productivity gap: A literature review.' *Community, Work and Family* 2,1.

Lewis, S. and Taylor, K., (1996) 'Evaluating the impact of family friendly employment policies: A case study', in S. Lewis and J. Lewis (eds), *The Work Family Challenge. Rethinking Employment* London, Sage, London: Sage 112-127.

McQuarrie. F. (1994) 'Telecommuting: who really benefits?' *Business Horizons* 37, 6: 79-84., Nov-Dec.

Mirchandani, K. (1999) 'Reforming organisation: contributions of teleworking employees' in Jackson, P. (Ed.) *Virtual Working Social and Organisational Dynamics*. London: Routledge.

Nilles, J. M. (1994) *Making telecommuting happen: A guide for telemanagers and telecommuters*. New York: Van Nostrand Reinhold.

Olson, M. H.. and Primps, S. B. (1984) Working at home with computers: work and non-work issues, *Journal of Social Issues,* Fall, 97-112.

Pleck J. (1997) 'The Work Family Role System' *Social Problems* 24, 417-427.

Pollert A. (1988) 'The Flexible Firm Fixation or Fact?' *Work, Employment & Society* 2, 3: 281-316.

Poole, M. (1989) 'Time To Tackle The Labour Supply Problem', *Personnel Management* July.

Riley, A. P. (1994) Teleworking: Ten keys to ensuring a successful program. *Solutions,* 16 April-May.

Risman, B. J. and Tomaskovic-Devey, D. (1989) 'The social construction of technology: microcomputers and the organization of work', *Business Horizons,* May-June, 71-75.

Simkin C. and Hillage J. (1992) *Family Friendly Working: New Hope or Old Hype?* Brighton IMS report No 224.

Stanworth, C. (1997) 'Telework and the information age'. *New Technology Work and Employment* 13:1 51 – 62.

Steward, B. (1997) 'Telework and Health: Time, Space and Identity Boundaries', in Jackson, P. and Van der Wielen, J. M. (Eds.) *Building Actions on Ideas,* Tilburg: WORC.

Toffler, A. (1981) *The Third Wave* , London: Bantam Books.

Toynbee, P. (2000) *The Guardian*: Manchester (UK); Jan 14, 2000.

Verespej, M. A. (1994) 'The anytime, anyplace workplace'. *Industry Week,* July 4, 243, 13: 37-40.

Weiss, J. M. (1994), 'Telecommuting boosts employee output', *HR Magazine,* 39, 2 February 51-54.

Wilkes, R. B., Frolick, M. N. and Urwiler, R., (1994) Critical Issues in Developing Successful Telework Programs, *Journal of Systems Management* July 30–34.

13 Home-Based vs. Mobile Telework: The Interrelationship between Different Types of Telework

Karsten Gareis

Empirica Gesellschaft für Kommunikations- und Technologieforschung mbH
Bonn, Germany

Introduction

Teleworkers are defined at least partly by the technology they use. This fact poses considerable problems for statistical measurement because of the rapid development of information and communication technologies (ICTs) and their tendency to gradually penetrate every sphere of life. In fact, the telework bracket has been extended further and further with the introduction of new technologies to the workplace, so much that it will soon be possible to call a majority of EU employees 'teleworkers'.

With regard to these developments it becomes increasingly important to make distinctions between different types of teleworkers, among them those who work at home (home-based teleworkers) and mobile teleworkers. Research by Julsrud (1998) and Jackson & Brewer (1999) have raised the issue of different types of telework practised at the same company. In his research in Norway, Julsrud concluded that mobile and home-based telework stimulate each other. Jackson and Brewer have mentioned his work as an exception from the rule of treating all kinds of telework 'as either similar phenomena, cut from the same telework cloth, or else as separate subject matter' (Jackson and Brewer 1999: 329). They suggest that the relationship between working at home, on site activity and mobile working is a field still waiting to be explored in depth.

The characteristics of such relationships have strong implications for the effect of telework on traffic and settlement patterns.

In this chapter the inter-relationship between home-based and mobile telework is investigated based on the ECaTT dataset on e-commerce and telework collected in 1999 (see ECaTT Consortium 2000 and the contribution of Kordey and Korte in this collection).

Factors Behind the Rise of Mobile Teleworking

In the last two decades companies began to realise that it is no longer sufficient to *push* a set of predefined products on the markets as the demand is becoming more volatile and differentiated. Instead, they have to let customers *pull* what they want from suppliers. This means that all processes which constitute value chains have to be re-evaluated and redesigned according to what customers ask for (*business process reengineering*). Companies 'move closer' to their customers.

As a result, just-in-time production is transfering the warehouse onto the roads in order to respond more quickly and adequately to the demands of the customer. For the same reason, mobile telework transfers work onto 'the road'. We might speak of *just-in-time-working*. Getting in touch with customers (still) means getting face-to-face with them. Physical proximity to great numbers of customers spread over the territory requires mobility.

In a parallel development, the organisation of economic activities has changed towards greater parts of the production process being executed as market transactions instead of intra-organisational movements of goods and information. Collaboration and network building between independent companies have increased (Wigand *et al* 1997). A higher number of employees spend more time collaborating with external parties. This implies more frequent travels, and more time spend travelling.

Office space is expensive. When rates of utilisation for office space decrease because workers spend more time with their customers and less in their office, breaking the link between staff and their desks can potentially lead to huge savings. Against this background, a number of concepts have been developed such as *desk-sharing* (staff losing their right to exclusive use of personal workspace), *hoteling* (workspace has to be booked in advance) and the *touchdown office* (staff are allotted a workspace when they arrive at the facility: 'first come - first serve'). In any case, sharing desks means organising access to resources which have to be available to every staff member.

There are still a number of factors that act as barriers to the implementation of innovative office space management. Employers are reluctant to take away central office work-desks from workers because of evidence that employees might feel threatened when deprived of their designated space (see e.g. Glaser and Glaser 1995). In such cases, teleworkers often fear being excluded from their work teams.

However, a bigger stress on the return on investment together with evidence that social isolation can be avoided through alternating telework meant that today all successful large-scale teleworking projects include at least desk-sharing, many of them a redesign of office space as well. From a social perspective, the most successful schemes have been those where desk-sharing was introduced for complete teams of employees and not only selected ones such as home-based teleworkers (Rimpler *et al* 1999).

Traditionally, sales agents and other mobile staff had a full workplace at a central office while working for the most part of their working time in the field, supplemented by some additional paperwork at home. Fieldwork has been an important application field for small computing and telecommunication devices from the very beginning. The development of ICTs that match the needs of salespeople, maintenance staff, drivers, couriers, and emergency staff, has long been a driver of mobile computing developments.

In addition to these, more and more professionals and executives have in recent years started to use mobile computing as a means to stay in contact with their company and co-operation partners. With the help of advanced mobile computing technology (a 'virtual office'), these people can today access central databases via GSM, ISDN or PSTN data connections during travel, (e.g. at railway stations, airports, conference sites and at the premises of partner companies). As mobile voice and data communication is now commonplace and available in a large part of the human-inhabited world, the virtual office can be assumed to exist everywhere where a mobile worker has a mobile phone and mobile computing device.

In practice, however, most workers will still prefer an office environment to do their work except maybe for checking and sending e-mails and emergency cases. Teleservice centres that offer travellers a temporary workplace equipped with PC, Internet access, printer, fax etc. are beginning to crop up at the nodes of international traffic networks, i.e. at central locations in large cities as well as airports (Roberts 1997). The spread of teleservice centres will contribute to making mobile work attractive for an increasing number of business travellers.

Definitions and Methodology

Home-based teleworkers – in the definition deployed for ECaTT surveys – are those who work from home (instead of commuting to a central workplace) for at least one full working day per week, use a personal computer in the course of their work, use telecommunications links (phone/fax/e-mail) to communicate with their colleagues/supervisor during work at home and are either in salaried employment or are self-employed, in which case their main working place is on the contractor's premises. Individuals who are teleworking from home for more than 90% of their overall working time are referred to as permanent teleworkers, while those working from home for less than 90% of their overall working time – but for more than one full day per week – are referred to as alternating teleworkers. *Supplementary teleworkers* have the same characteristics with the exception of working time spent at home which is less than one full working day per week. They are not included in the number for 'regular teleworkers' but can be regarded as 'occasional teleworkers'.

Mobile teleworkers are those who work at least 10 hours per week away from home and from a main place of work, (e.g. on business trips, in the field, travelling or on customer's premises), and use online computer connections when doing so.

Self-employed teleworkers in SOHOs (small offices, home offices) are those who work self-employed or effectively self-employed (e.g. persons employed by their own company or employed by an organisation they have considerable managing power over) and whose main place of work is at home (or they claim not to have a main place of work) and who use advanced ISTs for communicating with clients and/or (other) business partners.

The survey part of the study consisted of (a) representative surveys of individuals (aged 15 and older) in private households with a sample of 1000 in larger and 500 in smaller countries and (b) representative surveys of establishments in each of the participating countries with a sample of 500 in larger countries and 300 in smaller countries. Respondents in the latter case were head of the DP department, senior professionals in the DP department (in large organisations) or the managing director, general manager or proprietor (in small organisations). Because of the size-weighted sampling employed, reference in reported results such as '50% of all establishments in country A' are properly interpreted to mean 'establishments accounting for 50% of all employees in country A'.

The ECaTT database includes data on 10 EU Member States that together account for more than 90% of the total EU population.

Results from ECaTT on Telework and Mobile Working

Establishment survey

20% of establishments in the EU have mobile teleworkers, 14% have home-based teleworkers and 9% work with self-employed teleworkers (see Table 1). Therefore, the type of telework practised by the largest proportion of establishments is mobile telework. Two thirds of all establishments that have teleworkers also have mobile teleworkers.

Finland, Denmark, the UK and Sweden are the countries with the highest share of establishments practising at least one kind of telework. In these countries, every second establishment will soon make use of telework. Spain and Italy, on the other hand, lag behind. One might speak of a north-south-divide regarding the use of telework which is also reflected in the general population survey data (see below). The ranking order with regard to mobile telework is pretty similar. Denmark, the UK and Ireland are countries with a comparatively high share of establishments practising mobile telework among all users of telework.

These data alone give no indication as to the reason behind the differences in mobile telework take-up. Is the high proportion of establishments with mobile teleworkers in the Nordic countries and the U.K. a result of more companies deploying sales reps and other mobile workers, or does it stem from a high penetration of mobile workers with ICTs enabling online access?

	Establishments practising ...				
	(1) home-based telework	(2) self-employed telework	(3) mobile telework	(4) any kind of regular telework	(3) of (4)
Denmark	26.9	17.3	37.0	47.2	78.5
Finland	22.4	25.9	28.2	48.2	58.6
France	8.3	14.4	19.9	31.7	62.7
Germany	13.3	7.4	16.1	25.5	63.3
Ireland	13.5	7.2	23.1	32.6	71.0
Italy	4.7	4.8	9.0	15.3	58.8
Netherlands	18.7	11.0	23.3	35.7	65.4
Spain	7.8	5.7	10.4	17.6	59.0
Sweden	22.4	18.4	27.8	43.3	64.2
UK	24.5	8.3	33.8	43.5	77.8
EU10	13.9	9.2	20.0	29.7	67.3

Base: All establishments (n = 4,158), weighted © *empirica: ECaTT 2000*

Table 1. Establishments Practising Different Types of Telework in Europe 1999 (in % of All Establishments)[1]

1 All *EU10 averages* in this chapter are mean values weighted according to total population aged 15 and higher (Population Survey) and total number of employees (Establishment Survey).

	establishments with ...		
	mobile workers in % of all establishments	mobile teleworkers in % of all establishments	mobile teleworkers in % of establishments with mobile workers
Denmark	59.9	37.0	61.8
Finland	54.9	28.2	51.4
France	53.6	19.9	37.1
Germany	48.1	16.1	33.5
Ireland	58.9	23.1	39.3
Italy	32.3	9.0	27.8
Netherlands	57.3	23.3	40.7
Spain	41.9	10.4	24.8
Sweden	49.0	27.8	56.7
UK	58.5	33.8	57.8
EU10	49.1	20.0	40.7

Base: All establishments (n = 4,158), weighted *© empirica: EcaTT 2000*

Table 2. Mobile Work and Mobile Telework in Establishments in Europe 1999

Table 2 presents an answer to this question: In all EU10 countries except for Italy, between 40% and 60% of establishments employ mobile workers from which between one quarter (Spain) and almost two thirds (Denmark) let their mobile staff at least partly access resources on the company computer network online.

These findings indicate that differences in the share of establishments using mobile working are indeed much smaller than differences with regard to mobile telework. In the laggard countries, the majority of establishments do not use mobile telework, although many would have an application field for it because they have mobile workers. On the other hand, the Nordic countries are not as far ahead as might have been expected from the very high mobile telephony penetration rates in countries like Finland.

As ICTs for mobile use are filtering into everyday business life with great speed, and companies are eager to better integrate activities of their field-staff with their back-office, it is highly likely that an increasingly higher percentage of all companies with salespeople or other mobile workers will start to implement mobile telework. From those 29% of establishments that have mobile workers (but which do not use mobile telework at present), 6% already have concrete plans to introduce and another 5% are interested in mobile telework (see Table 3). 31% of all establishments in EU10 have mobile teleworkers or are at least interested in introducing it, whereas the corresponding values for home-based teleworking are 23% and for telework by self-employed workers 13%.

	mobile telework practised	Mobile work practised: concrete plans for introducing	interest in introducing	no interest in intro-ducing	n.a. on interest	mobile work not practised	d.k./ n.a.	total
Denmark	37.0	5.7	3.7	12.5	1.0	39.8	0.3	100
Finland	28.2	4.3	5.7	15.7	1.0	44.1	1.0	100
France	19.9	7.0	6.5	18.8	1.5	46.0	0.4	100
Germany	16.1	8.4	5.4	16.4	1.8	51.6	0.3	100
Ireland	23.1	4.4	7.2	20.7	3.5	40.9	0.3	100
Italy	9.0	1.7	3.2	15.0	3.4	67.0	0.7	100
Netherl.	23.3	7.7	3.7	21.7	1.0	40.7	2.0	100
Spain	10.4	4.6	2.2	22.2	2.5	57.6	0.6	100
Sweden	27.8	3.7	3.6	12.7	1.2	50.1	0.9	100
U.K.	33.8	5.4	5.6	13.2	0.6	40.7	0.8	100
EU10	20.0	5.9	4.8	16.6	1.7	50.3	0.6	100

Base: All establishments (n = 4,158), weighted *© empirica: ECaTT 2000*

Table 3. Practice, Plans and Interest in Mobile Telework in % of All Establishments

Julsrud (1998) has concluded from his research in Norway that mobile and home-based telework stimulate each other. Analysis of ECaTT establishments survey data at first seems to confirm this finding as a positive correlation between practise of home-based telework and practise of mobile telework can be found. The result is confirmed even when adjusting for establishment size (the strongest determinant of ICT use by establishments) and industry sector. However, a comparable correlation exists between other ICT-related variables on establishment level, (e.g. between Internet use and teleworking practice). Therefore, we must conclude that the ECaTT survey data does not give sufficient evidence for supporting the claim that mobile and home-based telework stimulate each other – that there is a causal nexus between both. The impulse to implement both seems to come rather from a general amenability to ICT-related innovations. More research on this topic is needed.

Population (labour force) survey

General findings

In the EU10 there are almost 2.7 million home-based teleworkers, or 2% of the labour force (see contribution of Korte and Kordey in this collection). Home-based telework is in average the most widespread form of telework in the EU, ahead of mobile telework, an order that is established in most of the countries surveyed. Exceptions are Germany, where all three organisational forms are equally spread, and the Netherlands where mobile telework is particularly widespread. 2% of all employees are supplementary teleworkers, working at home only occasionally.

	mobile workers	mobile teleworkers	mobile teleworkers in % of mobile workers
Denmark	14.6	2.1	14.3
Finland	15.7	2.6	16.7
France	10.5	0.8	7.8
Germany	23.6	1.5	6.2
Ireland	13.0	0.3	2.4
Italy	15.7	1.4	8.6
Netherlands	19.8	4.3	21.7
Spain	12.5	0.5	4.1
Sweden	12.5	2.3	18.5
U.K.	16.3	2.1	12.7
EU 10	16.8	1.6	9.4

Base: All respondents in paid work (n = 3,765), weighted *© empirica: ECaTT 2000*

Table 4. Mobile Teleworkers and Mobile Workers in % of Labour Force

The relation between the number of mobile teleworkers and all teleworkers gives an indication about how large a role mobile telework plays in the overall telework development. 38% of all teleworkers in the EU are mobile teleworkers. Above-average shares can be found in the Netherlands, Italy and the UK, whereas in Ireland and Spain – but also Finland – home-based telework is comparatively much more widespread.

As Table 4 shows, the share of mobile teleworkers among workers that spend a considerable time per week 'on the road' is still modest even in the forerunner countries of Scandinavia and the Netherlands. While 41% of all EU10 establishments that have sales representatives or other mobile staff practise mobile telework (see Table 2 above), only 9% of all mobile workers are mobile teleworkers. Therefore, until now accessing the company's computer system while travelling is a privilege (or duty?) only a small share of mobile workers take part in.

It is not clear from the data if the group of mobile teleworkers who also can be classified as home-based teleworkers or self-employed teleworkers in SOHOs has evolved from traditional groups of mobile workers (e.g. salespeople) or if workers who have taken up working from home have subsequently used the new locational flexibility to spend more time with customers and business partners 'on the road'.

Mobility of teleworkers

Are home-based teleworkers more likely to spend a significant share of their working time in the field in comparison to non-teleworkers? This question is central to the topic of interrelations between mobile and home-based telework. A positive answer would indicate that teleworking is indeed practised mainly as a way to increase the flexibility of where the work is done, beyond the simple duality of working at home and in the office.

Table 5 shows that a very high share of regular teleworkers (excluding mobile teleworkers) spend 10 hours or more per week in the field (42% against 15% among non-teleworkers), while supplementary teleworkers are more likely to spend less than 10 hours per week away from their main place of work and their home, but still much more than non-teleworkers.

As there was found to be a strong correlation between the likeliness of an individual to be teleworking with gender, level of formal education (men and the high-educated being significantly more likely to telework) and contractual status (employment versus self-employment)[2], there is a need to deepen the analysis before making judgements about the apparently stronger mobility of teleworkers. For this reason, cross-tabulation was also executed for sub-groups of the sample which are thought to be sufficiently homogeneous in regard to teleworking (male respondents from the two higher levels of formal education, male employees with

---

2 On the other hand there was found to be only very limited correlation with economic sector, age and household composition; see EcaTT Consortium 2000.

work contracts and male self-employed). In all four cases, results largely confirm the original findings that regular teleworkers are more likely to spend a considerable part of their working time away from home as well as the central office. A part of the explanation lies in the fact that teleworkers are more likely to be self-employed, and the self-employed more often spend a considerable part of their working time in the field. This does not, however, fully explain the differences, as 30% of male respondents with a contract of employment work mobile for more than 10 hours per week against only 19% of none-teleworkers in the same subgroup of the sample.

	regular teleworkers excluding mobile teleworkers	supplementary teleworkers	non-teleworkers
more than 10 hours/ week	42.1	24.3	14.9
less than 10 hours/ week	15.8	21.6	7.8
less than 10 hours/ month	23.0	33.2	12.6
not working mobile	18.0	21.0	63.1
n.a.	1.2	0.0	1.7
total	100.0	100.0	100.0
Base: All respondents in paid work (n = 3,765), weighted		*© empirica: ECaTT 2000*	

Table 5. Teleworkers and Non-teleworkers Practising Mobile Work in % of Labour Force

From these findings we can conclude that there is indeed a positive correlation between home-based telework and mobile working. It might be due either to teleworkers voluntarily changing their locational habits concerning at which places they do their job, or employers implementing telework explicitly as a means to make their staff spend more time with customers or co-operation partners.

Commuting distances of teleworkers

It might be argued that individuals choose to telework as a means to avoid long commutes. Indeed, among regular teleworkers large distances between the home and the central workplace are much more common than among the working population as a whole. 14% of regular teleworkers (excluding mobile teleworkers) have one-way commuting distances of 50km and more against 4% among non-teleworkers.

But looking at supplementary teleworkers, who by definition do not save commuting trips because they do not spend whole working days teleworking at home, a similar pattern appears: More than 15% of supplementary teleworkers live more than 50km away from their main place of work against only 4% in the working population as a whole. This might be evidence that while teleworking may be used to avoid commuting trips, it is also often used to avoid commuting at certain times of the day, namely peak hours.

	regular	regular excluding mobile	mobile	Supple-mentary	non-teleworkers
	teleworkers				
at home/ same building	25.1	36.0	8.9	4.7	4.2
up to 1 km	5.0	5.3	4.8	8.4	16.0
up to 5 km	11.7	11.0	13.7	16.4	27.4
up to 20 km	17.9	8.8	33.8	33.5	29.6
up to 50 km	17.1	16.6	12.7	21.6	16.1
up to 100 km	6.7	6.2	7.8	10.2	2.2
more than 100 km	9.4	8.2	12.0	5.2	1.5
no 'main place of work'	7.1	7.8	6.3	0.0	2.2
n.a./d.k.	0.0	0.0	0.0	0.0	0.8
total	100.0	100.0	100.0	100.0	100.0

Base: All respondents in paid work (n = 3,765), weighted *© empirica: ECaTT 2000*

Table 6. Distribution of Distance Home-to-Workplace Among Teleworkers (in %)

Conclusions

Although the evidence from an analysis of data collected as part of the ECaTT project and presented in this chapter is far from being comprehensive, it does support the proposition that telework that is fixed to just two locations (the central office and the home-office) is not as dominant as it has been seen to be. Already, 38% of teleworkers spend at least 10 hours per week away from their main place of work and their home to work mobile with the help of online connections to their company's computer network. Even from those teleworkers that cannot be classified as mobile teleworkers, 42% are out 'in the field' for 10 hours per week or more!

Against the background of these results, what can be said about probable impacts on traffic and settlement patterns (see Gareis & Kordey 1999)? Mobile telework means that the place of work is not the private residence, but other locations apart from home and office. Since this type of telework affects in particular individuals working in the field, prominent locations of customers determine the actual places where the work takes place. Mobile teleworkers are distinguished by – as their label implies – their mobility, for example the distance they cover in the course of their work. As a direct consequence of this, the growth of mobile telework will increase the total traffic load. Mobile telework also results in more demand for office space and accommodation facilities at the nodes of the traffic system, (i.e. central locations in cities as well as close to airports).

But in addition to mobile teleworkers in the narrow sense of the word, home-based teleworkers also seem to spend more time travelling than their centrally located colleagues. It is not possible yet to judge whether traffic reductions caused by a decrease in the number of commutes is made up for by additional non-commuting travelling. However, there can be no doubt that total traffic volumes have steadily increased in recent years in spite of the growth of telework – which at least in forerunner countries like the USA and the Nordic countries should have started to show a moderating effect on traffic volumes, if the original assumptions of telework proponents held true.

There have been very valuable and well-researched contributions to a better understanding of telecommuting's traffic impact lately (see for example Lyons *et al* 1998). However, projections about the likely volumes in traffic reductions (e.g. Mitomo & Jitsuzumi 1999) might just serve to highlight one of the main shortcomings of the research on this issue so far: they ignore that telework is in general only supported by private-sector companies when it brings a higher degree of flexibility and ultimately more interaction with customers. For this reason, telecommuting arrangements already bring with them a higher degree of non-commuting travelling, and will do so increasingly in the future.

There is a danger that research on social effects of telecommuting detaches itself more and more from the economic logic that has caused the rapid diffusion of teleworking in the first place. From the viewpoint of businesses, telework makes special sense when the time employees spend on commuting between place of work and place of living can be diverted to travelling to customers. Such a development would doubtlessly contribute to economic effectiveness, but not necessarily to traffic reduction.

However, it must be said here that telework has until now been used only very rarely by policy-makers as a means to assert socially desirable objectives *against* the dominant trends in traffic and regional development which are driven by private-sector imperatives. Publicly subsidised, centre-based telework is only one example of how telework might be used to achieve long-term social objectives, but hardly any national or regional government has had the courage to support telework centres with enough commitment to make them viable in the long run (see Korte 1999). Reductions in traffic volumes might also be achieved by making transport pricing reflect transport's real external costs. In this case, telework could be used to offset the negative effect of rising transport costs on household incomes. With that, telework might make it possible to increase the cost of private car traffic to a socially and economically reasonable level. It would then have contributed more than its share to environmental protection.

Literature

Davidow, W. H. and Malone, M. S. (1992) *The Virtual Corporation – Structuring and Revitalizing the Corporation for the 21st Century*, New York: HarperCollins.

ECaTT Consortium (2000) ECaTT Final Report, Luxembourg: Office for Official Publications of the European Communities.

Gareis, K. and Kordey, N. (1999) 'Telework - an Overview of Likely Impacts on Traffic and Settlement Patterns', NETCOM, 13, 3-4: 265-286.

Glaser, W. R. and Glaser, M. O. (1995) *Telearbeit in der Praxis*, Psychologische Erfahrungen mit Außerbetrieblichen Arbeitsstätten bei der IBM Deutschland GmbH, Berlin: Luchterhand.

Jackson, P. and Brewer, A. (1999) 'New Strategies for Telework Research', Proceedings of the Fourth International Telework Workshop 'Telework Strategies for the New Workforce', Tokyo: 327-335.

Julsrud, T. E. (1998) 'Combinations and Tracks: An Investigation of the Relationship Between Homework and Mobile Work', in Suomi, R. *et al.* (eds) *Telework Environments: Proceedings of the Third International Workshop on Telework*, Turku, 148-163.

Korte, W. B. and Wynne, R. (1996) *Telework - Penetration, Potential and Practice in Europe*, Amsterdam *et al.*: IOS Press.

Korte, W. B. (1999) 'Experiences with Telecentres in Germany and Abroad - Top or Flop?', http://www.gilgordon.com /downloads/empirica.txt, visited 13.07.2000, 14:30.

Lyons, G. D., Hickford, A. and Smith, J.C. (1998) 'The Nature and Scale of Teleworking's Travel Demand Impacts: Insights from a U.K. Trial', in Suomi, R. *et al.* (eds) *Teleworking Environments: Proceedings of the Third International Workshop on Telework*, Turku, 312-330.

Mitomo, H. and Jitsuzumi, T. (1999) 'Impact of Telecommuting on Mass Transit Congestion: the Tokoyo Case', *Telecommunications Policy*, 23: 741-751.

Rimpler, I., Glaser, M. O. and Glaser, W. R. (1999) 'Das Büro für mobiles Arbeiten: Von der Arbeitsstätte zum Kommunikationszentrum. Erfahrungen mit dem Business-Center von DIGITAL Equipment GmbH', in Godehardt, B., Korte, W.B., Michelsen, U. and Quadt, H.-P. (eds) *Managementhandbuch Telearbeit*. 4. Ergänzungslieferung. Hüthig: Heidelberg.

Roberts, P. (1997) 'Kinko's - The Free-Agent Home Office', Fast Company, 12/1, http://www.fastcompany.com/online/12/kinko.html, visited 10.7.2000, 14:25.

Wigand, R. T., Picot, A. and Reichwald, R. (1997) *Information, Organization and Management: Expanding Markets and Corporate Boundaries*, New York: John Wiley & Sons.

14 The Impacts of Telework on Quality of Life: A Revised Model for Research

Sigmund Akselsen[1], Tomas Bjarnason[2], Debra Diduca[3], Bente Evjemo[1], Emma France[3], Sigrún Gunnarsdóttir[2], Mary Jones[3], Asdis Jonsdottir[2], Tom Erik Julsrud[1], Roberto Marion[4], Maria Pereira Martins[5], Francisco Costa Pinto[5], Karina Tracey[3] and Birgitte Yttri[1]

[1]Telenor AS, Norway, [2]Iceland Telecom Ltd., Iceland, [3]British Telecommunications plc., UK, [4]Telecom Italia S.p.A., Italy, [5]Portugal Telecom S.A., Portugal

Introduction

Teleworking appears as one major area where new technology has a potential to change the way people are 'doing things' (in this case working) and thereby bring about a better life for the individual. This potential has raised interest in using telework among European decision-makers, employers and employees. The Quality of Life (QoL) issue has in particular been put on many employers' agenda, as the individual employees' well-being seems to be decisive for their professional contributions. In a knowledge-based economy, the knowledge and creativity of employees are companies' main capital. Thus, these companies are especially vulnerable to human malfunctioning. Knowledge workers, who feel miserable due to personal problems or poor living conditions, are not able to cope with their jobs (even if they could have managed doing simple routine tasks or hard physical labour tasks under the same circumstances). Increased QoL will have a great impact on productivity in knowledge-based activities, while a corresponding reduction may lead to dramatically negative effects. This motivates employers to take more responsibility for the individual employee's QoL. A telework arrangement is in this connection regarded as one of several possible ways to increase workers' (and families) QoL, and the arrangement also appear to be used as an attractor for recruiting and retaining workers with key skills.

For telecommunications companies (TelCos) this situation is representing an important business opportunity emerging partly in the business and professional market, and partly in the residential market. Despite the large market potential in this field, the take up of telework arrangements has been slower than expected. This seems in part to be caused by a lack of knowledge, not just on the impacts of telework on management issues such as productivity, work quality, team spirit and organisational commitment but also the impacts on the workers and their social and work network.

On this background EURESCOM (European Institute for Research and Strategic Studies in Telecommunications) launched a project to explore the connections between telework and QoL. The project included researchers from five TelCos (BT, Iceland Telecom, Telecom Italia, Telenor and Portugal Telecom) with educational backgrounds in sociology, social anthropology, psychology, informatics and telecom engineering. Its main aim was to study the possible links between telework from the home and quality of life for the individual teleworker and his/her families and the quality of the worker's results. This chapter reports briefly some findings from the study but goes on to put more emphasis on the revision of a model for doing research within this area. For a more detailed discussion of the separate findings, see Akselsen *et al* (2001).

Possible connections between telework and QoL

The impact of telework on workers' general well-being have for some time been an issue for research. One attempt to integrate this research has been done by Van Sell and Jacobs in their model of links between telework (or telecommuting as they term the field) and quality of life (Van Sell and Jacobs 1994: 82). We have used this model as a basis for our research but have extended it with more specific knowledge of the QoL concept. This extension builds on the work done by Sørensen and Næss (1996), The WHOQOL (World Health Organisation Quality of Life) Group (1995; 1998) and the Centre for Health Promotion, University of Toronto.

Defining quality of life

When talking about quality of life (QoL) we refer to subjective satisfaction that human beings have with their everyday life including their social and working life. Sørensen and Næss discuss the concept and how it can be measured:

> 'Quality of life is related to individual feelings. It is subjective and includes a global assessment. It is seen as both a cognitive evaluation and some degree of positive and negative feelings.' (1996: 29)

The Centre for Health Promotion defines Quality of Life as 'The degree to which a person enjoys the important possibilities of his/her life' (Raphael, *et al* 1998: 2). The enjoyment of important possibilities is relevant to three major life domains (Renwick and Brown, 1996):

Being reflects 'who one is' and has three sub-domains. Physical Being encompasses physical health, personal hygiene, nutrition, exercise, and general appearance. Psychological Being includes the person's psychological health and adjustment, feelings, and evaluations concerning the self, such as self-esteem and self-concept. Spiritual Being refers to one's personal values, standards of conduct, and spiritual beliefs.

Belonging concerns the person's fit with his or her environments. Physical Belonging describes connections with the physical environments of home, workplace, neighbourhood, school, and community. Social Belonging is the links with social environments and acceptance by intimate others, family, friends, co-workers, and neighbourhood or community. Community Belonging represents access to public resources, such as adequate income, health and social services, employment, educational and recreational programs, and community activities.

Becoming refers to activities carried out in the course of daily living, including those to achieve personal goals, hopes, and aspirations. Practical Becoming describes day-to-day activities, such as domestic activities, paid work, school, or volunteer activities, and seeing to health or social needs. Leisure Becoming includes activities carried out primarily for enjoyment that promote relaxation and stress reduction. Growth Becoming activities promote the maintenance or improvement of knowledge and skills, and adapting to change.

Based on this conceptualisation, a Quality of Life Profile, (in this case a 54-item instrument that assesses the importance and enjoyment in nine domains of life), has been developed by the Centre for Health Promotion (Raphael, *et al* 1998).

Research model

Our extension of the research model proposed by Van Sell and Jacobs allows for more explicit measures of QoL, and we have used the model to formulate and position a set of hypotheses on the possible links between the two concepts. The detailed list of hypotheses is presented in Table 1. As well as hypothesising a direct relationship between teleworking and Quality of Life (H1), our model proposes the existence of three key variables, which are hypothesised as acting as mediating variables between the practice of teleworking and specific aspects of Quality of Life (H2-H9). The research model includes four parts: context, work style, mediating variables and quality of life outcome factors (see figure 1).

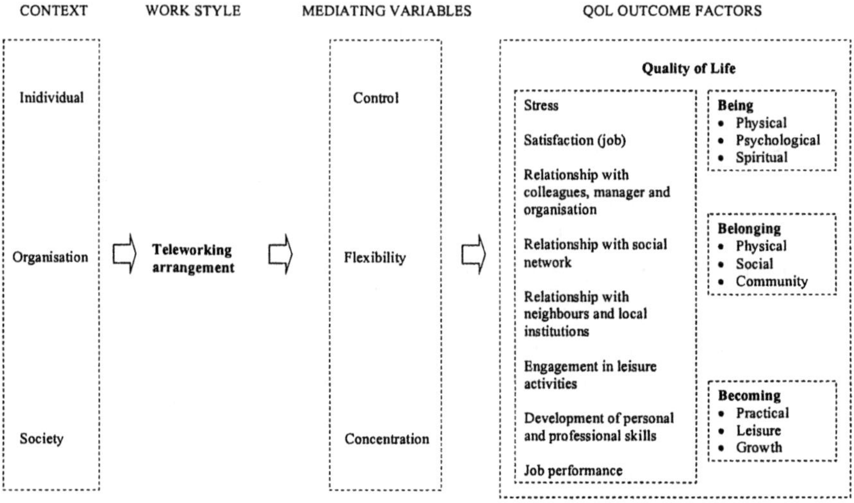

Figure 1. Simplified research model (not including details on context and work style)

Context

This part of the model describes input factors that may have a decisive influence on a telework arrangement. These factors include characteristics of society – for example environmental concerns – characteristics of the organisation and characteristics of the individual workers.

Work style

This part of the model describes how the telework arrangement is carried out by the individual teleworkers (and their colleagues and managers). In this chapter telework refers to '… work performed at a distance from the employer or client for whom the work is being performed, and where work is mediated by information and communications technologies' (Murphy, 1996: 47). This definition encompasses a family of work styles and we are especially interested in the number of days worked at different locations (in particular at home), the time spent overall on work and the regularity of the working arrangement.

Mediating variables

Van Sell and Jacobs argue that 'the influence of TC [telecommuting] on the individual's quality of life appears to be explained by the telecommuter's improved concentration, flexibility and control over time' (1994: p 82). Concentration, flexibility and control are believed to be mediating variables, that is, they explain the influences of telework on the quality of life variables. Teleworkers cite these variables as reasons for teleworking, and further, researchers in this field speculate that these contribute to the improvements in individual productivity, cost savings and affective reactions that are characteristic outcomes of telework arrangements:

- *Concentration*: Working at home rather than in an office, enhances the ability to concentrate on work for most, but not all individuals. This is mainly due to less interruption.
- *Flexibility*: A number of researchers have identified the need for more work flexibility to balance work and family demands or to pursue some personal goal outside work as the major impetus for telework.
- *Control*: Autonomy, which includes control over time, is a dimension of good job design. A large proportion of people who work at home say they want to work at their own pace, in their own way.

Quality of life outcome factors

The right-hand side of the research model (Figure 1) includes a set of quality of life outcome factors. We have chosen to examine the links between telework and the different domains of QoL from two perspectives:

- Through the overall Quality of Life score and in addition the separate Being, Belonging and Becoming components of the Centre for Health Promotion, University of Toronto, Quality of Life Profile.
- Through individual (independent) constructs within these domains, including Job Satisfaction, Job Performance (self and manager assessed), Stress, Closeness of personal relationships (self and other assessed), Closeness of working relationships (self and other assessed), Organisational commitment, Community involvement, Development of new skills and Leisure activities.

This approach allows for an assessment of the overall impacts of telework on QoL as well as a comparison of impacts on individual constructs that have been used in previous studies. It will also be of interest to see how the effects on the individual constructs relate to (and accounts for) the effect on the total QoL.

List of hypotheses

The hypotheses examined in the study are listed fully in table 1.

	Hypothesis
H1	The higher the number of days worked at home by a worker, the higher that worker's Quality of Life, and that of his/her friends and family.
H2	The higher perceived flexibility and control by a worker as a result of his/her work arrangement, the higher the worker's job satisfaction.
H3	The higher perceived control over work by a worker as a result of his/her work arrangement, the lower the worker's perceived stress.
H4	The higher perceived (opportunities for) concentration by a worker as a result of his/her work arrangement, the higher the worker's job performance.
H5	The higher perceived flexibility by a worker as a result of his/her work arrangement, the closer the worker's relationship with his/her immediate social network.
H6	The higher perceived flexibility by a worker as a result of his/her work arrangement, the closer the worker's relationship with neighbours and local institutions.
H7	The higher perceived flexibility by a worker as a result of his/her work arrangement, the closer the worker's relationship with colleagues, manager and organisation.
H8	The higher perceived flexibility by a worker as a result of his/her work arrangement, the more active the worker's development of personal and professional skills.
H9	The higher perceived flexibility by a worker as a result of his/her work arrangement, the more active the worker's engagement in leisure activities.

Table 1. List of hypotheses

Field Study

The overall design of the study was a between-subjects comparison of workers who work different numbers of days per week at home. The study included two stages, first a quantitative stage, consisting of self-administered questionnaires addressing each of the hypotheses and second a qualitative stage including interviews focused on a more limited set of issues.

The informants for the study were recruited from four participating countries: Iceland, Norway, Portugal and the UK. Within each country, a number of companies were approached using a variety of formal and informal contacts. The companies approached were found in sectors where we had reason to believe that some telework was going on. 14 companies agreed to participate in the study. Of these, 5 were companies in the computer (hardware and software) sector, 4 in the telecom sector, 1 in the insurance sector, 1 in the finance sector, 2 in the consultancy sector, and 1 in the seismic/oil sector. Once agreement had been obtained from a company, individual workers were then approached with the company's permission, as it was important to have the cooperation of workers, their managers and their colleagues.

Of a total of 531 workers that had agreed to take part in the study, 224 responded. 7 of these were excluded because they were missing essential information (number of days worked at home). This left us with 217 valid responses from workers that carried out different amounts and types of telework in occupations that can be characterised as knowledge work. Among the 217 workers was also a group of non-teleworkers included for comparison, see table 2 for details on the number of days worked at home by the workers. 88 workers came from the UK, 54 from Norway, 42 from Iceland and 33 from Portugal. 135 (62%) were males and 82 (38%) females. The majority (76%) had received a college education or higher. The average age of the workers was 38.25 years, and 37% of the workers were between 30 and 39 years. Most of the workers (64%) were married; with a further 12% living with a partner. 24% described themselves as single or divorced. Approximately half (48%) of households included at least one child. The mean number of hours that workers in the joint sample were contracted to work per week was 38.9 hours. However, the mean number of actual hours worked per week was nearly 10 hours more, namely 48.6 hours. In addition to the 217 worker responses, information was collected from their managers (127), colleagues (239) and social network members (281).

Days worked at home	Frequency	%
0	49	23
0.1 - 0.9	29	13
1.0 - 1.9	45	21
2.0 - 2.9	43	20
3.0 - 3.9	29	13
4.0 - 4.9	10	5
5.0 -	12	5
Total	217	100

Table 2. Days worked at home per week by the workers

Furthermore, in stage 2 a limited sample (42 workers, 18 partners, 8 children, 3 friends, 9 managers and 9 colleagues, a total of 89) was selected and interviewed in more depth on a set of issues. The choice of workers to take part in this stage was a mixture of premeditation and pragmatism, where the former aspect was decided by the following guidelines:

- Both teleworkers and non-teleworkers (in order to make comparison and deepen our understanding).
- Workers with the highest and lowest Quality of Life scores (to give a range of experiences).
- Different household structures (to ensure that we had a mix of partners with no kids, people living alone, lone parents and people with partners who have kids under 12).

These guidelines were blurred by the more pragmatic aspects of initial self-selection (expression of interest at the quantitative stage) and individual availability in the time span of the study. Also the number of people to choose from impacted on the final sample, as in some countries we could choose from several within each category, whereas the limited numbers of informants available in other countries hardly represented a choice.

Results

This section combines results from the quantitative as well as the qualitative stage of the study. Note that the quantitative and qualitative data are considered as complementary in that they provide a 'triangulation' – in other words, a view from different perspectives and hence better understanding. As the focus of this chapter has been the revision of a model for doing research, we have chosen to present findings related to the set of hypotheses rather briefly. The presentation is given in the form of a large correlation table (Table 3), followed by a set of multiple regression analyses (to determine the relative contributions of the different factors of the model to the informants' QoL), and finally some selected issues are discussed in slightly more detail using findings from the qualitative data. Also note that the study was conducted within a group of partly overworked knowledge workers that we make no claim are representative for European teleworkers in general, and that care therefore should be taken in making broad generalisations. However, we argue that the study has contributed more understanding that justify a revision of the research model laid out above.

Correlations related to each hypothesis

Within this section the main correlations found in the data material are summarised (see table 3). In the presentation of findings we refer to bivariate correlations, which measure how two variables or rank orders are related, indicated by the value rho-score – or 'r' for short. The absolute value of the correlation coefficient indicates the strength, with larger absolute values indicating stronger relationships. The sign of the correlation coefficient indicates the direction of the relationship (positive or negative). The significance levels 'highly significant' and 'significant' are usually expressed by the use of ** and *. Significance is the probability that the relation is random. Usually the 2 levels of significance considered in statistical studies are 0.01 (**) and 0.05 (*). These values indicate that the probability of a random relation is less than 1% and 5%, respectively. For example: In our study the variable 'Stress' is significantly negatively related to 'Control', displaying that correlation; r= -.249** (see table 3). The negative score indicate that the Stress score is low when Control is high, and vice versa. The two stars means that chances for a random relation is less than 1 percent.

Table 3. Significant correlations for hypothesised and unhypothesised relationships

		days at home	**flexibi-lity**	**control**	**concent-ration at home**
H1	worker's QoL	.121*	.186**	.210**	.136*
	worker's QoL being score	ns			
	worker's QoL belonging score	.212**	.238**	.244**	.138*
	worker's QoL becoming score	ns	.166**	.147*	.158*
	partner's QoL	-.244**			
	children' QoL	ns	.505*	.542*	
	friends' QoL	ns	.287*		
H2	job satisfaction		.342**	.535**	
H3	Stress		-.164*	-.249**	-.175*
H4	job performance			.171*	.193**
	rating by manager				ns
H5	closeness to all social network members		.114**	.129*	.145**
	rating by all social network members		.179**	.235**	
	closeness to partner		ns		.218*
	rating by partner		.179*		
	closeness to children		ns		
	rating by children		ns		
	closeness to friends		ns		.293*
	rating by friends	.234*	ns	.315*	
	closeness to other social network members		ns	.560**	
	rating by other social network members		ns	.283*	
H6	closeness to neighbours and local institutions		ns		

		days at home	flexibi-lity	control	concent-ration at home
H7	closeness to colleagues		ns		
	rating by colleagues		-.126*		
	closeness to manager		.165**	.272**	0.244**
	rating by manager		ns		
	organisational commitment		.165**	.363**	
H8	development of skills		ns		
H9	engagement in leisure activities		ns		
	Days at home	-	.310**	.131*	.171*

Note: Hypothesised results in bold; white cells = 1-tailed tests; shaded cells = 2-tailed tests.

Table 3. Continued

Table 3 should be understood as follows: Cells in bold are explicitly hypothesised relationships (*c.f.* Table 1). Other cells are 'found' relationships, (i.e. significant correlations found within the data but without being explicitly hypothesised). 'Found' correlations where the expected direction of the relationship is directly derivable from the hypotheses use 1-tailed tests (white cells); those which are not directly derivable, use 2-tailed tests (shaded cells). For clarity, we have added the symbol 'ns' (not significant) for hypothesised relationships where no significant correlation was found. Cells with no text included represent unhypothesised relationships where no significant correlation was found.

It should be noted that although we report several significant correlations, most of the correlation coefficients are small (typically 0.2 or 0.3). So how should the 'significance' be interpreted here? We suggest that 'significance' in this context should be interpreted more in the sense of 'confidence' that the correlation we are observing (however small) is reflecting some genuine relationship between the variables in question. In that context, the small size of many of the coefficients should probably be interpreted as indicating that although the variables seem to be related; there is not a direct or uniquely causal relationship present (insofar as any correlation should be taken to indicate a causal relationship!).

What explains variations in the individual QoL scores?

An important question raised in this project is how telework and other possible factors influence on individuals' QoL score. Table 3 shows that teleworking, when measured by the number of days spent working at home, has some positive impact on workers' QoL (r= .121*). However it does appear to have a moderate negative effect on Partner's Quality of Life (r=-.244**).

The question is then, how do the other factors influence the QoL of the informants? To shed some light on this we conducted a regression analysis where the factors on the left hand of the research model (see Figure 1) worked as independent variables influencing on the QoL factors as dependent variables at the right hand.

We conducted the analysis in a four-step procedure starting with the individual variables and then adding variables describing work pattern, the mediating variables and then all the outcome variables. The regression shows that the individual factors; age, gender, number of children in the family and self-efficacy together predict as much as 22.7% of the variance in the QoL score. Adding scores from the work pattern adds little to this (28.6%). Then, adding the variation on the three mediating variable doubles the predicting values to 44.7%. The last step includes all the outcome variables in our study, which all together explains 63% of the variance in QoL score (figure 2).

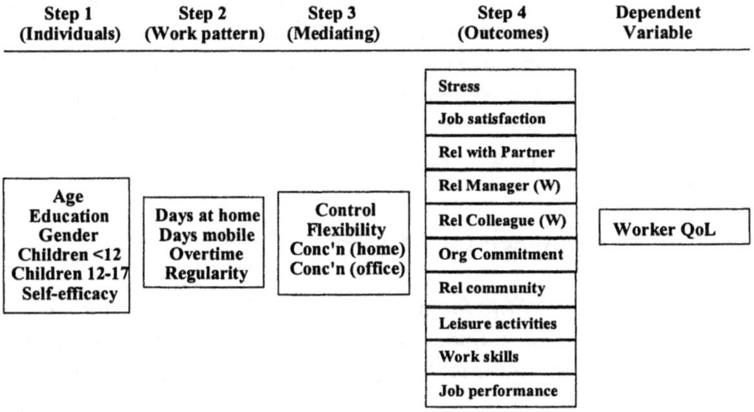

	Step 1	Step 2	Step 3	Step 4
Increase in variance explained after step	22.7%**	+5.9%*	+16.1%**	+18.3%**
Cumulative variance explained	22.7%	28.6%	44.7%	63.0%

(* = significant at p<.05; **=significant at p<.01)

Figure 2. Regression for Quality of Life using main Outcome variables at Step 4 showing percentage variance explained after Step 1, Step 2, Step 3 and Step 4

Figure 2 shows graphically the variables considered at each stage of the multiple regression analysis and the percentage variance explained after each step. Each step produces a significant increase in percentage of variance explained (indicated by the presence of asterisks after each figure). It is interesting to note that the work pattern variables (Step 2) produce the least amount of increase (only an extra 5.9% which is significant at the .05 level). This indicates that although work pattern variables are having a significant effect on Quality of Life, it is a much smaller effect compared to individual factors and the mediating variables. This is consistent with the weak correlation between Days at home and Worker Quality of Life (r= .121*) and our general conclusion that Quality of Life is the result of many variables acting together.

This shows that altogether we have included variables that have a clear predicting power on the QoL score. It appears however that variables other than work pattern and days at home have the strongest impact. Individual characteristics are clearly of importance, broadly covered under the concept of self-efficacy (Staples, Hulland and Higgins, 1998). Also education and work characteristics seem to have a clear impact (flexibility turned out as a significant factor). Exactly what these work characteristics are however is not very clear, as we found no significant variations when comparing the QoL scores of workers with different occupations. The simple correlations analyses (table 2) showed that control (r= .210**), flexibility (r= .186**) and concentration at home (r= .136*) correlated significantly with the workers' QoL.

Elaboration on selected issues

Impact on quality of life for workers and their close social network. Teleworking, as measured by the number of days spent working at home, has a weak, but significant, impact on quality of life (r= .121*). The teleworker's perception of belonging towards his place of living is part of this picture. Among other aspects we will emphasize: increased possibilities to concentrate (at home) and to control how to do the work, and reduced stress (even if teleworkers seem to overwork more than non-teleworkers). The overall impression is that quality of life is, not unexpectedly, affected by multiple factors all working together and that individual characteristics of the worker seem to be of special importance. Unexpectedly teleworking, still measured by the number of days spent at home, appears to have a moderate negative effect on Partner's Quality of Life (r=-0.244**). This finding seems relevant in particular to partners being full-time workers themselves. The children however, seemed to benefit from telework arrangements, indicated by a positive correlation between their QoL score and the worker's flexibility and control.

Relationship to close social network. The findings indicate that telework (mediated through flexibility) impacts positively on the worker's perception of closeness to the social network. However, we cannot find the same correlations when different types of social network members were analysed separately (possibly due to a small sample). When the effects related to concentration at home is analysed, we find a positive association with the worker's perception of closeness to the separated groups of partners and friends. Assessing these relationships the other way around, all social network members taken together the flexibility aspect seem to contribute positively to the perception of closeness, and this observation is significant for the partners (viewed separately) as well.

Relationship to professional network. Flexibility due to work arrangements does not seem to impact on the worker's perception of closeness to colleagues, whereas the colleagues assess this situation a bit more negatively. Further, the workers' perception of their relationship with their manager is improved (mediated through flexibility), but their feelings are not reciprocated by the managers, who in general are unaffected by the workers' increased flexibility. Workers, colleagues and managers emphasized the importance of trust and confidence to make teleworking arrangement a positive experience for the ones involved.

Assessment of efficiency and productivity. The workers seem to consider themselves as more productive due to flexible working arrangements, and the improved possibilities for concentration at home and control over how to do the work explains part of this tendency. The managers do not recognise this improvement in job performance, as they regard it as unchanged regardless of the number of days worked at home. This is however not the case for female workers whose performance are lower rated by the mangers the more days they work at home!

Which working style is 'best'? Instead of confirming the existing of a strong linear correlation between QoL and Number of days working at home, this study indicates connections between particular working styles and increased quality of life. In particular a combination of home working and office working seem to be favourable (according to among other factors stress and job satisfaction). We have demonstrated that working SOME days per week at home does indeed produce benefits, it is not a linear effect - and that more can be less! This finding from the quantitative analysis is directly supported by the qualitative study in which people report 1-3 days at home per week as being the ideal situation rather than 5 days per week. The preference with regard to number of days worked at home is in line with findings of previous studies (see, for example, Haddon and Lewis, 1994: 197). Furthermore, workers preferred the 1-3 days per week to be a regular arrangement, rather than long chunks of time in and away from the office. Workers perceive that regular days at home combined with regular time in the office maximises the benefits of home working (greater concentration and flexibility for family) and minimises the problems of home working (social isolation and maintaining relationship with manager and colleagues). It can be argued that this finding is not very surprising but we claim that we have added empirical evidence to the body of research that holds this position.

Discussion

We have seen through a set of regression analyses that a subset of the variables defined in the research model (see Figure 1) explains 63% of the variation in the worker's QoL scores (see Figure 2). A timely question to ask then is what accounts for the rest of the variance. There are possible candidates within the range of variables in the model not examined by this study, and there are additional variables to be examined, actualised by the findings of this study. In the following we will argue for a revision of the model to reflect the findings of the study, including additional variables and relations suggested by the findings, and to make it more explicit (see Figure 3). In doing this we have strongly felt the tension between abstraction and specificity. This means that we have tried to produce a model that is general enough to cover a variety of arrangements and outcomes, and at the same time is specific enough to be applicable to real situations.

The individual, organisational and societal characteristics provide the context or the 'preconditions' for the outcome of the working arrangement. Several demographic variables are examined by this study and we suggest that these are shown explicitly in the model. We also suggest an expanded list of input variables as this study (in particular the qualitative part) suggested additional variables to be candidates for explaining the relationship between telework and QoL. These are: motivation, stage of life, special needs and special events (INDIVIDUALS), and further, work regulations and culture (SOCIETY). We would also like to note that the preconditions of course also influence on people's QoL beside their working arrangement. In the revised model this is represented as an arrow bypassing the telework and mediating variables and influencing outcome variables directly.

Our study has shown that individual factors have a great deal of impact upon outcomes, and that the teleworking arrangements are also related to these outcomes (i.e. the teleworking situation influences how individual factors impact upon outcome variables rather than the teleworking variables defining the outcome variables directly). We therefore view the input factors as 'working through' the teleworking situation as a 'lens'. A key finding from the study was that work pattern variables do not act in a linear way and that 'clusters' of variables produce distinct work styles which in turn produce distinct patterns of outcome. To sum up the interaction between these variables the revised model includes reference to a non-linear function operating as part of the 'lens': f(Home, Mobile, Office, Regularity).

The mediating variables seem to be connected in some circumstances, but we still want to keep them separated because of clarity reasons when describing possible connections to the QoL outcome elements. We even suggest splitting up one of the existing variables and adding another one. Flexibility in time and place of working has distinct connections to, amongst others, the relationship between worker and partner, and we therefore suggest that the flexibility variable should be divided into two separate 'boxes'. When it comes to control, the research model holds that we can refer to control with regard to how, with what and with whom to work. In the questionnaire used all questions adding up the control construct, refer to control over how to work. The qualitative material however, indicated that a teleworking situation could give control with regard to assignment of tasks and project members (e.g. by finding excuses for not attending 'set-up' meetings). We keep the control variable unchanged through the revision of the model, but emphasize the importance of examining the control aspects more thoroughly in further studies. Regarding concentration, our findings clearly distinguish between the nature and effects of concentration at home (being connected with days at home and positively influencing outcomes) and concentration in the office (appearing to affect the workers' need for and interest in spending days at home due to various amounts of noise and interruptions). We therefore clarify the model by retaining concentration at home as a mediating variable and placing concentration in the office as an input variable (ORGANISATION). Finally, as overtime can be viewed as both an input variable and as an outcome variable, we suggest introducing overtime as a mediating variable (among other between days mobile and stress but also with connections to job performance).

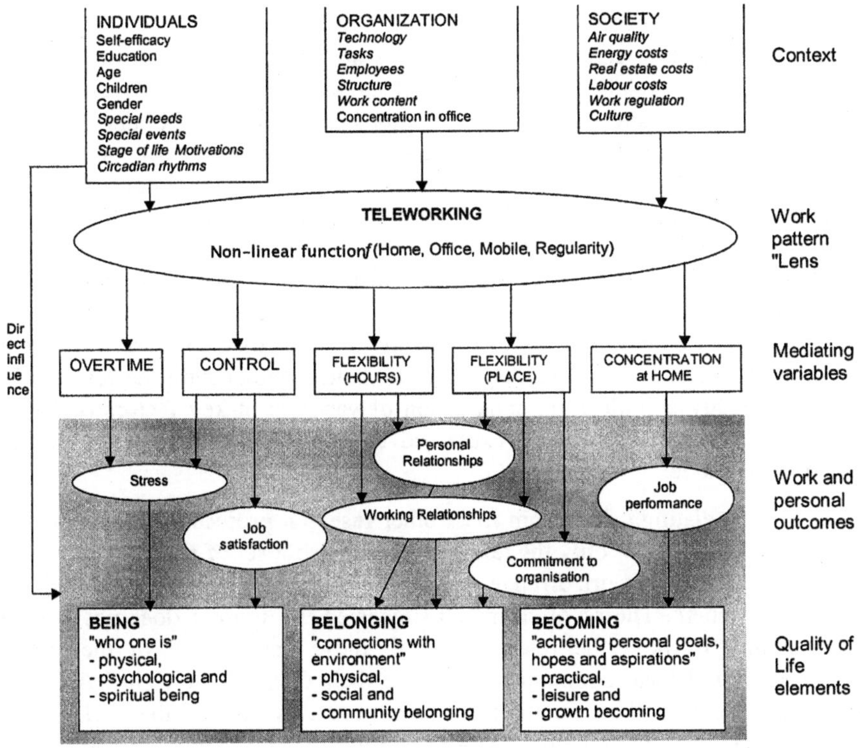

Figure 3. Revised research model based on study findings (items in italics not measured directly by this study). Connecting arrow implies influence, positive or negative

As we found no relationships between work pattern variables and three of the outcome variables in our model (relationship with local community, skill development and leisure activities), we recommend, perhaps controversially, that these outcome variables are deleted from the model. We might still feel that there is potential for these outcomes to be related to telework and be tempted to keep them in the model – but it is hard to justify presenting a revision of the model, based on the study findings, which still includes them. Further, organisational commitment has been extracted out as a separate outcome, distinguishing it from working relationships with people. The findings also indicated that only Flexibility of place had an impact on organisational commitment and there is therefore no link shown between Flexibility of hours and this variable (although we acknowledge this may be erring on the side of specificity here).

The right hand side of the model (see Figure 1) is rather complicated and not easy to understand at first sight. It is not obvious how the special constructs – stress, job satisfaction, relationship with colleagues, manager and organisation, relationship with social network, relationship with neighbours and local institutions, engagement in leisure activities, development of personal and professional skills, and job performance – relate to the QoL construct. In the revised model we have described more in detail the being, belonging and becoming parts of the model with characteristics given by the Toronto conceptualisation of the terms and distinguished these QoL elements from the work and personal outcome variables (the multiple regression analyses support the idea of selected outcome variables predicting these elements separately). Further, we suggest that the revised model should be held together with the results of the regression analyses indicating explanation of variance in key factors (*c.f.* Figure 2). The percentage of variance explained by each (group of) factors could be added to the model.

This study is distinguished from most other research projects in this area by the fact that it includes not only the teleworker, but also a set of people that might be influenced by the telework arrangement, including manager, colleagues and social network members. The research model suggested in Figure 1 does not provide a clear picture of how the relationships to these people and to the workers' organisation and local community influence their QoL. In the right hand side of the model we find these relationships mentioned as part of the QoL concept, especially in the belonging domain. A possibility to capture this issue would be to add feedback loops between relationships with network members and the worker's QoL (i.e. the closer relationship, the better the worker feels about his life, the even closer the relationships become, the even better the worker feels about himself and so on). A look at an extended correlation matrix shows significant correlation between the workers' relationship to social network members – and the workers' QoL. Thus, we see some support for including such connections (even loops). However, we view this suggestion as a bit problematic because it introduces a different dimension of time into the model and also the question of where to stop the addition of loops (recursive processes). We think, however, that the possible existence of feedback loops should be described in the text explaining the model.

Conclusions

In this chapter we have presented a revised model for doing research on the impacts of telework on quality of life. We have based our discussion on an existing theoretical model proposed by Van Sell and Jacobs (1994). This model has been made more specific by the inclusion of recent work on the measurement of QoL. It has further been informed by the results of a field study of European workers and their close social and vocational networks. The fitness of the research model has been tested through (amongst others) regression analyses showing that a subset of the variables defined in the research model explains a large part of the variance in the worker's QoL score. This implies we have included variables that have a clear predicting power on the QoL score. There are still variables in the model not examined, so the percentage might be even higher. All in all, we are looking at complex, non-linear relationships between different aspects of jobs and personalities, not simple or strong linear relationships looked for by correlations. This is confirmed by the multiple regressions and by the qualitative findings. The initial model has been revised to reflect the findings, including additional variables, and to make it more explicit. We argue that the extension of an existing model with recent quality of life research, including empirical testing, is a contribution to research in itself.

References

Akselsen, S. *et al.* (2001) *Telework and quality of life. Basic concepts and main results*, Heidelberg: EURESCOM, EDIN 0084-0904. Website:

http://www.eurescom.de/public/projects/P900-series/p904/P904.htm.

Haddon, L. and Lewis, A. (1994) 'The experience of teleworking: an annotated review', *International Journal of Human Resource Management*, 5, 1: 193-223.

Murphy, E. (1996) *Flexible work. The home-office partnership*, Cambridge: Directors Books.

Raphael, D., D'Amico, J., Brown, I. and Renwick, R. (1998) *The Quality of Life Profile: A Generic Measure of Health and Well-Being*, Toronto: Quality of Life Research Unit, Centre for Health Promotion, University of Toronto, Toronto, Canada, M5G 1L5. Website: http://www.utoronto.ca/qol.

Renwick, R. and Brown, I. (1996) 'The Centre for Health Promotion's conceptual approach to quality of life: Being, belonging, becoming', in Renwick, R. Brown, I. and Nagler, M. (eds.) *Quality of life in health promotion and rehabilitation: Conceptual approaches, issues, and applications*, Thousand Oaks, CA: Sage.

Staples, D.S., Hulland, J.S., and Higgins, C.A. (1998) 'Self-Efficacy Theory Explanation for the Management of Remote Workers in Virtual Organizations', *Journal of Computer Mediated Communications*, 3, 4. Website:

http://www.ascusc.org/jcmc/vol3/issue4/staples.html.

Sørensen, T. and Næss, S. (1996) 'To measure quality of life. Relevance and use in the psychiatric domain', *Nord J Psychiatry*, 50, Suppl 37: 29-39.

The WHOQOL Group, 1995. 'The World Health Organization Quality of Life Assessment (WHOQOL): position paper from the World Health Organization', *Social Science and Medicine*, 41, 1403-1409.

The WHOQOL Group, 1998. 'Development of the World Health Organization WHOQOL-BREF quality of life assessment', *Psychological Medicine*, 28, 3, 551-558.

Van Sell, M. and Jacobs S.M. (1994) 'Telecommuting and the quality of life: A review of the literature and a model for research', *Telematics and Informatics*, 11, 2: 81-95.

Communication Dynamics and Consequences

In this section of Part Two our attention turns to the dynamics and consequences that result from developments in new methods of work, particularly where they concern communications and social interaction.

Chapter 15, by Gunnela Westlander, kicks this off by examining the question of what researchers want to know about people who are teleworkers. She notes that while there are many perspectives and units of analysis that can – and have – been adopted in the study of telework, researchers have arrived somewhat late in the field of analysing the *human conditions* emerging from such arrangements. The chapter hence illustrates analytical views of teleworkers as 'actors' and 'learning human beings', and shows the important role such approaches can make to research and intellectual development in the area of ICTs and work innovation generally.

Carl-Johan Petri and Nils-Göran Olve , in Chapter 16, focus on the planning and monitoring of information processing activities in geographically dispersed organisations. The authors argue that in order to take advantage of ICTs along teleworking lines, organisations need to change their systems of management control. The chapter draws on published empirical work to describe how management has commonly acted in this regard. Control, they suggest, involves a range of influences, depending on the situation involved, including 'structure', 'procedures' and 'culture'. This leads them to argue that the changes produced by teleworking may require a number of management refinements – from authority structures and monitoring procedures, to behaviour regarding information sharing.

In Chapter 17, by Jon Rognes, the focus is on how spontaneous interaction is affected by teleworking. Using empirical data collected via work diaries, Rognes examines the time spent on spontaneous interaction in two groups: one working remotely part time and the other operating at one location. The chapter shows that time spent in spontaneous interaction is directly linked to the amount of time people are present in given work locations. In contrast to what is sometime assumed, Rognes shows that teleworkers do not therefore 'make up' for their remoteness by engaging in more spontaneous interaction when they are in central workplaces. The fact that interactions are not compensated for has important implications, says Rognes, for work such as R&D and management, where spontaneous interaction may be vital to performance.

Andrea Whittle also touches upon spontaneous interaction, particularly where it concerns personal networking, in the following chapter. The focus here is on the career implications of teleworking; namely, the often expressed fear of being 'out of sight, out of mind'. Whittle points out that while this issue is frequently talked about in the literature – and raised as a source of anxiety by teleworkers themselves – little empirical work has gone into exploring the subject. One important question raised here is whether presence can in some way be substituted for by electronic accessibility. The chapter addresses these points by drawing together theory from technology studies, organisation theory and career theory. The chapter concludes that a controversy remains at the heart of debate into telework and its career implications. On the one hand, notes Whittle, technology is seen as a means of promoting connectedness, and thus of ameliorating the problem of remoteness. On the other hand, teleworking is also seen as a source of career costs, due to social isolation. For Whittle, though, the debate on whether technology can or cannot bridge the social divide (particularly where career issues is concerned) misses the point. Differences in local contexts, particularly regarding social processes and knowledge transfers, means that the same technologies may have quite difference consequences for individuals and their career dynamics. We therefore need, she suggests, a more sophisticated theoretical grasp of the subject matter, and one that should be informed by empirical work.

The final chapter in this section, by Ewa Gunnarsson, looks at work dynamics and identities inside the ICT department of a knowledge-based consultancy company. In a similar way to Whittle, Gunnarsson is less concerned with telework as a work concept, and more interested in the working practices, experiences and emotions of people who use ICTs as part of their day-to-day work – and in so doing engage in a range of local and remote interactions with other, both conventionally and virtually. The chapter shows that as people exploit the flexibilities provided by ICTs, they necessarily produce a reworking of organisational and social boundaries. This has consequences for the very meaning of work, of course; but more fundamentally, Gunnarsson shows, for people's sense of who they are. The chapter puts particular analytical focus on matters of *masculinity* here, and the way the national Swedish – and ICT professional – cultures interact with the new work dynamics to influence experiences, self-perception and identity.

15 What Researchers Want to Know About 'the Teleworking Person'

Gunnela Westlander

Department of Work Sciences, Linköping University, Sweden

Introduction

Telework has aroused considerable interest, and many are involved in developing, testing and reporting on its applications (experts, practitioners, and *researchers*).

Taking a rather philosophical standpoint, let us talk about the researchers. Do we have a special role, a special task in this area? I would say yes. We are not necessarily better informed about the technology than the experts, but our *exclusive* contribution is that we can reflect upon the way analyses are performed to acquire information about the technical-organizational-human complex called teleworking.

In the inevitable technical-organizational discussions about the implementation of a telework system, human beings are often concealed or more or less ignored. How then do we then describe the teleworking person as a human being?

Researchers are confronted with a choice of principal focus:

> Alternative (1): *Technology* is the centre of attention; organizational issues are secondary factors to be considered; workers as human beings are virtually ignored.
>
> Alternative (2): *Organizational strategies* make up the primary subject, whereas technology and workers are regarded as instrumental.
>
> Alternative (3): Principal attention is paid to *human conditions*, and efforts are made to understand them in terms of their technological and organizational impacts.

The choice of main focus has of course something to do with the researcher's academic domicile. In my experience - looking at teleworking as a research field - the two following rather provocative questions come up at periodic intervals:

- Is not technological-managerial analysis good enough to arrive at satisfactory solutions?

- Is it even necessary in research on business development to pay attention to individual human beings and their conditions; if so, what is then important?

As organization researchers we do not completely neglect the working members of an organization. But we have a strong tendency to describe them at aggregate level. Staff as staff, so to speak! The questions this raises run as follows: 'For a business development, planned or accomplished, what importance should be attached to staff and professional groups?' If you are curious about the significance of individuals for teleworking, does putting the question this way encourage adequate information?

Now, I want to reflect upon what we, as researchers, seem to be curious about with regard to teleworking persons as human beings. About what are we really concerned?

Who do we define as teleworking persons from among the great diversity of human beings who are involved in and/or affected by telework?
What strikes me most is the contrast between the individualistic work lifestyle, nowadays proclaimed as some kind of ideal, and the individual worker's seemingly restricted freedom to choose IT systems. Managers or central decisionmakers seem to have a kind of preferential right with regard to interpretation. Their judgements on functionality and usability are generally worth more than those of the workers.

Looking at current research as a whole, the individual user's freedom to choose his or her mode of teleworking seems to be more respected, the higher his or her position in the organization. There is no doubt that researchers have sets of quite different spectacles when investigating teleworking persons of various categories.

Let me take an example: Managers' habits and preferences have, in recent years, interested a number of business researchers. Findings indicate that, in their jobs, these persons prefer face-to-face communication and natural language to electronically transferred information. They are strongly attracted to mobile equipment. They do not want to be forced to use IT systems that are not immediately enabling. The conclusion of the business researchers is that 'these views must be respected'.

But, do researchers adopt the same attitude towards non-management people? In other words, are non-management workers asked questions like:

- Are you free to inform people by way of direct or natural communication?

- Is it possible to report explicitly about the intentions underlying the information sent, and is it possible to grasp the receiver's reactions?

- Is it possible to grasp your communication partner's social context and to give him or her enough insight into your own?

Such questions concern social conditions related to telework systems introduced in businesses. They emerge from critical psychosocial issues in the arenas of social identity and recognition. Thus, a matter of vital importance is whether we, as researchers, regard people as active agents or as 'the exposed'? And this has epistemological consequences. *Do we choose a study approach to the teleworking person:*

- as *EXPOSED*,
- as a *LEARNIN*G human being,

or

- as one *ACTOR* among others.

I would like to comment on each one of these approaches separately. The findings they generate are strategic, and they are useful for very different purposes.

The Teleworking Person as Exposed

This approach is usually adopted *late* in the technological-implementation process. Researchers direct their attention at individuals when the process has gone on for a while and the situation is becoming more stable. The task of the researcher is to 'post-evaluate' the human conditions emerging from the new arrangement (already introduced) and, if possible, to distinguish different outcomes depending on variation in working conditions.

The world view here is that teleworking persons are exposed to technological-managerial systems allowing for a certain amount of self-discretion (personal influence on how work is carried out). This can be limited or more-or-less sufficient.

The field of occupational-health research offers many good examples. One is provided by Pekka Huutanen and colleagues' study *of telebanking services* in Finland. People in back-office work were moved to telebank-service duties. Work content changed. After four months, the following stressors were reported: new rules and instructions, a hectic pace of work, closer supervision, and increased customer expectations. But there were also experiences of positive learning opportunities. The findings are dramatic, and were reported recently in an article entitled 'Terrorized by Technology' .

This example of monitoring research, focusing on various categories of teleworking people and their wellbeing, demonstrates a new impact pattern on human conditions that has been found in many other recent studies. There is a *combination* of increased stress factors *and* new learning opportunities (or perhaps rather 'learning obligations'). The problem is that, from the point of view of occupational health, the positive experience cannot make up for the negative. This problem has to be solved in order to avoid burnout and similar long-term psychic consequences, while at the same time allowing the creation of learning possibilities that are meaningful and attractive to the teleworking human being.

One of the first broad surveys of teleworking was performed by Ursula Huws. Following her suggested taxonomy of teleworking settings (home-based full-time, part-time, mobile, satellite, telecottage, and freelance), there emerged a picture of different psychic wellbeing-illbeing patterns and one common feature, that of social isolation (felt or real, or both).

Another way of studying the conditions of stabilized (established) telework settings might be to search for knowledge about processes in the preceding convergence phase in order to find out when, and especially how, the initial adaptation period passes on into a stabilized one.

I find it very important to apply *prospective* approaches, however timeconsuming these may be. This is the only way of learning something about the worker *as a learning creature - a learning human being.*

The Teleworking Person as a Learning Human Being

Although it is the case that, in occupational-health impact-oriented research, learning receives the greatest attention, this is only in terms of the person's *perceived* or *experienced* learning opportunities - a supposed psychosocial reward.

However, the task of research now has become one of demonstrating *how* learning takes place and proceeds. In this context, there are two major features of interest:

1. Studying how the individual learns to cope with and master a telework system in a technological sense. Traditional educational psychologists, cognitive psychologists and experts in cognitive science are involved.
2. Exploring what kind of learning at work is going on in organizations where telework facilities are accessible. The core question is 'How does learning function and grow *in practice*?' This question concerns non-manipulated reality. Practice is the object of investigation - something quite the opposite of what an experimental or controlled situation (as favoured by traditional educational psychologists) has to offer.

The world view on *what learning is*, in this second sense, may be expressed in the following, rather indefinite, way:

- Learning is an aspect of everyday practice as a whole

- Learning and knowledge are elements in concrete change processes, which in turn depend on existing actors and power relations
- Non-learning is not a personality characteristic but another side of learning. Non-learning must be understood as 'situated', meaning that it has its roots in the specific context where it appears.

As we know, such a conception of human learning has been adopted by social scientists of different disciplines (social, cultural and cognitive anthropologists, ethnomethodologists, educational psychologists, and cognitive psychologists). Their methodology for studying human learning involves some kind of scanning and scrutinizing of practice, in this case the practice of work. Its purpose is to find out how learning takes place.

I would like briefly to mention an ongoing research project within the Department of Computer Science at Linköping University in Sweden, which aims to develop interorganizational collaboration and competence in a local community's rehabilitation activities for the long-term unemployed. It is intended that three local agencies should abandon a time-consuming parallel-work model, and embark on client-centered multiperspectival synchronous collaboration in order to speed up the rehabilitation process (thereby helping the client more effectively). The researchers' guiding question is 'How can we - in the best way - support strivings to reach a good, workable solution?' Further, there is the question: *'Which telework support systems* would be helpful?'

The research has a participative-action design, covering the entire process of integration, and is strongly influenced by practitioners. Office workers in three local agencies are asked to drive change *at their own pace*. The computer engineer involved, who will prepare the telework systems, is waiting for the practitioners' considered and final decision about the best collaborative structure (including what ICT equipment would be most suitable). The problem is discussed in dialogue between the practitioners involved and the research team, in particular the team member charged with the task of designing the telework system. In this project, all regard themselves as learners.

Considering the teleworking person as a learner is to see him or her as an individual with active potential. But even greater stress may be placed on the active side of the person by taking what I call an 'actor's perspective'. What might this mean?

The Teleworking Person as an Actor?

Viewing the teleworking person as an ACTOR is based on the idea of a <u>dynamic</u> rather than an established organization/business. For precisely this reason, the term 'organizing' is preferred to 'organization' in the context of this practice. The dynamic is visible in that individuals continuously handle, change, and perhaps renew material and technical resources, and also everyday administrative procedures. They are involved in organizing and reorganizing. As researchers, we want answers to questions such as:

- How do workers negotiate over who shall do the tasks to be performed?
- What circumstances limit their options?
- Are there any leading change agents?
- If so, who gives them legitimacy?
- Are there any persons with the role of 'gate keeper'?
- Are there people who remain passive when confronted by suggestions for change?

Questions of this kind are crucial to consultants involved in corporate development projects. They are also highly relevant across the entire period of a project - not only at its start or in terms of the final outcome. For the researcher, a useful way of positioning an ongoing development activity, and thereby of obtaining a better understanding of involved people's situational conditions and potential influences, is to be aware of the stage of development. Are they at the preconvergence, convergence, or continued (more stabilized) phase of an organization's life?

I would like to conclude my chapter by pointing to an example of a specific ICT-supported implementation issue - one where I think a researcher, by choosing an actor's perspective approach, would offer the most useful and thought-provoking findings.

The example is taken from my own professional field, psychology. At least in practitioners' core tasks, face-to-face relations are a 'must'. Indeed, even the most standardized assessment instruments require interpersonal contact. As in all other fields, assisting persons and working with delicate personal and often confidential problems, computer use and telecommunication technology are introduced relatively late and with much caution. This is also true for the branch of professional psychology called psychotherapy!

Confidentiality and face-to-face interaction are unavoidably the most critical issues in discussions of the applications of so-called *telehealth* to psychotherapy. As an occupational-health practice, this is defined in terms of providing 'health services in which health-care professionals - psychotherapists and others - and their clients use interactive, real-time communication media to connect across distances'.

The media referred to today include:

- Internet chat rooms,
- Video and audio-only transmissions via the Internet,
- Closed-circuit television,

and even

- The traditional telephone.

(Excluded are e-mail and facsimiles, since they are not synchronically interactive or in real time.)

Providing psychotherapy at distance is still in its infancy. For two reasons professional psychotherapists hesitate, and are unwilling to take the line of least resistance:

1. Current technology is not able to support face-to-face discussions with *high*-quality images.
2. Psychotherapy as a 'telework' is a mode of therapy that has been very little tested. Knowledge is scarce.

Nevertheless, in this slowly growing field, different kinds of actors have crystallized. Besides *professionals themselves*, psychotherapists and clinical psychologists, acting through their professional associations and (in large countries) their coordinating national organizations, there are *telecom industries* competing hard in product development. Further, there is the *research funding system*, steered by national future-oriented policies, and - at least in the US - dedicated specifically to the area of *telehealth and health care communications*. All these "institutional" actors have different interests, attitudes and insights, and also inside knowledge concerning the concrete, very delicate and personal interactive situation of the carer providing psychological health services to his/her patient or client/consumer.

1. Professional associations form the psychotherapists' channel for declaring standpoints and acting cautiously, prudently, or even with hesitation. Intense discussions take place. Usability, professional quality and integrity, risks and threats to patients/clients (and so indirectly to themselves) are the main issues in their discussions.
2. As well as such professional core issues there are still others that emerge from the *technical facilities specifically coupled to the Internet*. In particular, it is now possible for a health-provider to offer service to a help-seeking person living in another state. Perhaps the most pressing problem to be solved is whether it is legal for an authorized psychologist/psychotherapist in one state or nation to treat a client in another state or nation by telephone or over the Internet. Must the practitioner be licensed in/and by the state authorities where the client lives? So far, no state legislature has addressed this problem with regard to psychologists (although some nation states have begun restricting

physicians' practices across this line). However, it is highly relevant in times of the Internet and globalization that European nations adopt a coordinated approach to these complications. The *national, coordinating boards* of the professional associations are currently working on such legal and regulatory issues.

3. To the contrary, the attitude of the *telecommunications industry* is *offensive*. It does not wait for answers to psychotherapists' doubts and questions, or for legislative problems to be solved. The industry will survive on the market only by developing affordable high-quality distance technologies in the near future.
4. Research centres involved in issues of *telehealth and health care communications* are most concerned with one question: 'How and under what conditions do telecommunications-mediated health lead to positive psychological health outcomes?' They take an in-between position, and act adaptively - in the sense of wanting to find out how to comply with the strivings of the telecom industry's proinnovative intentions.
5. Yet another set of actors consist in *national research funding systems*, with their accompanying investment policies. It is said that the *US research funding system* supports financially technological innovations and infrastructures for telework but has no interest in evaluation research concerning the activities this entails (such as telehealth in terms of treatment effectiveness). By contrast, in Scandinavia, Australia and other countries, national funding policies cover cross-disciplinary research for evaluating qualities of human-computer interaction, and even business development based on human-technology organization interaction.

The small numbers of studies of long-distance psychotherapy so far published have been much critized. In the critics' view, their focus is too narrow - largely on patient-provider satisfaction with the technology, but seldom on what is most important (namely treatment effects and cost-benefit outcomes). There is an urgent need to find out how services of this kind work. How, for example, does video-conferencing affect different disorders?

Technology should not drive mental-health services. To the contrary, the services must drive the technology. This slogan is not new, but it is strikingly relevant when the product/outcome/goal is people's health.

Concluding Words

The *potentials of future teleworking* extend far beyond the occupational contexts now observed in telework research. In my view, they represent new, possible, future work forms, which inexorably demand the following:

- Quality research, in order to address the real impacts of using a particular kind of telecommunication technology.
- A rethinking of *who* is "the teleworker" - *from* a person or a category of persons within a profession, or one or several occupations who perform certain tasks, *to* a dual relationship, consisting of two persons (a professional provider and a service consumer) in a subject-to-subject relation. Both should in fact be looked at as teleworking persons - in the sense that they use an ICT system in order to transfer information and keep conversation going in order to attain a specific goal.

Both parties, the health provider and the patient/client, must be able to:

- *cope with* the technology operatively in order to offer preconditions for conversation
- *understand* how to utilize the ICT setting in the best way in order to have desirable information transferred.
- *realize* how long-distance contact imposes greater limits than the rich and multimodal relation enabled by face-to-face discussion.

This case of potential use of ICT in the future may be unique concerning details and specific aspects of effectiveness. But it may as well be regarded as a metaphor for a range of professional activities not yet invaded by ICT systems. Thinking about the future involves trying to envisage the interests of extending ICT to new areas of application, and to act proactively for its best qualitative use.

16 Increasing the Bandwidth in Telework Control

Carl-Johan Petri and Nils-Göran Olve

Economic Information Systems, Linköping University and Concours Cepro AB, Stockholm
Sweden

INTRODUCTION

This chapter focuses on information providing activities in geographically dispersed organizations, and how these activities can be visualized, planned and monitored. Our belief is that the management control systems influence what is regarded as important in an organization (Simons, 1995). The organization can consequently redesign their management control systems to manifest the importance of information sharing.

Control in the sense of influencing individual actions within the context of an organization can be executed in a variety of ways. Olve (1990) proposed a simple triple to identify what kinds of influences are important in a given situation: *structure*, *procedures* and *culture*. Introducing telework means that the structure is changed (division of tasks, localization of units), work procedures are altered, and a modified culture may evolve.

The purpose of this chapter is to discuss how organizations may need to change management controls in order to take advantage of modern ICT[1] in situations where telework has been introduced. We are especially concerned about the potential presented by remote information-provision activities by the teleworkers that will usually not be the main focus of their work. Telework represents a change in structure, which may require complementing and compensating changes in other types of control. This is especially important as the telework structure will often present new contacts with the organization's environment, and consequently a potential to identify valuable information. Much of this will not be recorded automatically but require a conscious effort by the teleworkers in order to be made available to others in the organization.

The chapter starts with a theoretical discussion, and we then turn to four previously presented empirical studies for reports on how management has acted

---

1 Information and communication technologies

with regard to the management control systems' implications on the organizational information provision. As these studies were not performed with a focus on this particular question, we have to glean some evidence from more incidental mentions of such practices. As a first attempt to investigate this topic, however, we feel that our re-use of previous studies is very much in the spirit of our general theme of asynchronous information sharing, and that it makes possible some conclusions that may encourage further work in this field.

Control in Geographically Dispersed Organizations

The concept of management control has, over time, been given many interpretations. In this chapter, we use the definition of Anthony et al. (1992, p. 10): "*the process by which managers influence other members of the organization to implement the organization's strategies*". Control in the sense of influencing individual actions within the context of an organization can be executed in a variety of ways. Olve (1990) proposed a simple triple to identify what kinds of influences are important in a given situation: *structure*, *procedures* and *culture* (see also Bakka et al., 1993, who suggest the same triple). The mix can be designed differently, and different ingredients should complement, and may sometimes substitute for, each other.

By *structure* we mean the physical locations of people and facilities, their roles and tasks, and the reporting structure. In focusing on control we are concerned with the conscious design of these. When talking about how activities are organized, or reorganized, structure often seems to be perceived as the most important part, or at least the most visible. Locations, roles, tasks and reporting structure are usually designed to be valid from a specific date. There are of course also informal structures, but the more formal structures typically continue to be the first thing a visitor to an organization may be told about.

When a firm decides to implement telework it chooses a certain structure regarding physical locations. This chapter essentially deals with the problem how other aspects of structure, as well as procedures and culture, will then need to be reconsidered.

By control through *procedures* we mean the administrative routines that members of an organization are expected to perform. They often involve several actors and use of the organization's information systems, and are expected to occur at regular intervals or triggered by certain events. Like the structure, these are usually designed to be in force from a specific date.

By *culture*, finally, we here mean the socially conditioned behaviors of organization members that are a result of their membership in the organization. In focusing on control we disregard these. Instead we concentrate on how people are made to share a common way of thinking (for instance, "customer orientation" or "willingness to change") through the way they are trained, the information they receive, how they are rewarded, and so on.

The combination of structure, procedures, and culture should be designed so that they together provide the "influence" mentioned by Anthony et al. However, in most cases "to implement the organization's strategy" should not be seen as a static goal. Rather, control (especially procedures and culture) should make it possible for management to receive feedback on new conditions and opportunities, to enable a dynamic view of desirable actions (Simons, 1995; Hedberg and Jönsson, 1978).

In this chapter we consider the case of outsourced and remotely located functions that are part of an organization. Location is an important part of structure, and locating tasks at a distance from each other will influence how tasks are "bundled", i.e. the roles in the organization. A comparison can be made with so-called virtual corporations (Davidow and Malone, 1992) or imaginary organizations (Hedberg et al., 1997), where the concept of the organization is extended to encompass collaborating but legally or physically separate firms. We would expect this type of situation to affect the mix or controls chosen, or indeed available, to the managers in what Hedberg et al. call the lead organization.

Successful telework may be linked to the use of more elaborate procedures than before the introduction of telework, and require efforts to influence the culture of the teleworkers. Both will require considerable exchange of information between managers and teleworkers. While the procedures may be described in rules communicated once and for all, there will be a need for communication between management and local agents in order to follow the procedures. Affecting the culture can only be done through communication. We therefore expect successful telework to be associated with a larger amount of structured communication between managers and employees as well as between employees, compared to when the corresponding tasks are performed in the proximity of the organization. This should be especially true when the functions performed by the teleworkers are highly integrated with those performed elsewhere in the organization.

So what are the indications so far that existing telework arrangements have recognized this need for improved controls? According to Rognes (1999, p. 48), the issues of managing teleworkers have not been focused to the same extent as for example issues of communication patterns in geographically dispersed organizations, telework resistance, telework appropriateness, telework efficiency/productivity and more general exploratory studies of telework. Managing teleworkers is often said to require a high level of trust:

> "*...the general characteristics needed for leading an organisation based on a higher level of trust than historically is particularly important when dealing with telecommuting or other forms of geographical dispersion*" (ibid, p. 48).

The trust issue is also highlighted by Forsebäck (1995), but in this case derived from the necessity for the teleworker and her manager to agree on a set of clear goals and defined processes.

Other writers seem to suggest lines of thought that are similar to ours. Kelly (1988) argues that the relationship between the employee and the job specification is reciprocal: "*Managers must choose not only individuals who are suited to working at home, but also jobs that are suitable to telework*" (Kelly, 1998, p. 31). Suitable characteristics are for example: possibility to define milestones or 'deliverables' at specific time, and project-oriented job activities with tasks involving a structured flow of information in a defined time frame.

Larsen (1996, p. 157, 160) also argues that the teleworker needs explicit feedback. In the absence of an everyday spontaneous feedback mechanism from colleagues and managers, the teleworkers might wonder whether or not they are doing a good job. "*The teleworkers [...] feel unconfident whether they work enough and good enough*" (our translation). Her hypothesis (ibid, p. 157) is that unambiguous goals are of greater importance for co-ordination when the work is performed remotely than if not.

Information Provision in Geographically Dispersed Organizations

Asynchronous information sharing enables employees of a firm, or users of a web site, to interact with each other regardless of time and space. One person can post a question on an intranet and all users of that system can answer her, regardless of where they are.

Older techniques, such as the bulletin board in the library, have enabled individuals to communicate independent of time. One person can communicate with another person supported by paper notes, without having to show up at the same moment. The note can be posted, and read at any other point in time. These examples are trivial, but the basic principle is still important – the principle of time and space independence. Individuals can use different techniques to communicate bilaterally or multilaterally, transcending time and space (Gunton, 1989, p. 125).

The way an organization creates, shares and utilizes information has become one of its most important competitive weapons. All processes, internal as well as external, are becoming more and more information intense (Davenport, 1997; Keen, 1991; Porter and Millar, 1985), and the way information and IT resources are managed internally defines whether the IT investments will be valuable or not (Strassman, 1990).

Information-providing activities are, however, rarely shown in the organizational models. They are often implicit in both the systems operation model, and in the departments' business processes. Information generation and retrieval are activities that are expected to follow naturally for each employee, in her daily work. But these activities are unfortunately neither natural nor obvious. They are often regarded as bureaucratic and time consuming, taking time from what the employee really thinks she should do. *Documentation* is thus seen as an optional extra activity that can be performed in case of any spare time (Davenport, 1997, p. 196).

The responsibility to produce and record information in joint information systems is especially important in geographically dispersed organizations. This intention is however challenged in many geographically dispersed organizations, as described by Larsen (1996, p. 90), since employees working remote from the office tend to focus on their primary activities. As they spend more and more time away from the office, they focus more and more on their core responsibilities: selling, servicing, calling and so on. Consequently they perceive a decrease in dependency of others, thus reducing the need for synchronous as well as asynchronous information sharing.

Controlling Information Provision and Telework: A Tentative Perspective

Our discussion so far can be summarized as follows. Control practices in organizations where work units are geographically dispersed need to be reconsidered. Increasing geographical distances will change "how managers influence other members of the organization to implement the organization's strategies", to borrow Anthony's definition of management control referred to above. We suggested that this could be seen as a change in *structure*, i.e. how a firm has designed organizational roles and tasks, where they are performed, and authority relationships. *Ceteris paribus*, we expect that increasing the distance between workers or units will be perceived as a move towards less control, i.e. more independence, or self-dependency.

When everyone works in the same place, there will be subtle signals that encourage treating information as an important resource. With telework this disappears. At the same time as IS-enabled information sharing probably becomes even more potentially important, there is a danger that it declines. Task descriptions, performance measures, and reward systems will usually focus on short-term achievements: new sales, handling customer complaints, and so on. The potential long-term benefits from collecting and utilizing stored information are much harder to explain and evaluate. It will thus be desirable to modify the *procedures* and *culture* which we also include in our concept of management control.

Management needs to take action to compensate for the lack of spontaneous, synchronous communication. Otherwise information sharing will erode and efficiency may decrease. We drew support for this partly intuitive thesis from the literatures on virtual communities, roles associated with IS use, and different forms of information-sharing organizations. In the following section, we will look to a number of practical cases for support. Control in telework has not to our knowledge been addressed as a topic for detailed research, but we may be able to find some evidence on the issues discussed so far.

Empirical Illustrations

Our empirical illustrations are compiled from research to which we have had primary or secondary access. We present the cases to show situations where information sharing in geographically dispersed organizations can be viewed through management control lenses.

Ericsson Business Network

Background[2]. The studied unit was responsible for key accounts, and belonged to the business area Ericsson Business Networks. It consisted of seven employees working as liaisons between corporate customers and different Ericsson companies, helping the customers to develop business practice around Ericsson's products. They simultaneously facilitated feedback from the customers into the Ericsson organization.

Work routines and information sharing. The prime responsibility of the employees was customer interaction, mostly via the telephone. The employees described their job as a typical consulting practice, where they worked as project leaders or project members in the customer's organization, developing the client's processes and practice using various Ericsson products. When working with the customer, the employee often travelled to that customer's office. Other duties, such as writing reports and preparing meetings, were also suitable for distance work. These activities were previously done at the office, but were now carried out in the home of the teleworker. The employees found the telework arrangement more flexible and efficient than having to travel to the office.

---

2 The case is presented in Kristina Larsen's licentiate thesis (1996, pp. 63-71) at Economic Information Systems, Linköping University.

There were no explicit changes in work routines or responsibilities after the introduction of telework. Instead of the weekly meeting, the unit scheduled one monthly meeting, which was more formalized. The employees could brief each other on present and future activities during these meetings. The physical arrangements in the office were however changed. Instead of having their own room, the employees shared one office. This open forum was an important information-sharing device: "*By passive listening to discussions or taking part in them, enlarge the awareness of the business*" (ibid, p. 66, *our translation*). Another important channel was the joint database, which was created to enable cooperation. Sales data, information about customers and client history were stored in the database. It was critical for the unit to keep this database updated, to enable individual teleworkers to replace each other in ongoing projects.

Control practice. The procedures in the unit were not changed in any formal sense to support the new work pattern. The structure was changed as an intervention from management, in order to improve efficiency: office costs would drop since the home-office solution (combined with a shared room at the office) was cheaper than having separate rooms for each employee in the corporate office, plus productivity would go up as an effect of greater flexibility.

A new information system was developed and introduced in the organization, in which the employees were supposed to record information about customers and projects. Still, no mechanisms appeared to lay emphasis on this responsibility. On the contrary, Larsen says: "*The control in the operation is budgets and cost outcome. Other feedback and follow up is often informal*" and "*No written reports on progress is given, but to some extent are activities written down in the joint database*" (ibid, p. 68, *our translation*). Neither was the operation measured in any new way.

Rather than aligning procedures and responsibility structures to the new telework arrangements, the employees seem to have adjusted to the new situation voluntarily. The employees tended to lean towards synchronous modes of communication, where the recurring monthly group meeting became an important forum for information sharing. The shared office space also functioned as a sharing device, where employees could overhear each other's conversations.

Dial

Background [3]. The unit of analysis was a group in the department of Technology and Motor in the insurance company Dial. The department was responsible for car insurances, and was geographically structured in eight regions. Every region had a group of eight to eleven field technicians whose responsibility was to inspect

---

3 This case is also compiled from Larsen's thesis (1996, p. 85-96).

wrecked cars before they were fixed by an auto repair shop, in order to calculate and accept how much the insurance company was willing to pay for the repair.

Work routines and information sharing. The field technician's duty was to handle the company's relations with auto repair shops in his district. When the customer, the car owner, handed over his wrecked car to the mechanic, the mechanic estimated the repair costs. The insurance company would pay for it, so it was in their interest to see that the mechanic did not overcharge. The field technicians monitored the mechanics and accepted or rejected the proposal. The work procedures were explicitly defined, so it was easy for the technicians to relate to the expectations.

As the organization shifted to a telework arrangement, a new computerized information system was installed, and the procedures were redesigned to reflect the intention of the new system. As the system enabled compilation of cost estimates of typical repair jobs from a broader population, the organization got a better picture of what a certain job "should" cost. To enable this compilation, the field technicians had to spend more time on reporting and information gathering. After the system was introduced, the technicians estimated that they spent approximately 50 % of their time on reporting (ibid, p. 87). Often this had to be done in the evening (ibid, p. 86), after normal working hours.

The interviewees commented on the shift in working procedures – from more contact with mechanics and customers, towards more reporting and documentation. This was found somewhat boring, since the other activities were perceived as more creative and problem solving (ibid, p. 89). The technicians felt that these interesting activities had been replaced with more administrative and boring duties.

Control practice. The new structure of geographically dispersed field technicians, working from home instead of from the office, was explicitly reflected in the responsibility structure of the organization. The group leader used the information in the system as an agenda for the meetings (ibid, p. 93). He thereby justified some of the time spent on reporting – by showing interest for the data in the system. The importance of feedback, for example established through the group leader's utilization of the data, was noticed by one of the interviewees. He found that the new structure required more feedback than the previous one, due to the fact that the employees and the group leader met less often than previously (ibid, p. 93).

Another important issue was to ensure obedience with the established procedures (ibid, p. 95). This could not be monitored, since the technicians worked remotely from the office. The group leader thus spent much time on discussing how and why the activities should be done. If the technicians started to report information based on their own definitions and structures, the common frame of reference would erode – and the data in the system would be uninterpretable.

The monthly meeting was a vehicle to create some sort of bond within the group. During these meetings the technicians were given a chance to compare their work with that of their peers. These meetings were also a channel to inform about events in the company, and to influence the culture of the group.

Virtual Helpdesk Organization

Background[4]. The virtual help desk is run by one of Sweden's biggest export companies, with representation in more than 130 countries. The study focused on the helpdesk agents' actions when interacting with the helpdesk system, and how existing management-control mechanisms and responsibility structures influenced their behaviour. The interviewed users belonged to a unit within the internal IT-department.

Work routines and information sharing. The structure of the global helpdesk solution was based on the idea that every problem should be handled as close to the end-user as possible. It was thus important that the helpdesk agent entered as much relevant information into the system as possible, so that the system could suggest a solution. The solutions were based on the collective knowledge of problems previously handled by all the helpdesks connected to the global system – all over the world. The system also allowed the company to diagnose the status of their infrastructure. Since all problems were recorded and stored, it was for example possible to find hardware with recurring problems, systems that were difficult to use or subdomains in the network with bad performance. These aggregate observations could also be used in order to put pressure on the companys' suppliers, as well as being used for internal decision-making on the future development of the infrastructure (ibid, p. 118).

Another important function of the system was the ability to escalate problems (ibid, p. 120). If the first line of support was unable to solve a problem, it could be escalated either to a local expert (internal or external) or to the second line of support.

Control practice. One procedural goal had been defined: 80 % of the problems should be solved in the first line of support (ibid, p. 117). Local experts should solve 16 % of the problems and the remaining 4 % should be handled by the second line of support, or by external experts. Two other important procedural performance indicators were used in the operative performance evaluation system. The first one, which was measured automatically in the switchboard, measured how much time each agent spent on each customer. The goal was three minutes, in order to minimize the queue of end-users on hold. The other goal was the number of subjects handled per agent and day. These two indicators stressed the

---

4 This case is presented, in its full length, by one of the authors in Westin (1998, pp. 111-125).

importance of finishing a subject as soon as possible, unfortunately discouraging from recording problems and solutions in the database. From the perspective of the management control system, it was better to handle more subjects per day than contributing with new information. It was also better to pass on difficult problems as soon as possible, rather than to "throw away" valuable time on endless reporting. This, however, forced the experts and second line of support to collect information that should already have been in the system.

The reverse was also perceived as a problem. The experts interpreted their role in the system as operative advisers. When a problem was solved, the experts turned to the next issue in line (ibid, p. 121). Their role as information providers in the system was not procedurally addressed. Therefore, instead of documenting the solution or the answer, they moved on to the next problem, and razed the possibility for downstream technicians to draw from advanced expert's advises. The consequence was a reinforcing loop whereby the experts had increasing amounts of work, since the first line of support did not have access to documented solutions, yet increasingly limited time to record their solutions (due to the fact that the problems were not being handled by helpdesk personnel downstream).

Folksam

Background[5]. At the time of the study (1991-1992), Folksam was the biggest insurance company in Sweden, with approximately 4100 employees. The studied unit was a customer-care satellite office located in the archipelago of Stockholm. The customer-care group belonged to a full service branch, which had one additional customer group. The function was thus separated in two different sites: at the branch in Nacka on the outskirts of Stockholm, and the satellite office at the island Möja. The duties and responsibilities of the two groups were identical, with the exception that the Nacka office also occasionally handled walk-in customers.

Work routines and information sharing. The activities of the customer-care center ranged from answering incoming telephone calls through updating information in existing customer databases to selling boat and home insurance. The number of incoming calls was around 50 per day and employee (ibid, 109). Documentation appeared to be tightly integrated into the work procedures, so information was available to other colleagues regardless of where they worked: at Möja, in the Nacka office, or in the headquarter in Stockholm.

Control practice. The structural change in Folksam was to add a remote customer-care centre. The employees at the remote site did not have to learn a new behavior, since the procedures in the remote office were their only experience of customer care in Folksam. They could however compare their situation with the conditions

---

5 The description of Folksam is found in Anna Moberg's licentiate thesis (Moberg, 1993) at Economic Information Systems, Linköping University.

of their peers in the Nacka office or at the headquarters. According to the interviewees, one problem, from a structural point of view, was that some activities could only be performed at the HQ, which limited the career opportunities for the Möja employees (ibid, p. 112).

The procedural control mechanisms were fairly elaborate, and embedded in the systems. Existing systems could be used to evaluate performance on group as well as individual level, but the company had chosen against this. Neither did they follow the amount of information that was contributed. The coordination and performance evaluation was instead based on mutual trust (ibid, p. 109).

The company was aware of the potential problems that could follow from geographical dispersion, especially regarding the remote workers' feeling for the department and for the company. To create a sense of belongingness, the Möja employees travelled into Stockholm a couple of times every year for education and information as well as social activities (ibid, p. 108)

Conclusion

In this chapter we have addressed one dimension in particular of telework: management control of the information-sharing activities performed by teleworkers. Our thesis was that the changed structure, compared to traditional organizations, should require revised controls: contingent changes in the structure (e.g. tasks, authority relations, etc), procedures (e.g. monitoring), and culture (e.g. signalling the importance of information sharing through the use of corporate information media). We looked at four cases of telework in the literature and tried to find examples of these changes. As these studies had not focused control, we looked for more incidental signs of changes in control, and several were identified:

- The Virtual Helpdesk may be considered an example of changes in control in terms of *structure*. A very specific set of roles and tasks were set up, where problems were routed to more advanced experts, first locally, then – if necessary – to central experts, or even outside the company. Goals for process times and number of cases helped communicate how this routing structure was expected to work. However, we argued that these controls discouraged employees from recording information and may have prevented desirable learning. Therefore, rather than providing an example of how management controls can compensate for the possible problems of too little information sharing in telework, we feel that the Virtual Helpdesk is an example where management has reinforced these tendencies by the structure they have imposed!

- Both Dial and Folksam can be considered examples of changes in control in terms of *procedures*. Dial appears to have increased its use of goals, feedback and measuring, both for individuals and on the group level. The interest in reported data shown by the group leader is a way of encouraging data recording. The Folksam case shows some of the same traits. There may be a subtle difference in the kind of roles expected of the teleworkers. Dial's employees were used to work rather independently, and some of them resented having to spend so much time on sharing information.

- Finally, in the Ericsson example management seems to have relied only on its ability to influence the *culture*, or even the culture already engrained in the new teleworkers from their previous career with Ericsson. Only traditional control procedures were used, in combination with informal contacts and briefings. With long-time organization members who are well versed in the ways of the organization, this may be thought to be sufficient. However, if there are new possibilities for information sharing associated with the new structure, there is an obvious danger that these will not be exploited, as there are few incentives encouraging them, and management may not even be aware of them. Over time, new employees may be hired who have not been groomed into the existing ways, before the introduction of telework, and the existing employees may gradually change their work habits.

These examples provide some illustrations of the kind of thinking we believe management needs to engage with in connection with the introduction of telework. To do this would be perfectly natural as most telework arrangements already involve the technical ICT solutions needed for increased communication between managers and teleworkers. We believe that intranets, for instance, could be used in much more creative ways to encourage and reinforce information sharing. It is not so much a matter of technical bandwidth, although it is likely that video will be a part of this in the future. Rather, we use bandwidth here as a metaphor: management must combine structure, procedures, and culture in order to influence actions.

Our message, then, is essentially a normative one, as yet without much empirical proof. Nevertheless, it is based on some arguments that we think are logically convincing, and fairly widely accepted:

- Information sharing is increasingly important in many organizations, as information becomes widely regarded as a source of strategic advantage.

- Telework-like situations, sometimes involving partners outside one's own organization, may come into use for a variety of reasons. By increasing the contact surface between an organization and its environment, it should provide opportunities for finding, recording, sharing, and using information derived from such contacts – i.e., new information sharing may become possible and attractive.

- Asynchronous information use, especially if it involves one person recording information that is to be used by others, will rarely happen spontaneously, at least not in a way which reflects the organization's best interests. It requires a conscious effort on part of management to control information provision and sharing.
- Management can use various controls to influence activities in an organization. These may be thought of as a control 'mix', where changes in some ingredients may motivate changes in others as well. To realize an organization's potential for information provision and sharing, the control mix must identify and emphasize these.

References

Anthony, R. N., Dearden, J. and Govindarajan, V. (1992) *Management control systems (7th ed.)*, Boston: Irwin.

Bakka, J. F., Fivelsdal, E. and Lindkvist, L. (1993) *Organisationsstruktur: struktur – kultur – processer*, Malmö: Liber-Hermods.

Davenport, T. H. and Prusak, L. (1998) *Working knowledge : how organizations manage what they know*, Boston: Harvard Business School Press.

Davenport, T. H. (1997) *Information ecology – mastering the information and knowledge environment*, New York: Oxford University Press.

Davidow, W. H. and Malone, M.S. (1992) *The virtual corporation*, New York: HarperBusiness.

Forsebäck, L. (1995) *20 sekunder till jobbet – distansarbete från bostaden*, Teldok rapport # 101, Stockholm: Teldok.

Gunton, T. (1989) *Infrastructure – building a framework for corporate information handling*, Hemel Hempstead: Prentice Hall.

Hedberg, B., Dahlgren, G., Hansson, J. and Olve, N-G. (1997) *Virtual organizations and beyond – discovering imaginary systems*, Chichester: John Wiley & Sons.

Hedberg, B. and Jönsson, S. (1978) Designing semi-confusing information systems for organizations in changing environments, *Accounting, Organization and Society*, 3(1), p. 47-64.

Keen, P. G. W. (1991) *Shaping the future – business design through information technology*, Boston: Harvard Business School Press.

Kelly, M. M. (1988) The work-at-home revolution, *The Futurist*, November-December, p. 28-32.

Larsen, K. (1996) *Förutsättningar och begränsningar för arbete på distans – erfarenheter från fyra svenska företag*, (licentiate thesis.), Department of Computer and Information Science, Linköping University.

Moberg, A. (1993, *Satellitkontor – en studie av kommunikationsmönster vid arbete på distans* (licentiate thesis), Department of Computer and Information Science, Linköping University.

Olve, N-G. and Ekström, G. (1990) *Decentralisering i verkstadsindustrin*, Stockholm: Mekanförbundets Förlag.

Petri, C-J. and Olve, N-G. (2001), Increasing the bandwidth in telework control. Chapter 3 in Petri, C-J., *Organizational Information Provision* (Diss.), Department of Computer and Information Science, Linköping University.

Porter, M. E. and Millar, V. E. (1985) How information gives you competetive advantage, *Harvard Business Review*, July-August, p. 149-160.

Rognes, J. (1999) *Telecommuting – organisational impact of home-based telecommuting* (diss.), Stockholm School of Economics.

Simons, R. (1995) *Levers of control – how managers use innovative control systems to drive strategic renewal*, Boston: Harvard Business School Press.

Strassmann, P. A. (1990) *The business value of computers – an executive's guide*, New Canaan: The Information Economics Press.

Westin, C-J (1998) *Informationsförsörjning: en fråga om ansvar* ("Information provision: a matter of responsibility", in Swedish) (licentiate thesis.), Department of Computer and Information Science, Linköping University.

17 Telecommunicating and Spontaneous Interaction

Jon Rognes

Stockholm School of Economics, Sweden

INTRODUCION

This chapter investigates how spontaneous interaction is affected by telecommuting. By using work diaries to collect data on time spent on spontaneous interaction, two groups are studied, one working form a remote location for part of the time, and one working at one location. The assumption is that spontaneous interaction is either constant during time of co-presence, or it is saved until time of presence. In the latter case this would result in more spontaneous interaction when present. The results from the study show that the spontaneous interaction is directly linked to the amount of time the person is present, and that no compensation is made for the time of absence. Spontaneous interaction takes place when opportunities occur, and lost opportunities are not compensated for by more spontaneous interaction when opportunity is given later. This has implications for telecommuting in environments where spontaneous interaction is vital such as in R&D settings and in managerial roles. Telecommuting will decrease the amount of spontaneous interaction in the group, which may influence the outcome.

Telecommuting, in this case spending a few days at home instead of at the office, constrains the opportunities for face-to-face communication during that time. This has consequences for the possibilities for informal interaction for the telecommuters. Spontaneous interaction, or unplanned informal interaction, is a part of everyday life in organisations, and has been studied in many settings. One aspect of spontaneous interaction that is little studied is the temporal dimension, or when in time the interaction takes place, including the question 'can it be delayed in time?' This study sets out to investigate this question by studying a group of telecommuters, who are separated geographically from the rest of the organisation for part of the time. The study asks: 'In what way is co-presence influencing the amount of spontaneous interaction in a group?' The chapter begins by looking into previous studies on informal interaction and communication, in order to specify the area of this study. The study is performed using a work diary, which is described in the following section. This is then followed by the results of the study, and discussion on the theoretical and practical implications of these findings.

Spontaneous Interaction

Communication, and informal interaction, plays a central role in organisations, as discussed already by the Human Relations School in the middle of the 20th century (Barnard, 1956, McGregor, 1960, Rogers and Rogers, 1976). Taking this further, social interactionism (Blumer, 1969) and social constructionism (Berger and Luckmann, 1966) stress the centrality of social processes and informal interaction to the way groups and organisations function.

Communication can be viewed as a vehicle to solve problems or unclear situations (Bensau and Venkatraman, 1996). A traditional or rational approach to problem solving is that more information will solve a problem, or, in other words, that the problem is a matter of uncertainty (Fulk and Boyd, 1991). Tushman (1988) observes that high-performing research projects showed extensive and decentralised communication within the project. A more turbulent environment was associated with mote intense and decentralised communication. Intra-firm communication was also found to be intensive in successful projects. Tushman is basing his investigation on an information processing perspective (Bensau and Venkatraman, 1996), where the issue is one of finding the right mechanism to increase the amount of information.

Another view on the role of communication in problem solving assumes that the real problem is not information on how the problem can be solved, but the formulation of the problem itself. This approach discusses ambiguity rather than uncertainty (Weick, 1979). In this case, more information will not solve the problem, but this is dependent on mutual agreement. The communication need is different in the two cases. This categorisation may also be labelled "problem finding" for the more ambiguous situation and "problem solving" for the reduction of uncertainty (Schön, 1983). Problem finding involves clarification and agreement between parties. Problem solving mainly involves information processing. Problem finding is a less structured activity, and may be more dependent on rich communication with possibilities for feedback and agreement on redirecting the focus. When dealing with ambiguous issues, face to face communication is found to be central (Noriah and Eccles, 1992a).

Informal communication has been studied by Rogers using a network approach (Rogers and Rogers, 1976, Rogers and Kincaid, 1981). The focus in the network procedure is identifying communication links and their strengths, between individuals or between cliques, within an existing system. The approach also measures various structural indexes, such as connectedness. One problem in this approach is that different communication patterns appear for different types of communication (professional, social) within the same group. Another problem is the immense number of connections that exist in a large organisation. This problem is handled by limiting the study object and by studying cliques instead of individuals. A normal procedure is to 1) gather sociometric data, 2) identify cliques and 3) superimpose these cliques on the formal organisation, to look for correspondence or misfits. For the personal communication network, a relevant variable is integration. Integration measures links *between* the persons included in the personal network.

It is suggested that there is a minimum amount of face-to-face interaction required for any type of social organisation to work effectively (Noriah and Eccles, 1992b). Forms of communication other than face-to-face media are in this situation primarily useful when presence is not possible, or when the task is not important enough to justify the possible cost of co-location. The distancing from colleagues and the use of other communication media rather than face-to-face communication may influence the result in a negative way (Noriah and Eccles, 1992a).

Creative activities such as product development seem to require some form of informal interaction to resolve ambiguities (Allen, 1984, Weick, 1995). The relationship between professional communication and physical closeness has been studied in an R&D setting by Allen. Communication is found to be greater within organisational units than between units (Allen, 1984). A physical distance of less than 30 meters is highly influential on communication. When people are more than thirty meters apart, communication decreases drastically. The findings are used to argue that separation in a group should be minimised, preferably by a circular layout. The advantage of integration-promoting facilities is also discussed, such as copiers, coffee machines and water coolers (Allen, 1984). The highlighting of such contact-points shows the importance of non-controlled and non-planned communication. Keller has investigated predictors of successful R&D projects (Keller, 1986), and finds that group coherence is the most important factor in a successful project. This, and related studies, are summarised by Brown & Eisenhardt (Brown and Eisenhardt, 1995), who suggest that internal communication improves team performance. Cross-functional teams with fluid routines and a variety of internal communication flows is thought to improve performance.

These studies all show that informal interaction is important for activities dealing with complex and ambiguous issues. A similar type of task is the task of the manager. This is studied by Mintzberg (Mintzberg, 1973, Mintzberg, 1975), who notes that managers prefer verbal communication, and that written communication is given less time and a more cursory treatment. Mintzberg characterises unscheduled meetings and telephone as informal media. These are used by managers when the parties are well known or/and when information and requests must be transmitted quickly. Unscheduled meetings are preferred to telephone calls. Very current information is also preferred by the managers, and gossip, hearsay and speculations are favoured, routine reports and written information is not. The manager is not characterised as a planner but as an adaptive information manipulator. In this role, the unplanned, informal meeting plays a vital role.

Previous studies on communication and social networks deal mainly with who talks to whom, or what communication media are used, but not when the informal interaction takes place. Allen noted the importance of proximity, but not how this is handled if the proximity varies over time. The question then arises: how is informal interaction influenced when proximity varies over time? This is the focus of the present study. To study this we need to introduce a time dimension in informal interaction. Thus we choose to label what we study 'spontaneous interaction', as will be discussed further below.

Informal interaction can either imply a non-formalised way of communicating, or communication through non-formal channels. Informal communication as communication through non-formal channels focuses on whom you communicate with. The non-formalised communication is concerned with the form of the communication, or how the exchange takes place. This is sometimes also labelled informal interaction. In this study the focus is on the form of the communication, or informal interaction. The informal interaction may be planned, but performed in an informal way, thus not having a set agenda or subject. The focus of this study is on unplanned informal interaction. To distinguish this from informal interaction, it is labelled spontaneous interaction. Spontaneous interaction is here defined as unplanned, informal interaction, and not necessarily related to a specific issue. It can be many forms of work-related chat, exchange of unfinished ideas, ad-hoc opinions, and off-the-record assistance. Spontaneous interaction is not necessarily related to work issues. Even if the interaction is social, this may have impact on mutual understanding and future co-operative activities. In the present study we have chosen not to distinguish between work related and non-work related spontaneous communication.

A further limitation is that spontaneous interaction is seen as dependent on a face-to-face situation, which means that presence is required. This limitation excludes all other media than face-to-face communication from being defined as spontaneous interaction. There may be possibilities for other definitions or other forms of spontaneous interaction, as will be discussed at the end of this chapter, but for the purpose of this study, physical presence and face-to-face interaction is seen as a requirement for spontaneous interaction. Spontaneous interaction can thus be described as unplanned and informal face-to-face interaction.

The Study

The following section will describe the organisational settings for the study, starting with a brief overview of telecommuting. Since other chapters of this book go deeper into telecommuting and its history, this chapter choose to focus on defining what is considered telecommuting in this study, to come back to telecommuting in the discussion at the end. The definition of telecommuting is followed by an elaboration on the research question, and methods used in the study.

Telecommuting

Telecommuting, or working part of the time from another location than the regular office, has been tried in several organisations over recent years (Rognes, 1999). Since the geographical distancing from colleagues during working hours makes spontaneous communication, as defined above, impossible, the telecommuting situation is ideal to study how this is handled. There may be different ways to deal with the fact that one is deprived of spontaneous communication for part of the time. One may not handle it at all, and thus have less spontaneous communication. One may become more active when at the work site, and in that way make up for the time at home. One may also use other media more, and change communication patterns, and in this way substitute the spontaneous communication with other forms of communication. In this study we have chosen to focus on two of these possibilities, and find out whether spontaneous communication is saved until later.

There is no general agreement on how to define telecommuting, and several groups have tried to establish their own definition (Rognes and Rogberg, 1996, Qvotrup, 1998). Telework is sometimes used synonymous to telecommuting, but telework is generally used in a broader sense, covering a wider array of distributed work. In most attempts to set a general definition, telecommuting is very broadly defined. When telecommuting is studied scientifically, the problem or interest area is often more specific, and more stringent definitions than the general ones are needed. In this study the following choices and limitations are made. The present study focuses on telecommuting on a part time basis, at least 1 and no more than 4 days a week should be used for telecommuting (working from home), counting only regular working hours. Overtime at home is not considered telecommuting in this case. The category of work studied is professional non-routine tasks, with an interaction component in the work. The selected and preferred group of telecommuters is a group of skilled professionals, working with R&D projects. Both solitary work and interaction is to be parts of their tasks.

Research question

This study takes interest in how the total amount of spontaneous interaction over time is affected when face-to-face communication is not an option for part of the time. In this case, we have two possibilities. One possibility is that the need to communicate is left for a later occasion. In this case, the amount of time spent on spontaneous interaction will be higher during the time when this is possible; that is when face-to-face communication is possible. In other words, the spontaneous interaction is buffered, and time at the office will be used for more spontaneous interaction by those not present all the time.

The other possibility is that the amount of spontaneous interaction is dependent on the opportunities given, and that these will be more or less constant over time. In a given organisation a certain person will have a number of instances of spontaneous interaction during a given time period. Irrespectible of the underlying mechanism, this will be observed as a constant level of spontaneous interaction, regardless of previous absence. Spontaneous interaction is not buffered, but is instead constant during presence

These two possibilities may be stated as the following two propositions:

- ***Proposition 1***
  The need for spontaneous interaction is "saved up" during absence, leading to increased spontaneous interaction during co-presence.
- ***Proposition 2***
  Spontaneous interaction is constant during co-presence.

These propositions are tested by studying a group of telecommuters, absent from the office for part of the time, as will be described in the following section.

Method

This study needed to measure how much time is spent on spontaneous interaction in various situations for selected groups. Work diaries, communication diaries, or duty studies, is a data collection method where the respondent himself logs his activities during a study period. This is an option for collecting data on spontaneous interaction. The advantage of this approach is the rich information possible to obtain, the directness of the data (not dependent on the respondents memory, but logged continuously) and that large amounts of data can be gathered with limited effort from the researcher (Yin, 1989). Disadvantages are the high need for co-operation, and the willingness of the study object to devote time to fill in the diaries. Due to the close cooperation with the studied organisation, it was considered to be possible to get full cooperation from the respondents, and thus a full set of data.

To be able to compare between the two situations - spontaneous interaction when absent for part of the time, and spontaneous interaction when present - the study was set up with two groups, one which were working from home two days a week, and one working at the regular work site. These two groups filled in detailed work diaries. Three sets of data is thus obtained, spontaneous interaction for time spent at home and at the office for the telecommuters, and spontaneous interaction (at the office) for the control group.

The diaries were designed as pre-printed schemes with one row per hour and columns for various activities. The diaries have 8 main categories, and a possibility to comment in text on each entry. The categories are as follows: e-mail, writing, reading, other computer related work, incoming telephone, outgoing telephone calls, spontaneous meetings, planned meetings, Pause and Others. After a reclassification of some activities coded in others (all of these have a written comment attached to them) others accounted for only around one per cent of the total, and were therefore excluded from the rest of the analysis. In this case, the category spontaneous meetings is the one of primary interest.

To select statistical tools, a test on normal distribution for the data had to be made. Since the fit was low, with a more flat distribution, and distribution tails was limited by the total time available in one day, the approximation to the normal distribution was rejected. This left us with non-parametric test tools. To examine if the difference in mean values between two independent groups, not normally distributed, is significant, the Mann Whitney test is recommended (Siegel and Castellan, 1988). This test investigates if the two tested samples are drawn from the same population. Since the telecommuters and the control group were selected to be similar, but not paired, a paired test was not viable in this case. On testing the difference between telecommuters at home and at the office, a paired test might be used, and in this case both a Mann-Whitney test, as above, treating each day as a sample, and a Wilcoxon test, treating each person as a sample, may be performed. The chosen approach was to use the standard module of a Mann-Whitney U - Wilcoxon Rank Sum W Test from SPSS. This approach gives an answer to where the difference between the two groups tested is significant.

The studied organisation

To study the impact of geographical dispersion on spontaneous interaction, we need to choose an organisation with spontaneous interaction, as well as with geographical dispersion. In this study we had the opportunity to follow the introduction of telecommuting in an R&D organisation. This fulfils both these criteria. The studied organisation can be described as a knowledge intensive organisation. The studied group is a unit within the research and development department in an IT-company. Of the employees, more than 70% has a university degree. The research division as a whole has basically a matrix organisation, with a line manager taking care of personnel responsibilities and administrative responsibilities. All activities are organised in projects of various sizes, and people have their main belonging in projects, which is also the main production structure. The tasks for the two groups were similar, and a parallel study showed that the organisation and the overall formal communication patterns were not significantly influenced by the telecommuting introduction. The main changes due to the geographical dispersion were found in the personal work patterns and planning for the telecommuters.

Each organisational member has a high degree of discretion on how to manage and perform his or her own work. This permits a highly flexible managerial approach, with little constraint set on subordinates. As standardisation of work process or output is difficult in this type of activity, the organisation has to rely on mutual adjustment for co-ordination. The level of bureaucracy can be described as low, with few (coercive) rules and a high amount of freedom left to each member of the organisation. The administration and the actual work tend to blend into a single effort, which calls for a high degree of communication between project members. Planning is difficult and frequent contact between project members is essential. Formality is low, and communication structures are complex and shifting. Persons can hold several roles simultaneously, and roles change frequently. This situation implies that unplanned and spontaneous interaction is a central part of the communication patterns.

The test set-up

The study is performed on an organisation where telecommuting was introduced as an option for part of the studied department. 11 out of 40 persons were allowed to work from home for two days a week. These were followed closely, together with the control group. The groups were selected from a population of possible telecommuters, where the control group and the telecommuter group were selected for posessing as similar characteristics as possible, with the same mix of tasks, age and experience. This selection was made by representatives of the company, who had previous knowledge of the participants. The groups were followed over two years, using both interviews and a detailed work diary to collect data on their work situation.

Work diaries were handed out to be filled in during a full day, either at the office or at home. The diaries were to be filled in on a minute-to-minute basis, but some respondents filled in the diary on a more aggregated level, with 5-10 minutes accuracy. This was repeated on five occasions. Each time the diaries were prompted by the project group, and support was given if respondents were unsure of how to use the form. The process of collecting the diaries included several reminders to the respondents, since there was some reluctance at first to spend time to fill them in.

The work diaries were handed out and collected during a chosen week, for both groups. The respondents were allowed to choose two typical days. This logging procedure has been followed up by telephone calls during the week and short interviews afterwards, to identify problems and adjust the diaries if necessary. The reliability of the data in the diaries was ensured by following up the first sets of diaries with short interviews. Differences were adjusted and the filling in of diaries was co-ordinated between the respondents. When prompting for the diaries, spontaneous comments were collected, and the habit of filling in the diaries was checked. The follow up procedure resulted in a high answer rate; all respondents returned at least 3 diaries per situation, with a total of 86% of all diaries returned.

Findings on Telecommuting and Spontaneous Interaction

The telecommuting initiative was followed during a period of 6 months using these diaries, with a total of 129 diaries, covering approximately 1000 hours of work time. Each diary gives us approximately 10 to 50 data points, stating activity, time and duration, and comments when needed. The time spent on each activity during the day is recorded. After collecting the diaries, the total amount of time spent at each activity is summed, and the percentage of time spent at each activity in each setting is calculated. Differences between groups and between work sites in use of time for different activities were examined using statistical methods as described above.

To investigate the propositions three tests were made on the collected data. First, the difference between telecommuters at home and at the office is tested, to see if there is a significant difference in spontaneous interaction at home and at the office. This is assumed in the set-up of the study, but needs to be verified. Then the two groups are compared for time at the office and for total time, to see if there is a significant difference in time spent on spontaneous interaction in any of these situations. If there is a significant difference between telecommuters and the control group when being at the office, with more spontaneous interaction for the telecommuters, it is likely that the spontaneous interaction is buffered by the telecommuters, and proposition 1 is supported. If there is no significant difference at the office, but a significant difference regarding overall aggregated time spent on spontaneous interaction, it is likely that spontaneous interaction is not buffered, and proposition two is supported. The results of the Mann-Whitney test are presented below, in figures 1-3.

The first test is on the difference between the amount of spontaneous interaction for telecommuters at home and at the office. The numbers in figure 1 shows that the two groups clearly differ in this respect. The probability for the two groups (telecommuters spending time at home and control group spending time at the office) to be from the same population is 0.00% regarding time spent on spontaneous interaction.

	Telecommuters at Home	Telecommuters at Office
% of time spent on spontaneous interaction	**0**	**10,3**

Probability of being from the same population P = **0,0000**

Test Statistics	Spont int.	Ranks		N	Mean Rank	Sum of Ranks
Mann-Whitney U	171,000					
Wilcoxon W	874,000	TC home	1,00	37	23,62	874,00
Z	-6,367	TC off	2,00	38	52,00	1976,00
Asymp. Sig. (2-tailed)	,000		Total	75		

Figure 1. Comparison between telecommuters meeting activities at home and at the office

The second test is on the difference between the amount of spontaneous interaction for telecommuters at the office and the control group at the office. In this case we cannot show that the two groups differ. The probability for the two groups to be of the same population is 41%.

	Telecommuters at Office	Control Group
% of time spent on spontaneous interaction	**10,3**	**8,6**

Probability of being from the same population **P = 0,412**

Test Statistics	Spont int.	Ranks		N	Mean Rank	Sum of Ranks
Mann-Whitney U	941,000					
Wilcoxon W	2481,000	TC off	2,00	38	49,74	1890,00
Z	-,821	C GR	4,00	55	45,11	2481,00
Asymp. Sig. (2-tailed)	**,412**		Total	93		

Figure 2. Comparison between telecommuters meeting activities at the office and the control group

The third test is on the difference between the amount of spontaneous interaction for telecommuters overall and the control group at the office (which is also their overall situation). Given a limit of 1% for significant differences, we can assume that the two groups differ. The probability for the two groups to be of the same population is 0,002.

	Telecommuters average	Control Group
% of time spent on spontaneous interaction	**5**	**8,6**

Probability of being from the same population **P = 0,002**

Test Statistics	Spont int.	Ranks		N	Mean Rank	Sum of Ranks
Mann-Whitney U	1453,000					
Wilcoxon W	4303,000	TC avg	3,00	75	57,37	4303,00
Z	-3,033	C GR	4,00	55	76,58	4212,00

Asymp. Sig. (2-tailed)	,002	Total	130

Figure 3. Comparison between telecommuters meeting activities overall and the control group

These tests show that the level of spontaneous meetings is not significantly different for the telecommuters and the control group for the time spent at the office. The level of spontaneous meetings is approximately at the same level for both groups for the time spent at the office. There is a slight difference in absolute figures, but this is not shown to be significant. The overall time spent on spontaneous interaction is significantly lower for the telecommuters. The telecommuters have less spontaneous meetings than their colleagues, when the total work situation is compared. This is since the telecommuters do not have any spontaneous interaction during the time at home, and the same amount of spontaneous interaction when at the office.

This answers the research question, where the first proposition; "*spontaneous interaction is "saved up" until the opportunity is given, and is increased after absence*", is shown to be incorrect, and the second proposition; spontaneous interaction is constant during the period when it is possible" is supported. This situation may result from a number of mechanisms, and in the following section we will examine a few possible underlying mechanisms for the lack of buffering of spontaneous interaction.

Discussion

The practice of telecommuting has not been as high expected in the past years (Baruch, 2000), and this may partly be explained by the effect telecommuting has on spontaneous interaction. Since a large group of telecommuters are knowledge workers with characteristics such as managerial aspects of their work, and the need to relate to complex and ambiguous issues (Moktharian, 1997, Moktharian, 1994), telecommuting will influence the ability to do this in a negative way. In an R&D environment the importance of informal interaction and face-to-face communication is stressed (Allen, 1984, Rogers and Kincaid, 1981, Tushman, 1988). This study complements these findings with the observation that the amount of spontaneous interaction is directly related to the time of presence. If spontaneous interaction is important, the amount of time when group members are co-present is also important, since this is directly related to the amount of spontaneous interaction. In activities such as the creative phase of product development, where a high level of spontaneous interaction may be positive (Allen, 1984, Tushman, 1979), co-location may be preferable for a major part the total time. Other activities where spontaneous interaction is seen as important are management-related situations and situations that are seen as ambiguous (Mintzberg, 1973, Weick, 1995). Also in these cases the level of co-presence determines the amount of spontaneous interaction, and thus the possibility to resolve minor issues that may otherwise grow into larger issues or may slow down progress. If spontaneous interaction is seen as important, co-presence is necessary, and directly related to the amount of spontaneous interaction.

Telecommuting reduces the time of co-presence, and thus the amount of spontaneous interaction, and this is less desirable for certain groups and tasks. Besides the rational, output-related issues discussed above, there is a symbolic aspect to presence and telecommuting. Telecommuting is shown to be problematic due to symbolic and cultural reasons (Perin, 1991, Perlow, 1998). The need to be present and visible at the work is linked to the concept of work and commitment to work (Perin, 1991, Bailyn, 1988), and these factors have been shown to have influenced the development of telecommuting over time in organisations (Rognes, 1999). This can be linked to the visibility aspects, which in its turns is linked to the spontaneous interaction taking place when present at the work site. Since absence is not compensated for regarding spontaneous interaction, this becomes an issue for the telecommuters.

The lack of opportunity for face-to-face communication at home is not compensated for by having more spontaneous interaction during time spent at the office. What might be the reason for this? The low impact on the level of spontaneous interaction found in this study may be parallel to the concept of communication genres (Yates and Orlikowski, 1992). Communication patterns and media use are found to be stable over time, and can be described as local institutions (Jepperson, 1991, Powell and DiMaggio, 1991). If a parallel is drawn to spontaneous interaction, the frequency in which persons in a group interact may be hard to change. If this is the case, a pattern of informal interaction is established in a group, and this is not changed even if members are absent for part of the time. This could imply, as shown in this study, that patterns of interaction in a group are relatively stable in a given situation, and not affected by temporary absence.

Another possibility is that the wish for informal interaction is not fulfilled even when persons are constantly present at the work site. If this is the case, an increase of spontaneous interaction is not possible for those who have been absent. This is not shown in the present study, but may be an explanation for the found observations, and needs to be examined further. There may be a greater need/wish for spontaneous interaction than the amount actually taking place; a latent need for spontaneous interaction that is not fulfilled. In this case every opportunity for spontaneous interaction needs to be taken care of, and utilised when possible. To find opportunities for spontaneous interaction a person needs to be alert to every chance to interact with other persons with whom he has an issue to resolve. This can be labelled opportunity scanning for spontaneous interaction, which is going on all the time in the presence of other people. With opportunity scanning we propose that each person has a number of issues he would like input on pending at each time, and takes the chance to resolve one or more of these when the chance appears. The chance appears when an unplanned encounter takes place, and an issue may be resolved by exchanging a few words. Each of these issues may not be enough to call for a regular planned contact, but can be raised at the spur of the moment when a person is at hand. When colleagues are temporarily in sight, colleagues can take advantage of this. The concept of opportunity scanning for spontaneous interaction can be linked to the favoured geographical proximity in teams discussed by Mintzberg and Allen (Allen, 1984, Mintzberg, 1973). Persons in close range rely more on unplanned meetings than colleagues located at a distance. This is in itself not surprising, since the planning and formalisation phase may be left out if the meeting can be taken care of at the spur of the moment. These instances when spontaneous meetings can take place is likely to happen when paths cross, and this happens more frequently for closely located colleagues than for more distant colleagues. On the other hand, a deliberate "path-crossing" is in many cases not an option, the opportunity needs to be grasped when present, when the colleague happens to be available, and the issue is fresh. These opportunities may be scarce, thus operating as a limiting factor for increasing the amount of spontaneous interaction. If the opportunities for spontaneous interaction are the critical factor, this would hinder an increase in spontaneous interaction during presence. In this case, when the possibility for spontaneous interaction is limited, absence will increase the need for spontaneous interaction during presence, but this cannot be compensated for.

Summary and Conclusions

The role of informal interaction in tasks involving a high degree of complexity and ambiguity has been reviewed, and the dimension of when this informal interaction is undertaken introduced. This is linked to temporary absence, and a research question was formulated around how the interaction is handled when persons are absent for part of the time. Two propositions were made; either the communication is buffered when absent, i.e. saved until later, or the spontaneous interaction is not saved, but it is constant during presence.

This study shows that the level of spontaneous interaction during co-presence is found to be constant. The conclusion is that dispersed groups do not have the same overall level of spontaneous interaction as co-located groups with an otherwise similar situation. Loss of spontaneous interaction during time of absence is not compensated for during time of presence.

Proposed future studies

These findings need to be examined further, by capturing the perceived importance of spontaneous interaction, and the reason for having more spontaneous interaction than at present. The present study will be followed by a further examination of the perceived change in spontaneous interaction in the same group, and the reasoning around this. This will indicate what importance is placed on spontaneous interaction, and what may lie behind the lack of buffering of spontaneous interaction in this case.

A limitation of this study is the definition of spontaneous interaction as dependent on a face-to-face situation. There may be possibilities for spontaneous communication using other media than face-to-face. One major difference between face-to-face communication and other forms of communication is the possibility of opportunity scanning. When physically present, coincidental presence of other persons may trigger communication. This option is at the present time not possible for most other media, except for some forms of computer presence indicators, such as ICQ and AOL instant messenger[1]. Another determining factor is that communication media other than face-to-face communication have no established pattern of spontaneous interaction.

Spontaneous interaction decreases with absence, but this may possibly be compensated for by changing the opportunities for spontaneous interaction while present. This is not covered by this study, but may be an interesting avenue to examine further. If it is possible to increase the overall spontaneous interaction at the office by some means, this may be used to balance for absence. A possibility is to increase the opportunities for unplanned meetings. Another issue to look into is if there is a optimal level of spontaneous interaction. Too much spontaneous interaction will probably take time from other activities, and will influence the amount of solitary work, which may lead to lower output.

Acknowledgements: This research has been made possible by the Swedish Council for Work Life Research (RALF) and by the Swedish Board for Communication Research (KFB). The project was performed within a program at the Institute for Management of Innovation and Technology (IMIT) at the Stockholm School of Economics.

---

1 ICQ is an acronym for I seek You. ICQ and AOL online are both programs that monitors choosen persons on the net,and makes it possible to send messages and to see if colleagues are currently on line.

References

Allen, T. J. (1984) *Managing the Flow of Technology*, Cambridge, Mass: MIT Press.

Bailyn, L. (1988) 'Freeing Work from the constraints of location and time', *New Technology, Work and Employment,* **3,** 143-152.

Barnard, C. (1956) *The Functions of the Executive*, Cambridge, Mass: Harvard University Press.

Baruch, Y. (2000) 'Teleworking: benefits and pitfalls as perceived by professionals and managers', *New Technology, Work and Employment,* **15,** 34-49.

Bensau, M. and Venkatraman, N. (1996) 'Inter-organisational relationships and information technology: a conceptual synthesis and a research framework', *European Journal of Information System,* 84-91.

Berger, P. and Luckmann, T. (1966) *The Social Construction of reality*, London: Penguin Books Ltd.

Blumer, H. (1969) *Symbolic Interaction: Perspective and Method*, Englewood Cliffs, NJ: Prentice-Hall.

Brown, S. L. and Eisenhardt, K. M. (1995) 'Product development: Past research, present findings, and future directions', *Academy of Management Review,* **20,** 343-.

Fulk, J. and Boyd, B. (1991) 'Emerging Theories of Communication in Organizations', *Journal of Management,* **17,** 407-446.

Jepperson, R. L. (1991) 'Institutions, Institutional Effects, and Institutionalism', In *The New Institutionalism in Organisational Analysis* (Eds, Powell, W. W. and DiMaggio, P. J.) University of Chicago Press, London, pp. 143-163.

Keller, R. T. (1986) 'Predictors of the Performance of Project Groups in R&D Organizations', *Academy of Management Journal,* **29,** 715-726.

McGregor, D. (1960) *The Human Side of Enterprise,* Penguin Books.

Mintzberg, H. (1973) *The Nature of Managerial Work,* New York: Harper & Row.

Mintzberg, H. (1975) 'The Manager's job. Folklore and fact', *HBR,* **Jul-Aug,** 49-61.

Moktharian, P. L. (1994) 'Modelling the choice of telecommuting: setting the context', *Environment and Planning A,* **26,** 749-766.

Moktharian, P. L. (1997) 'Modelling the desire to telecommute. The importance of attitudinal factors in behavioural models', *Transportation Research A,* **31,** 35-50.

Noriah, N. and Eccles, R. G. (1992a) 'Face-to-Face: Making Network Organisation Work', In *Networks and Organisations* (Eds, Noriah, N. and Eccles, R. G.) Harvard Business School Press, pp. 288 - 308.

Noriah, N. and Eccles, R. G. (Eds.) (1992b) *Networks and Organisations,* Harvard Business School Press.

Perin, C. (1991) 'The Moral Fabric of the Office: Panopticon discourse and Scheduled Flexibilities', In *Research in the Sociology of Organizations* (Eds, Tolbert, P. S. and Barley, S. R.) JAI Press, Greenwich, pp. 241-268.

Perlow, L. A. (1998) 'Boundary Control: The Social Ordering of Work and Family Time in a High-tech Corporation', *ASQ,* **43,** 328-.

Powell, W. W. and DiMaggio, P. J. (1991) *The New Institutionalism in Organisational Analysis*, Chicago: University of Chicago Press.

Qvotrup, L. (1998) 'From teleworking to networking: definitions and trends', In *Teleworking: International Perspectives* (Eds, Jackson, P. J. and van der Wielen, J. M.) London: Routledge, pp. 21-39.

Rogers, E. M. and Kincaid, L. D. (1981) *Communications networks*, London: The Free Press.

Rogers, E. M. and Rogers, R. A. (1976) *Communication in Organisations,* London: Free Press, Macmillan.

Rognes, J. (1999) *Telecommuting: Organisational Impact of Home-based Telecommuting,* Stockholm: EFI Publishing.

Rognes, J. and Rogberg, M. (1996) 'Telecommuting, Field, Fad or Fashion'. In *New International Perspectives on Telework. From Telecommuting to the Virtual Organisation*, Vol. 2 (Eds, Jackson, P. and van der Wielen, J.) WORC, Brunel University, London, pp. 335-346 (+2).

Schön, D. A. (1983) *The Reflective Practitioner: How professionals think in action,* New York, NY: Basic Books.

Siegel, S. and Castellan, N. J. J. (1988) *Nonparametric Statistics,* McGraw-Hill.

Tushman, M. J. (1979) 'Managing Communication Networks in R&D Laboratories', In *Readings in the Management of Innovation.*

Tushman, M. L. (1988) 'Managing Communication Network in R&D Laboratories', In *Readings in The Management of Innovation* (Ed, Tushman, M. L.) Harper Business, pp. 261 - 274.

Weick, K. (1979) *The Social Psychology of Organizing,* MA: Addison-Wesley, Reading.

Weick, K. E. (1995) *Sensemaking in Organisations,* Cal: SAGE, Thousand oaks.

Yates, J. and Orlikowski, W. J. (1992) 'Genres of Organizational Communication: a Structurational Approach to Studying Communication and Media', *Academy of Management Review,* **17,** 299-326.

Yin, R. K. (1989) *Case Study Research - Design and Methods,* Newbury Park: Sage.

18 Keeping Connected: An Analysis of Teleworking Careers

Andrea Whittle

Centre for Research Into Innovation Culture and Technology, Brunel University, UK

Introduction

This chapter presents a debate about the career implications of teleworking. Choice of the topic was prompted by numerous teleworking studies, both qualitative and quantitative, which uncovered a concern for the career implications of teleworking (Olson and Primps, 1984; Parliamentary Office of Science and Technology, 1995; Huws, 1997; Perin, 1998; Johnson, 1998). Teleworkers were expressing fears of being 'out of sight, out of mind' regarding career development opportunities because they were not physically present in the office; where they could communicate informally and socially, put in 'face time' and network. Indeed, Galpin and Sims (1999) found that many teleworkers deliberately go the office for these purposes.

Wellman *et al* (1996: 14) claim that

> despite the proliferation of telework and great public interest in the subject, there has not been much systematic research into what teleworkers actually do, their connections with their main offices, their links with co-workers (peers, subordinates, and supervisors), and the implications of their physical isolation for their careers within organisations.

This chapter attempts to address these issues, all of which can theorised as career issues, given the new model of career.

Most research has focused on *perceptions* of career impacts. Research results presented at the 1998 "Teleworking Environments" conference in Turku found that as many as 85% of respondents feared that telework at home could reduce their promotion possibilities. Even now, though,

> there is relatively little knowledge about the consequences of telework on career development (Araujo, 1998: 65).

Nevertheless, it was noted that this fear does not necessarily equate to the reality. A negative relationship was assumed because of the invisibility of the teleworker.

McCloskey and Igbaria (1998: 342) similarly conclude that

> it has been suggested that the level of telecommuting participation will have a negative impact on visibility and consequently career advancement prospects, yet empirical research has not yet addressed this issue.

However, the authors recognise that

> just because employees who have never telecommuted *believe* telecommuting will result in less career advancement opportunities does not necessarily mean that limited career advancement *will* be an outcome ... instead of focusing solely on perceptions, future researchers may choose to address whether employee and supervisor perceptions have an impact on actual telecommuting outcomes (*ibid*: 341).

Nevertheless, the fear may itself be significant enough to warrant attention. Perin (1991) suggests that the awareness of the long term career costs of working at home is a major reason why the uptake of teleworking by professional employees is much lower than predicted. Few authors have considered whether technology can reduce this invisibility, thereby alleviating career concerns. One crucial question, therefore, is whether technology can overcome this physical absence, or whether Kompast and Wagner (1998) are correct in stating that presence is not always substitutable by electronic accessibility.

This chapter attempts to address this deficiency of understanding in the field by synthesising literature from studies of technology, organisations and career into an analysis of teleworking careers. It may be argued that career research is especially pertinent in the year 2000 and beyond, given the current instability of job markets and organisational structures. It is to this issue that we shall now turn.

Career in the 21st Century

The traditional ladder metaphor of career suggests a linear, unbroken progression of occupational positions, moving upwards in the hierarchy over time. There are at least two arguments as to why this metaphor may be outdated in the 21st century. Firstly, the UK has witnessed massive changes in the *labour market* since the 70s. Increases in female participation in the workforce, especially working mothers, and shifts to part-time work, temporary contracts, self-employment and flexible work arrangements (Office of National Statistics, 1997; 1999), make the (predominantly male) full-time, unbroken, nine-to-five working patterns appear to be in the minority.

Secondly, changes in *organisations* have made the ladder metaphor outdated. It depended on steep hierarchies and cradle to grave employment. In fact, the average length of employment with firms has remained fairly constant, and the 'job for life' security only ever applied to the minority (Vandevelde, 1997).

However, high profile downsizing operations of large organisations have resulted in widespread fear over job security.

Downsizing is just one part of the move from Fordist bureaucracy to flatter hierarchies and more flexible, adaptive business structures: often labelled the 'network' form. Teleworking is believed to a crucial tool for achieving such decentralisation and flexibility. Telework is often associated with ad-hoc, as-needed solutions to individual problems, whereas the transformation into a 'virtual organisation' is often a more strategic, corporate level investment. Therefore, telecommuting is seen as only the first step toward more sophisticated working environments that we call the virtual workplace (Grensing-Pophal, 1999).

The implications of these new business structures for career is said to be clear.

> Each business environment and organisational form created its own requisite career pattern and set of managerial competencies (Hall, 1996: 15).

Career ladders were assumed to have been supported by the stability and bureaucracy of old, but the current pace of technological and market change, fierce competition and the challenge of globalisation is said to have created the need for networked organisations and therefore much more flexible careers (*ibid*).

Not only do I find myself critical of such technological and economic determinism, I also concur with Nicholson (1996) in viewing the new networked form as largely mythical and unreal. Just as bureaucracy existed more in paper than in practise, both represent ideal types rather than widely operating paradigms. However, one must acknowledge the power of this rhetoric, which has the career literature currently gripped in a state of fear and panic.

A cursory glance at the 1996 Special Issue of the *Academy of Management Executive* entitled "Careers in the 21st Century", with it's articles entitled "Career Systems in Crisis" and "Career Pandemonium", sums up the panic over career without the need to go into more detail. The articles are littered with reminders of the scope of the revolution, like "it's the end of the paternalistic model" and "the covenant between employer and employee has been broken", coupled with strategies for surviving in the 'new economy', like "pack your own parachute", "do-it-yourself careers", "portfolio careers" and "free agents".

Clearly this new career discourse displays a pervasive belief that individuals, through their actions, are the main determinants of their careers: "careers in today's world are what you make of them" (Arthur and Rousseau, 1996)! Agency is emphasised at the expense of any consideration of structural forces acting upon the individual. Research into career in new forms of work like telework is most pressing if individuals in the 21st century are to be increasingly responsible for career management.

Individuals who are organisationally important or 'core'[1], such as professional and managerial employees and contractors, but are spatially and temporally peripheral, offer an interesting position from which to analyse teleworking careers. Professional and managerial roles are those traditionally associated with 'career', as opposed to being merely a 'job'.

Telework arrangements are part and parcel of the transformation occurring in the workforce. Tolbert and Simons (1994) describe how this transformation can be labelled "externalisation": the weakening of the structures that have traditionally tied employers to employees. These structures include the geographic centralisation of work activities, regular interaction between colleagues, long-term employment and career development within a single organisation. They call for research into teleworking careers because

> given the growing pressures on most organisations for more flexible employment arrangements, including the use of work at home, such research can contribute both to immediate practical knowledge as well as theoretical understandings of career patterns in a changing workplace (*ibid*: 16).

The labour market does seem to have witnessed a transfer of *risk* from government and firms onto the individual. This is a common complaint about the new 'knowledge economy' or 'information age' (Coyle, 1999). Indeed, many teleworking schemes are set up to give firms flexibility, transferring risk and uncertainty from the firm onto the individual (Jackson, 1997). Huws (1996) terms this the 'exploitation model', with it's associated gender dimensions.

A new Theory of Career

A career theory applicable to working life in the 21st century also requires a change in definition of 'career failure' and 'career success'. Flat organisations without steep hierarchies that supported career ladders cannot define career success as simply about 'making it to the top' anymore. Instead, the career aim is said to be psychological success, with its multiplicity of goals, like family happiness or self-development. The new career contract is believed to infer that "the path to the top has been replaced by the path with a heart" (Hall, 1996: 9).

---

1 The labels 'core', 'professional' or 'expert' are not obvious categorisations, nor a natural result of the 'skill level' or 'strategic importance' of the role (Prichard *et al*, 2000). Indeed, Jackson (1997) argues that firms often wrongly categorise jobs which are crucial to customer perception of the firm as peripheral, such as customer facing salespeople. Definitions of expertise are socially constructed through power struggles (Hull, 2000). What counts as 'core' therefore has to be actively negotiated and can change over time.

This is surely a pleasant way to conceptualise the future of management without tall hierarchies and seniority-based pay, and appears at first glance fairly 'female/family friendly'. But as Nicholson (1996) points out, old attitudes still die hard. The 'promotion culture' still values promotion as the only true measure of success.

> [These] old structures persist in people's minds - in what individuals want and expect. ... people talk the change better than they walk the change (*ibid*: 43).

Although any idealistic notion of an altruistic corporation offering teleworking to give individuals flexibility may be unrealistic, there is often a business rationale behind such an idea. The primary motivation for offering teleworking schemes is the retention of trained, experienced and skilled staff (Phizacklea and Wolkowitz, 1995). This is a strategy under threat if long-term career development is not provided; staff will take their skills elsewhere eventually. Yet the career model of the year 2000 and beyond suggests career development will be decided on an individual basis. Assistance will seemingly not be forthcoming from the bureaucracy of organisations or the state, who have the scope to intervene to reduce social inequality.

Without the bureaucracy of the state or corporations, social equity is instead thought to arise from the innate fairness of the capitalist competitive system. This concept of Social Darwinism is very popular, especially in the US, as it complements the popular values of Western Society. The underlying assumption is that corporations will select fairly and objectively, that it is 'survival of the fittest'. This argument places the emphasis on structure over agency. Individuals do not have to actively promote their careers, the 'cream rises to the top' naturally through the workings of the system.

But the very idea of an 'objective' measure of performance is problematic. Although most literature on Human Resource Management would like to believe objectivity is possible, offering advise on how to eliminate what they call 'evaluator bias', I would like to content that there is no such thing as an objective evaluation. Managers invariably use *signals* of ability, which necessarily include contextual factors, such as race, sex, dress and speech, along with other intangibles like 'reputation' (*ibid*).

In interviews, the impression management skills of the applicant can influence ratings over and above actual qualifications (Gilmore and Ferris, 1989). In any case, precisely because there are usually many more able candidates than positions available, selections based on criterion like these are made even if competitors are equal, thereby *creating* inequalities (Arthur *et al*, 1989). But career is not simply about individual promotion decisions, rather it is an ongoing, everyday process of managing your impressions, maintaining relationships and constructing a good reputation. It is to these processes which teleworking career research must address itself.

A theory which understands career as based upon *personal networks* takes account of these everyday social processes. Career is not understood as an objective economic system based on the technical skill of the individual which comes into play at critical junctures like recruitment interviews or pay reviews, but as a social process which pervades the very nature of work itself. Teleworking research itself is slowly beginning to realise that the crucial issues are not technological or economic, but that teleworking developments are themselves innately *social* (Jackson, 1999a). Work does not occur in a social vacuum (*ibid*).

> Many people's jobs rely on the support, assistance and advice of others (Jackson, 1999b: 2).

Career success therefore depends not only on intelligence, skill and experience, but social skills. Goleman (1999) terms these skills emotional intelligence. He estimates that IQ only accounts for at most 10% and probably as little as 4% of career success. Personal capital includes not just intelligence, experience and qualifications, but crucially personal networks.

> Networks are a kind of personal capital. Doing well in our jobs depends to a greater or lesser extent on the work of a web of others. ... This is particularly crucial for advancement from the lower rungs of an organisation to the higher levels: these human links are the routes through which people come to be known for their abilities (*ibid*: 209).

The phrase 'come to be known for' is important: abilities and competencies do not speak for themselves but require publicity. Management are more likely to hear about an 'up and coming star' through the grapevine than through formal reporting mechanisms. The aim for the individual is to 'get your name known' with organisationally powerful people in order to construct a favourable impression in the eyes of those who could benefit your career in the future. A new set of issues arise when these processes cannot be conducted *in person* because the workforce is spatially and temporally distributed, perhaps even distributed across the globe.

Teleworking alters the relationship between importance and proximity, which have traditionally been correlated (Sproull and Kiesler, 1991).

> Further, for professionals in our society, work provides a substantial measure of self-identity. Going to the office is an important component of that identity. It takes a strong person to maintain that identity in isolation from peers and the social context of work (*ibid*: 122).

However, the issue of whether isolation may be overcome by technologies which can socially connect workers to their colleagues and superiors is not addressed here. It is to this question that the chapter shall now turn.

Technology and Social Connection

The key question is whether a lack of presence (along traditional notions of time and space) can be substitutable by electronic accessibility? If, as Jackson (1997: 7) suggests, shared temporal and spatial processes can be seen as central to the dynamics of informal networks, social connection may be hampered by electronic media that alter the conventional time and space dimensions of office work.

There is much debate over whether technology can facilitate or restrict social connectivity. Most research has been undertaken on computer-mediated communication (CMC), most recently on e-mail and the Internet. On the pessimistic side, many authors believe CMC is inferior to face-to-face (FTF) interaction, attributing this the nature of the medium as anonymous, asynchronous or low 'richness' (the number of channels for expression).

Each of these arguments can be questioned, not only for their technological determinism. Firstly, the anonymity argument cannot be easily applied to work contexts where workers are rarely anonymous. In any case, anonymity would be counter-productive for career where personal reputation and personal networks are critical. Secondly, many technologies are now synchronous or 'real time', such as Inter-Relay Chat, electronic whiteboards and video- and audio-conferencing.

Therefore, Haywood's (1998: 82) contention that synchronous communication tends to build relationships more quickly than asynchronous communication does not restrict itself to FTF interaction. Yet Durkin (1996: 9) maintains that people who have met each other personally relate to each other much better electronically than people who have not met each other. Stanworth (1991) agrees that personal, FTF contact is critical for career. She suggests that because

> management development is based as much on *who* you know as *what* you know, ... this is certainly a barrier for workers who are home-based and only have limited face-to-face contact with colleagues and superiors (*ibid*: 94, emphasis in original).

Finally, the Media Richness Theory (MRT) argument has difficulty with evidence demonstrating groups 'overcoming' the supposedly 'inherent' limitations of the medium. For example, e-mail does not 'make' people flame each other nor automatically limit social connection. Internet groups have developed 'netiquette' to implicitly or explicitly shape communication and facilitate discussions. 'Emoticons' can be used to express non-verbal signals, such as laughter or sadness, within text based interaction.

Individuals can also strategically use a medium for political means, for example by 'dropping bombs' (Brown and Lightfoot, 2000) or to deliberately circumvent face-to-face interaction in order to diffuse problematic relationships (Sproull and Kiesler, 1995). Such intentional behaviours can be mistakenly attributed to characteristics of the technology, with FTF being seen as the remedy. FTF is not necessarily superior or unproblematic, nor does it necessarily facilitate social connection. Minority groups have for a long time experienced career exclusion and marginalisation even when there are physically present in the workplace, with plenty of informal FTF networking opportunities.

It is just as inadequate to attribute career problems to physical absence as it is to criticise the electronic media for being less 'real' than FTF communication.

> When critics of electronic media argue that the new symbolic environment does not represent 'reality', they implicitly refer to an absurdly primitive notion of 'uncoded' real experience that never existed. All realities are communicated through symbols (Castells, 1996: 373).

Even if electronic media are not denigrated in this way, connection to other people by a computer network does not guarantee connection into a social network. Access does not imply inclusion. For example, a study by Steward (2000) showed that, in spite of experiencing similar health problems and having electronic connection to colleagues in the same position, teleworkers did not use these connections to discuss problems or provide social support for each other. The contention of Wellman *et al* (1996: 213) that "when computer networks link people as well as machines, they become social networks", is not strictly accurate.

Career motives may be the motivation for such *un*-connectivity: teleworkers did not want to give the impression of being ill, preferring to maintain a 'fit and committed' identity, and didn't want to be seen complaining about the 'privileged' position of teleworking. Teleworkers were also devoid of the office conversations which define what is 'unfit for work'. Although this study focuses on issues of health, the findings are pertinent to career research also. They reveal the political motives behind technology usage, the importance of performing virtual identity and the implications of being absent from office discourses.

Where does this debate leave the communication critical for teleworking careers? At the one extreme, one could extrapolate that social connection (and hence career success in the 'who you know' adage) is hampered by mediated communication because it cannot be as 'rich' or 'real' as FTF interaction, because it does not include the office discourses, or is not even used to socially connect. This fits nicely with the 'out of sight, out of mind' scenario. But another extreme position exists which would suggest exactly the opposite.

Keeping Connected

A utopian school of thought exists which believes that new media can generate communities and social inclusion, even producing emancipatory effects. Rheingold (1994) believes that Internet groups can accurately labelled 'communities' because the relationships and sense of belonging generated by virtual communication are sufficiently strong and cohesive.

Wellman *et al* (1996) also argue that people find social support, companionship, and a sense of belonging through virtual networks, even when they are composed of people they hardly know. Levels of workgroup communication can actually *increase*, and people can greatly extend their number and diversity of social contacts through membership of virtual networks (*ibid*).

The theory which underpins these arguments is that, because technology overcomes spatial distance, social connections develop out of shared interests rather than physical proximity. From this point of view, one could posit that groups of professionals, often called 'communities of practise' (Campbell, 1999), can be adequately developed and sustained, if not enhanced, within virtual environments just as in 'real world' contexts.

If teleworkers experience connection and inclusion in virtual networks without the need for FTF contact, this would be good news for teleworkers' careers. Indeed, Sproull and Kiesler (1991) believe technology can overcome career costs by giving greater visibility to people who work at home. The very title of one chapter - "Increasing Personal Connections" - summarises their optimism regarding technology.

This view is supported by the ethnographic study of Nardi, Whittaker and Schwartz (2000), aptly entitled "It's Not What You Know, It's Who You Know: Work in the Information Age". The authors describe how workers use mobile phones, Palm products, instant messaging and pagers to 'plug into' their social network. These 'intensional networks' are 'egocentric' networks that arise from individuals and their communication and workplace activity (*ibid*). This is almost the opposite of 'out of sight, out of mind', with the technology not only 'solving' the communication problem, but even facilitating increased 'connectedness'.

Recent statistics may also support this contention and cast doubt onto previous research findings. An American survey by AT&T found that over 60% of respondents saying teleworking had *positively* affecting their careers, a third reporting no impact, and only 3% said teleworking had a negative influence on career advancement. (McCune, 1998). Similarly, quantitative research by Tolpert and Simons (1994) of around 400 professionals which measured actual impact on salaries and promotion, not simply attitudes and opinions, also produced findings which contradict the common argument that working at home is associated with career costs.

> Contrary to expectations of negative career effects, employees who work at home actually have *higher* salary levels than employees who do not (*ibid*: 8). [Yet] the positive effect of working at home on salary levels may reflect organisational practises of permitting only higher status, more "trusted" (and hence higher paid) employees to work at home (*ibid*: 8).

Still, their findings reveal that the longer an employee has had work at home arrangements, the slower his or her rate of promotion (*ibid*). There may another explanation for these results than the 'out of sight, out of mind' argument.

> Typically, such employees are older, more experienced and higher salaried - i.e. employees who are probably near the top of their career ladder and hence, who should have slower rates of promotion (*ibid*: 13).

The career impact of teleworking may not be as negative as was first assumed. The issue is not as clear cut as invisibility invariably resulting in career costs, because technology may be used in ways which mitigate this problem.

Conclusion

The conclusion of this chapter is that there remains controversy over the career implications of teleworking. There exists two opposing opinions. On the one hand, teleworking is said to generate career costs due to the isolation and invisibility of teleworkers, in spite of technological connection. On the other hand, the suggestion is that career may actually benefit from teleworking, with technology offering increased connectedness. It is clear that more empirical research is needed to bring further insight into the complex dynamics of teleworking careers.

The debate over teleworking careers may be assited by reviewing the wider debates about sociality within dispersed and virtual organisations. Recent studies have brought insight to the debate over whether technology makes distance, space and place irrelevant, and that the 'virtual' can substitute (or even improve upon) the sociality of the 'real'. Contemporary thought in related fields which do not explicitly address career, but which cast doubt upon these assertions which are so often made about technology, may provide firmer answers to the career debate:

- Olmstead and Smith (1997) recommend that teleworkers attend the office regularly (note that this cannot be done with globally situated teleworkers);
- Britton *et al* (1999) maintain that cities remain important in spite of teleworking because businesses need FTF networking opportunities to build trust with clients and partner firms;
- Haywood (1998) recommend that senior staff can work away from the office, but junior staff need to at the office in order to learn;
- Prichard *et al* (2000) find that Management Information Systems cannot fully capture the knowledge of workers, and that data transfer does not guarantee learning and innovation;
- Jackson (1999c) content that a lack of FTF interaction makes knowledge creation problematic, because knowledge is not only tacit but situated;
- Handy (1995) believe that the more virtual the organisation, the more members need to meet FTF to establish trust in their relationships;

The findings emerging from the British ESRC Virtual Society? programme are also sceptical of the above contentions regarding technology. Virtuality often makes things more local, not more global. The virtual can only supplement the real, not substitute for physical contact. Virtual interaction frequently generates even more of the real variety. In fact, striving for one universal conclusion about technology may not be desirable. Teleworking career outcomes depend upon the local context. In different contexts, the same technology can produce different effects; the same effect can be produced by different technologies.

The European Union are actively promoting telework as part of their 'Information Society' project, which aims to make Europe the leading economy Knowledge Economy. The UK Government are also now promoting teleworking as part of the drive towards all things electronic: e-commerce, e-government, e-work. Technology is seen as representing economic progress and is by default conflated with social progress. It may be useful to reassess why teleworking is assumed to be a positive development (and for whom ?) and analyse more carefully the social dynamics of new 'technologically enabled' work arrangements.

References

Araujo, E. R. (1998) 'To a Problematic about Telework: Social Representations', *Proceedings of Third International Workshop on Telework* Turku, Finland September 1998: 54-74.

Arthur, M. B. *et al* (eds) (1989) *Handbook of Career Theory,* Cambridge: Cambridge University Press.

Arthur, M. B. and Rouseau, D. M. (1996) 'A Career Lexicon for the 21st Century', *The Academy of Management Review* 10, 4: 28-40.

Britton, J. *et al* (1999) 'The Potential for Home-Working in the Information Age: Case Studies from Machester's Financial and Business Services', *Proceedings of Exploring Cyber Society Conference* Newcastle, 5th-7th July 1999.

Brown, S. and Lightfoot, G. (2000) 'The Politics of Electronic Communication: E-mail, for instance', Paper presented at *Virtual Society? Get Real !* Conference, Ashridge, May 2000.

Campbell, A. (1999) 'Knowledge Management in the Web Enterprise: Exploiting Communities of Practise', in: Jackson, P. (ed) (1999) *Virtual Working: Social and Organisational Dynamics,* London: Routledge.

Castells, M. (1996) *Rise of the Networked Society,* Oxford: Blackwell Publishers.

Coyle, D. (1999) *The Weightless World: Strategies for Managing the Digital Economy,* Oxford: Capstone.

Durkin, T. (1996) 'Some Virtual Observations on Face Time: Face-To-Face Interaction vs Electronic Communication', *Telecommuting Review: The Gordon Report,* 13, 10: 9-12.

Evetts, J. (*ed*) (1994) *Women and Career: Themes and Issues in Advanced Industrial Societies,* London: Longman.

Galpin, S. and Sims, D. (1999) 'Narratives and Identity in Flexible Working and Teleworking Organisations', in: Jackson, P. (ed) (1999) *Virtual Working: Social and Organisational Dynamics,* London: Routledge.

Gilmore, D. C. and Ferris, G. R. (1989) 'The Effects of Applicant Impression Management Tactics on Interviewer Judgement', *Journal of Management,* 15: 557-564.

Goleman, D. (1999) *Working with Emotional Intelligence,* London: Bloomsbury.

Grensing-Pophal, L. (1998) 'Training Employees to Telecommute: A Recipe for Success', *HRMagazine,* December 1998.

Grint, K. (1991) *The Sociology of Work: An Introduction,* Cambridge: Polity Press.

Hall, D. T. (1996) 'The New Career Contract', *The Academy of Management Review,* 10, 4: 8-17.

Handy, C. (1995) 'Trust and the Virtual Organisation', *Harvard Business Review* May-June: 40-50.

Haywood, M. (1998) *Managing Virtual Teams,* Boston: Artech House.

Huws, U. *et al* (1996) *Teleworking and Gender,* Report 304, Brighton: Institute for Employment Studies.

Huws, U. (1997) 'Different Spheres, Different Places', in: NUTEK (1997) *Virtually Free? Gender, Work and Spatial Choice,* Swedish National Board for Industrial and Technical Development and Swedish National Resource Centre for Women, March 1997.

Jackson, P. (1997) 'Flexibility and Rigidity in New Forms of Work: Individual versus Organisational Issues', *EAWOP Symposium: Flexible Working and Employer-Employee Relations,* Verona 1997.

Jackson, P. (1999a) 'A Crisis of Identity or Too Many Hats ? The Challenge for the Modern Teleworker', *Proceedings of the 6th European Telework and New Ways of Working Assembly,* Aarhus, Denmark.

Jackson, P. (1999b) 'Teleworking with Emotional Intelligence', Unpublished article.

Jackson, P. (1999c) 'Organisational Change and Virtual Teams: Strategic and Operational Integration', *Information Systems* 9: 313-332.

Johnson, S. A. (1998) 'Teleworking Service Management: Issues for an Integrated Framework', in: Jackson, P.J. and Van Der Wielen, J. M. (eds) (1998) *Teleworking: International Perspectives: From Telecommuting to the Virtual Organisation,* London: Routledge.

Kompast, M. and Wagner, I. (1998) 'Telework: Managing Spatial, Temporal and Cultural Boundaries', in: Jackson, P.J. and Van Der Wielen, J. M. (eds) (1998) *Teleworking:*

International Perspectives: From Telecommuting to the Virtual Organisation, London: Routledge.

McCloskey, D. W. and Igbaria, M. (eds) (1998) 'A Review of the Empirical Research on Telecommuting and Directions for Future Research', in: Igbaria, M. and Tan *The Virtual Workplace,* London: Idea Group Pub.: 338-358

McCune, J. C. (1998) 'Telecommunicating Revisited', *Management Review,* 87, 2: 10-17

Nardi, B. A., Whittaker, S. and Schwarz, H. (2000) 'It's Not What You Know, It's Who You Know: Work in the Information Age', *FirstMonday,* 5, 5 May 2000

Nicholson, N. (1996) 'Career Systems in Crisis: Change and Opportunity in the Information Age', *The Academy of Management Review,* 10, 4: 40-52.

Office of National Statistics (1997) *Labour Market Trends.*

Office of National Statistics (1999) *Labour Force Survey Historical Supplement 1984-1998.*

Olmstead, B. and Smith, S. (1997) *Managing in a Flexible Workplace,* New York: Amacon.

Olson, M. H. and Primps, S. B. (1984) 'Working at Home with Computers: Work and Non-Work Issues', *Journal of Social Issues,* 40: 97-112.

Parliamentary Office of Science and Technology (1995) *Working at a Distance: UK Teleworking and it's Implications,* Parliamentary Office of Science and Technology: London.

Perin, C. (1991) 'The Moral Fabric of the Office: Panoptical Discourse and Schedule Flexibilities', *Research Series in the Sociology of Organisations,* v8, 'Organisations and Professions', New York: JAI Press: 241-268.

Perin, C. (1998) 'Work, Space and Time on the Threshold of a New Century', in: Jackson, P.J. and Van Der Wielen, J.M. (1998) *Teleworking: International Perspectives,* London: Routledge: 40-56.

Phizacklea, A. and Wolkowitz, C. (1995) *Homeworking Women: Gender, Racism and Class at Work,* London: SAGE Publications.

Prichard, C. *et al* (eds) *Managing Knowledge: Critical Investigations of Work and Learning,* London: Macmillan.

Rheingold, H. (1994) *The Virtual Community: Finding Connections in a Computerised World,* London: Secker and Warburg.

Sproull, L. and Kiesler, S. (1991) *Connections: New Ways of Working in the Networked Organisation,* London: MIT Press.

Sproull, L. and Kiesler, S. (1995) 'Increasing Personal Connections', in: Kling, R. (ed.) (1996) *Computerisation and Controversy: Value Conflicts and Social Choices,* New York: Academic Press.

Stanworth, C. (1991) *Telework: The Human Resource Management Implications,* Institute of Personnel Management: London.

Steward, B. (2000) 'Telework: Good for Whose Health ?' Paper presented at *Virtual Society? Get Real !* Conference, Ashridge, May 2000.

Tolbert, P. S. and Simons, T. (1994) 'The Impact of Working at Home on Career Outcomes of Professional Employees', Working Paper 94 - 04, Centre for Advanced Human Resource Studies, School for Industrial and Labor Relations, Cornell University, USA.

Vandevelde, H. (1997) *Beyond the CV: Securing a Lifetime of Work in the Global Market,* Oxford: Butterworth-Heinemann.

Virtual Society? Programme: see www.virtualsociety.org.uk.

Wellman, B. *et al* (1996) 'Computer Networks as Social Networks: Collaborative Work, Telework, and Virtual Community', *Annual Review of Sociology* 22: 213-239.

19 Balancing Flexibility and Stability: The Case of and ICT-department in a Knowledge-based Consultant Company

Ewa Gunnarsson

National Institute of Working Life, Sweden

INTRODUCTION

Teleworkers and teleworking in Swedish surveys are often limited to comprise employees that have a *formal* agreement with the employer to practice multi-locational work, typically given the possibility to work partly from the home and partly from a central office. This conceptual limitation then excludes teleworking categories of high-skilled professional and executive occupations. These employees have become a symbol of the modern professional worker with a *powerful* impact on defining the norm and characteristics of modern working life. These professional employees are *not* seeing themselves as teleworking, although in performing their work they have many similar characteristics in relation to spatial and temporal dimensions. These professional employees are also interesting with respect to their relatively high degree of freedom at work, as an example of modern individualised work; allowing them to '*design*' their work and working conditions according to individual preferences to a higher extent than other employees.

In this chapter I will take the opportunity to discuss and problematise some organisational challenges with respect to temporal and spatial dimensions at work at an ICT department in a knowledge-based consultant company. The case described in the chapter is part of the research project: *ICT, new ways of organising work and the construction of masculinities* (financed by the former Swedish Council for Work Life Research, today part of the Swedish Agency for Innovation Systems). The project started two years ago and will be completed in 2001.

To clarify the conceptual framework used in the project in defining the field of telework and the typology of different forms of teleworking I will here refer to the article *–Teleworking in Europe*, where Ursula Huws problematises in an interesting way the concept teleworker and teleworking (Huws, 1998). She argues that:

'We can conclude that 'teleworking' is a useful verb in that it is something that a large, and growing , proportion of the workforce engages in for at least some of their working time. But 'teleworker' is no longer a useful noun.'

...'In considering their impact, however, it is important to remember that teleworking is a tool, not an occupational category. While it forms a component of many jobs, it is rarely if ever the defining feature. Before we are teleworkers we are something else: manager, artist, programmer, secretary, translator, sales assistant or whatever. In other words, teleworking may be what we (sometimes) DO but it isn't necessarily what we think we ARE.'

(Huws,1998 p.76)

Despite the diverse forms of teleworking it is though useful to identity some types, both that are of specific interest in relation to spatial and temporal dimensions and that are developing on a numerically significant scale, such as: multi-locational teleworking, tele-homeworking, freelance teleworking, mobile teleworking (Huws, 1998)[1]. This diversity in teleworking could also be expressed as

---

1 The following typology is used by Huws (1998):
Multi-locational teleworking – this form of teleworking involves working from more than one location, typicallay partly from the home and partly from a central office. This form is developing rapidly in Northern Europe especially UK and Sweden, involving relatively high-skilled professional and executive occupations being in general a preferred choice.
Tele-homeworking- this form refers to work carried out exclusively in the home for a single employer, often associated with poor working conditions. This form is prevalent in the UK and to a lesser extent in the Netherlands but very rare in the Nordic countries. This form of teleworking typically involves low-skilled work, carried out predominantly by women.
Freelance teleworking – this form may also involve work carried out execlusively in the home, but the work is for a number of different employers and the worker is self-employed, this form is found throughout the EU and increasing in many countries, involving a diverse range of occupations.
Mobile teleworking- This form of teleworking is carried out on the move by mostly nomadic workers with telematic support. This form of teleworking is found throughout the EU but is more prevalent in the Northern countries. It is found in sales, inspection and maintenance occupation with a overwhelmingly male workforce.
For a discussion around the compatibility of different Swedish surveys see e.g. Gunnarsson, 1998a in Swedish, and 1998b in English).

'Each of these variants can be seen as corresponding to a set of connected or layered work spaces, some of them material and immediate, others distributed and virtual.'

(Wagner and Kompast, 1996)

The Case[2]

The case described, with the teleworking consultants at an ICT department, displays features from multi-locational teleworking as well as mobile teleworking. In practice of course the categories are often overlapping each other. At the time when the empirical data were collected (mainly during 1999), teleworking, by the interviewed manager, secretary and the consultants, was understood as multi-locational teleworking, working partly from the central office or clients' premises and adding the possibility to work from home. It was working from home that was seen as the teleworking part. This possibility had just recently been discussed and more formally accepted and become an option for the consultants and the secretary. To work from home was seen more as a bonus than something the consultants and the secretary planned to do on a regular basis. In this case the teleworking parts then consisted of teleworking between the clients' premises to the central office, on the move and to a minor extent from home. However, in one case the option to work from home some days/week had enabled one consultant to solve a problematic family situation.

Semi-structured qualitative interviews were carried out with the staff at the ICT-department in the consultant company. The department manager, the secretary (a more appropriate title in this case would be co-ordinator) and 14 (out of the 18) consultants, 8 men and 6 women, aged between 28 to 52 years, were interviewed about the following themes:

- *work and work-life balance,*
- *work culture,*
- *work organisation,*
- *ICT*
- *the construction of gender with focus on masculinities.* [3]

---

2 A full research report with empirical data from the project's two main cases will be published during 2001.

3 For an extensive overwiew over this field see i.e. Korvajärvi, 1998 or Kvande, 1998. Korvajärvi uses what she calls 'contextual reading' as a fruitful tool to explore and analyse gendering dynamics in white-collar work organisations.

The relatively even distribution between the male and female consultants is the result of an outspoken wish and strategy from the department manager to recruit women as well as men. This in turn is reflecting the strong societal policy in Sweden to promote equal opportunities for women and men.

The quotations used in this chapter are mainly based on the interviews with the department manager, the secretary/co-ordinator and four of the consultants (two female and two male). The quotations used are not representative for all interviewed persons but are chosen to highlight important dimensions and thought patterns in the organisation. In this chapter I have chosen to focus particularly on the following issues:

-How and by what means is a balance between flexibility, mobility and stability achieved to obtain cohesion in an organisation with continuously changing boundaries?

-How is company culture and connectedness between people created? The use of discourses, family imaginary and emotion work, as well as information- and communication technology (ICT), will be discussed as means.

-The construction of gender, with focus on masculinity, is an important issue in the project. Different gender aspects in relation to temporal and spatial dimensions as well as the sex-segregation of work, work-life balance and emotion work will be discussed and problematised.[4]

Flexible work

Flexibility has become the symbol of modern society. As a symbol the concept is used in many different ways or speaks with many different voices. Translated to the field of organisation it has been given different meanings. It could mean flexibility in the working process or in the organisational structure. Rapp and Rapp (1999) make for example a distinction between flexible work and multiflex. Flexible work then refers to an adjustment to work in different situations, both at the office and/or at home. The work is done at several places and/or with flexibility in time. Multiflex on the other hand refers to an organisational solution where the group or the department work in a flexible way and this flexibility concerns several dimensions such as: the use of ICT, the intensity of knowledge, internal contacts in the organisation and external contacts, and location. Rapp and Rapp also point at two current contradictory trends, a flexibility aiming at a division of work without organisational ties and towards the free market and another *'back to office'* trend where team work (project work) is emphasised (Rapp and Rapp, 1999).

---

4 For an overview over the field of gender and teleworking se for example: Huws et al. 1996, Gunnarsson,1994,1996,1998a, b och c, 1999, and NUTEK Förlag, 1997.

These new models of organising work are, as in the described case, often reflecting and supported by strong societal discourses focusing on flexibility expressed as an individual flexibility in time and space. This poses several problems for the researcher and some of them will be shortly mentioned here.[5] When focusing on the individual level, limiting structures and patterns in the organisation are often obscured or even made invisible. Organisational requirements and dilemmas can easily be transformed to be seen as individual dilemmas in this type of organisation.

These framing discursive contexts are of course reflected in the interview situation. The interviewed staff in the department consequently placed a stronger emphasis on organisational flexibility than stability. This must be carefully dealt with by the researcher. Focusing on flexibility, as one of the major dimension in this case study, easily makes its less glamorous but necessary *'twinsister'*[6] stability less visible.

Another characteristic for this type of white-collar organisation is that negotiations, to a larger extent than before, take place in informal arenas. This is particularly important to keep in mind when we are exploring the dynamics of gendering practices and patterns. A fruitful approach to handle this has been elaborated by Korvajärvi with her method of *'contextual reading'* (Korvajärvi,1998).

To capture this type of organisation with constantly changing spatial boundaries, traditional perspectives on organisations as structures have to be combined with more process oriented views on organisations and organisational cultures. Some are even arguing for a perspective where organisations are discussed as discourses. In this research project a combination of a structure/agency perspective and a processual view on organisation and organisational culture has been found to be most appropriate.[7]

The company and the ICT department

This Swedish company has around 1100 employees (82% men and 18% women) and has three main business areas: product- and production development,

---

5 Methodology dilemmas in relation to the project's two cases will be more elaborated and discussed in the forthcoming full research report.

6 Twinsister is here used to point at the fact that stability in the flexible organisation is gendered. Stability is often maintained by female dominated tasks or positions in the organisation.

7 For an interesting and elaborate discussion on different views on organisational cultures se e.g Korvajärvi, 1998 and Kvande, 1998. Gendering processes in organisations are also discussed by e.g. Acker, 1990. See Rapp and Rapp, 1999 for a discussion on perspectives on organisations in relation to teleworking.

industrial ICT, and competence- and process development. The company's main customers are Volvo, Ericsson and SAAB and recently Telia. The ICT department under study is part of the industrial ICT division. This division offers services in the field of system development, programming, communication, and sells IT-based tools for product development such as CAD- and PDM (Product Data Management) products. The company has been very successful and still is - its strategy has been to grow in an organic way and not to buy other companies. The manager sees this as an important advantage when building up a homogeneous company culture. When a department exceeds more than 20-23 persons a new department is created.

This particular ICT- department is seen as one of the most modern departments in the company. It is modern in the sense of having a relatively flat organisation, a modern management style and an open and friendly work culture. The quotation below shows how the department manager formulates this conception:

'I don't look upon myself as the manager for this department, but I realise that I am the manager, and I have of course a certain authority but I am not authoritarian. I see this group of people who are supposed to perform their best on their commissions, and my commission is to recruit commissions. Mentally I have positioned myself as a member of the group. I am very little the type of boss that has the door closed and you have to knock the door before you enter or positions myself through different status attributes.'

This managerial attitude has been a recruitment potential. Many of the consultants have experience from more hierarchical international organisations and they have deliberately moved to this less hierarchical Swedish company and this department in particular. They also strongly emphasise the more family friendly culture including among other things the possibility to use their right to take parental leave for young children without being punished. This will be further discussed in the part on the construction of gender later on in this chapter.

The consultants' emphasis on the desire to work in a less hierarchical organisation can be partly explained by the Nordic context with a long tradition of a democratisation process in Swedish working life. This now goes hand in hand with the new less authoritarian managerial style. This combination perhaps offers a specific Swedish/Nordic advantage in flexible organisations and in future flexible work configurations in particular.

Balancing flexibility, mobility and stability

The challenge for this ICT department is to create what could be described as a *'continuously changing balance'* between organisational flexibility and stability. This balance is aimed at maximising simultaneously the demands from the company, the clients and the individual consultants. A special dilemma lies in recruiting and retaining a workforce, the consultants, that are highly attractive on the labour market. To recruit consultants that at the same time take responsibility and identify themselves with the company, transcend boundaries and are open to new challenges, leads to particular requirements on the management to present enough interesting commissions. One strategy has also been to balance the young consultants' mobility with more experienced consultants stability.

Creating company cohesion and connectedness between actors on different spatial arenas is obtained by different means such as company culture (including modern leadership style and family imaginary), in-house commissions, emotion work and ICT.

Embedded in the company and department culture, strong and partly contradicting discourses are actively reflecting this need to balance flexibility, mobility and stability. For example the symbol for the consultant illustrates flexibility and mobility with a brave parachuting man, ready to meet challenges and transcend boundaries. The text below the picture tells us on the other hand that: *'I think there are many similarities between parachute jumping and the role of the consultant, both in jumping and in my work I prepare myself very carefully'*. Transcending boundaries and taking on challenges are then carefully planned and *'restrained'* movements and activities. In the department culture a strong emphasis is not only put on flexibility and mobility, strong discourses are also found promoting informalisation and individualisation. On the other hand, family metaphors are at the same time used in different ways as cohesion means, a company glue in connecting people.

Partly contradictory to this is the Swedish equal opportunities discourse expressed in the company culture by an active recruitment of both female and male consultants and a more family-friendly work – life contract than usually is ascribed to the ICT sector in general. Overtime work is not given status any longer and is not a desired norm in the department. The male consultants also take parental leave.

These contradicting discourses embedded in the company culture are rarely problematised and avoided by the strong emphasis that it should, to quote the secretary, *'be fun to work here'*. This also means that when interviewing the staff at the department there are more sunny stories told than sad ones, giving a picture strongly emphasising the advantages of the work place. The disadvantages in the working conditions are faded out. This is of course a methodological problem to be aware of when analysing the interviews.

The contradictions mentioned above could also be seen as a reflection of what is often discussed in terms of modern organisations being, to quote Kvande, both 'seductive and greedy' (Kvande,1999) . The work becomes at the same time an arena for individual challenges with a high degree of responsibility for the results but at the same time more demanding than traditional organisations. These modern organisations often transcend traditional boundaries between the public and the private spheres. One of the most interesting discussions in this field is the recently published book by Arlie Hochscild, Time Bind – When work becomes Home and Home becomes Work (Hochschild,1997). This book illustrates how the company Americo, well known for its great company culture, empowered independent work teams and a very family-friendly policy, from being an attractive and seductive organisation turns out to be an increasingly greedy organisation.

The family as an useful imaginary[8]

Real and virtual families are used in an intertwined way as a cultural support in the organisation. In the company culture the virtual *'company family'* is created through metaphors, concepts and symbols borrowed from the real private sphere. Most commonly used is the concept 'home' for the main office. For example the consultants talk about *'visiting home'* when they pay a visit to the main office, and the secretary is called *'the little mother'*.

The involvement of the real partners and families is seen as an important part of the company culture. When recruited to the company you are informed that you are supposed to share these values and to bring your partner and your family to the monthly social activities. You are also invited to bring your partner to different training courses if there are empty places. Different kinds of social activities are also arranged for the company children. Family involvement is by the department manager seen as an important means to create *'participation and understanding'* for overtime at dead-lines and travelling for example. Expressed in another way, the time structure of paid work is given priority when necessary and the family is supposed to be a sympathising co-worker. Research in this field even reports that while teleworking from home is part of the work, the home-based wife of a male salesmen co-worked with her husband for his company (Wagner and Kompast, 1996). Overtime is not today given high status as such in this department and more normal working hours are in general kept. But on the other hand you are supposed to contribute with *'private social time'* so brought to a head paid overtime is exchanged with unpaid private time. These family contributions are on a discursive level strong and often outspoken but, studying the practices of the individual consultants, great variations are accepted - from hardly being present at all at the social activities to a more regular presence.

---

8 The familiy as an important and useful imaginary in modern society is discussed in an interesting way in the article 'Our virtual families: Toward a Cultural Understanding of Modern Family Life, by John Gillis (unpublished, 2001).

The 'home' as a multifunctional space

The main office *'the home'* is an important hub for different activities. It is a common spatial arena for information and company identification as well as learning. In the main office you find the department manager and the secretary, and a few consultants, heading large projects, having permanent work places. The recently recruited consultant often starts with some short in-house commissions and then moves on to work on the clients' premises. These commissions are generally of long durability, from 6 month to a year and even longer. The balance between the consultants working in-house and on the clients' premises is another dimension of balancing flexibility and stability. In-house based commissions are promoting company identity and prestige. To quote the department manager:

'With the in-house commissions you get another company identity and promote company legitimacy as a knowledge-intensive company. The work done at home is seen as more prestigious and having higher quality. If you have done the commission at home you can also say that this is fully done by the company.'

A desirable balance was to have 50% of the consultants working with in-house commissions and 50% at the clients′ premises. To balance the flexibility, initiatives have been taken to create an in-house based team (inter-department) in order to develop a '*learning arena*' for a specific technical field.

Experiences from the other case-study with highly mobile inspectors show interesting parallels in the necessity to create common arenas at work. These arenas for meeting colleagues in person serve different aims for the inspectors. Here difficult judgements are discussed and praxis in relation to the rules are negotiated. The main office can also be interpreted as the location where most aspects of the *'work norm'* is continuously negotiated and where the individual confirms his or her affinity with the work.

The secretary, when asked about her own freedom and flexibility at work, states that she experiences a high degree of freedom and responsibility. Her flexibility though refers mainly to how and to some extent to when she is able to perform a certain task. Her flexibility in time could be more appropriately described as an availability, *'tailing'* the managers. If the managers are coming in late, she says, she also has the flexibility to come late and when they work over-time she adjusts her working hours to them. In other words her stability and availability is necessary to balance the flexibility for the managers (she is serving more than one) and the consultants.

Emotion work

Emotion work for example in the form of caring for the wellbeing of the consultants plays an important role, *'a key role'* according to the department manager, as a means to retain this attractive dispersed workforce.[9] It is also a means for nourishing the *'virtual family'* and the *'it should be fun to work here'* feeling, and as one of the consultants said, *' consultant companies have their faces and they work in the same way to create a feeling'*

A central person in carrying out this aspect of emotion work is the department manager, emotion work being part of modern leadership. When asked how he dealt with having so many consults working on the clients' premises and the loyalty and identification with the company, he said:

'It is a question of keeping in touch with people. Give them a ring and chat. It is a bit tricky because not everyone is interested in being contacted. They are satisfied with their technical task or whatever it is and if you phone them you feel sometimes that you are disturbing them.'

His aim is to keep in touch with every individual consultant weekly, preferably by phone but also by mail. Another cohesion and strategic means is the so-called GLUE group, with himself, the secretary and two consultants (one female and two male). The group is created as an advisory and a visionary team to support him in decision-making.

The crucial actor though for carrying out emotion work is the *'home-based'* secretary (or more appropriately co-ordinator). Keeping continuously in contact with the consultants has become an increasingly important task for the secretary. Talking to the department manager about the secretary's social role he confirms the importance of it and says *'she becomes the little mother here.'* This type of emotion work is by Hochschild referred to as *'a motherly culture'* (Hochschild, 1997). A main task for this secretary/ co-ordinator is to be the hub in the network connecting the consultants with the *'mother'* department. Maybe it is not a coincidence that the recruited female co-ordinator has a background as a guide. By the use of e-mail as well as telephone contacts and to some extent personal meetings she is *'mothering'* people. She underlines herself the importance to contact the consultant on the phone and to give them attention and care for them in different ways.

The secretary also has the main responsibility for organising the monthly social event, she says:

'I am very much occupied with organising different social activities. We are so dispersed so we need to meet each other. I organise something enjoyable so that people like to come and get to know each other and bring their families.'

---

9 A more elaborated discussion on the content embeddied in the concept of emotion work, with particular focus on gender, is found in the work of e.g Gunnarsson, 1998c, Hochschild, 1997 and Mirchandani, 1998.

ICT

ICT is a major means in connecting different spatial arenas and people. It could be described as a technical glue in the organisation. The tools used for communication between the different locations are the traditional telephone, computers connected to the internet (no portable computers) and the mobile phone. When work is done 'at home' information from different databases and so on are easily accessible through the intranet. Working on the client's premises, however, only a limited part of the information is accessible from the outside of the company through the extranet. This limited accessibility is currently a problem, for example when you have an urgent need to reach a particular competence within the company. This is not yet possible from the extranet. This limitation is mainly due to safety aspects, not opening up for competing companies to trace interesting persons to recruit. Nowadays increasing amounts of information is available on the extranet. For example, work reports are done this way and an extended homepage (with the manager's information sheet, general company news, notes from the meetings etc,) is currently updated by the secretary. This *'virtual home'* is, to quote the secretary:

'It is another way of communicating. Here the consultants can see what is happening in the company. We can inform them in a better way. They can say that this is also ours, this is in a way our home, this is where we work. Here you find pictures of all the staff and a short description of who they are. You find the notes from the meetings and the information sheet from the manager. So here they can go home without coming to the office.'

E-mail is the most frequent mode of communication used by both the department manager and the secretary when distributing company information to the consultants. Important information is sent out daily by the secretary using the different mailing lists. The mail harvest has, according to the department manager, increased enormously the last years. Personal meetings and the telephone are still the most important means in carrying out the necessary emotion work.

The technical visionary at the department argues that there are still more obstacles embedded in people's traditional communication patterns than in technology itself. What he sees as necessary is to have more visionaries than at present and a home-based arena for working with technical ideas and solutions. Other more challenging technical solutions should also be opened up for, he says, and below he is illustrating a possible shift in the use of group wear:

'What we are talking about today is to see and use information from outside the company. That is something you already have decided to present for someone, that is you have the mail function and different types of databases and you find resource persons etc. But what I mean is when you work efficiently with group wear. You use the group wear as a dynamic interactive tool and information is created by everyone in the organisation. That is different. As soon as someone is

creating information for someone else you loose this dynamic and interactive way of creating new knowledge and information.'

The *'freedom under responsibility'* discourse that permeates the organisational culture is shifting focus from formal and collective arenas to informal and individual arenas. In this shift modern ICT is also transcending boundaries between the public and the private spheres. Here the disciplining feature embedded in technology is not experienced as a forced choice giving priority to paid work (when for example opening your mail at breakfast at the start of the day), but experienced as an individual choice. The requirements of the organisation are transformed to an individual level where they are *'privatised'* and most often experienced as individual choices.

The construction of gender

On a symbolic level a traditional gender contract is very visible when you approach the company[10]. The top manager and most of the department managers are men and the secretaries and assistants are women. This is also true for the ICT department, the department manager is a man and the secretary/co-ordinator is a woman. The department manager's closest man is also a male consultant, a technical visionary. The vertical sex-segregation shows a traditional gender pattern with the men at the top and the women at the bottom. The Norwegian researcher Elin Kvande discusses this in an interesting way in relation to these un-hierarchical modern organisations. In her article, *Women in male dominated organisations – 10 years after*, she argues, referring to international research, that when organisations are decentralised through de-hierarchisation it is the middle management layer where you also find the women who are cut out (Kvande, 1999). At the same time as the job is decentralised and more responsibility is put on individuals there is a tendency to centralise strategic management. This in turn strengthens male domination at the top level.

At the consultant level you find a much more complex picture where traditional gender patterns are found in parallel with more untraditional ones. The expected sex-segregation common in the IT-sector is not found here mainly due to an outspoken policy to also recruit women framed by a shortage of consultants in general. There is neither among the consultants a conspicuous salary sex-segregation. Discussing gender at the consultants' level calls for a need for new analytical and comparative tools. For example, Thuren discusses gender with

10 The concept *'gender contract'* has been coined by Nordic researchers to describe the sex-segregated division of labour (paid as well as unpaid). Aspects of power and negociations are important elements within this concept. Gender contracts are expressed on different levels: on a structural level, a work-place level, between paid and unpaid work and within the family.

respect to *force, scope and hierarchy* (Thuren, 1996). This will be discussed more in detail in the forthcoming research report from the project.

What you also see at the consultant level is the expression of a modern Swedish construction of masculinity influenced by the strong Swedish equality policy in existence for decades, expressed for example in the use of parental leave taken by the male consultants. Contradictory to the stereotyped picture of the IT-sector, those male consultants having small children were all five using their rights to take parental leaves, from a few months to half a year on a part-time basis. On the other hand you also find traces of a horizontal sex-segregation, where the male consultants are more of technical experts than the female consultants, but both sexes are equally project leaders.

The expansion of ICT is very closely linked to global processes and not only comparative tools are needed when analysing the meaning and expressions of gender. There is also a need to link the local level to what Connell describes as *'the global gender order'* (Connell, 1997). In his theory of the construction of masculinities he argues that in the hegemonic form of masculinity in the contemporary world, the gender order is the masculinity that is linked to those who control dominant institutions. This form of masculinity is by Connell conceptualised through *'transnational business masculinities'*[11] This masculinity does not require bodily force but corporations increasingly use the exemplary bodies of elite sportsmen as a marketing tool and indirectly as a means of legitimacy for the whole gender order. Interesting features are found in the construction of masculinities within this ICT department linking it to features of the global gender order – one example is the picture of the parachute jumping male consultant as a symbol for the dominant masculinity at the company. At the same time you find features of a local masculinity, for example the parental leave among the male consultants. This modern Swedish masculinity found at this ICT-department could perhaps be conceptualised as - *men of reason and emotion.* At the consultant level you also find new forms of femininities with very similar features found in the construction of masculinities.

Concluding Remarks

The challenge for this ICT department is to create a *'continuously changing balance'* between organisational flexibility and stability. Important means in creating this cohesion and connectedness between actors on different spatial

---

11 Transnational business masculinities is according to Connnell characterized by a limited technical rationality (management theory), which is increasingly separate from science and a growing tendency to commodify relations with women (Connell, 1995 and 1997)

arenas are ICT, a strong company culture including emotion work, and in-house commissions. Partly contradictory discourses are reflecting this need to balance flexibility, mobility and stability. A strong emphasis is not only put on flexibility and mobility, you also find strong discourses promoting informalisation and individualisation. The embedded contradictions are rarely problematised. When focusing on the individual level, limiting structures in the organisation are often obscured. The interviewed persons consequently put a stronger emphasis on organisational flexibility than stability. Focusing upon flexibility easily makes its less glamorous twin-sister stability less visible.

The main office *'the home'* is an important hub for creating stability. It is a common arena for information and company identification as well as learning. The balance between the consultants working in-house and on the clients' premises here plays an important role. In-house based commissions also promote company identity and prestige. Emotion work carried out from *'home'* is an important cohesion means. The secretary is a crucial person to carry out this work. By predominantly the use of the telephone and to some extent personal meetings, she is then *'mothering'* people.

Real and virtual families are also used in an intertwined way as a cultural support in the organisation. The virtual *'company family'* is created through metaphors, concepts and symbols borrowed from the real private sphere. Involvement by real families are expected - you are for example supposed to contribute with *'private social time'*. These family contributions are strong on a discursive level but, studying the practices of the individual consultants, great variations are accepted.

The *'freedom under responsibility'* discourse that permeates the work culture is shifting focus from formal and collective arenas to informal and individual arenas. In this shift, modern ICT is also transcending boundaries between the public and the private spheres. Here the disciplining feature embedded in technology is not experienced as a forced choice giving priority to paid work, when for example opening your mail at breakfast at the start of the day, but experienced as an individual choice. The requirements of the organisation are transformed to an individual level where they are *'privatised'* and most often experienced as individual choices.

Approaching the company, a traditional gender contract is conspicuous, with the men as the managers and the women as the secretaries. At the consultant level you find a much more complex picture where traditional gender patterns are found in parallel with more untraditional ones. The expected sex-segregation common in the IT-sector is not found here.

What you see at the consultant level is a construction of masculinity influenced by the strong Swedish equality policy, expressed for example in the use of parental leave taken by the male consultants. Contradictory to the stereotyped picture of the IT-sector, those male consultants having small children were all using their rights to take parental leave. In the construction of masculinity, some features are also linking it to global business masculinities. This local/global construction of masculinity found at the ICT-department could maybe be conceptualised as - *men of reason and emotion.*

References

Acker, J. (1990) 'Hierarchies, Jobs, Bodies: A Theory of Gendered Organization', *Gender and Society*, 4:4, 139-158.

Connell, B. (1995) Masculinities, Camebridge, MA:Polity.

Connell, B. (1998) 'Masculinities and Globalization', Men and Masculinities, 1, 1:3-23.

Gillis, J. (2001 unpublished) 'Our Virtual Families: Towards a Cultural Understanding of Modern Family Life'.

Gunnarsson, E. (1994) 'News Technologies – New Opportunities for Integrating Work and Living, in G. E. Bradley and H.W. Hendrick (eds.) *Human Factors in Organizational Design and Management IV*, North Holland.

Gunnarsson, E. (1996) 'Ett äventyr med manliga förtecken – distansarbete och maskuliniteter', Dokumentation från forskarsymposiet, 5c: *Kvinnor och män i dialog om regionernas framtid*, Östersund/Stockholm: SIR och NRC/NUTEK.

Gunnarsson, E. (1998a) 'Distansarbete ur ett jämställdhetsperspektiv', i Distansarbetsutredningen, bilaga nr 4, SOU 1998:15.

Gunnarsson, E. (1998b) 'Telearbeit in Schweden aus geschlechts-spezifischer Sicht/Teleworking in Sweden from a Gender Perspective. Arbeit 2002- Zukunft der Frauen/ Employment 2002- The Future for Women . EU Commission DGV/Institute for Arts and Technology Archimedia, Linz, Austria.

Gunnarsson, E. Et al. (1998c) *Känsla och regelverk i balans*, Arbetslivsinstitutet/Folksam.

Hochschild, A. R. (1997) *The Time Bind. When Work Becomes Home, and Home Becomes Work*, New York: Metropolitan Books.

Huws, U. et.al. (1996) *Teleworking and Gender*, The Institute of Employment Studies, IES report 317, Brighton.

Huws, U. (1998) 'Teleworking in Europé', Arbeit 2002- Zukunft der Frauen/ Employment 2002- The Future for Women . EU Commission DGV/Institute for Arts and Technology Archimedia, Linz, Austria.

Korvajärvi, P. (1998) *Gendering Dynamics in White-Collar Work Organizations*, Acta Universitatis Tamperensis 600, University of Tampere, Tampere.

Kvande, E. *Paradoxes of Gender and Organizations. Gender, Organizations and Change*, Dr.polit.-avhandling. ISS, NTNU, Trondheim.

Kvande, E. (1999) 'Kvinner i menns organisasjoner – 10 år etter', Kvinneforskning, nr 3:99, 6-13.

Mirchandani.K (1998) 'Protecting the Boundary: Teleworker Insights on the Expansive Concept of "Work"', Gender and Society, no 2, April.

NUTEK Förlag (1997) *Virtually Free? –Gender, Work and Spatial Choice*, Stockholm.

Rapp, B. And Rapp, B (1999) *Flexibla organisationslösningar – om flexibla arbetsformer och flexibla kontor*,Telematik 2001, KFB 1999:30 och Teldok 36, Stockholm.

Thuren, B. 'Om styrka, räckvidd och hierarki, samt andra genusteoretiska begrepp', Kvinnovetenskaplig Tidskrift, nr 3-4, 69-85.

Wagner, I. And Kompast, M. (1996) 'Telework: Managing Spatial, Temporal and Cultural Boundaries', in New International Perspectives on Telework, P. Jackson and J. Van der Wielen (eds.) WORC Report 96.10.005.

International Perspectives

The final section of the book provides a window onto new work developments worldwide. In her reflection chapter on this topic, which introduces the chapters, Wendy Spinks identifies just some of the places around the globe where initiatives have taken place. These have produced, she shows, a rich array of experiences, although one thing is common: each one has required people to change the way they think and behave. Experiences of work innovation can be productive, rewarding and exciting; but they can also be a source of anxiety and concern. Understanding the nature of developments, and planning for and managing change effectively will be a cornerstone of success, wherever in the world this may take place.

Our journey starts in Chapter 21 with the European Union, and analysis of a major study by Werner Korte and Norbert Kordey into teleworking in 10 member countries. The data details types of teleworking, such as home-based work, SOHO-working and mobile work, and examines the relationships between them in each country. Korte and Kordey show how the EU has broadly met the ambitious goals laid down some years ago for 10 Million teleworkers by the year 2000. The popular spread of such working methods can be explained, they say, by the falling costs and improving efficiencies of ICTs, the demonstration of benefits by forerunner organisations, and by a number of EU supporting activities and promotional campaigns. The chapter goes on to discuss the barriers that still exist in teleworking and takes a look at the possibilities for future developments. Over the coming years, the authors conclude, the issues surrounding telework are likely to shift: from a focus on technological and management problems, to a concern with self-employment and more general social innovation.

The next chapter, by Lennart Sturesson, focuses on Sweden, and the discrepancies between rhetoric and practice in teleworking developments. Using discourse analysis, the chapter explores what Sturesson sees as a 'double function' of telework: that it carries with it *symbolic* values while also having an *instrumental* purpose. The former is reflected where telework is discussed as an icon of the 'information society'. The latter sees telework as a source of practical work utility: for example to bridge distances or as a means of work flexibility. Understanding these two functions helps us, says Sturesson, understand the gap between rhetoric and reality in telework, a gap that may vary between different countries and cultures.

Chapter 23, by George Lafferty, Gillian Whitehouse and Chris Diamond, moves the action down under. The chapter draws on research from a large Australian project concerned with trends and problems in the implementation of telework.

Data from the project is presented, which details, among other things, the prevalence of teleworking in different industrial sectors, the types of telework being undertaken and the reasons for telework (non) adoption. The chapter concludes that telework is not something that can easily be categorised. In Australia, the authors note, teleworking remains limited, even in those industries that are at the forefront of developments. This leads them to predict that for the foreseeable future, it is unlikely to become a mainstream form of work innovation.

From Australia we head next to Singapore, and a chapter by Geoffrey Dick and Lai Lai Tung. The authors look at the reasons that might explain a preference for teleworking among workers in Singapore, and the factors that govern the suitability of tasks for teleworking. The chapter goes on to address reasons for the amount of teleworking being undertaken in the country. It concludes that telework is still not widespread in Singapore. One reason for this, they suggest, is the negative perceptions that may exist among management and fellow workers. This leads the authors to consider the issue of culture, and how this may differ between different countries, and even companies. Culture, they conclude, is an crucial mediator in telework adoption, and is an important variable that can explain differential rates of telework adoption between and within countries.

We travel next to the United States. In Chapter 25 by Joanne Pratt, telework developments are addressed as part of the flexible deployment of workers in virtual organising structures. Data is presented that looks at the growth of teleworking and the use of ICTs in the home. Pratt also touches on the issue of culture, as raised in the previous chapter. For Pratt, the evolving culture of work that is bound up with telework developments demands new values, attitudes and practices, particularly on the part of management. Individuals must also learn to adjust, she says, as we adapt to working in domestic domains and handling the interpenetration of work and non-work relations. Pratt concludes that future work developments are likely to be increasingly caught up with the mobilisation of work and workers.

From North America we move next to the South, and Alvaro Mello and Luiz Sakuda's research, which produced the first major survey of teleworking trends in Brazil. The chapter discussed the diffusion of ICTs in Brazil, before going on to address flexibility issues and employment contracts in Brazilian work relations. It then goes on to outline the findings from their survey. This found that the major reasons for implementing telework were to make working hours and workplaces more flexible, to increase quality and productivity, and to reduce commuting times. The major inhibitors concerned a lack of management knowledge on how to plan for and organise telework; problems relating to security, confidentiality, insurance, health or legislation; and difficulties of managing and supervising telework. These issues, of course, mirror findings in other parts of the world, and the authors conclude that in Brazil, too, telework is likely grow in importance in organisations. However, greater awareness and management knowledge will be needed, they caution, for this to happen.

The final chapter of this section takes us to the East, and the teleworking opportunities for women in India. Chapter 27, by Shiri Ahuja, notes that understanding such opportunities has to take into account of the more general role that women play in the Indian workforce; in particular their lower socio-economic status and advantage, which begins back in childhood. The chapter provides details of men and women's prevalence in terms of education levels and experience of unemployment categories. It also discusses issues wrapped up with the deployment and application of ICTs in the country. The new technologies, and work innovations such as telework that they support, are a potential boon to women in India, says Ahuja. Despite a tradition in which a career came second to women's family obligations, women in India are becoming increasingly career-oriented. The search for greater educational and vocational fulfilment may prove essential, the chapter shows, given developments in the economy as a whole and the demand for ICT skills. This is particularly so, concludes Ahuka, in rural areas, where ICTs and telework provide a way of empowering women, in terms of access to the labour market, as well as enhancing their skills through tele-education. Such developments hold open the promise of bridging the gender divide – and in the process produce both micro and macro economic and social benefits.

20 Reflections

Wendy A. Spinks

Science University of Tokyo, Japan

The truly interesting aspect of flexible work arrangements, especially telework and other forms of e-work, is their universal appeal. Despite differences in national and organizational culture, examples can be found in countries as diverse as India, Australia, Japan and Brazil, not to mention the major North American and European economies. Moreover, applications range from seeking productivity gains and accommodating work/life balance in the corporate sector to combating urban environmental issues and rural problems such as depopulation or declining economic activity. In an age when globalisation is increasingly the leitmotif, albeit a controversial one, the spread of telework would certainly seem to indicate that our social and business issues are indeed global, or at least the need for new, flexible ways of tackling them.

I have had virtually identical conversations with rural residents in Wales, Tasmania and the hills of Yamagata expressing the same fears and hopes for turning their communities around. Moreover, not only does the policy planner in Helsinki voice the same concerns as the policy planner in Tokyo, what is truly remarkable is the similarity in responses to telework around the globe. One can find a business manager just as eager to implement telework in Vancouver as in the Outer Hebrides, and one who is just as adamant that it cannot possibly work in Leeds as in Sao Paulo. If the appeal of telework is truly as universal as the literature infers, what is at play here? What is the deciding factor that makes an individual, a company or a branch of government willing to adopt it and so many others refuse to entertain it?

The obvious answer is, of course, fear of change. In another blow for globalism, Spencer Johnson's *Who moved my cheese?* (G.P. Putnam's Sons, Inc., 1998) is now climbing the bestseller list in Tokyo. For those unfamiliar with this modern-day parable of two mice and two "littlepeople" prowling a maze in search of cheese, the central message is that how we react to change is a key determinant of our success in life, however we choose individually and as societies to measure that success. Sniff and Scurry, the two simple-minded mice, react to change – that is, the disappearance of their cheese – by immediately setting off in search of new cheese. Hem and Haw, the smarter, more complicated littlepeople, however, go into denial, procrastinate and cling to the hope that the status quo – a regularly replenished stock of cheese - will magically return. Convinced eventually of the finality of the disappearance of the cheese, Haw sets out on a journey of discovery about the nature of change, his reaction to it, and the location of new cheese.

Telework is also a journey of discovery. While it brings its own challenges concerning the nature of interaction, communication and just what it means "to get the job done" equitably, its primary value lies in its utility as a diagnostic tool. While the answering machine and the facsimile heralded the arrival of asynchronous communication, which has since been expanded exponentially by the advent of electronic networks and the now ubiquitous e-mail, leveraging these new technologies into aspatiality – the "unsharing" of physical space if you will – is telework's true contribution to change. In other words, by freeing us to choose where we work, telework calls into question all our location-dependent assumptions. This, in turn, allows us as individuals, businesses and societies to reassess our modi operandi and to make more informed choices about which area of the maze we wish to explore.

It is my personal view that the international appeal of telework lies in this simple fact. Namely, irrespective of nationality, natural environment, stage of economic development, religion or culture, we have all been bounded by physical location. Where do our capital cities stand? Where are our traditional engines of industry located? Where were battles lost and won? Much of our history and social fabric have been shaped or framed by physical environmental factors. It should therefore come as no surprise that breaking this link, particularly when such physical dependency has been the result of force not choice, should have a broad appeal.

So whether it is English Stilton, French camembert, Dutch edam, Danish blue, Italian pecorino, Greek feta, Californian Monterey jack, Indian paneer, or even Japanese soybean curd you are after, telework and other electronic modes of flexible work are useful additions to the general arsenal of responses to change. We may not be able to build a better mousetrap, but we can certainly experiment with the cheese. It is in this sense that the diagnostic powers of telework come into their own and span international boundaries.

21 Telework in Europe

Werner B. Korte and Norbert Kordey

empirica Gesellschaft für Kommunikations- und Technologieforschung mbH, Bonn, Germany

Introduction

In the beginning of the 1990s a working group of top-class experts in the EU laid down the goal of 10 million teleworkers by the year 2000. While this seemed hugely ambitious at the time, a representative survey of the EU population (ECaTT 2000) in 1999 arrived at a figure of a total of 8 million teleworkers in the 10 countries surveyed. Projected for the whole European Union (and counting regular as well as supplementary teleworkers), the 9 million limit has been exceeded, making it most likely that the 10 million threshold has been passed at some time during the year 2000.

With regard to absolute numbers of teleworkers, Germany and the United Kingdom lead Europe. Between them, there are more than 4 million teleworkers, i.e. almost half of all teleworkers in Europe. The Netherlands follows ahead of Italy, France, and Sweden.

	home-based teleworkers (as % of labour force)		all teleworkers (as % of labour force)	
	1999 (ECaTT)	2005 (estimate)	1999 (ECaTT)	2005 (estimate)
Denmark	4.5	10.2	10.5	19.4
Finland	6.7	16.7	16.8	29.4
France	1.2	2.4	2.9	4.8
Germany	1.5	4.0	6.0	12.6
Ireland	1.0	2.1	4.4	7.7
Italy	1.6	4.2	3.6	7.1
Netherlands	4.0	9.7	14.5	25.2
Spain	1.3	2.7	2.8	5.4
Sweden	5.3	11.2	15.2	24.3
U.K.	2.4	4.3	7.6	11.7
EU10	***2.0***	***4.2***	***6.1***	***10.8***

Table 1. The spread of telework in Europe (Gareis and Kordey 2000)

A number of factors can explain the current spread of teleworking and the dynamic behind it. Efficient and inexpensive information and communications technologies allow employees to work when and where they wish. Successful forerunner organisations have demonstrated that telework can be applied to the advantage of businesses as well as employees, and have urged many other businesses to follow suit. A great number of campaigns, support measures and support programmes of the EU commission and the various political platforms of the individual Member States were probably also of assistance.

Comparison with the TELDET study that was carried out in 1994 in the United Kingdom, France, Italy, Spain and Germany (Korte and Wynne 1996) shows that the number of teleworkers increased most in Germany. In 1994 there were only a few hundred thousand teleworkers in Germany. This figure has risen to more than 2 million within 5 years, which corresponds to an annual increase of 34%. The corresponding growth rates are 29% in Italy and only 11%, 10% and 8% in Spain, France and the U.K. respectively.

In Germany telework has developed very rapidly in the 1990s, commencing from a very low starting point. This may be explained not least by the efficient telecommunication infrastructure as well as - due to the liberalisation in the telecommunications sector - the recent strong decrease in telecommunication costs. A further reason might be the supposed German reluctance to innovate. In the United Kingdom on the other hand, negative experiences with particular forms of telework (freelance) as well as businesses' motives (cost savings, flexibility forced on workforce) may have contributed to the slow growth in telework. It may also be that there is some kind of upper limit to teleworking prevalence, which the UK and now other countries may be approaching.

However, Germany's performance looks less bright when considering relative figures: 6% of European employees already practice telework – roughly the same level as in Germany, but much less than in the Scandinavian countries (Finland, Sweden and Denmark) as well as in the Netherlands. The U.K. is also above average, while the diffusion of telework in Ireland, Italy, France and Spain is trailing behind. These figures confirm that there is a considerable North-South decline in telework: Finland have the highest rates of telework penetration with 17%, Spain, France and Italy are at the bottom with 3%. Generally, barriers for telework diffusion in Southern Europe are to be found in relation to negative attitudes, more cramped conditions in private homes, and the poorer quality of the technological infrastructure.

Types of Telework and Interrelationships

In the EU there are almost 3 million home-based teleworkers, i.e. individuals who work from home for at least one full working day per week and use a personal computer as well as telecommunications links to colleagues/ supervisor in the course of their work (see

Table 2). The majority by far practice alternating telework, i.e. they switch between their workplace at home and in the business location. 1.4 million employees can be classified as self-employed teleworkers in SOHOs (small office, home office) and 2.3 million mobile teleworkers (some of them also counting as home-based teleworkers because they spent more than one working day per week at home, or as self-employed in SOHOs). Home-based telework is thus the most widespread form of telework in Europe, ahead of mobile telework, an order that is established in most of the countries surveyed. Exceptions are Germany where all 3 organisational forms are equally spread, and the Netherlands where mobile telework is particularly widespread.

	all regular tele-workers	home-based tele-work	self-employed in SOHOs	mobile telework	mobile tele-workers, also other type of telework	mobile in % of all regular tele-workers
Denmark	6.6	4.	1.4	2.1	1.4	31.6
Finland	10.8	6.	2.2	2.6	0.8	24.2
France	2.3	1.	0.2	0.8	0.0	36.4
Germany	4.4	1.	1.5	1.5	0.1	33.2
Ireland	1.9	1.	0.6	0.3	0.0	16.5
Italy	2.9	1.	0.5	1.4	0.5	46.2
NL	8.3	4.	2.3	4.3	2.3	52.0
Spain	2.0	1.	0.3	0.5	0.0	25.0
Sweden	8.0	5.	1.6	2.3	1.2	28.9
U.K.	4.8	2.	0.9	2.1	0.5	43.3
EU10	***4.1***	***2.***	***0.9***	***1.6***	***0.4***	***38.2***

Base: All respondents in paid work (n = 3,765), weighted © *empirica: ECaTT 2000*

Table 2. Regular Teleworkers as % of Labour Force

The ECaTT survey also covered the phenomenon of so-called supplementary telework (see

Figure 1). 3 million teleworkers in the EU, i.e. 2% of all employees, telework at home occasionally. As supplementary teleworkers already have experience of working from home linked up to their employer/client via telecommunications networks, it may be that many of them turn into regular teleworkers in the near future. With regard to supplementary telework there are also country specific features. In contrast to telework in the stricter sense, supplementary telework is particularly widespread in Ireland, Sweden and the Netherlands. In these countries there is roughly one supplementary teleworker for every regular teleworker.

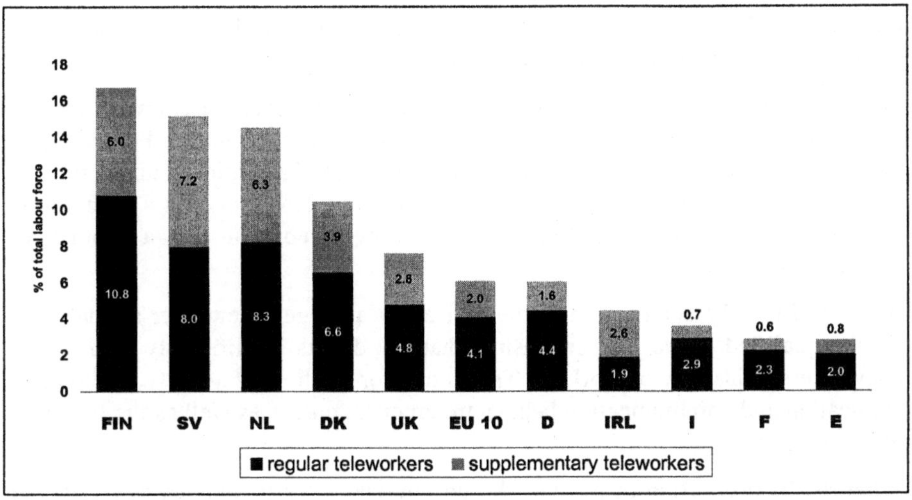

Figure 1. Regular And Supplementary Teleworkers In % Of Labour Force (Empirica 2000)

Key Characteristics of the Teleworking Population

In contrast to the labour force as a whole, results from ECaTT surveys show that 75% of teleworkers in Europe are male and only 25% female. This finding stands in sharp contrast to the widespread opinion that telework is a predominantly female domain. The image of the female clerk or typist, who via telework manages to combine work and family more satisfactorily, as often presented in the media, only represents a minority of teleworkers in Europe.

The majority of teleworkers belong to the middle age range. 63% of all teleworkers in Europe are aged between 30 and 49 years of age (compared to 56% of non-teleworkers). The average age of the European teleworkers lies, as with all other employees, at around 39 years.

However, there are significant differences to non-teleworkers with regard to education and self-employment. Teleworkers are mostly highly qualified. Every third teleworker is furthermore either self-employed or employed but enjoying freedom to decide his own terms of employment due to his position in the business. Such employees need to be involved in the business activities more often, even outside normal office surroundings.

Obviously there are also groups of people with other motives for telework such as better compatibility of family and work or reduction of commuting. For example, every 2nd woman who practises home-based telework has children under the age of 6. Every 6th teleworker (against every 27th non-teleworker) has a commuting distance of more than 50 km. Such groups, however, represent only a minority of teleworkers.

In view of the characterisation of the typical or 'average' teleworker as male and highly qualified, it is not surprising that he differs significantly from non-teleworkers in his way of working. This is true for the field of activity, technology application and communication behaviour, amongst others, as well as the length of working hours.

Whereas the proportion of people who do physical work is understandably lower among teleworkers than non-teleworkers, a disproportionately high number of teleworkers have managerial functions or carry out tasks that require a high level of qualification. A large number of teleworkers are also characterised by long commutes. Furthermore, teleworkers are significantly keener to communicate: almost all teleworkers report to having frequent external business contacts.

The average amount of working time spent teleworking is rather low. Permanent home-based telework - which many expected to become the dominant form at the beginning of the telework discussion in the 80s - did not come about. In fact, as

Table 3 shows, only a small percentage of all (home-based) teleworkers are working at home *permanently*. Most spend the larger share of their working time at a central office. This may also be the reason why telework is less 'visible' in society, as it might be assumed on the basis of the large number of individuals teleworking.

about 1 day	51.3%
about 2 days	30.3%
about 3-4 days	4.6%
almost 5 days or permanent	6.3%
n.a.	7.5%
all home-based teleworkers	100.0%

Table 3. The intensity of telework in the EU[1] (Gareis 2001)

Alternating telework, with its switching workplaces, has clearly become the norm throughout Europe. For the majority of job tasks, a part-time presence in the office continues to be necessary or desirable. Further research is necessary to establish whether the amount of time teleworkers spend away from the central office, i.e. at home or on the road, tends to increase or decrease as teleworking spreads to more and more workers.

Finally, differences between actual and contractually fixed working time deserve consideration. Whereas every 2nd non-teleworker works more hours per week than contractually agreed, this figure increases to 80% for teleworkers. However, the data does not explain what the principal cause is: Is the extra workload a consequence of telework - or do people who tend to be workaholics become teleworkers more often than average? This finding has particular implications for the quality of life of teleworkers and their households – it may be that quality of working and non-working life is in many cases compromised by this work form.

Establishments Applying Telework

30% of all establishments in Europe already practise regular telework. Including supplementary telework the diffusion rate is 36%.

1 Numbers are weighted averages for the EU10, see Empirica 2000.

Again there are significant differences between the European countries. Diffusion of telework amongst establishments has spread farthest in Scandinavia and the United Kingdom. The Netherlands, Ireland and France are in the middle, Germany takes on 8th position with Spain and Italy behind. The latter countries have a business size structure that differs noticeably from all the others, with a considerably higher share of micro-companies.

In the course of time the number of establishments practising telework has increased noticeably; it has grown even faster than that of teleworkers. Obviously, a large number of establishments have introduced telework in the second half of the nineties. Throughout Europe, less than a third of establishments have been carrying out telework for 5 or more years. Half of the establishments have introduced telework over the last 2 years.

However, the extent to which telework has diffused inside of establishments, i.e. the number of teleworkers as a share of total establishment workforces, is on average still modest.

Telework is still mainly practised by large organisations. Nearly ¾ of all European establishments with 500 or more employees offer tele-workplaces. This figure is significantly lower for smaller establishments. Only 15% of all establishments with less than 10 employees employ teleworkers.

Establishments from the financial and business services sector take a leading role. The number of teleworkers working in this sector is above average. Other service sectors' representation as employers of teleworkers lies below the average.

There are significant differences between single-site companies and establishments belonging to multi-site companies. Amongst the single-site companies only a quarter practise telework, compared to more than half of the establishments belonging to multi-site companies.

Almost every 2nd business that employs teleworkers uses them for specialised activities. The second most mentioned tasks are management tasks. In spite of evidence of some negative attitudes, telework is obviously suitable for managers. By far the least practised forms of telework are secretarial duties. The strong need for communication and impromptu acts as the main barrier here.

As has already been mentioned, the number of teleworkers per business is rather low. The majority of establishments have less than 10 teleworkers. On the other hand, the number of mobile teleworkers per business is comparatively high. There still exists a large growth potential in those establishments that already practise telework.

Teleworkability and Interest in Telework

The further development of telework requires, amongst others:

- sufficiently large numbers of jobs which are suitable for this work form,
- sufficient interest of employees to practice telework as well as
- establishments' willingness to provide tele-workplaces.

Suitability

Two thirds of European employees carry out activities suitable for telework on at least one day per week. This includes office work, tasks such as writing and telephoning that are generally carried out at a desk, as well as working on the computer or with machinery controlled by a computer. Thus, at least part-time telework is 'technically' feasible in 2 out of 3 cases.

Employee interest

There is no lack of interest in telework by employees. In addition to employees who already practice telework, an average of 60% of employees show an interest in working from home either occasionally, alternating or permanently throughout Europe. As might be expected, the interest of those looking for work is even stronger. When comparing the result with the 1994 findings, interest has increased even further. Today by far the strongest interest is expressed in Sweden; all other countries are relatively close to the average.

Establishment interest

The situation on the establishments side is not quite as clear cut. Amongst telework practising establishments, almost half show an interest in extending telework.

Amongst those establishments which do not so far practice telework, interest in implementation is comparatively low. In addition to 36% of telework practising establishments a further 12% show an interest in an introduction. Germany had highest levels of interest with 17%.

However, the growth potential of telework is not limited to additional establishments introducing telework. The largest, as yet untapped potential lies in further intra-company diffusion (i.e. expansion of already existing schemes), taking into account that the average number of teleworkers per establishment is still very low.

From the Past to the Future

Telework has benefited strongly from the political support it has attracted in the last decade, but is developing somewhat differently than expected. Permanent home-working continues to be rare, whereas the numbers of alternating teleworkers (spending no more than one day per week at home) and supplementary teleworkers (spending even fewer hours outside of the office) has grown considerably. Teleworkers are not necessarily recruited from segments of the population that many think would benefit most, namely women and mothers/fathers of young children. Rather it seems that teleworkers are generally hard-working, highly qualified men. Teleworking is being used as a means to make work more flexible in line with the demands of present-day business. More flexibility also often seems to mean more physical mobility, casting doubt on the original hope that telework might decrease traffic volumes.

In spite of a readiness to introduce telework, European decision makers continue to see major barriers for telework diffusion (see

Figure 2). They regard data protection and data security problems as particular obstacles: 62% rank them as important or very important. Other barriers mentioned by a large share of establishments are: concerns regarding productivity and quality of work (55%), insufficient knowledge of how to plan and organise telework as well as problems regarding management and supervision of teleworkers (54% each). Lack of employee interest plays only a minor role (37%) while possible resistance from works councils and trade unions (25%) ranks last.

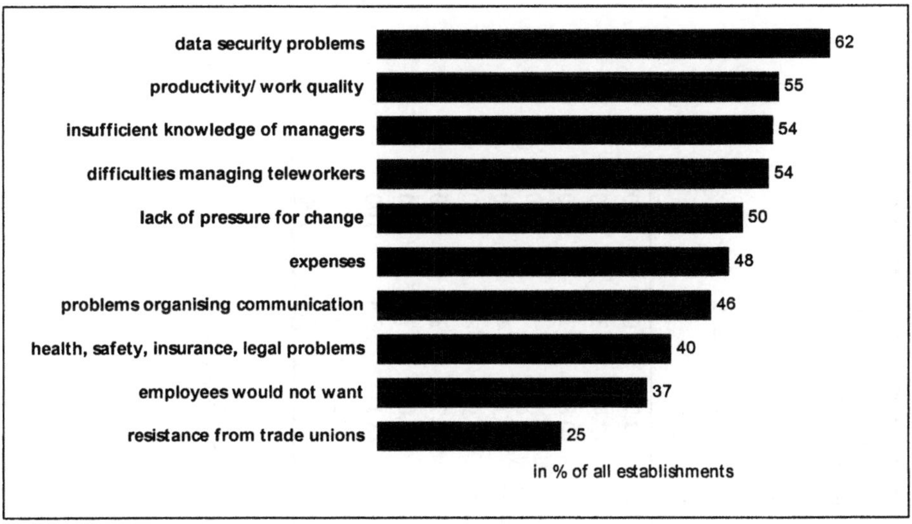

Figure 2. Barriers to telework In Europe 1999 (in % of all establishments) (Empirica 2000)

These concerns are reflected in the behaviour of employers with regard to current teleworking practice and plans for future implementation.

	establishments that do not practise telework already (as % of all est.)				establishments that practise telework already (as % of all est.)				total
	concrete plans for introducing	interest in introducing	no interest in introducing	n.a . on interest	concrete plans for extension	interest in extension	no interest in extension	n.a. on interest	
Denmark	5.3	6.0	28.8	2.0	25.4	12.6	9.7	10.2	100
Finland	1.5	9.2	28.7	1.3	15.6	18.2	12.4	13.1	100
France	4.4	7.0	49.8	3.8	4.5	6.5	10.8	13.3	100
Germany	5.6	11.6	50.6	2.3	5.2	10.8	5.0	8.9	100
Ireland	3.6	8.7	43.6	5.0	7.3	9.7	7.1	14.9	100
Italy	2.3	8.0	62.2	10.2	1.9	4.3	2.9	8.1	100
Netherlands	5.0	7.7	37.0	4.3	5.0	16.3	11.7	13.0	100
Spain	4.5	6.1	60.8	8.6	1.9	6.4	4.0	7.7	100
Sweden	2.2	4.5	29.3	2.4	17.0	13.3	18.1	13.3	100
U.K.	2.1	3.7	37.4	1.8	10.8	12.8	11.2	20.2	100
EU10	***3.9***	***7.6***	***48.3***	***4.4***	***6.3***	***9.6***	***7.7***	***12.1***	***100***

Table 4. Practice, plans and interest in any kind of telework in % of all establishments 1999 (Gareis & Kordey 2000)

Gareis and Kordey (2000) have developed a model for the projection of teleworker figures in European countries to the year 2005. For this purpose, establishment-side data on interest and plans regarding the introduction (or extension) of telework was used. In

Table 4 establishments currently using and not using telework are differentiated according to these variables. These findings are now integrated in a model of the future development of telework that takes into account the following data derived from the ECaTT representative surveys: (a) current spread of telework, (b) current share of establishments employing teleworkers, (c) share of establishments with concrete plans for or only interest in introducing/ extending telework.

Using a calculation model based on certain (conservative) assumptions (see Gareis and Kordey 2000), 2005 diffusion rates for all countries surveyed in ECaTT can be estimated (see

Table 1 on the first page of this chapter). They range between 5% in Spain (up from 3% in 1999) to 29% in Finland (17%).

Telework will increasingly become a normal work form for Europeans in the coming years in view of rapid technological development, significant decreases in costs, businesses' urge for more flexibility and employees' willingness to work outside the traditional office. Whereas making work locationally flexible was considered a technological problem in the 1980s and an organisational and management problem in the 1990s, in the first decade of this century we expect the main focus of the telework debate to shift to the issues surrounding self-employment, with possibly much more far-reaching (and controversial) implications for the social status quo in the European union.

References

ECaTT Consortium (2000) *ECaTT Final Report*, Luxembourg: Office for Official Publications of the European Communities.

Gareis, K. (2001) 'The Electronic Freelancing Economy: Myth or Reality? An Overview of Evidence', STAR Issue Report No.9, http://www.databank.it/star.

Gareis, K. and Kordey, N. (2000) 'The Spread of Telework in 2005', in Stanford-Smith, B. and Kidd, P.T. (eds) *E-business – Key Issues, Applications, Technologies*, 83-90, Amsterdam et al.: IOS Press.

Korte, W. B. and Wynne, R. (1996) *Telework - Penetration, Potential and Practice in Europe*, Amsterdam et al.: IOS Press.

22 The Role of Telework: In Rhetoric and Practice

Lennart Sturesson

Department of Technology and Social Change, Linköpings University, Sweden

Introduction

Thinking about discrepancies

The concept of telework (alternatively termed telecommuting) was established in the USA in the 1970s. In Sweden, which is the focus of interest in this chapter, the idea took life in the 1980s. Since then different names have been tagged on the phenomenon, and a lot of interpretations have been made. One of the key expectations was that the use of information and communication technology (ICT) would lead to a rapid and wide increase in telework. However, in statistics we find discrepancies, still existing, between the visions of quantitative growth and what actually has occurred. This has been noted but seldom made the central issue of discussion (Huws et. al. 1990, Korte et. al. 1996).

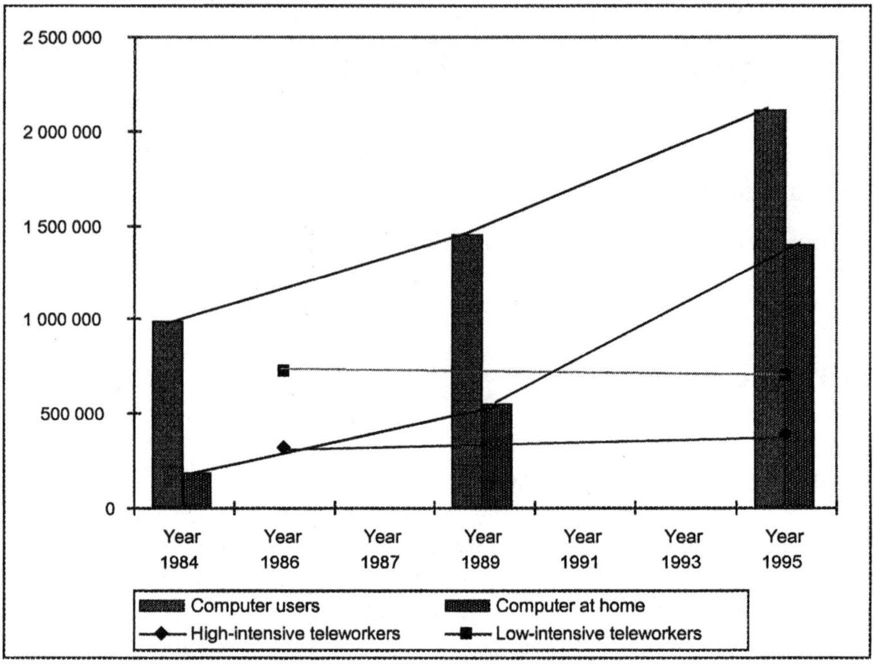

Figure 1. Users of personal computer and teleworkers in Sweden.

In European statistics, Sweden seems to be one of the leading countries regarding teleworking at home (see preceding chapter). However, the number of teleworkers has not risen since the middle of the 1980s, when about 8% of all employed were teleworking. This was also in a period when computers at home were rare. Related to this development, a second discrepancy is visible, but even less discussed: the availability and use of ICT has increased, while the growth of telework has been much slower (Figure 1). The number of personal computers has increased dramatically, first in the work place and then in households. But the number of persons working at home has increased slightly between the middle of the 1980s and 1990s respectively. On the other hand, the discussion about telework has continued, the interest in telework has increased in the media, and more people have expressed interest in working remotely.

Telework is a phenomenon that has been expected to solve many different issues: decreasing transport and commuting, decreasing air pollution and energy consumption, providing flexibility for enterprises and individuals, and resulting in productivity gains, lower office costs and easier recruitment, among others. Some of these visions have been fulfilled, yet there are a number of discrepancies connected to the expectations. For example, telework has not become the means to bridging temporal and geographical distances, or decreasing travel, and in particular, commuting to work. This was an early theme in the USA as well as in Sweden, and in both countries the expectations regarding telework seem to have been triggered by research reports. Examples are those of Jack Nilles in California and the research institute Nordplan in Sweden. Researchers looked at the method of working at home, or in neighbourhood offices, as a solution to traffic congestion and long commutes (Nilles et al 1976, Engström m fl 1985).

The aim of this chapter is to show how rhetoric and discourse analysis can be used in order to understand better the discrepancies between telework *rhetoric* and *practice*, mostly based on material from the case of Sweden. A key to the analysis is the double function of telework: *symbolic* and *instrumental*. These two pairs of concepts will also be coupled together in the analysis. The empirical base of the chapter has been presented extensively in the thesis *Telework: technology, rhetoric and practice* (in Swedish) with Sweden as the arena of discourse and two Swedish municipalities promoting telework as primary cases for the study of teleworkers' practice (Sturesson 2000).

Theoretical Framework: Actors, Rhetoric and Discourse

Many actors are involved in the rhetoric as well as the practice of telework. Individuals and organisations try to promote or inhibit telework. In order to understand telework – its rhetoric and practice – we must consider the actors' different interests and goals. Actors may have very concrete aims, such as selling computers, increasing telecom traffic, protecting the environment, handling everyday life for oneself and the family. There are also many means to achieve such aims, for example starting a local project, constructing suitable technology, advertising, changing laws and rules, etc.

The aim of rhetoric, generally, is to convince or persuade the public (or some part thereof). With a linguistic term, speech acts are used to convince others of something – for example, that one's products are the best, or that certain claims and ideas are worth consideration and adoption. In the case of telework, the aim could be to introduce 'telework', with its symbolic or instrumental functions, to sell products needed for telework, or to spread the actor's specific view of telework. Thus rhetoric is short-term as well as long-term used to shape a 'preferential right of interpretation'. Different groups of actors try to get their interpretation established as *the* meaning of telework.

In order to stipulate that there is a *discourse of telework* one must make it plausible that there is a shared view of what telework is. In that case, some things will be regarded as self-evident and not needing to be declared, and some beliefs will not be questioned as they are *taken for granted*. The search for these 'taken for granted' issues is the main procedure in this discourse analysis.[1]

Characteristic of a discourse used in a social-scientific analysis is that it has an influence on individuals and society. In analysing discourses, it is also important to understand that discourse is shaped and reshaped not only by actors, but also by the context of the discourse and by other discourses. The discourse is always existing in a textual context, and this textual context always exists in a social context (Fairclough 1992). Therefore, the analysis of the discourse of telework also comprises the search for other discourses that have had impact on it.

To summarise, an analysis of rhetoric and discourse can cast light upon interpretations of the notion of telework that are produced by different actors. Successful rhetoric can shape a discourse, where the actor's ideas are prominent, and make other actors take up his arguments consciously or unconsciously. But the final aim of rhetoric is not winning a rhetorical or discursive victory, but influencing other social groups to take action.

Symbolic and instrumental functions

Some researchers on telework have noticed that telework, beside its more obvious instrumental functions, also has symbolic meanings, but they have not elaborated the issue (Huws et. al. 1990, Aune 1996, Gunnarsson 1997, Armstrong 1997, Rognes 1999). At a first glance, it is easy to think that the symbolic meanings are connected to the rhetoric, and that the instrumental meanings are to be found only in practice. However, a closer study of the discourse shows that this one-dimensional scheme is insufficient: there are instrumental functions present in rhetoric while telework sometimes functions in a symbolic way even in practice. Therefore, both pairs of concepts are relevant: rhetoric—practice and symbolism—instrumentalism. Putting those two pairs together in a co-ordinate diagram, as in figure 2, provides a strong instrument for analysing the concepts of telework, and it works as a tool for the *researcher's interpretation* of telework.

---

1 The expression 'taken for granted' thus is closely related to concepts like figure of thoughts, paradigm, spirit of the time and culture.

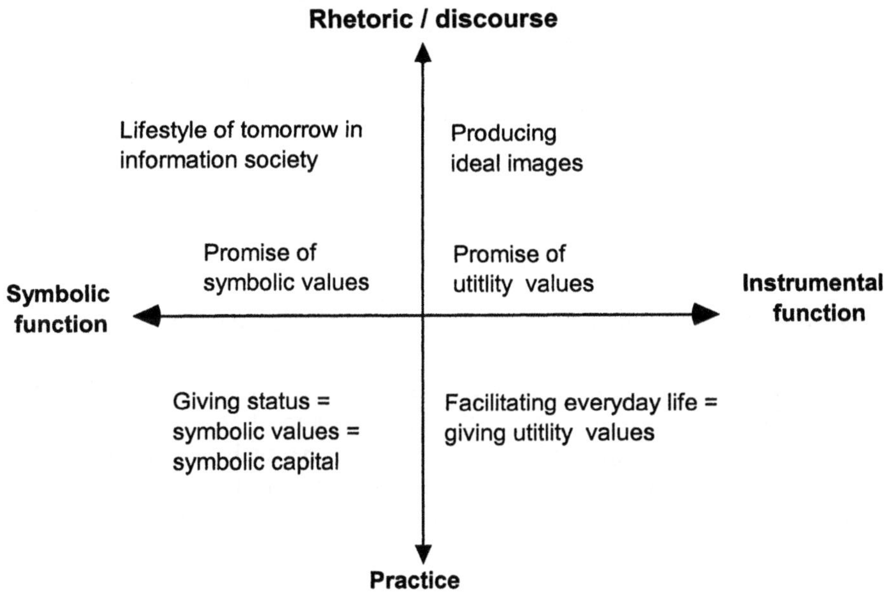

Figure 2. Analytical interpretations of telework

The symbolic function of telework in rhetoric (upper left quadrant in figure 2) turns out as a symbol for lifestyles and for a type of society that is believed to be attractive to the teleworker. At the same time, telework is a totem pointing towards this society. It is heavily inspired by modern society's belief in Progress, and in the Information Society as something we are supposed to adopt (Beckman 1995 analyses 'IT' in this way).

> Examples from rhetoric: A man with golf set and laptop on Arlanda Sky City, or a man performing his work in the little red cottage of his garden (a Swedish archetype).

In practice, the symbolic function of telework (bottom left quadrant) can give status to the performer; teleworking increases his/her symbolic capital.

> Example: The freedom to "work where you want" (Canon advertisement), and to be trusted to regulate one's own work and working conditions.

The instrumental function of telework in rhetoric (upper right quadrant) is to produce ideal pictures, describing all the things telework can do and accomplish.

Example: Saving energy, resolving congestion, coming home to children when they are awake instead of working overtime in the office.

The instrumental functions of telework in practice (bottom right) are those promises that are fulfilled in everyday life.

Example: Working more effectively at home. Better handling of work time and leisure time.

The Swedish Case of Discourse and Practice

In this section we will outline how the discussion of telework has developed in Sweden. The focus is on the rhetoric and the development of a discourse, in order to find those taken-for-granted issues relevant to the analysis suggested by the diagram above (Figure 2). Here, they are found in the history of telework in Sweden. This is contrasted to the practice of telework and the way in which Swedish teleworkers experience it.

Discourse

The Swedish discussion of telework begins around 1980 in a little town named Nykvarn near Södertälje, about 50 km south-west of Stockholm. By this time there were stories about telecommuting in the USA and telework in the UK and other European countries. Swedish human geographers, as an experiment, started a neighbourhood working centre for employees working in Södertälje and Stockholm. The project, the idea of a neighbourhood working centre, and the notion of telework in common were discussed in the media from the time of preparation, during the time of the experiment, 1982-84, and during 1985, when the centre was managed by a private enterprise.

In the beginning, many researchers, trade union journals and other specialist magazines were engaged in the debate. Daily papers also reported on the project and soon also joined the discussion about telework. Early on the discussion was polarised between the promoters of telework and its critics. Researchers wishing to reduce commuter traffic were in support of telework, while unions, afraid of isolating female homeworkers, were against it. After a few years the two conflicting discourses were melded into one, and telework was accepted as a way of solving practical problems for employees. This occurred after TCO (The Swedish Confederation of Professional Employees) had concluded that the 'trap for women' was really not an issue, since most teleworkers appeared to be men with qualified positions.

The statements taken for granted in the discourse of the 1980s were the following: ICT is distance bridging; it makes work possible from any location; telework gives more flexibility to individuals; telework can provide jobs to rural districts; travelling is decreased by teleworking; neighbourhood working centres are socially 'good' solutions.

After a sharp drop in interest and almost no public discussion of telework in the latter part of the 1980s, the issue re-emerged strongly around 1990. One issue was a new public project promoting telework. This was a huge building project in Nyköping 100 km south of Stockholm, named 'Nya Nyköping' (New Nyköping). The project was presented in 1989 with its first stage projected for 1992-93. When the building market began to collapse in the first years of the 1990s, the project was sharply reduced, but the marketing of telecommunications, telework, and telework centres sped up. In the marketing, a rhetorical figure, 'the intelligent society', was invented. The meaning could be interpreted as either 'living intelligently' near nature and not spending time on long commutes – or using 'intelligent technology' like telecommunications and computers. The two ingredients in this figure, nature and technology, were thoroughly mixed in the marketing, and it is possible to identify the 'intelligent society' with an older rhetorical figure, the 'technical pastoral', a notion used by Leo Marx (1964) and, in Sweden, Martin Kylhammar (1985).

The local discourse of telework was reinforced by the talk of 'cable bundles' and digital ISDN technology, demonstrated in Nyköping. In Nynäshamn, another city within commuting distance from Stockholm, the municipality promoted a telework project together with committed users. The project aimed at informing the public about telework and encouraging commuters to stay home one or two days per week instead of making the long journey to Stockholm.

The national discourse was strengthened when Telia, Canon and other suppliers of ICT services and equipment started to promote telework in late 1994. At that time, every paper and magazine 'had to' write about telework, and most of them did so in positive, not to say enthusiastic, terms. Thus, the discourse of telework was stable for some years in the middle of the 1990s, with the interest (measured in the number of articles and books) decreasing somewhat after 1997.

What was taken for granted in the discourse of the 1990s had not changed much from the beginning of the 1980s. Two differences are significant, though. The 'information society' became a main component in the discourse in the 1990s. Nya Nyköping, with its 'intelligent society', inspired this talk. So did the Swedish prime minister, Carl Bildt, and his IT commission, both of whom mixed telework into the 'information society' and 'information highways' following an international trend (Karlsson 1996). The other difference was that telework in the 1990s was described as individual work, at home or otherwise. The neighbourhood centre as a community of workers was no longer a central concept, and telework was not spoken about as contributing to the social life of the neighbourhood.

The fact that telework had not yet 'taken off' was of course a problem. It was often explained away with reference to resistance from employers, and through noting that working rules, insurance, and taxes were not (yet) adapted to telework.

Swedish actors

Actors with a strong interest in the phenomenon have tried to influence the discussion and interpretation of telework. Five groups of actors are identified in my thesis. Three of them are usually mentioned in the literature: 1) employers, 2) governmental and local authorities, plus politicians, and 3) teleworkers. The new ones that I introduce are *suppliers* and *knowledge brokers*.

Employers seem, in general, to have been reluctant or indifferent to telework, with some exceptions, especially in the ICT industry. *Politicians* were interested in telework as a means of reducing transport and saving energy, and municipalities in order to guarantee jobs to their area. This interest, however, grew slowly. From the third group, *teleworkers*, only a few showed up in the discourse at the beginning, and their spokesmen, trade unions, started out as opponents. From the study of the Swedish discourse, two additional actor groups emerge. First, there are producers and sellers of ICT services and equipment, named *suppliers*, who together have formed the strongest and most active actor group in the 1990s. Second, the history of telework points strongly to another, fifth, group: researchers, consultants, and journalists jointly named *knowledge brokers*. Some of these knowledge brokers are strong promoters of telework, others are neutral analysts, and in a few cases they are sceptical or critical. Researchers, whatever their stance, however, are like public authorities encouraging the phenomenon by giving it respectability. The interest from journalists and the media is also crucial in order to make the discourse accepted.

Practice

For a full analysis according to the dimensions of figure 2, we need to look at the practice. How is telework in fact performed in Sweden? We can learn specifically, from the two above mentioned towns where telework was promoted, how teleworkers there describe and regard their practice. The teleworker is not a typical Swede. Few blue collar workers are teleworkers, and only a minority are women. Most are self-employed men or professional employees. They are well educated and established in their professional roles, they have a high level of independence, work many hours, and travel in their jobs.

Questionnaires and interviews show that there was a widespread and expanding interest in telework in Sweden in the 1990s. The messages from the promoters of telework seemed to have been accepted by large groups; the critical voices in the media became more rare and media interest in telework appeared high. Whether the interest depended on good arguments or on the needs of individuals is difficult to know. The conclusion, however, is that there were some factors that slowed down the expansion of telework. For example, the lack of, or poorly functioning, ICT for use in homes was shown to be the most evident discrepancy between the visions and practice.

Most teleworkers have had an instrumental view, using telework to solve problems in everyday life. A few interviews have indicated, though, that telework has also been used as a status symbol or as a marker of lifestyle. The fascination with communication technology that could occasionally be seen with teleworkers also indicates that the devices for telework have had a meaning beyond their function as work tools. But the idea that telework means freedom has not been accepted by all. Even though most teleworkers have said that it provides flexibility, they don't find it advantageous in every situation – it also involves an adjustment of everyday life to the demands of work, regarding both scope and scheduling of time.

To summarise, the message in general is tempting, especially when dealing with the instrumental advantages of telework. But the message contains exaggerations that soon become apparent to people beginning to practise telework. Tempting messages are not enough; they must be capable of being transformed into something that is perceived as having either symbolic value or utility value.

Understanding the Discrepancies

This study shows that most of the discrepancies between rhetoric and practice still remain. They have not disappeared with time, which suggests that deeper understandings are needed, rather than only references to simple time-lags. Now we will argue that these discrepancies can be better understood by looking at them in the two dimensions of figure 2: on the one hand, the rhetoric/discourse—practice of telework, and, on the other, its symbolic—instrumental functions.

Telework, pastoral and the information society

In rhetoric two symbolic functions of telework have been found: it is a symbol for the 'information society' and an example of 'technical pastoral'. The latter connects the modern 'information society' to an older metaphor, the idyllic countryside (upper left of figure 2). For this telework is a perfect tool, according to the rhetoric, because of its capability to bridge distance in time and space; it is possible to be modern in the pastoral countryside. This has been a convincing picture, widespread in the media and in peoples' minds. But in fact most teleworkers have not been rural people; rather, they have been commuters near large cities.

In the recent history of Swedish telework, there have been many connections between the telework discourse and the discourse of the information society, as well as 'IT'. Those three are often described together. Information technology is the basic technology of the information society, and will bring about great social changes and development. For telework, 'IT' is the technology that makes telework interesting in the discourse – by itself the old habit of professionals to bring work home hardly seems worthy of notice. For true believers in the 'information society' there is a need for good and concrete examples of the advantages. Telework seems to have been such an example. If we suppose that the main aim is not to promote telework, but to establish the image of the information society, telework may be seen as a good, concrete example that has been well publicised and positively received.

Telework thus works both symbolically and instrumentally, as a sign of modernity and as an example of a concrete content: we can embrace it both with our heart and our brain. Telework – as the lifestyle of tomorrow and part of the information society (upper left quadrant) – is acting into all other quadrants of Figure 2: it gives Ideal images, Symbolic value and Utility value. However, its degree of success has not lived up to the expectations, which can be explained by the teleworkers' tendency to rank Utility value first.

Ideal images and utility value

In rhetoric, telework is also described with instrumental connotations. These can be found in a line of ideal images (upper right quadrant, Figure 2). These images promise utility value (bottom right) to the teleworker, but there are also some important discrepancies here. In the empirical material, nine ideal images are identified and listed in table 1 below, with a brief evaluation of practice (elaborated in Sturesson 2000: 326-346).

Ideal image	Practice summary
ICT is a bridging technology that implicates telework	ICT have been seen more in and between organisations than for home based work
Telework is a mode of organisation for the flexible company	It is possible to understand telework as part of changes in organisations towards flexible companies and flexible work
Telework brings about higher efficiency and productivity	Individuals experience higher efficiency. There is little evidence for this as well as company productivity, however
Telework is a manifestation of mobility	A majority of teleworkers also work on journeys. Many teleworkers have duties that make travelling a part of their job
Telework gives space of action to the individual – and the home becomes an 'electronic cottage'	Many teleworkers but not all experience a large amount of flexibility. There are hints that it is the total situation of life that determines the degree of utility value of telework
Telework makes possible more integration of functions into living areas	Evidence for this has not been found
"IT to every household"	Telework can be seen as a contributing factor for diffusion of ICT into households
Telework is a solution of energy and environmental problems	Hitherto measurable effects have been small, but these are expected in the future
Telework is an instrument for regional policy (decentralisation)	There are, in Sweden, very few examples of teleworking bringing new work to rural areas

Table 1. Ideal images and their outcome in practice.

Many of the ideal images have not been realised. This seems to depend on several different hurdles for telework, but mostly it seems to be a question of exaggerated expectations. Many of these have their ground in the belief in the power of technology, specifically ICT, to bridge distances and solve problems that are in reality not technical but part of the complex interaction of social and economic as well as technical factors.

Conclusion

The use of discourse analysis in studying telework in a historical context makes it possible to analyse the discrepancies in rhetoric and practice in an integrated manner. This gives deeper understanding of the mechanisms between conceptions in rhetoric and the outcomes in practice. It makes it possible also to study the activities of proponents compared to the activities and expectations of the teleworkers and their families. Further, it is obvious that telework has many dimensions. The phenomenon is more understandable if we accept its symbolic as well as its instrumental functions, and if we include these dimensions in the same analytic scheme as the rhetoric/practice dimensions. Here, we have found that the 'symbolic rhetoric' has been a strong one in peoples' minds, but that the outcomes in activities in practice have been modest. On the other hand different ideal images depicted in 'instrumental rhetoric' have been transformed into utility value in different ways and scope. Thus, in Sweden the utility values seem to have been most important to teleworkers. The model used, integrating discourse analyses with the study of practice, can not be generalised to other countries directly. However, it may be suggested that it can be used to identify cultural differences that impact upon both rhetoric and practice.

References

Armstrong, N. (1997) 'Negotiating the boundaries between 'Home' and 'Work': A case study of teleworking in New Zealand', in E. Gunnarsson and U. Huws (eds.) *Virtually Free? – Gender, Work and Spatial Choice.* (B 1997:7) Stockholm: Nutek.

Aune, M. (1996) 'The computer in everyday life', M. Lie and K. Sørensen (eds.) *Making technology our own? Domesticating technology into everyday life.* Oslo: Scandinavian University Press.

Beckman, S. (1995) 'A world-shaping technology', in M. Karlsson and L. Sturesson (eds.) *The World's Largest Machine. Global Telecommunications and the Human Condition.* Linköping: University.

Engström, M., Paavonen, H. and Sahlberg, B. (1985) *Grannskap 90. Närarbete på distans i informationssamhället.* (Report 16) Teldok. (Neighbourhood 90. Close work at a distance in the information society).

Fairclough, N. (1992) *Discourse and social change.* Cambridge: Polity Press.

Gunnarsson, E. (1997) 'Gendered faces? Teleworking from a Swedish perspective', in E. Gunnarsson and U. Huws (eds.) *Virtually Free? – Gender, Work and Spatial Choice.* (B 1997:7) Stockholm: Nutek.

Huws, U., Korte, W. and Robinson, S. (1990) *Telework: Towards the elusive office.* Chichester: Wiley.

Karlsson, M. (1996) *Hi-tech visions as global fashion – The international diffusion of information technology policy.* (Working Paper Nr 168) Linköping: Tema T.

Korte, W. and R. Wynne (1996) *Telework. Penetration, potential and practice in Europe.* Amsterdam: IOS Press.

Kylhammar, M. (1985) *Maskin och idyll – Teknik och pastoral hos Strindberg och Heidenstam.* Malmö: Tema and Liber Förlag. (Machine and idyll – Technology and pastoral in Strindberg and Heidenstam).

Marx, L. (1964) *The machine in the garden: Technology and the pastoral ideal in America.* New York: Oxford University Press.

Nilles, J. M. et al (1976) *The telecommunications-transportation tradeoff. Options for tomorrow.* New York: Wiley.

Rognes, J. (1999) *Telecommuting. Organisational impact of home-based telecommuting.* Stockholm School of Economics (Diss).

Sturesson, Lennart (2000) *Distansarbete: teknik, retorik och praktik.* (Studies in Arts and Sciences no. 204) Linköping: Univ. (Telework: technology, rhetoric and practice).

23 Telework in Australia: Findings from a National Survey[1]

George Lafferty, Gillian Whitehouse and Chris Diamond

The University of Queensland, Australia

Introduction

This chapter is based on research undertaken as part of a larger, on-going project on current trends and problems in the implementation of telework in Australia.[2] It draws on a national organisational survey which examined the extent and type of teleworking in different industry sectors, and managers' perceptions about the advantages and problems of this form of work organisation. The goal of the chapter is to provide an overview of the survey findings and what they suggest about the prospects for an extension of teleworking in Australia in the near future.

Since the 1970s, there have been numerous predictions of the rapid growth of telework (for example, Nilles 1998). However, reliable estimates of the extent of teleworking are rare, with cross-national comparisons particularly difficult. The general consensus in the existing literature is that the United States has the highest incidence of telework, while Australia ranks low-to-middle among developed economies (see Diamond and Lafferty 2000; Di Martino 2001; Lafferty and Whitehouse 2000: table 1). Cross-national comparisons have been inhibited by the widespread variations in definitions of telework and the survey methods used to identify the incidence of telework. There has also been a dearth of research on the implementation or non-implementation of telework at organisational level, and the experiences of managers, employees and unions within those organisations. Given this lack of consistency and organisation-based research on the incidence of telework, we devised a national survey to provide basic information about the prevalence, problems and advantages of telework in Australian organisations.

Our initial task was to adopt a suitable definition of telework. In the telework literature, definitions have varied according to the number of days or hours per week that people are engaged in telework, types of technology being used (for example, computer and modem, mobile phone), location (for example, home, mobile office), and the types of work relationship (for example, employee, sub-contractor or self-employed). For this project, we used a definition which included four important elements. First, we focused on 'regular' teleworkers, which we defined as employees consistently working 40 per cent or more of their hours (that is, two days per week for full-time employees, or the pro rata equivalent for part-time employees) away from the central workplace. Second, teleworkers in the project had to have the legal status of employee, rather than being sub-contractors or self-employed; that is, they had to be integral members of the organisation. Third, we focused on telework that was integrated into organisational management and planning, rather than occurring in an *ad hoc* fashion. Finally, teleworkers had to be utilising telecommunications and information technologies, so that they were performing work on-line. Some researchers also include, within their definition, individuals who use a non-networked computer and then mail a disk to the office, but this leads to an extremely broad definition of telework (see Qvortrup 1998: 24).

The main focus of our research was on teleworking that was consistent with all four of our criteria. However, we also collected material on teleworking without definitional restriction, in order to contrast the prevalence of this with 'regular' teleworking. Overall, our survey was designed to identify:

- the prevalence of telework in selected industry sectors;
- the types of telework being undertaken – that is, the alternative location being used and the types of technology adopted;
- the characteristics of teleworkers;
- the reasons for adoption or non-adoption of telework;
- the perceived advantages and disadvantages of telework.

Survey Design and Implementation

We used a commercial database of Australian organisations to construct a sampling frame, concentrating on those industry sectors that we identified from earlier analysis as most likely to introduce telework. These were: Finance and Insurance; Property and Business Services; Communications; Government Administration; and Manufacturing. Incorrect industry coding in the original sample meant we also ended up with organisations in other industry sectors, particularly Wholesale and Retail. Our final industry breakdown thus also includes Wholesale and Retail, and an 'Other' category covering the remainder of industry sectors. We limited our sample to organisations with 10 or more employees as the management and organisational issues we were interested in are unlikely to be as relevant in smaller organisations. In order to ensure a sufficiently large database of responses, we began with a sample of around 7500, which covered all Australian states and territories and included public and private sector organisations with both single and multiple locations.

The survey questionnaire was suitable for administration through an in-house Computer Aided Telephone Interview (CATI) system. The CATI system offered a number of advantages: a good response rate; relatively accurate survey data; and rapid data collection. Since it is based on direct personal contact with respondents, response rates tend to be maximised. Moreover, the accuracy of the data is enhanced as interviewers can deal with misunderstandings immediately and respondents cannot miss questions.

Working with a team of interviewers, we implemented the survey in late 1999. Interviews were conducted with human resource managers or their equivalents. The interviewing process was checked throughout by supervisors who monitored phone calls and conducted random call-backs to check answers to specific questions. The latter process showed an accuracy rate of around 99 per cent on the questions selected for checking. A response rate of over 80 per cent meant that we did not need to access the full sample in order to attain our goal of around 2000 responses. On completion of interviewing we had obtained responses from 2595 organisations – the first large-scale national survey of telework in Australian organisations. Subsequent data cleaning reduced the number of usable cases to 2528.

Survey Findings

Our first concern was to identify the prevalence of telework in the selected industries. The results are reported in Table 1 for two different categories of organisation: (A) those with any types of telework (without time or other definitional restrictions); and (B), those with 'regular telework' (in line with our definition above, this required having employees teleworking for at least 40 per cent of their working time). Table 1 shows that around 44 per cent of the organisations in our sample had used telework in some form, although only around 15 per cent had used 'regular' teleworkers.

Although we had deliberately selected organisations in the industry sectors we considered most likely to have telework, these are clearly not the only areas where telework is utilised, as the 'Other' category in Table 1 shows. Consequently, applying weights to correct for our industry imbalance does not change our estimates of the prevalence of telework across Australian organisations significantly, and figures reported throughout are unweighted.

For both populations A and B, a similar industry distribution is evident. As Table 1 shows, the use of teleworkers in both categories is higher than the overall average in Property and Business and Government Administration, and considerably higher in Communication Services (although caution is required in this case given the small sample size for this industry). In comparison, the use of telework is low in Wholesale and Retail Trade – not one of the original industries we selected for investigation.

	N	A. Organisations with telework, percentage in industry (N)	B. Organisations with regular telework[1], percentage in industry (N)
Manufacturing	726	36 (262)	10 (73)
Wholesale and Retail	120	28 (33)	8 (9)
Communication Services[2]	21	64 (13)	32 (6)
Finance and Insurance	215	42 (91)	14 (31)
Property and Business	817	51 (417)	18 (150)
Government Admin	435	52 (228)	18 (80)
Other	194	40 (77)	15 (29)
Total	***2528***	***44 (1121)***	***15 (378)***

Table 1. Organisations with telework, by industry

Notes

1. 'Regular' telework, as defined above, involves employees consistently working 40 per cent or more of their hours away from the central workplace.
2. Due to low numbers in this industry, estimates should be interpreted with caution.

When the two populations are broken down by private and public sector (Table 2), a further difference in the uptake of telework is evident. A higher uptake of telework is evident in public sector organisations where 53 per cent have some telework, and 20 per cent have some regular telework; compared with 43 per cent and 14 per cent respectively in the private sector (see Table 2). As a whole, the survey sample contained a majority of private sector organisations (some 82 per cent). The apparent higher public sector uptake of telework contrasts with US data gathered at the same time and using a similar definition of telework which identified over 9O percent of teleworkers being employed in the private sector (Di Martino 2001: 30)[3].

	N	A. Organisations with telework, percentage in sector (N)	B. Organisations with regular telework[1], percentage in sector (N)
Private	2079	43 (886)	14 (287)
Public	449	53 (235)	20 (91)
Total	***2528***	***(1121)***	***(378)***

Table 2. Organisations with telework, by sector

Note

1. 'Regular' telework, as defined above, involves employees consistently working 40 per cent or more of their hours away from the central workplace.

Table 3 sets out the distribution of organisations with teleworkers by size. It is clearly the larger organisations (those with over 150 employees) that are most likely to have teleworkers. Around a quarter of these organisations record the use of some regular teleworkers, compared with less than 10 per cent of organisations with fewer than 50 employees. These findings complement the international data, which have consistently shown that larger organisations have a higher incidence of telework (see Johnston and Botterman 1999: 32-33; Johnston and Nolan 2000: 69, 110-111).

	N	A. Organisations with telework, percentage in size category (N)	B. Organisations with regular telework[1], percentage in size category (N)
<50 employees	1205	33 (394)	9 (112)
50-149 employees	647	44 (287)	15 (95)
150+ employees	676	65 (440)	25 (171)
Total	***2528***	***44 (1121)***	***15 (378)***

Table 3. Organisations with telework, by size

Note

1. 'Regular' telework, as defined above, involves employees consistently working 40 per cent or more of their hours away from the central workplace.

Turning to the types of telework being utilised, among the 378 organisations with some regular teleworkers, most (332) employed teleworkers who worked from home using a computer linked electronically to the office. This was the most prevalent form of teleworking among the organisations in our sample as a whole (reported in close to 40 per cent of organisations in the sample). Mobile teleworking was less frequently reported (around 30 per cent of all organisations in the sample), while the employment of workers in telecentres was extremely rare (only around 1 per cent of organisations).[4]

The survey also provided us with some information about the characteristics of teleworkers, in particular the occupational groups most frequently employed, gender composition and the extent of part-time and casual employment. The most frequently cited occupational groups are shown in Table 4. 'Manager' was identified most frequently, followed by information technology (IT) professionals, administrative and clerical workers, salespeople and other professionals. This suggests that telework is more prevalent among occupations where employees are likely to have considerable autonomy over the way their work is organised and conducted – the main exception being administrative and clerical workers. Market researchers and telemarketers were comparatively rare in the organisations in our sample.[5] Although the industry breakdown produces extremely small cell sizes for some sectors, it does illustrate some significant differences. Organisations in Government Administration, for example, are more likely than those in most other industry sectors to employ administrative and clerical workers as teleworkers, and – understandably – there is an absence of salespeople as teleworkers in Government Administration, although this is quite prevalent elsewhere.

	Sales pple	Tele-mrkts	Admin /cler.	Trans-lators	Mrkt resrch	IT prfess	Other prfess	Man-agers	Total N
Manufacturing	56	4	23	4	3	25	21	43	73
Wholesale and Retail[3]	56	11	33			33	11	33	9
Communications[3]	50		17		17	83	33	33	6
Finance and Insurance	48	3	26	3	3	29	29	26	31
Property and Business	31	2	22		3	41	30	41	150
Government Admin.			49		1	20	36	28	80
Other	21	3	48		7	17	28	45	29
All industries	***31***	***2***	***30***	***1***	***3***	***31***	***29***	***37***	***378***

Table 4. Occupational groups teleworking, by industry[1], row percentages[2]

Notes

1. Sample is comprised of organisations with some *regular* teleworkers, as defined above.
2. Respondents could identify more than one occupational group, hence rows do not add to 100%.
3. Due to the low number of organisations in this industry, percentages in this row should be interpreted with caution.

We also examined the respective representation of women and men in telework, and the prevalence of part-time and casual workers. The most recent European evidence indicates that telework is predominantly a male area of work, with men teleworkers outnumbering women by a factor of 3 to 1 (Johnston and Nolan 2000: 31). However, our evidence suggests a more equal gender distribution in Australian organisations. Table 5 shows that, in slightly less than one-third of the organisations with regular teleworkers in our dataset, teleworkers are all male. Discounting occupations with very small numbers, this situation is most prevalent in sales, where over a third of the organisations with regular teleworkers employed no females in this type of work. At the other end of the spectrum, around a quarter of the organisations with regular teleworkers stated that over 75 per cent of their teleworkers were female (and for 76 organisations, or around 20 per cent of those with regular teleworkers, all of their teleworkers are female). High proportions of female teleworkers were most prevalent in the administrative and clerical group, and least evident in sales, with cell counts in some of the other occupational groups too low to make a valid comparison.

The higher proportion of female teleworkers in administrative and clerical teleworking, compared with areas such as IT professionals, reflects patterns of occupational sex segregation evident in the labour market more broadly. However, given the lack of detail available in our sample on this issue (as respondents could select multiple occupational categories and we did not ask them to specify numbers of teleworkers in the different occupations), we cannot provide an accurate assessment of sex segregation in telework.

	N	Proportion of regular teleworkers who are female 0	1-25%	26-50%	51-75%	>75%
Salespeople	116	36	19	25	11	9
Telemarketers[3]	9			78		22
Admin. & Clerical	115	16	9	21	17	38
Translators[3]	4	50		25	25	
Market researchers[3]	12	8	25	42	8	17
IT professionals	118	28	20	25	13	15
Other professionals	109	23	17	32	13	16
Managers	140	30	22	26	9	14
All occupations	***378***	***30***	***15***	***20***	***11***	***24***
		(114)	*(55)*	*(76)*	*(42)*	*(91)*

Table 5. Proportion of regular teleworkers who are female, by occupation[1], row percentages[2]

Notes

1. Sample is comprised of organisations with some *regular* teleworkers, as defined above.
2. Due to rounding, rows may not add to 100%.
3. Due to the low number of organisations identifying this occupational category, percentages in this row should be interpreted with caution.

Turning to the issue of 'irregular' employment (such as part-time and casual work), the survey data suggests that regular telework is rarely performed by casual employees. In Australia, casual workers are defined as those employees who lack access to the entitlements associated with regular full-time or part-time employment (such as holiday and sick pay), but who in most cases receive a financial loading in recompense. Casual workers can also be dismissed or can leave without a period of notice. In our survey, 90 per cent of organisations with regular teleworkers had no teleworkers employed on a casual basis. This finding is consistent with the prevalent idea that teleworkers are most likely to be trusted permanent employees who are well acquainted with the organisational expectations and culture. It also counters the perception of teleworkers as simply a 'peripheral' workforce. Part-time work[6] was slightly more evident in the survey data, but still not widespread. Seventy-two per cent of organisations with regular teleworkers had no teleworkers employed on a part-time basis, and part-timers accounted for over 50 per cent of regular teleworkers in less than 15 per cent of organisations. Overall, these figures indicate that Australian telework is not typically casualised or 'irregular' employment.

Our survey also investigated pressures leading to the adoption of telework. The data suggest that this tends to be primarily a senior management decision, with little support from unions. Among organisations with regular teleworkers, CEOs or Managing Directors were cited most frequently (in 43 per cent of cases) as having an important role in supporting the introduction of telework. In around 31 per cent of cases middle management was cited as playing an important supporting role. Other groups were cited much less frequently (other employees in 17 per cent of cases, human resource managers in 11 per cent, customers in 3 per cent, and unions in only 1 per cent of cases). This comparative emphasis on middle managers as initiators is of some note, since middle managers have often been identified in the literature as opposing the introduction of telework, given perceptions that it might create difficulties for management and supervision (Christensen 1992; Kugelmass 1995; Johnson and Botterman 1999: 42).

Among those organisations with regular telework, the main reasons cited as highly important in the decision to adopt telework were hopes for greater productivity and allowing employees more flexible hours. As Table 6 shows, responses from over half the organisations with regular telework (56 per cent) rated increased productivity as highly important in the decision to introduce telework. Equally frequent was the desire to allow employees more flexible hours (57 per cent),[7] although the number of respondents specifically identifying more specific work and family reasons was lower (38 per cent). Government Administration was most likely among the industry sectors to record this rationale for introduction. Reducing commuting time was noted as important in around a third of organisations, but reducing the cost of office accommodation was identified as a reason for introducing telework in only 7 per cent of cases.

	Manu-facturing	W'sale/ retail[3]	Commun -ication[3]	Finance& ins.	Prop.& business	Govt admin.	Other	Total
Increase productivity	59	33	33	74	61	49	41	56
Allow employees more flexible hours	44	33	50	48	63	65	55	57
More effective use of communic. tech.	52	22	67	36	51	34	48	46
Assist employees w/ family commitments	25	22	17	42	43	46	31	38
Reduce commuting time	40	44	67	29	36	20	38	34
Retain employees	19	22	33	36	28	28	35	27
Reduce cost of office accomm.	10			10	7	8	7	7
Total N	***73***	***9***	***6***	***31***	***150***	***80***	***29***	***378***

Table 6. Factors rated as 'highly important' in the decision to introduce telework[1] column percentages[2]

Notes

1. Sample is comprised of organisations with some *regular* teleworkers, as defined above.
2. Respondents could select more than one reason hence columns do not add to 100%.
3. Due to the low number of organisations in this industry, percentages in this column should be interpreted with caution

Respondents to the questionnaire were also asked to identify the main advantages and disadvantages associated with telework. Table 7 provides an overview of the advantages cited. These responses largely parallel the reasons for introduction shown in Table 6, with the emphasis particularly on productivity gains. Over 60 per cent of the respondents in organisations with regular telework cited increased productivity as a highly important advantage of telework. This was highest among the Finance and Insurance organisations, and lowest in Wholesale and Retail Trade and Communication Services (where – as noted earlier – the number of respondents is low and estimates may be unreliable). We emphasise that these are perceptions of respondents and that our survey data do not provide information on actual changes in productivity, which is notoriously difficult to estimate, especially in service sector industries. Further analysis is necessary to ascertain whether any monitoring of productivity is occurring, and whether it is being perceived in terms of cost reductions or efficiency gains. Preliminary case study evidence we have gathered as part of the project would suggest that productivity is rarely monitored in any meaningful way, although many teleworkers state that they are more productive when teleworking. This is often seen as due to receiving fewer interruptions to their work (interruptions that their colleagues at the workplace presumably have to deal with).

	Manu-facturing	W'sale/ retail[3]	Commun-ication[3]	Finance & ins.	Prop.& businss	Govt admin.	Other	Total
Higher productivity	63	33	33	73	69	54	48	62
Increased adoption of communic. tech.	60	22	50	45	53	47	63	53
More flexible use of staff	52	22	50	55	58	63	50	56
Better retention of experienced staff	30	44	33	47	44	41	36	40
More flexible use of infrastructure	30	11	17	26	35	22	32	30
Improved employee morale	21		17	32	37	38	32	32
Greater commitment to company goals	22	11	17	30	25	30	29	26
Reduced cost of office accomm.	12	11		7	9	10		9
Total N	*73*	*9*	*6*	*31*	*150*	*80*	*29*	*378*

Table 7. Perceived advantages from the use of telework[1], column percentages[2]

Notes

1. Sample is comprised of organisations with some *regular* teleworkers, as defined above.

2. Respondents could select more than one reason hence columns do not add to 100%; responses are those rating the factor as 'highly important'.

3. Due to the low number of organisations in this industry, percentages in this column should be treated with caution.

Table 7 also shows that more flexible use of staff is cited in over half of the responses. This result cannot be directly equated with the item in Table 6 – allow employees more flexible hours – since the latter specifically implies concern for employees' interests. However, questions on staff retention were more similarly worded, and we note that better retention of skilled staff rated somewhat higher in Table 7 than might have been expected from the figures in Table 6. Table 7 shows that around 40 per cent of respondents cited this option (the lowest response being 30 per cent in Manufacturing), compared with the 27 per cent of respondents in Table 6 who saw this as a reason for adopting telework. Around one-quarter to one-third of organisations also reported increased employee morale and commitment to company goals. Again, only a small proportion reported reduced accommodation costs as highly important.

Perceived problems with the use of telework were also investigated. Among the organisations with regular teleworkers, data security was the most frequently identified concern – this was seen as highly or moderately problematic by around 44 per cent of organisations. Issues raised in the literature including difficulties for teleworkers (for example, isolation) and management problems (for example, training, supervision, communication) were identified as highly or moderately problematic by around 30 per cent of organisations. Occupational health and safety issues were apparently less of a concern (around a quarter of cases), and industrial relations issues more broadly were noted by less than 10 per cent of respondents. A number of respondents registered problems unanticipated by the questionnaire by selecting the 'other' category. A large proportion of these were issues relating to the technology involved in telework: speed, systems or computer problems, difficulties with maintenance and skills training. Case study work suggests that another outstanding problem may be pressures on teleworkers to attend the central office regularly. While many of the teleworkers we have interviewed in our case studies have agreements with their managers to be home-based for one or two days a week, they often find that they must come into the office for meetings or team work.

When we compare the problems identified by respondents in those organisations employing regular teleworkers with anticipated problems identified by respondents in those organisations where telework had been considered but not introduced, some contrasts are evident. In particular, the proportion of non-teleworking organisations expressing fears about problems with management of teleworkers and loss of employees' identification with the company was higher than the proportion of 'regular telework' organisations actually perceiving these problems in practice. On the other hand, industrial relations issues and problems with support from staff and unions were noted more frequently as problems in the organisations actually using telework than as anticipated problems in organisations where telework had been considered but not introduced. It is thus possible that telework may introduce some unforeseen difficulties for staff – perhaps for non-teleworkers as well as teleworkers – and our case study work to date does suggest some tensions over access to the 'privilege' of teleworking and perceptions that those left behind in the central office carry an additional burden when their colleagues telework.

Conclusion

The data from our survey have illustrated several features of the incidence and implementation of telework in Australian organisations. While a substantial proportion of organisations have adopted telework in some form, only a small number have *regular* teleworkers. Teleworkers are most likely to be managers, IT and other professionals, and clerical and administrative employees; with telemarketers and market researchers rare in our sample. Proportions of female and male teleworkers appear to vary according to industry and occupation in much the same way as in the labour market overall. The incidence of casual and part-time workers, though, appears considerably lower than the labour market average. Management (particularly CEOs and middle managers) have been the most important promoters of telework, and greater productivity is the main advantage organisations perceive as arising from the introduction of telework. While concern for employee flexibility and, to a lesser extent, work/family balance are evident in the sample, there is also some suggestion of management and employee relations difficulties with the implementation of this form of work organisation. Continuing case study work will be crucial to investigate these issues more fully.

Overall, the data show that telework cannot be categorised simply, and that – unlike traditional outwork – it is not necessarily secondary labour market employment. Its incidence, however, remains limited in Australia, even in those industry sectors most likely to implement it. Also, there is no indication in our data of a widespread intent among organisations without telework to adopt it in the near future. Among those organisations without telework in our sample, only around 8 per cent had plans for its introduction within the next two years. In Australia, telework remains a relatively novel form of work arrangement, and the 'mainstreaming' predicted for some countries (Johnson and Botterman 1999: 9) is apparently not on the short-term agenda.

Endnotes

1. This chapter draws on material previously published in a journal article: George Lafferty and Gillian Whitehouse (2000) 'Telework in Australia: findings from a national survey', *Australian Bulletin of Labour*, 26, 3: 236-252. Our thanks go to co-editor, Mark Cully, for permission to use this material.

2. The project is funded through an Australian Research Council Strategic Partnerships with Industry (Research and Training) grant. Research partners are the University of Queensland, Unisys Australia and the Queensland Department of Employment, Training and Industrial Relations. The research team on this project also includes Paul Boreham, Bill Harley, Richard Hall and Michelle Nesic.

3. There are important structural differences between Australia and the United States that would exaggerate this contrast. Firstly, Australian public sector organisations tend to form a greater percentage of larger Australian organisations than US public sector organisations form in relation to all larger US organisations. Secondly, public sector employment accounts for a greater share of overall Australian employment than public sector employment does as a proportion of overall US employment.

4. Around 7 per cent of our respondents reported the use of teleworkers in call centres, but in line with our definitional requirement that telework be conducted away from the central workplace, we excluded from our analysis any organisations for which this was the only form of teleworking identified.

5. This is unlikely to be due to our elimination of organisations only employing teleworkers in call centres as this was such a small proportion of our sample. The most likely explanation is that these types of workers most commonly work at a main office in facilities provided for this purpose.

6. Although a high proportion of part-time workers in Australia are employed on casual employment contracts, casual and part-time work are not synonymous, and permanent part-time has increasingly been an issue in pay negotiation and public policy.

7. The proportion of responses rating 'allowing employees more flexible hours' and 'assisting with family commitments' as highly important is around 10 percentage points lower if the population is organisations with any form of telework (rather than organisations with regular telework).

References

Australian Bureau of Statistics (ABS) (1998) *Use of the Internet by Householders*, November 1998, Cat. No. 8147.0, Canberra: ABS.

Christensen, K. (1992) 'Managing invisible employees: how to meet the telecommuting challenge', *Employment Relations Today*, 19, 2: 133-143.

Diamond, C. and Lafferty, G. (2000) 'Telework: issues for research, policy and regulation', *Labour & Industry*, 11, 1: 115-128.

Di Martino, V. (2001) *The High Road to Teleworking*, Geneva: International Labour Organization.

Johnston, P. and Botterman, M. (1999) (eds) *Status Report on European Telework: New Methods of Work 1999*, Brussels: European Commission.

Johnston, P. and Nolan, J. (2000) (eds) *eWork 2000: Status Report on New Ways to Work in the Information Society*, Brussels: European Commission.

Kugelmass, J. (1995) *Telecommuting: A Manager's Guide to Flexible Work Arrangements*, New York: Lexington Books.

Lafferty, G. and Whitehouse G. (2000) 'Telework in Australia: Findings from a National Survey in Selected Industries', *Australian Bulletin of Labour* 26(3): 236-252.

Nilles, J. (1998) *Managing Telework: Strategies for Managing the Virtual Workforce*, New York : John Wiley & Sons.

Qvortrup, L. (1998) 'From teleworking to networking: definitions and trends', in P. J. Jackson & J. M. van der Wielen (eds) *Teleworking: International Perspectives: from Telecommuting to the Virtual Organisation*, London: Routledge.

24 Telecommuting in Singapore

Geoffrey N. Dick[1], Lai Lai Tung [2]

[1]University of New South Wales, Australia

[2]Nayang Technical University, Singapore

Introduction

Telecommuting is a global phenomenon – countries in Asia, the Americas and Europe all report some of their countrymen working from home – in most cases this number seems to be gradually increasing, although not as fast as some of the earlier predictions. However, the research would indicate that telecommuting is here to stay, at least for the foreseeable future. Why do staff and their employers embrace telecommuting? The literature points to a series of reasons in the areas of advantages and disadvantages, personal attitudes to work and the tasks involved. This chapter, which looks at workers in Singapore, attempts to identify the reasons explaining the preference to telecommute, what governs the suitability of tasks for telecommuting, and what factors explain the amount of telecommuting being practiced.

In Singapore it seems that telecommuting has not been as popular as might have been expected, particularly given the type of work performed there and the extent of industrialization of this Asian country. For instance, a survey by the National Computer Board (NCB) in Singapore (1994) revealed that 43% of the workforce is engaged in information-related activities, which are highly appropriate for telecommuting. Additionally, telecommuting is a new phenomenon in Singapore, with most entrants having less than 5 years of experience with telecommuting (Endeshaw et al 2000). Therefore, it is still unclear if telecommuting will become a significant trend over the next few years. The chapter will review literature on factors motivating and inhibiting telecommuting to shed light on factors that may affect this progression.

While previous studies have hinted at the impact of cultural difference on the utilization of telecommuting between Singapore and other countries (for instance, see Khan et al. 1996 and Khan et al 1997) none of these studies had made direct comparisons to explain its influences. The chapter seeks to relate the conventional telecommuting literature to some of the work defining and explaining national culture in the hope that there may be some clues here for researchers and managers of telecommuters alike.

Why Telecommute (or why not)?

The reduction or elimination of long periods of commuting time is a principle benefit to the telecommuter (Ford and Butts, 1991; Mokhtarian and Salomon, 1994). Working from home provides the telecommuter with a degree of flexibility (Ford and Butts, 1991) which is impossible in the conventional workplace - typically this flexibility will revolve around scheduling of tasks, possibly by extending the working day and allowing time to do personal or private tasks during normal working hours, such as collection of children from school, facilitating tradesman's visits or looking after a dependent child or relative. This 'better form of working' is cited to be of utmost importance in a recent study of telecommuting in Singapore when the 56 respondents ranked a set of motivators for telecommuting (Endeshaw and Tung 2000)· Other Singapore studies that found similar motivators include Tung et al. (1997). In general: an improved family life (Turban and Wang, 1995), while enabling the employee to take advantage of the general move from an industrial-based society to a knowledge-based one. (Palmquist, 1992). This opportunity to take advantage of increased leisure and family time is seen as an important component in the individual's choice as to whether to participate in a telecommuting programme (Mokhtarian and Salomon, 1994). Contrary to the above, however, Singapore respondents ranked social reasons such as taking care of dependents or one's own disability lowest according to Endesaw and Tung (2000).

Transport costs can be a significant item of expenditure for the employee (Gray et al. 1993), particularly for the lower-level employee who is unlikely to benefit from taxation advantages or salary packages which might include the provision of a car. Other expenses that might be reduced if working from home include clothing, lunches and cosmetics (Turban and Wang, 1995). Control over one's working environment (Mokhtarian and Salomon, 1994) and avoidance of colleagues one might prefer to avoid are put forward as potential benefits, as is improvement in health due to reduction in stress (commute or workplace induced).

Available data also shows that there is an increasing base of workers in occupations and industries that are likely to lend themselves to telecommuting (National Board of Employment, 1995 and National Computer Board 1992), and with the technology available in the home (Vitalari and Venkatesh, 1987) one might expect that the conditions are right for telecommuting. In general terms also the data indicates that decisions to work at home are being made by a better educated workforce, with more males choosing to telecommute than in the past for work-related reasons, and on the basis of personal choice rather than being required to be at home to care for dependent children. The proportion of the workforce most suitable to telecommuting is that working in what is generally known as 'knowledge work' (Mokhtarian, 1998) and as this proportion increase, the number of workers able to telecommute also increases. While it seems that telecommuting is more *possible* (in terms of allowed by one's tasks) for many workers, how many of these workers have the *ability* (comfortable with the working arrangements and competent) to telecommute has yet to be determined.

Community reasons and organisational reasons are important too and these have particular relevance in Singapore. Telecommuting was highlighted in Singapore's IT2000 Plan (National Computer Board 1992) as a possible work option for reasons such as more balanced lifestyles, higher job satisfaction and increased productivity. Organisations (and therefore the community) would benefit from reduced rental costs, easier recruitment and lower turnover (Teo, et al 1999). Additionally, Singapore, with its excellent IT infrastructure, is well equipped for telecommuting in terms of the technology that enables telecommuting (see Tung and Turban 1996 for a discussion of technologies as enablers)

Perhaps the most frequently expressed concerns are those of feelings of isolation from one's fellow workers and being out-of-sight and out-of-mind (Ramsower, 1985). Exploitation of the individual is another concern - referred to only in passing or in a light-hearted manner in most of the literature (Turban and Wang, 1995; Filipczak, 1992). It gets somewhat more serious treatment in studies reporting on the involvement of industrial organisations in the telecommuting implementation process or critical of the supposed benefits (McQuarrie, 1994; Gordon, 1992; Pagonis, 1995). There are other potential drawbacks for the telecommuter - the use of a private home for a workplace may contravene local government regulations and may have taxation implications (Spinks and Timbrell, 1996).

From a Singaporean organisational perspective, the perceived disadvantages were security, supervision and management of telecommuters, responsibility for equipment in an employee's home, the initial investment to set up home offices and the evaluation of work performance Teo, et al 1999).

Several models setting out behavioural frameworks for the individual's choice to telecommuting have been proposed (Bernardino and Ben-Akiva, 1996; Mokhtarian and Salomon, 1994). Typically, these models have referred to such desires as a need to have more flexibility and increase productivity, spend more time with one's family and to have more job autonomy. In one case (Mokhtarian and Salomon, 1994) the choice set is incorporated into the decision process and this identifies the need for 'drives' which motivate the employee to telecommute. This work and the identification of these drives raise the question of the necessary attributes in a person contemplating working in this mode. For example, in order to take advantage of more flexible working arrangements and increase productivity, it might be expected that the employee will have the ability to concentrate for long periods of time, be a 'self-starter', produce work without the external imposition of deadlines and be able to seek required information. Moreover, it will also be necessary for him to have a suitable work arrangement and work space that will enable him to accomplish this.

A number of authors have mentioned job types suitable for telecommuting (Moskowitz, 1995; Goodrich, 1990). Drawing on the work of others, Fritz (Fritz et al. 1996) provides a range of job types - programmers, analysts, data entry clerks, planners, accountants, support service staff and governmental employees. By way of a simple validation of the above model, it can be fairly readily seen that these jobs are likely to fit the model at least to some degree for at least some of the time. Obviously, some tasks are not suited to telecommuting. The issue is whether a significant portion of the job may lend itself to telecommuting. A job is comprised of a series of component tasks, some of which may be suitable to telecommuting and others will demand the employee's presence in the conventional workplace (Filipczak, 1992), suggesting that many jobs have task components that facilitate telecommuting. As such, the reasons for adopting telecommuting will also vary according to the nature of the job.

It is recognised that an examination of the official data will not provide definite numbers for telecommuting; rather by examination of trends and the growing numbers of people involved in working from home, broken down into the professions mostly likely to be undertaking this type of work, some more reliable insight into the magnitude of this mode of working may be gained. An understanding of the influences will provide management with an improved ability to manage the introduction of telecommuting into the workplace.

Perhaps a word here on definitional problems would be appropriate – in an authoritative and wide-ranging discussion on telework, telecommuting and so on (Lindstrom et al. 1997), the authors draw attention to the need to be as exact as possible in defining the concept when discussing it to ensure a clear frame of reference and eliminate unnecessary confusion and imprecision. The authors point out that the differing results in telecommuting studies can often be traced back to the researchers using different definitions of the same concept. For the results of the study underpinning this chapter, telecommuting was defined as:

> Work for an employer which takes place at the worker's home, for a significant amount of time, involves knowledge work, and where the worker makes at least occasional use of telecommunications and computing equipment to interact with his/her organisation and colleagues.

There is some support for the belief that national culture may affect work patterns and such practices as telecommuting. (Tan et al. 1998; Adler et al. 1986; Rice et al. 1998) An examination of national cultures across the world (Hofstede, 1994) proposed a series of dimensions by which national culture could be measured. His work is controversial, but does enjoy significant support (Rice et al. 1998). The concept of inequality is assessed by the dimension Hofstede calls *power distance*. In an attempt to measure the degree of inequality in society he developed the Power Distance Index. Singapore ranks high on the Power Distance Index. These PDI scores inform us about dependence relationships within a country. Low power distance countries are likely to prefer consultation between supervisor and subordinate; in high power distance countries, the subordinate is quite dependent on his supervisor. Given the degree of trust necessary for telecommuting (Handy, 1995) it is conjectured that high power distance countries will be less amenable to telecommuting and management attitudes would be a significant factor in the preference to telecommute.

Hofstede's next dimension is *individualism versus collectivism*. A somewhat controversial nomenclature, at least in a political sense, it can be considered as personal issues versus family issues. Singaporeans rank quite low on the Individualism index. In a telecommuting context, it might be expected that family issues would figure prominently in a Singaporean decision to telecommute, while countries which ranked higher on this index might be expected to put greater emphasis on individualist issues.

Masculinity/femininity – the next dimension in Hofstede's work, suggests that those countries ranking as more 'masculine' might be expected to attach higher importance to such things as earnings, recognition, advancement and challenge. For the countries ranked as more 'feminine', issues such as having a good working relationship with the one's supervisor, co-operation, living in a desirable area and employment security will be more important. Singapore ranks midway on the Masculinity index. Accordingly, it is conjectured that although the group may show some of these factors as influencing the decision, they would be unlikely to be significant factors.

The final dimension, *uncertainty avoidance* (the extent to which members of a culture feel threatened by uncertain or unknown situations) ranks Singapore as the lowest. It might be construed from this that Singaporeans are less likely to base their telecommuting decisions on things such as working in familiar situations, at their own pace and without too many interruptions. It seems possible, therefore that the national culture may have an influence on one's willingness to work as a telecommuter.

The study was partly motivated by the desire to investigate whether this was likely.

The Data

A survey was administered to groups of students (almost all part-time) undertaking MBA-type programmes in Singapore during 1998. There were 63 respondents. As the surveys were administered during class, the response rate was close to 100%. The respondents were predominantly male, aged under 40, in managerial or professional positions, had worked less than 5 years in their current section and were highly educated.

The average time spent travelling to and from work each day was 1 hour and 10 minutes with 50% of the respondents taking between 50 minutes and an hour and a half for the round trip.

The respondents were asked how much telecommuting they would like to do, how much they saw as possible given the component tasks of there jobs and how much telecommuting they were doing at present. The following graphs summarise their responses.

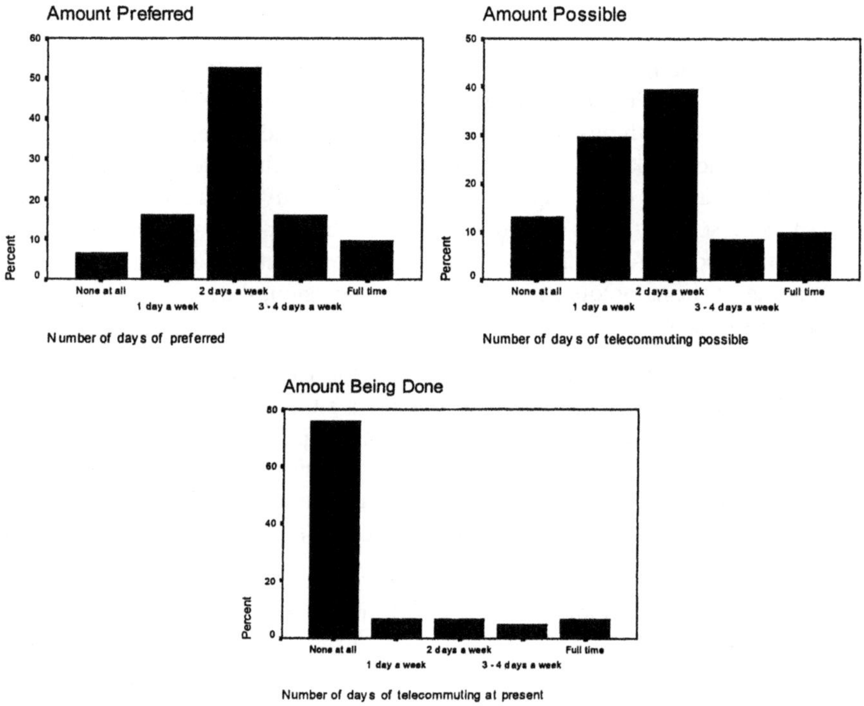

Figure 1. Telecommuting: Preferred, Possible and Being Done

Clearly there is a significant difference between the amounts considered possible and preferred and the amount being done, and while there is scope for much more, at first glance 25% of this group working as telecommuters for at least some of the time is not out of line with what might be expected in other countries (Mokhtarian, 1998; Dick, 1996). Against that it must be remember that this group of 'knowledge workers' are the group most likely to work as telecommuters and the overall figure for all industries is likely to be much lower.

Data Analysis and Discussion

In order to better understand the influences on telecommuting in Singapore, the data analysis conducted on this sample commenced with a series of stepwise regressions against the amount of telecommuting preferred, the amount seen as possible and the amount being done.

Preference for telecommuting

The dominant factors explaining the amount of telecommuting preferred were:

- the flexibility provided,
- that it would be viewed negatively by management, and
- the inability to schedule tasks restricting telecommuting.

These three factors had an adjusted R^2 value of .30, thereby explaining 30% of the variance. The first item that loaded in the regression, flexibility, defined in the data collection instrument as being better able to manage one's own affairs, more independence, control over one's physical working environment and to study or pursue personal interests, may be interpreted as the respondent desiring only to telecommute for a limited time. If for example, travel had been a particularly important factor to the respondents, with each facing a long or arduous journey to and from work each day, one might have expected the amount preferred to be somewhat higher. Against the preference for some telecommuting owing to flexibility, the individual's perception that it would be viewed negatively by management and his inability to schedule his tasks to facilitate telecommuting can be expected to have an effect on the amount preferred. In other words, if the amount of telecommuting preferred is taken holistically, one might expect the amount to be influenced by the managerial attitude and the possibility of organising his work to facilitate telecommuting supports the relatively low average desired amount of 2 days a week. This is borne out by the standardised regression coefficients with flexibility being positive, the other two negative.

Amount possible

The dominant factors explaining the amount of telecommuting possible were:

- the importance of co-ordination in the tasks undertaken
- the ability to work when sick or disabled,

- the feeling of being able to work better when away from the office, and
- the opportunity to get more work done.

These three factors had an adjusted R^2 value of .476, thereby explaining 47% of the variance. The analysis indicates that while the tasks the respondents were involved in frequently required significant co-ordination with one's fellow workers, this was countered to a considerable degree by the extra work that could be accomplished by being able to work when sick or disabled, being able to work better (perhaps without distractions or the improved ability to concentrate) and the opportunity to get more work done – longer hours, work on a specific task etc.

The graph shown at Figure 1 above indicates that most respondents saw their tasks as lending themselves to at least some telecommuting – only 10% saw none as possible. While the importance of the co-ordination issue (the only negative standardised beta coefficient in the above factors) clearly would be of concern to most respondents, we are left with the conclusion that in Singapore (as with similar jobs elsewhere) there is nothing in the tasks themselves that makes telecommuting impossible.

Amount being done

The dominant factors explaining the amount of telecommuting possible were:

- the risk to one's career in being away from the office, and
- having the confidence to make the necessary decisions.

These three factors had an adjusted R^2 value of .119, thereby explaining only 12% of the variance. The first factor, the risk to one's career fits with the previously discussed views of management – it might well be expected that this feeling would work against the respondents working in this way. The second factor, having the confidence to make the necessary decisions, may be an anomaly in the regression, based more on the individual respondent's position in the work force. An additional factor that is perhaps likely to explain considerably more of the variance and not included in the data collection instrument, is the limited acceptance of telecommuting by employers in Singapore, as mentioned above. In Figure 1 above we see that some 75% of respondents do no telecommuting, notwithstanding both the desire to do so and the apparent suitability of their tasks to telecommuting.

Culture

The data would indicate that there is some support for the issue of culture having an effect on the issues associated with telecommuting in Singapore. One of the factors explaining the desire to telecommute and the amount of telecommuting being done was the view that management would take, or at least as it was perceived by the respondents. This was underlined in a related series of tests comparing a similar group of Australians to the Singaporean group. The Singaporeans perceived that their supervisors would be more concerned about cost and control than the Australian group thought their supervisors would be. This might suggest that the Power Distance index is a useful factor in the decisions relating to telecommuting.

The individualism v collectivism index also receives some support from the data. Family issues seem to be a factor in Singapore more so than in Australia where individualist issues such as the importance of uninterrupted time (getting more work done?) and not being reliant on others figured more prominently. Against this, it should be noted that 'flexibility' was important in Singapore, perhaps due to high work pressure and related issues. As expected, there were no great differences due to masculinity/femininity – it is possible the concern that management might view telecommuting negatively reflects something of the desire to have a good working relationship with one's supervisor and build employment security. Finally, there was some support for the uncertainty avoidance dimension – Australians do seem to attach a higher importance to the issues of working in a familiar environment, at their own pace and without too many interruptions – for Singaporeans these issues do not rate highly.

It is important to recognise that there are limitations to these suggestions regarding the influence of international culture – first, the Hofstede work took place many years ago and there would be considerable support for the proposition that Singapore and Singaporean work practice has changed a great deal since that study. (It was beyond the scope of this study to re-assess the Hofstede indices for this group of respondents.) Secondly, these indices were intended as only a general guide and not in any way definitive explanations of an individual country's traits. Finally it should be reiterated that the Hofstede work is very controversial, although it does enjoy widespread recognition.

Conclusion

To date, telecommuting in Singapore has not become as widespread as might have been expected, notwithstanding several efforts by the government to encourage alternative work practices, of which telecommuting is one. There is at least a strong indication in this data that the reasons for this may be found in both managerial practices and employee perceptions of how telecommuting would be viewed by management and by fellow workers.

From a cultural perspective, the implications of these findings for management seem to fall into two main areas. For global organisations, it seems reasonable to conclude that telecommuting, as a work practice, does not necessarily translate seamlessly from country to country. An evaluation of cultural differences is likely to be required before deciding whether such practices will be suitable. For local organisations, an understanding that while a desire to work from home may be apparent in the workforce, local issues are likely to have an influence in either preventing or facilitating this happening.

References

Adler, N. J., Doktor, R. and Redding, S. G. (1986) 'From the Atlantic to the Pacific Century: Cross-Cultural Management Reviewed' *Journal of Management* 12, 295-318.

Bernardino, A. and Ben-Akiva, M. (1996) 'Modeling the Process of Adoption of Telecommuting: A Comprehensive Framework' *Transportation Research Record* 1552, 161-170.

Dick, G. N. (1996) 'Telecommuting in Australia: Tomorrow's Workforce or "A Pie in the Sky?"' *Telecommuting '96* Jacksonville University of Georgia.

Endeshaw, A. and Tung, L.L. (2000) 'Emerging patterns of teleworking in Singapore' *Human Systems Management* 19(4) pp. 161-167.

Filipczak, R. (1992) 'Telecommuting: A Better Way to Work?' *Training* 53-61.

Ford, R. C. and Butts, M. A. (1991) 'Is Your Organization Ready for Telecommuting?' *SAM Advanced Management Journal* 56, 19-23.

Fritz, M. E. W., Narasimhan, S., and Rhee, H. (1996) 'Adoption of Remote Work Arrangements: An Initial Analysis' *Proceedings of the 29th Annual Hawaii International Conference on System Sciences* Hawaii, USA pp.118-127.

Goodrich, J. N. (1990) 'Telecommuting in America' *Business Horizons* 33, 31-37.

Gordon, G. (1992) 'Telework Troubles, Traumas, and Triumphs: Confessions from Telework Planners around the Pacific Rim' *Pacific Telecommunications Council.*

Gray, M., Hodson, N. and Gordon, G. (1993) '*Teleworking Explained*' John Wiley & Sons.

Handy, C. (1995) 'Trust and the Virtual Organization' *Harvard Business Review* 40-50.

Hofstede, G. (1994) 'Cultures and Organizations: Software of the Mind' London: HarperCollins.

Khan, M., Kukalis, S., Tung, L. L. and Turban, E. (1996) 'Telecommuting on the Edges of the Pacific Rim: Singapore versus Southern California', *DSI.*

Khan, M., Tung, L. L. and Turban, E. (1997) 'Telecommuting: Comparing Singapore to Southern California' *Human Systems Management* 16(2) pp. 91-98

Lindstrom, J., Moberg, A. and Rapp, B. (1997) 'On Classification of Telework Situations' *European Journal of Information Systems* 6, pp.243-255.

McQuarrie, F.A.E. (1994) 'Telecommuting: Who Really Benefits?' *Business Horizons* 79-83.

Mokhtarian, P. L. (1998) 'A Synthetic Approach to Estimating The Impacts of Telecommuting on Travel' *Urban Studies* 35, 215-241.

Mokhtarian, P. L. and Salomon, I. (1994) 'Modeling the Choice of Telecommuting: Setting the Context' *Environment and Planning A* 26, 749-766.

Moskowitz, R. (1995) 'Let's Get it Straight About Telecommuting! A Reply' *Business Horizons* 84-86.

National Board of Employment, E.a.T. (1995) 'Converging Communications and Computer Technologies - Implications for Australia's Future Employment and Skills' *Employment and Skills Formation Council.* Discussion Paper.

National Computer Board, (1992) 'The IT2000 Report' *National Computer Board Publication*, Singapore.

National Computer Board, (1994) 'Report on status of Telework in Singapore' *National Computer Board Publication*, Singapore.

Pagonis, J. (1995) 'Teleworking Explosion: Fact or Fallacy?' Unpublished work.

Palmquist, R. A. (1992) 'The Impact of Information Technology on the Individual' *Annual Review of Information Technology* 27, 3-42.

Ramsower, R. M. (1985) "*Telecommuting: The Organizational and Behavioural Effects of Working at Home*" UMI Research Press.

Rice, R. E., D'Ambra, J. A. and More, E. (1998) 'Cross-Cultural Comparison of Organizational Media Evaluation and Choice' *Journal of Communication* 3-26.

Spinks, J. and Timbrell, P. (1996) 'Telecommuting: Working at the Speed of Light' Sydney: Toshiba.

Tan, B. C. Y., Wei, K. K., Watson, R. T. and Walczuch, R. M. (1998) 'Reducing Status Effects with Computer-Mediated Communication: Evidence from Two Distinct National Cultures' *Journal of Management Information Systems* 15, 119-141.

Teo, T. S. H., Lim, V. K. G. and Har, W. S. (1999) 'Assessing Attitudes Towards Teleworking Among Information Technology Professionals' *Singapore Management Review* 21 (1) pp 33-49

Tung, L. L., Palvia, S., Lee, C. H., Loy, Y. M. and Teng, M. Y. (1997). 'Telecommuting in Singapore: Current Status and A Comparison with Other Countries', *Journal of Global Information Management* 5(1) pp. 27-35

Tung, L. L. and Turban, E. (1996) 'Information Technology as an Enabler of Telecommuting', *International Journal of Information Management* 16(2) pp. 103-117

Turban, E. and Wang, P. (1995) 'Telecommuting Management: A Comprehensive Overview' *Human Systems Management* 14, 227-238.

Vitalari, N. P. and Venkatesh, A. (1987) 'In-Home Computing and Information Services: A 20 Year Analysis of the Technology and Its Impacts' *Telecommunications Policy* 11, 65-81.

25 Telework Trends in the United States

Joanne H. Pratt

Joanne H. Pratt Associates, USA

Introduction

Telework is not an isolated work process. Viewed in the larger context, it is part of the reorganization of work in response to new business opportunities. In the United States *telecommuting* began as a trip reduction strategy. It is evolving as *telework,* one form of the virtual organisation, which flexibly deploys workers where it makes the most sense to do so. With this reorganisation of the workplace new issues must be addressed to understand the impact on the workers and the corporate culture.

The Past

In 1983 we guessed wrong

In the United States, telework initially was championed as a strategy to reduce commuting trips to work. The early 1980s was a time of severe gasoline shortages. Although there was little standardised technology available to facilitate working in alternate locations, telecommuting, a coined term for working at a distance, was promoted as one way to alleviate the energy crisis. In 1983, the cover of *Forbes*, a business magazine, illustrated a future freeway with no cars. The caption 'It's 8:45 — do you know where your employees are?' implied, first, that all workers would work from home and second, that they would work in their homes full time. Nether prediction came true.

During the 1980s and 1990s the U.S. Congress funded pilot telecommuting programs within transportation and energy bills. That policy stimulated telecommuting programs starting in the western states of California, and Washington and gradually spreading East. State governments have generally followed their internal telecommuting programs with employer outreach programs. However, even with the incentives of free consultant help, and more recently, tax credits, employers remain reluctant to let their employees work out of sight. Thus, telecommuting has not been as effective in solving traffic and air pollution problems as initially hoped.

The Present

Finally, we are compatible and connected

In the early stages of telecommuting very few homes and not that many employers had personal computers to facilitate remote work. From the late 1980s through the end of the century, both the availability and compatibility of hardware and software increased. As of 2001, we are heavy users of e-mail--you can't work at home without it--and we are increasingly dependent on the Internet. Teleworkers are just being introduced to "always on" broadband connectivity, but it is not yet widely available.

Except for a dip in 1995 during the last recession, telework has grown steadily. The number of employees working at home one or more days a month was 19.6 million, or 10 percent of U.S. adults in October 1999 and estimated at 23.6 million one year later (Pratt 1999; Nilles 2000).

In a time of full employment, employers are using permission to telework as an incentive to retain and hire skilled employees. Corporations are less interested in how their employees get to work than they are in hiring and keeping the best employees in order to compete.

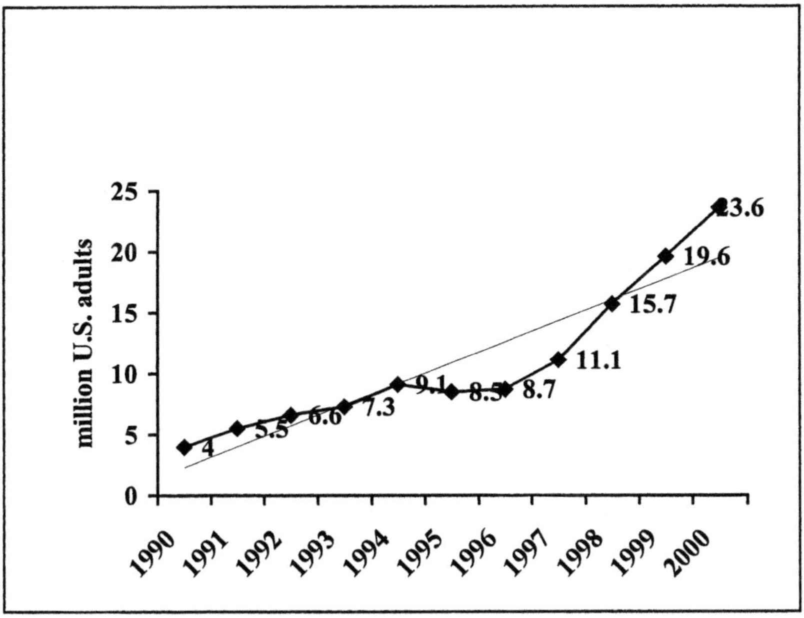

Figure 1. U. S. telecommuting population trend line
Source: CyberDialogue; Joanne H. Pratt Associates; Nilles

Technology enables working anywhere

The telework trend has paralleled the use of technology in homes. Teleworking is up because the use of PCs and the Internet is up. Ninety-four percent of U.S. homes have telephones, more than 40 percent have PCs and more than 33 percent are online as of 1999. Defined as employees who work at home during business hours, over half of the telecommuters already are online, as are nearly half of all homebased business owners.

Figure 2 shows that the number of teleworkers using the Internet has turned sharply upwards. Because the Internet connects the home office to the employer's LAN and to the world at large, this factor can be expected to increase the incidence of teleworking as well. Similarly, as "always on" broadband becomes more widely available throughout the country, it also, will facilitate homebased work. In a study of teleworkers who were provided with DSL, every participant 'reported that he/she enjoyed the enhanced speeds that allowed him/her to download and upload email or large data files, surf the web, etc., and reported greater productivity…'(Riley et al 2001).

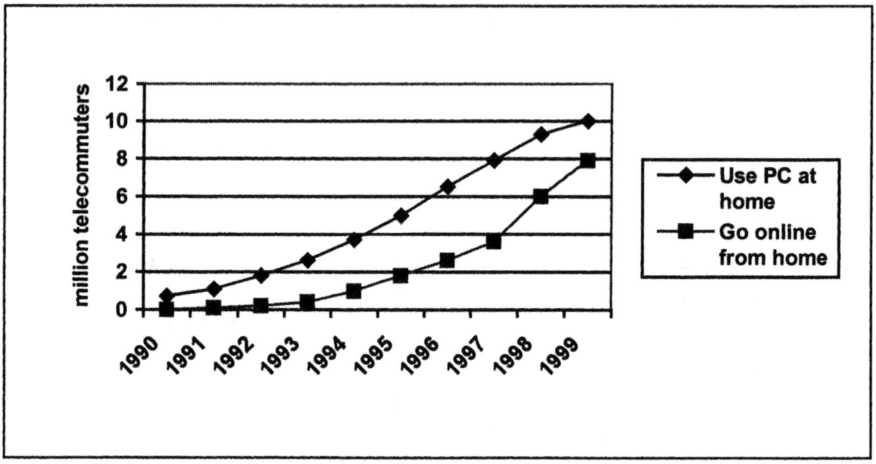

Figure 2. Technology enables working anywhere
Source: CyberDialogue

U. S. homes are becoming equipped for work

American homes are being remodeled to accommodate all kinds of teleworking. From 1995 to 1997, the number of homes with separate offices increased from 4 to 5 percent of all households (Pratt 2001a). An additional 7 percent of U.S. homes have offices in rooms that also are used for domestic functions. As Table 1 shows, most teleworkers set up their office in a bedroom.

Location of shared office	Percent
In bedrooms	67
In living rooms	11
In kitchens	5
In dining rooms	6
In other rooms	19
Total Shared	108

Table 1. Location of shared home offices
Source: 1995 American Housing Survey
Note: Total exceeds 100 percent because some homes have more than one shared office.

Both telework and after-hours work takes place at home

Over one-fourth of the U.S. adult population of 198 million adults works at home. In the past we thought that teleworkers would work either full time at home or on say, Tuesday and Thursday, each week. The reality is that 60 percent of the 55 million (1999) who do any work at all at home, work after hours. For Americans working longer hours in general, home is one of the places they can work those extra hours to reduce some of the stress. Twenty-seven percent of American teleworkers are *employees* who work at home during the business day but the remaining 25 percent constitute another important group, the *self-employed* who operate a business from home. Over one-half of small businesses are homebased.

U. S. teleworkers are about half men and half women. Those employees and homebased business owners who do telework average two or more days a week working from a home office but not necessarily working in the regular pattern that transportation planners had foreseen. Another 25 percent work at home only once or twice a month. The reason is clear if you look at work at home first, by the type of tasks individuals do at home and second, by their occupations (Figure 3):

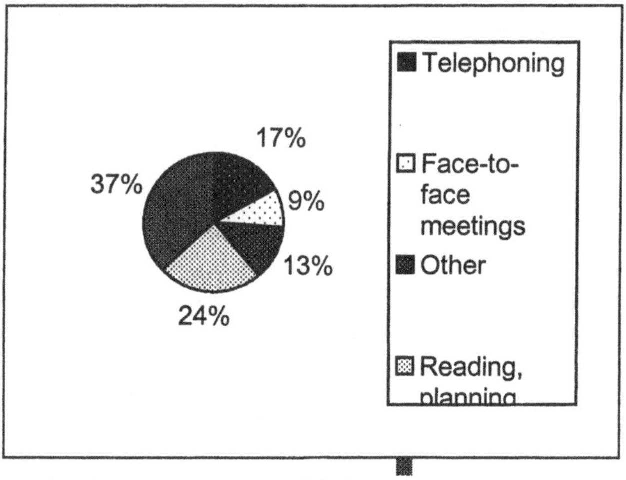

Figure 3. Work at home is computer and desk work
Source: Joanne H. Pratt Associates (Pratt 1999)

It is no surprise that people in their home offices work on their computer, do the planning and reading they can not get done at the office and telephoning. What may be surprising is that teleworkers include pilots, pediatricians, and cooks as well as the managers, professionals and sales representatives. The pilot, for example, works at home about once a week, spending 75 percent of his time on the computer and 25 percent reading and planning. Similarly, the pediatrician spends six days a month working 60 percent of the time on the computer and 30 percent on the telephone. Presumably he calls patients and updates their medical records. Self-employed construction workers prepare estimates of job costs and attend to their bookkeeping in their home offices. The point is that most occupations have some paper work. That paper work can often be carried out in a home office.

The Future

Telework is a pioneering form of the virtual organisation

At this stage in the evolution of telework, small, powerful and affordable technology is generally available in the U. S. for working at home. Provided by either the employer or more usually by the employee, equipment is not only available for work, but software incompatibilities also have largely been resolved.

Now teleworkers are becoming connected, a relatively few at broadband speeds. With the mechanics of equipping the home for work well in hand, attention can be directed to the role of telework in a global economy engaged in electronic commerce.

With the maturing or at least the adolescence of telework, we can analyse its role in a larger context. Teleworking is more than a commuting trip reduction strategy or a recruitment incentive. Seen in retrospect, it is an early form of flexible work, a pioneering form of the virtual corporation. Telework has been championed as a way to address environmental problems, help balance work/life responsibilities and gain competitive advantage in the e-commerce economy. Because it is motivated for such diverse reasons, it is time to examine the implications of teleworking for the worker and for the employer.

New organisational forms are less hierarchical and more collaborative

In the global world of e-commerce the organisation must soften its rigid boundaries in order to meet new challenges competitively. The new organisational form is referred to variously as virtual, imaginary, extended and collaborative (Cohen 1997). The virtual team may collaborate for a particular project, then dismantle when the work is completed. Team members may meet occasionally or never. They are likely to work globally.

Telework is a special case of virtual work. Typically employees who telework do not spend full time in their home offices. They continue to go to the employer's to work and to meet with co-workers. Although employees may work at home on a regular schedule of one or two days a week or on an episodic basis, the co-worker team lasts over an indefinite period of time (Pratt 2001). Teleworkers not only have a continuing face-to-face interaction with their employer but most live in the region, on average 18 miles from their central office (Pratt 1999).

The virtual organisation is reshaped as self-directed teams that work across space, time and organisational boundaries (Pratt 2001). This reorganisation of the workplace impacts the total organisation. It is expressed in the changing corporate culture as managers put into action the redefined "values of the organisation, its system of rewards and punishments, its spirit and its culture" (Drucker 1994). It impacts the employees and their families as formerly rigid boundaries between their work and their lives are blurred.

For managers, the evolving new corporate culture requires telemanaging virtual teams:

Telemanagers must learn to manage cultural differences

When their staff works virtually, outside the corporate center, there is less opportunity for the organisation to instill a common corporate culture. Therefore, one challenge supervisors face is how to manage cultural differences. The most effective approach emphasises transformational, rather than transactional leadership (Church and Waclawski 1999). That is, telemanagers help team members mutually define the culture and values applicable to the specific project, creating a 'situational culture' that does not necessarily last beyond the end of the project (Shakun 1999).

Telemanagers must learn to transfer power

Telemanagement requires transfer of power from the manager to the worker. The evolving information age organisation values the workers' intellectual capabilities rather than their brawn. No longer linked in the parent-to-child relationship reflected in the old nicknames 'Ma Bell' (AT&T), 'Mother Met' (Metropolitan Life) and 'Great Yellow Father' (Kodak), managers must free their workers to perform their work rather than wait for step-by-step instructions (Pink 2000; Pratt 2001).

Telemanagers must help bond work teams

Virtual teams are boundaryless. They lack the daily face-to-face interaction of formal meetings and informal encounters. Therefore it is incumbent upon telemanagers to substitute other forms of communication for the feedback provided by chit chat around the coffee pot and by body language as workers pass in the halls. For example, some telemanagers send daily e-mails; others hold a weekly brown bag lunch or pay for distant teleworkers to attend holiday parties. They must put conscious effort into keeping the project team bonded as a working group.

Telemanagers must promote trust

Trust underlies successful collaboration. Trust is based on positive feed-back that follows when each member of the team performs in accord with expectations (Pratt 1997). The manager has the responsibility to build and maintain trust among members of a project team. A particular challenge is to ensure that employees working in their homes are not inadvertently treated as somehow suspect. One set of instructions for team managers was to "Make it known that remote workers are 'at work'..." as if they, unlike other remote workers, needed justification (Fritz and Manheim 1998). Because perceived fairness is at the core of establishing trust, telemanagers in one U.S. federal office assign projects on a combined list of teleworkers and on-site employees (Langhof 2000).

For employees, the new challenges of a global workplace are to find new ways to demark their work and personal lives:

Teleworkers need to separate the public from the private domain when work moves into homes

Teleworking moves the boundary between public and private life from the street into the home. In the Industrial Age `the factory...took the worker and work out of the home and moved them into the workplace, leaving family members behind' (Drucker 1999). No longer does `going to work' mean literally getting into the car, commuting from the home through transitional time and space, before walking into the corporate office to "start" work. According to Mirchandani, `Teleworkers continue to organise their lives in terms of public and private, although the meanings of these terms shift from workplace-home to work-nonwork. In effect, the division shifts to one within the home, instead of one between the home and workplace' (Mirchandani 1999). Men and women set the new boundaries in different ways. For men, work comes first. They call the family a 'temptation'. Although most women do not try to combine work with simultaneous childcare, still women see their family, not work, as their priority responsibility.

However, neither for men nor for women, does telecommuting from bedroom to home office afford the same degree of transition or psychological relief from omnipresent domestic tasks as does getting into the car and driving off. Also, broadband "always on" Internet connecting us globally makes the world feel omnipresent in our homes.

Employees find they have to legitimise homebased work

Teleworkers feel they must legitimise their working at home as a defensive response to their managers, co-workers, family, neighbors and society—and even to their own children. For teleworkers, the public-private boundary shift raises new questions such as privacy. For example, supervisors telephone employees less often on work-at-home days than when they are on-site because they feel they are intruding on private space. Another problem can be that teleworkers are caught between wanting recognition for their higher productivity at home while fearing jealousy from co-workers who do not have the same privilege.

Teleworkers need to learn to "turn it off"

Teleworking in a global e-commerce world means an 'always on' 24-7 work/life. Being equipped to work at home or as mobile workers and grateful for the opportunity to do so, teleworkers are particularly vulnerable to making themselves available day and night. What will put the brakes on being available for work 24 hours a day and seven days a week? It is becoming habitual to respond to cell phone calls. However, lack of quality time 'as an economic and political issue, ...goes unacknowledged and ignored' (Kaplan and Chelton 1996).

What is uniquely American?

As a gross generalisation, but having elements of truth, citizens of the United States still express the culture of our founders. We were the rebels against British rule who made independence our greater virtue. The American personality retains elements of independence, resistance to central authority and entrepreneurism. That may partly explain why, in their gut, supervisors equate their workers' independence with irresponsibility and disobedience. As technology weakens the control of the physical corporate headquarters, managers are left ambivalent about the positive benefits of a self-actuating remote workforce.

Another American characteristic is the tendency to overwork, but at some point enough is enough. It is not at all clear in the U.S., if indeed it is anywhere else, what form the backlash will take to being 'always on'. The early signs are that the answer will arise in the open market, not as a result of action by unions or the government. Unions formed in response to overwork in the Industrial Age helped get the Wages and Hours (later Fair Labor Standards) Act passed in 1940, setting the 40-hour work week, which meant that people 'worked specified hours; the rest of the day was their own' (Lutins 2000; Drucker 1994). But from the early days of telecommuting, unions have rejected work at home even over the clamor of their own telework wannabe members.

Another possibility is government regulation. The Occupational Safety and Health Administration (OHSHA) quickly rescinded a ruling that would have monitored the home work place for safety. However, in the open market it is becoming usual to see or hear messages to turn cell phones off in theaters and concert halls. 'Silent' cars are a popular new addition to Amtrak commuter trains and one airline has a sign predominantly displayed on the ticket counter requesting that cell phone calls be completed before approaching the agent.

As employers, corporations need to link restructuring to work and family concerns in order to promote successful change. For their own workers they need to help establish new limits for expected hours of work, a new business ethic for doing commerce in a global universe and new business etiquette for use of intrusive technology.

In 2001 is Teleworking simply Mobile Business?'

Siemens, a German company founded in 1847, expressed in a 2001 advertisement a more likely future for telework than did the 1983 cover of Forbes (Business Week 2001). Picturing a worker barefoot on a sandy beach, the text inquires: `The head office, The car office, The home office, The beach office. How many offices would you like?' Now an international company itself, Siemens does not ask `Do you know where your employees are?' which was the question at the dawn of telecommuting, but the more relevant question for today's world of mobile business conducted over the Internet: `When will you let your valued employees go? The best talent may prefer to work *for* your company only if they don't have to work *at* your company.'

Telework in the United States—and very likely elsewhere—has evolved from an atypical way to work at home for a relatively few employees to a more flexible pattern of using cell phones, PDAs and combination handheld devices connected to the Internet, to work any time and anywhere—without necessarily giving that pattern a name. Continuing challenges are to maintain work/life balance and separation between public and private domains.

References

Business Week (2001) April 23: 12-13.

Church, A. H. and Waclawski (1999) 'The impact of leadership style on global management practices', Journal of Applied Social Psychology, 29, 7: 1416-1443.

Cohen, S. (1997) *Training and Development*, American Society for Training and Development 5, 5: 30-32.

Drucker, P. F. (1994) 'The age of social transformation', *Atlantic Monthly*, November. http://www.theatlantic.com/politics/ecbig/soctrans.htm. Accessed 4/18/01

Drucker, P. F. (1999) 'Beyond the information revolution', *Atlantic Monthly*, October. http://www.theatlantic.com/issues/9oct/9910drucker.htm. Accessed 4/18/01.

Fritz, M. B. and Manheim (1998) 'Managing virtual work: A framework for managerial action,' in *Organizational Virtualness*, Sieber, P.and Griese (eds), proceedings of the VoNet Workshop, April 27-28.

Kaplan, D. and Chelton (1996) 'Is it time to dump the forty-hour week?' *Conscious Choice*, September. www.consciouschoice.com/issues/cc095/dump40hourweek.html Accessed 4/16/2001.

Langhof, J. (2000) *ITAC TeleBytes*, August.

Lutins, A.(2000) 'An eclectic list of events in U.S. labor history', August 21. http://lutins.org/labor.html. Accessed 4/16/2001.

Mirchandani, K. (1999) 'Legitimizing work: telework and the gendered reification of the work-nonwork dichotomy', *Canadian Review of Sociology and Anthropology,* 36, 1: 87-107.

Nilles, J. M. (2000) *Telework in the U.S.: Telework America Survey*, Washington, D.C.: International Telework Association and Council (ITAC).

Pink, D. (2000) 'Understanding the free agent nation', keynote speech, International Telework Association and Council (ITAC), The World is Our Workplace conference, New Orleans, LA, September 17-20.

Pratt, J. H. (2001) 'Telework and society—implications for corporate and societal cultures', *Telework: the New Workplace of the 21st Century*, U. S. Department of Labor, 225-243.

Pratt, J. H. (2001a) *Policy and Travel Planning Implications of Work/Life Changes: Insights from the NPTS and Other Surveys*, Bureau of Transportation Statistics (forthcoming).

Pratt J. H. (1999) *Cost/benefits of Teleworking to Manage Work/life Responsibilities,* Washington, D.C.: International Telework Association and Council (ITAC).

Pratt, J. H. (1997) 'Teamwork, trust, and technology', Second International Workshop in Telework, Amsterdam, September 2-5.

Riley, P., Mandavilli and Heino (2001) 'Observing the impact of communication and information technology on 'net-work', *Telework: the New Workplace of the 21st Century*, U. S. Department of Labor, 140-154.

Shakun, M. F. (1999) 'An ESD computer culture for intercultural problem-solving and negotiation', *Group Decision and Negotiation*, 8, 3: 237-249.

26 Telework Trends in Brazil: Preliminary Research Results

Álvaro A. A. Mello[1] and Luiz Ojima Sakuda

Brazilian Society of Telework and Teleactivities

Introduction

Telework studies in Brazil are still little developed. The development of Internet and its great coverage by mass media encourage the discussion of Telework-related topics, but most writing "to date involves prescriptions based heavily on the experience of individuals and does not use existing theory or recent research." There were no great changes since the literature review made by Sakuda (1999), which presented the first research between Brazilian Teleworkers users of telecenters:

> "Telework is currently not a widely discussed topic in Brazil, and it has been approached only indirectly in the mass media. Some popular authors [...] emphasise the importance of Telework in the context of work flexibility because of the impact of information technologies on our society. Other authors [...], follow the trend previously detected by Lamond *et al.* (1997) in the database ABI/Inform: "Most writing on Telework to date involves prescriptions based heavily on the experience of individuals and does not use existing theory or recent research."
>
> The first specific academic work published in Brazil was Soares (1995). Published originally in Gattiker (1992), the article analyses a Telework research study made on two data processing centers in Brazil between 1989 and 1992. The author is

1 The authors would like to express their sincere appreciation to the following individuals and organizations, for without their support, this research would not have been achieved its purposes. For funding the research and institutional support: Brazilian Society of Telework and Teleactivities (SOBRATT), Consiel Management, Consulting E Formazione, São Paulo Council of the Administration Professional (CRA/SP), and Transamerica Services and Commerce. For the organizations selected and researched duly indicated in this chapter that allowed the authors to have their Telework programmes as case studies to this survey: Bayer S/A, Cebela – Centro Brasileiro de Estudos Latino-Americanos, Cisco do Brasil Ltda., Consiel Management, Consulting E Formazione, Cosipa –Companhia Siderúrgica Paulista, IBM do Brasil Ltda., Kodak Brasileira Comércio e Indústria Ltda / Kodak da Amazônia Indústria e Comércio Ltda., Natura Cosméticos S/A, Siemens Ltda (IT Division), Siemens Ltda (Telecommunications Division), Tess S/A, and Weg Automação.

critical regarding the myths of Telework and concludes that, "using Zuboff's terminology, the management tried to informate ORG1, but actually just automated it. As a result, ORG1's organizational structure became more rigid and static after Telework introduction even though the opposite result had been desired." This was the only academic work in this area with field research in Brazil until the publication of this article.

Two master theses, written by Oliveira (1996) and Troppe (1998), are also interesting. Oliveira examines home-based Telework, proposing ergonomics to study working conditions improvement. Troppe emphasises the differences between virtual organization and Telework concepts, basing his study mostly on European authors. Although he doesn't present a theoretical or empirical point of view, his work is valuable since he is the first Brazilian author to have a book about Telework published by a major publishing house which has contributed to the diffusion and debate of the concept. However, his glossary definition of Telework as "the act of working outside of an organization's facilities while communicating with the organisation through a personal computer, a modem, and communications software," is quite restrictive.

Mello (1997) was the first to publish a book on home-based Telework, released during the event "Home Office 97" organised by him. The book also presents a translation of several of Gil Gordon's "frequently asked questions." An enlarged and updated version of this work was released by the Brazilian Human Resources Association (ABRH) in the second semester of this year (Mello, 1999). In addition, other Brazilian specific books are the translations of Nilles (1994) and Kugelmass (1996)."

Telework involves many aspects - economic, social, cultural, technological, legal, ecological, transportation and others; and many actors - organisations, individuals, governments, employers' associations, workers' unions, equipment and services suppliers, disabled people and others. This chapter aims at showing the complexity of the theme, examining, for the first time in Brazil, the experiences in 12 outstanding Brazilian companies of distinct sectors, which are using Telework, formally and informally.

Favourable Conditions to the Development of Telework in Brazil

The Advance of Information and Communication Technologies

According to Gazeta Mercantil (2000), the main Brazilian business newspaper, the telecommunications sector can be considered an island of prosperity. The expansion of the conventional telephone network, the Internet, cellular operators, trunking, paging and optical fibres pull the investments. Industry's revenues are expected to grow 30% in 2000, achieving US$ 5.2 billion. Last year it achieved US$ 4 billion and in 1998, US$ 3 billion, according to the Brazilian Association of the Electric and Electronic Industry (ABINEE).

The population of cellular phones alone reached 13 millions last year, and it is expected to jump to 23 million in 2003. Of the ones produced in Brazil, which probably totalled 10 million in 1999, around 4.5 million were exported. The figures are estimates from ABINEE, because the companies do not present official numbers.

The Internet has become one of the main industry catalysts, both to the telecommunications and to the informatics industries. The 10th Annual Research on Informatics Resources Administration, carried out by the Applied Informatics Resources Centre of Fundação Getúlio Vargas (CIA/FGV, 2000) showed that 80% of the 1.5 thousand researched companies are in the Internet. All of them have at least two institutional pages in the web. Of the research universe, 60% are companies classified among Brazil's 500 biggest companies. Brazilian Internet is growing very fast. Brazilian bank industry is considered one of the most advanced in terms of technology. Bradesco, the largest private bank, was the only bank mentioned on Bill Gates' book "Business @ The Speed of Thought". New services are available, as cheaper broadband connection (DSL and cable), distance learning and others. The authors believe that this teleactivities' development will contribute to Brazilian Telework expansion.

The eLatin American Report, published by eMarketer on June 14, 2000, revealed that, according to their researches, Argentina, Mexico and Brazil, which all together represent 80% of Latin America's Internet users, total today 8 million of Internet users. It seems to be difficult for foreign companies to understand how to do their researches and methodologies in Brazil. How can these companies analyse Brazilian market's complexity beyond the comparative figures with the North-American market? An example that is seen as restricting the fast development of the Internet economy, always mentioned by international research institutes, is the high number of PCs per capita in the USA, compared to the extremely reduced number of Brazilian homes with on-line PCs.

As a good national initiative in this area, Datafolha, the respectable research institute of the Folha de São Paulo newspaper's Group, published its research on Brazilian Internet users. Conducted in the end of 1999, it presented an estimated number of 7.6 million of Internet users (only in Brazil). At that time, this number was accepted and confirmed by the main local access providers. With a growth rate of almost 170% per year, surely the Brazilian Internet users already total approximately 13 million, 60% of which do not have their own PC and use PCs from third parties, at the company where they work, at school or at friends and relatives' homes.

Brazilian Internet users represent the economic elite, which belongs to the upper classes. The rich Brazil, around 40% of the population, is bigger than Italy's population, composed of 64 million Brazilians, who are the major part of our middle class, especially in the south and southeast regions, including the extremely rich economic elite, which corresponds to less than 1% of the population. Of these, 60 million, based on the Datafolha's research and on the growth rate of the Internet in Brazil, representing approximately 20% "of this Brazil", and with purchasing power similar to that of the developed countries, use the Internet frequently. The rest of the Brazilian population, the unprivileged ones, the remaining 100 million of Brazilians, are excluded for the time being, waiting for cellular telephony, which, rather than the PC, will bring the mass of low income consumers to the Internet economy.

This second wave, which will reach the lower classes, is already being formed, pulled by 12 million cellular phone users, whose annual growth rate is 50% per year. That figure has been gradually increasing, with the possibility of surpassing the number of fixed telephones users in the short term. The millions of Brazilians who are excluded from access to the Internet due to the high cost of a PC and also due to the complexity of the interaction that this technology presents will be rapidly brought to the new economy.

In the next three years, great changes are expected to the use of WAP technology, that is cheaper, mobile, and that, even though it is more limited as media, is also more adequate to consumers with less sophisticated contents, such as the Brazilians with a lower educational level. This group of Brazilians are more interested in comfort and access to the consumption of global products, which nowadays are concentrated in shopping malls located at the great Brazilian cities, but very distant from the millions of consumers spread throughout Brazil.

The Flexibility of Work Relations and Employment Contracts

According to Pastore (2000), jobs all over the world are being exposed to international competition, directly or indirectly. It is impossible to keep them here or there. They arrive, stay for a while and go away, like travellers. Workers' unions cannot control them, being left in a weak defensive position.

All this has a tremendous impact on the labour institutions. In this context, collective negotiation is no longer effective, neither are the Brazilian laws. Work, which used to be called "a-typical", is getting more and more typical. Thousands of new activities and professions do not fit in the existing laws. This is the case, for example, for the Teleworker, the personal trainer and the teacher who teaches English to executives during lunch-time. None of them is an employee nor a small company owner.

In Brazil, the informal market has already achieved 60%. Part of this figure is constituted by fraud, but the greatest part results from new ways of working that do not adjust to the current laws. Consequently, people are forced to live without the conventional protections – all of which are linked to formal employment. For example, only those who were employed somewhere have the right to receive unemployment insurance, to have the Mandatory Fund for Unemployment Benefit, or to retire.

With the shrink of the employment world and the expansion of the work world, not only is the worker left unprotected, but social security suffers a capital loss, increasing the deficit of the public finances, which reduces even more the capacity of the State to protect those who need it most– youths, women, old people and the disabled. This is the problem: how do you protect the new ways of working, like Telework, that have nothing to do with employment? The existing institutions have become obsolete and are not being substituted by others. In sociology, this is called institutional crisis.

The few changes in the work field have been slow, timid and disorientated. Brazilian "informality" does not stop growing, while the reforms are done in a stop-and-go basis. They advance when the crisis worsens, but are forgotten when the economy starts to recover. This year (2000) Brazil started growing again, and there was a sensation that the labour problem was overcome. In the last 12 months, 822 thousand jobs were created, but only 62 thousand with the employer having signed the employee's working papers. And, from now on, work will be increasingly carried out under the new flexible contracting forms – subject to internationalisation and escaping from conventional rules.

The number of Brazilian companies that are adopting flexible contracting forms is becoming more and more significant. This is the conclusion of a research carried out in February 2000 by the University of São Paulo (USP). The survey, coordinated by Professor Hélio Zylberstajn, concentrated on the theme "Flexible and non-traditional contracting forms" and pointed out that 45% of the companies hire their employees exclusively by means of the traditional employment system. A mix, joining the traditional form to others, is used by 55% of the researched companies.

Within this group, in 14% of the companies the proportion of employees hired by flexible and non-traditional forms varies between 20 and 40% of the total. The research proved that flexible and non-traditional forms previously mentioned by Pastore are already a reality in the Brazilian labour market, but that formal employment will still predominate for a long period of time. The alternative contracting form that was most mentioned in the research was outsourcing, used by 91% of the companies. This predominance is natural, because it was the first flexible form of contracting that appeared in the country.

Other ways of working mentioned in the research were: temporary job (59%); contract over a pre-determined period of time (55%); self-employment (50%); work by project / task (32%); part-time work (23%); on call work (15%); home-based work (9%); and Telework (9%). A curious piece of information: the alternative “other kinds of contracting” was ticked by 18% of the sample. It is possible to conclude that there is a great diversity of flexible contracting forms.

With regard to the objectives alleged for the utilisation of alternative flexible contracts, cost reduction is the most cited in this research:

- To adjust the workforce to the floating demand: 76%
- To reduce the cost of social charges: 76%
- To reduce workforce cost: 67%
- To optimise equipment use: 48%
- To meet the characteristics of the used technology: 43%
- To test new employees: 29%

Finally, the research shows that 10% of the companies use flexible forms in order to fulfil an employee’s requirement.

The Research

The research was carried out between March and July 2000. The initial purpose was to conduct a national research on the theme, using the ECATT methodology (*Electronic Commerce and Telework Trends*); however, the authors ultimately decided to approach representative companies that already implemented Telework and carry out exploratory research. Thus, exploratory questionnaires were sent by e-mail to 30 companies, and 12 organisations sent their answers back. Some companies we contacted did not reply, which can be explained by two factors:

- generally speaking, the Brazilian companies are not inclined to provide information for the academic community, and they usually consider any data as “confidential”, especially concerning labour matters;
- as the legal aspects of Telework in Brazil are not yet quite formalized, additional risk may be perceived with deeper exposure on the theme.

However, the authors feel that this research has contributed to create an awareness concerning the issue, in order to have organisations that are interested in partnerships for the elaboration of further research on Telework in Brazil.

Methodology and Characteristics of the Sample

In order to guarantee the anonymity of the respondents, the sector of the companies are not presented in next page’s table, which presents the profile of researched organisations. The great majority of Teleworkers in the sample are company employees. However, the situation is slightly different in the other companies. In the majority of Telework cases that was detected outside the sample, the system is not formalised (it is informal or hidden from the directors) and there is an aversion to its study. The lack of clear and disseminated rules regulating Telework also inhibits the study of the real state of affairs in Brazil. The area with Telework most cited is sales (7 of the 12 organizations). Technical assistant, support, maintenance and related issues is the second most cited (4 of the 12 organizations). Then follows consulting (3 organizations), management (3), marketing (1) and training (1). (See table below)

Frequency data available is not conclusive, because many organizations did not made this item available. For example, in sales area, Teleworkers from 3 organizations spend more than 70% of their time teleworking; while in other 3 organizations, the Teleworkers spend between 30% and 70% teleworking. One organization didn't supply this data. The place of Telework also varies a lot, and suggests that both frequency and place are more related to the way of working of the organizations than to telework itself.

	Total of collaborators in the organisation (Teleworker and non-Teleworkers)	Functions / Areas with Teleworkers	Teleworker's Status		Frequency (Time)			Place of Telework		
			Employee	Autonomous	> 70%	30 – 70%	< 30%	At home	Mobile	Custo-mer
1	90	- executive board / management	10	-	-	X	-	X	X	-
		- marketing	4	-	-	X	-	X	X	-
		- training	1	-	-	X	-	X	X	-
		- sales	30	-	-	X	-	X	X	-
		- engineering	20	-	-	X	-	X	X	-
2	3900	- consulting	193	-		not available		-	X	-
		- maintenance	131	-		not available		-	X	-
		- sales	150	-		not available		-	X	-
3	1000	- sales	23	-	X	-	-	-	X	-
4	370	- engineering	1	-	X	-	-	X	-	-
5	5680	- technical assistance	18	2	-	X	-	-	-	X

6	20	- consulting	8	8	-	-	X	-	-	X
7	737	- sales	21	53	-	X	-	-	X	X
8	2930	- sales	392	-	-	X	-	-	-	-
		- maintenance, inspection and installation	535	-	X	-	-	-	X	-
		- product development	18	-	X	-	-	-	X	-
		- support	21	-	X	-	-	-	X	-
9	2405	not available	not available			not available			not available	
10	3000	- sales	610	-	X	-	-	X	-	-
11	1321	- sales, regional management, technical support	147	-	X	-	-	-	X	-
12	20	- executive board / management	2	-		not available			not available	
		- consulting	-	2		not available			not available	

Major Findings

The first question in the questionnaire about the reasons of the implementation of Telework and the result was as follows:

Reasons	Number of answers
To make working hours and workplaces more flexible	7
To increase quality / productivity	6
To reduce the employee's need to commute and the time he spends in the traffic / to avoid the system of cars rotation	6
Pressures concerning dates when work must be completed	4
To compensate lack of personnel	1
Employee's interest (taking care of old people, of their own children, physical handicap, moving out of their house...)	1
Space restrictions	1
To reduce costs	1
Work confidentiality	-
Others: Characteristic of the job	3

The new ways of working demand a spatial-temporal flexibilisation with an increase in quality and productivity. Telework emerges as a natural alternative. It is important to note that the concern about increase in quality and productivity is higher than the concern about cost reduction, which was mentioned just once in this question. The majority of the selected companies are located in the city of São Paulo, where traffic-jam problems are becoming increasingly critical. The system of car rotation has been implemented in the central zones. This scenario explains why the reduction of the need to commute is the second most cited item. The city of São Paulo has a population of ten million of inhabitants and five million of vehicles. This ratio of vehicles for inhabitants (1 vehicle for 2 inhabitants) is greater than New York City (1 vehicle for 3,7 inhabitants), and much higher than the Brazilian national ratio (1 vehicle for 9,4 inhabitants). We believe that in other medium sized Braziian cities, where traffic jams are not so critical, this item is not as relevant in the decision.

The process of implementation of Telework schemes was planned in only three cases, and it was perceived as arising out of technology in five cases. In one company, Telework was the solution found to keep a qualified employee that moved out of where he lived. In only two cases there were specific Telework training, and in four cases the selection process was considered enough for the choice of the Teleworkers. In four cases, there was neither selection nor specific training. This result shows that Telework, even in the few companies in which it is implemented, is not perceived as a work-form that requires formal training, and that the transition to this new work-form is considered to be simple.

The question about factors that inhibit Telework had the following answers:

Factors	Number of answers
Managers' lack of knowledge about how to plan and organise Telework	9
Problems relating to security, confidentiality, insurance, health or legislation	6
Difficulties to manage and supervise the Teleworkers	4
Reasons relating to work productivity or quality	2
Lack of pressure to change current practices	2
High investments in computers and telecommunications services and products	2
Communication problems with the Teleworkers	1
Workers unions' resistance	1
Employees' lack of interest	-

It is important to observe the absence of answers in the items "High investments in computers and telecommunications", "Employees lack of interest" and "Workers unions resistance". The three most cited items are clearly connected with the management and operationalisation of Telework, and the question of employment contract was specifically mentioned.

In the question about the tools used by the Teleworkers, the only unanimity was the telephone. The fax machine (10 cases) was cited more than remote access (9 cases) and telephone conference (7 cases). This shows that, in the researched sample, traditional technologies are considered to be enough for Telework. However, remote access and the use of computers will be part of the "basic Telework technology" in the coming years.

In the question about the advantages and disadvantages of Telework perceived by companies and individuals, answers obtained confirm many previous studies about the theme. The following advantages to the individuals were mentioned:

- Productivity gains due to real-time availability of information (access to permanent and up-to-date documentation);
- Productivity gains due to focus on specific work (reduction of interruptions);
- Freedom to work in a way they consider to be adequate (more autonomy);
- Facility to conciliate work and personal life;
- More flexibility;
- Higher quality of life;
- Better geographical distribution (regional manager in each area, in this case).

The following disadvantages to the individual were mentioned:

- Distancing from the company;
- Difficulty in having brainstorming meetings;
- Interruptions by home issues;
- Loneliness;
- Lack of contact with colleagues and lack of knowledge about daily information.

With regard to the companies, the advantages that were mentioned were:

- Faster processes and problem-solving activities;
- Increase in productivity;
- Increase in revenues;
- Productivity gains;
- Image of state-of-the-art technology;
- Liberation of physical space;
- Increase in customer satisfaction;

- Improvement of duration and frequency of customer's visit;
- Customer's proximity;
- Elimination of geographic limitations;
- Cost reduction.

The following disadvantages were mentioned by the companies:

- Collaborator's distancing from the company;
- Making "coaching" between managers and supervisors more difficult;
- Forces formal communication, which may have negative impact on content richness;
- Difficulty in transferring pre-programmed tasks;
- Lack of trustworthiness of the access system;
- Costs of extra structure.

It is important to notice that, again, the increase in productivity was emphasised more than cost reduction. Among the comments contained in the questionnaires, two were selected as being complementary and summarising the others: one company considers that Telework "is an innovative type of work, it improves the type of work, (but) it is not very disseminated" and the other company is "very satisfied with our experience, because Telework is no bugaboo" and it intends to extend it to its world-wide activities.

Limitations of the Study and Conclusions

Considering the sample of the companies researched, the authors foresee that Telework is becoming increasingly important within the organisations and that it shall be one of the main discussion themes in the coming years. The increasing use of ICT, the discussion of new ways of working, the environmental and public and individual health repercussions on society, all play a role in the dissemination of Telework in organizations in Brazil.

There is a clear need for activities to raise awareness amongst talented Brazilian managers, thereby making Telework a viable new method of working in Brazil. Awareness-raising activities need to be complemented with training programmes, including heavy behavioural and culture components of "learn by doing" for these potential Teleworkers, as mentioned in Mello and Sakuda (1999).

However, it is important to acknowledge that the evidence in this research is indicative rather than conclusive. Due to the small number and homogenous nature of potential Teleworkers included in this research, it was not possible to test various subordinate hypothesis of interest. The lack of comparable data in Brazil with other organizations' cases limits the research conclusions. Accordingly, further and comparable research would be necessary to assess successfully the implementation of Telework in Brazilian companies.

References

CIA-FGV (2000) *10a Pesquisa Anual de Administração de Recursos de Informática* ('The 10th Annual Research on Informatics Resources Administration'), Centro de Informática Aplicada da Fundação Getúlio Vargas. Fundação Getúlio Vargas: São Paulo.

EITO– European Information Technology Observatory (1998) 'Telework: Status, Development and Issues', in *European Information Technology Observatory 98.* European Information Technology Observatory: Frankfurt.

Gazeta Marcantil 'Oásis das Telecomunicações' ("Telecommunications' Oásis") *Gazeta Mercantil*, 03 de abril de 2000. Gazeta Mercantil: São Paulo.

Lamond, D.; Daniels, K.; Standen, P. (1997) 'Defining Telework: What Is It Exactly?' in Jackson, P.; Van der Wielen, J. (Eds.) *Amsterdam'97 - Second International Workshop on Telework. Proceedings of the Workshop: Building Actions on Ideas"* Work and Organisation Research Center and Brunel University: Tilburg, London.

Mello, A. A. A. (1997) *A Volta para casa: desmistificando o telecommuting (Back home: de-mithing telecommuting).* Alvaro Mello: São Paulo.

___ (1999) *Teletrabalho (Telework): o trabalho em qualquer lugar e a qualquer hora (Telework: work anywhere and anytime).* Qualitymark, ABRH Nacional: Rio de Janeiro.

___ Sakuda, L.O. (1999) 'Intrapreneurship Contributions to Telework' in Spinks, W. (Ed.). *Proceedings of the Second International Workshop on Telework: 'Telework Strategies for the New Workforce'* International Telework Foundation, International Flexwork Forum: Tokyo.

Ministério das Comunicações (1997) *PASTE - Programa de Recuperação e Ampliação do Sistema de Telecomunicações e do Sistema Postal (Brazilian Programme of Telecommunications Recovery and Expansion) – Edição 1997.* Ministério das Comunicações, Brasília.

Moraes Filho, E. (1994) *Trabalho a Domicílio e Contrato de Trabalho (Homework and Labours Contracts),* LTr: São Paulo.

Oliveira, M. M. V. (1996) *Ergonomia e o teletrabalho a domicílio (Ergonomics and home-based Telework).* Universidade Federal de Santa Catarina: Florianópolis.

Pastore, J. (1998) *O desemprego tem cura? (Does unemployment have a cure?)* Makron Books: São Paulo.

___ (2000) 'Obsolescência das instituições do trabalho' ("Obsolescence of work institutions") *O Estado de São Paulo,* 04 de abril de julho de 2000, O Estado de São Paulo: São Paulo

Sakuda, L.O. (1999) 'Telework in Business Centers and Virtual Offices in Brazil' in Spinks, W. (Ed.). *Proceedings of the Second International Workshop on Telework: 'Telework Strategies for the New Workforce* International Telework Foundation, International Flexwork Forum: Tokyo.

Soares, A. (1995) 'Teletrabalho e Comunicação em Grandes CPDs' ("Telework and Communication in Data Processing Centers in Brazil") *Revista de Administração de Empresas,* v.35, n. 2, Mar/Abr-95 pp. 64-77.

Troppe, A. (1998) *Organizações Virtuais e Teletrabalho (Virtual Organisations and Telework),* Qualitymark: Rio de Janeiro.

27 Teleworking: Opportunities for the Indian Woman

Shiri Ahuja

Institute for Integrated Learning in Management, Lodhi Institutional Area
New Delhi, India

Introduction

'Women constitute half the population of India, but do not represent the work force in the same proportion' This statement is a strong reflection of the position of women in India. There are various stages through which a slow elimination of women from the active work force takes place in India. This begins during childhood at lower socio-economic levels where a boy is sent to school while the girl child stays at home to help out the mother. In the higher socio economic classes, this discrimination shows itself in the way children are brought up. While boys get more and more technology toys, girls are encouraged to play with dolls and kitchen sets. Even if a girl gets school education, discrimination sets in at the level where professional or specialised education is to be imparted.

Once a woman has a family, double income is always preferred to contain the rising cost of living and fulfill the desire for better standards. Lack of right education, or education at all, now forces a woman to take up jobs which may add to the family income but do not give any satisfaction to her. Nor do such jobs have any future. Most women with such generalised education resort to jobs like teaching or jobs that are clerical in nature. At middle age many of them opt to drop out of these jobs because of various socio cultural reasons. Besides, too many professionally educated women, who are stressed with rising family expectations, react to this stress by dropping out of the workforce.

The various sections of this chapter suggest ways in which teleworking and the use of Information and Communication Technologies at micro and macro levels can improve the scenario for Indian women in the above mentioned stages, at various socio economic levels.

Women, Teleworking and India: A SWOT Analysis

Strengths of India

This section presents some factual information about India. These facts have long been taken as disadvantages in the case of India. However, in the new millenium, they are proving to be India's strengths as a country with huge potential for teleworking.

"Happiness is the end for which human beings are designed", said Aristotle. According to the survey the "1999 Happiness Barometer", Indians are second after Americans, with 37% (24% Global) declaring themselves happy (Times of India 2000). Relationships with family and friends seem to be the most important source of happiness to Indians. Besides, satisfaction with one's job is seen to be strongly correlated with the ratings in respect of possession of money and material goods.

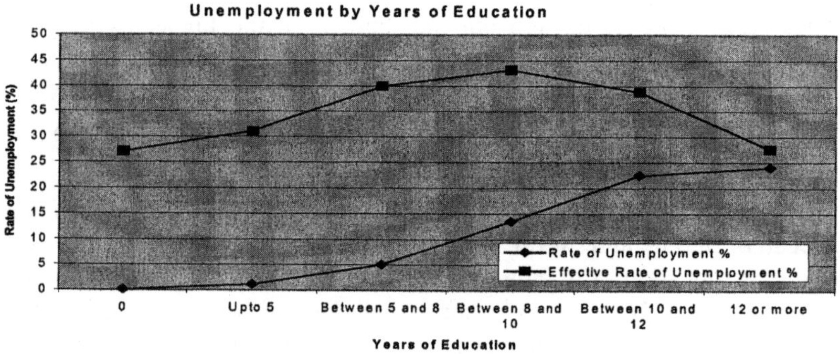

Figure 1. Unemployment by Years of Education

India has an enviable strength of numbers. The economically active age group of 15 to 64 years, comprises 59% of the Indian population, which is the most productive bracket (World Development Indicators, 1999). Even after discounting for illiteracy and low skill levels, the numbers are still large- at 180 to 200 million, providing India with the second largest pool of English speaking population after the US (Bhattacharjee 2000). Women make a third of this pool. (Table 1)

	Under graduate/graduate				Graduate/ postgraduate			
Year	**I**	**II**	**III**	**IV**	**I**	**II**	**III**	**IV**
1993-94	5,130,447	1,694,546	66.98	33.02	549,741	193,907	64.73	35.37
1992-93	4,900,537	1,589,071	67.57	32.43	510,317	181,837	64.37	35.63
1991-92	4,658,845	1,479,231	68.25	31.75	487,777	169,267	65.30	34.70

I= Total Enrolment III= Men's proportion to Total Enrolment

II= Enrolment of Women IV= Women's Proportion to Total Enrolment

Table 1. Levelwise Distribution of Men and Women Students in Higher Education
Source: University Grants Commission (1995)

Presently, the undergraduate population of India adds strongly to the number of educated unemployed (Figure 1) and contributes least in terms of GDP, but with IT based solutions to workplace and time, India's historical bane, its population has become the largest strength.

15.8 % of the total organised sector employment in India consists of women. The distribution of women employees in major industries reveals that community, social and personal services sectors continue to absorb the majority of women employees (India 1999). Indian women have always been considered to be more suited for such jobs, thus showing a higher rate of growth in their representation in services (21% in 1977-78 to 27%in 1993-94) as compared to men (11% in 1977-78 to 13% in 1993-94) (Ghosh 1999)

Until a few years back, these jobs did not pay very high salaries and were perceived as safe and less demanding on innovation and creativity, thus being highly suitable for women. With an influx of remote working opportunities and outsourced services, the Indian woman will still be the queen of the service world, but will have an increased ability to earn than in the past.

Among emerging markets, only India, China, Russia and Brazil offer continental scale economies. While a domestic market the size of the US or larger could eventually develop in India, it cannot develop in most other emerging market economies. To achieve such economies of scale, smaller IT producing countries like Israel and Ireland have no choice but to turn to export markets, where they may encounter trade barriers and greater competition.

The Weaknesses

Indian women suffer from disadvantages as a result of structural constraints, caused by the social environment dominated by patriarchy, legal frameworks which are not completely gender neutral and unequal access to education and training . Ironically, the two biggest happiness factors mentioned in the "1999 Happiness Barometer" also indicate towards the ongoing conflict an average Indian woman faces at work and at home. The cultural and social set up in India put all the onus of maintaining good 'relationship between family and friends' on the lady of the house. This factor gets even stronger with the continued tradition of joint families in India. The role of the woman as a working member is becoming increasingly acceptable in Indian society, but that has not reduced the family responsibilities or society's expectations from her.

Inspite of the social expectations, the career aspirations combined with her desire for economic independence are found to be in strong positive correlation with the level of a woman's education. The resultant contradiction between society's norms and individual aspirations is leading to some shocking developments within Indian society, such as singlehood or separation after marriage in order to fulfill their career aspirations.

Opportunities for India

While the introduction of location independent working is bound to support women and the disabled world wide, it is a boon for educated Indian women, irrespective of their level of education.

The entire scenario can be seen in terms of what it gives to the nation as a whole. Though the Information Technology Enabled Services cannot give India leadership in the next century, they will add very large amounts to the Indian GDP. A Nasscom study (National Association of Software and Services Companies) has projected that by 2008, 11,00,000 people will be employed in various IT enabled services being outsourced by companies or organisations located elsewhere in the world (www.teleworkingindia.com) The world wide ITES market is poised to grow from the present US $ 10 billion to US $180 billion by 2010. McKinsey and Company predicts that the number of teleworkers will rise to 1m- 3m people within 10 years (The Economist 1999).

The job opportunities being offered by Information technology, along with the freedom of time and place is attracting a very high percentage of technically and professionally qualified women in the workforce. This flexibility also has the potential to prevent working Indian women from dropping out of the work force in response to social and family expectations.

Threats facing India

A lot is being talked about India's strength given the global opportunity being made available by Information Technology. However, India may not be able to gain comparative advantage if the whole situation is not viewed critically, without any further delay.

Inspite of continued attention in each growth plan, the Indian education system has failed to link itself with employment. The feminine and masculine dichotomy of disciplines in higher education in India has not been diluted, but only strengthened by the patriarchal imprints on the disciplinary choices of women in higher education. The next section of this chapter will attempt to deal with these problems by suggesting strategies to align Indian education with newfound opportunities for employment.

The class and income levels of the family have always affected women's access to higher education in India. Over the years women have shown a constant inclination towards clustering in general disciplines which do not lead to specialisation and professional education. This tendency for generalised education is reflected more strongly as one moves towards middle and lower income families and socially lower classes. Consequently most technically and professionally qualified women belong to urban middle and upper strata of professional and salaried class in the metropolitan cities. Amongst these, a very high percentage of those belonging to top-level institutions pursue a career after their education. But as is observed at middle and lower end institutes, only about 30% of women students obtain jobs. Even amongst those who start pursuing careers as young executives, a very high percentage drops out after a few years. Thus, there occurs an absolute dearth of women at middle and top management levels. The section on 'Women, Work and Flexibility' will focus on strategies to attract and retain more educated women in the work force by providing them with the flexibility made feasible by location independent work practices.

Women and Employable Education

Globalisation has brought the question of education and skills development to the center of the employment scene. Statistics show that the Indian economy does not get full benefit of even low levels of education. (Figure 1)

The Problem of Unemployment

As reflected in Figure 1, part of the employment problem emanates from the mismatch between the skill requirements of employment openings and the skill bases of job seekers. The prime reason for this is that aspirations of educated tend to be inconsistent with their skill profile as well as with the requirements of the economy. It is therefore necessary to orient the education and training system towards improving its capability to supply - over the medium and long terms- the skills required by the potential sectors for employment. This is possible through an early reform of the education system so that the education policy can develop as a part of the employment policy or as a tool to achieve employment targets.

As the western hemisphere looks towards India as a suitable country for outsourcing several business activities, employment for the educated youth - those who have attained at least 12 years of education - can only be ensured through linking of education and employment policies of the country. Statistics also highlight that in India a higher percentage of girls forego education after 12 years of schooling thus adding to the observed positive relation between the level of education and rate of unemployment. This relationship is the most significant feature of unemployment in India.

This situation can be attributed to two factors. First, the level of educational attainment of an Indian is an indicator of wealth and income of the family. That means that only those people who can afford to remain out of the work force, as a result of the support they get from family income, opt for continued education. Thus higher the level of education, the weaker is the compulsion to participate in the active labour force.

Secondly, given the prevailing economic and socio-cultural context, education tends to incline young people to aspire for employment in non-manual occupations in the organised sector. They have very good reasons for doing this since the service sector actually offers the best quality jobs. Since aspirations, ability to afford unemployment and the level of education all move together, the outcome is a positive relation between the level of education and rate of unemployment.

General education in India does not equip the educated with particular skills other than perhaps clerical. The educated therefore may not necessarily find employment even when the organised sector generates employment at a rapid pace. Thus in Indian conditions, the rate of unemployment is more of an indicator of labour market mismatches generated by the spread of general education. The IT enabled services are being outsourced to India in time to correct the historical mismatches; provided again, the education and employment policies are tuned to complement each other.

Employment and Information Technology Advantage

Keeping in view the present labour market demand scenario, the Indian education system requires two important strategic changes to ensure that education leads to employment. Firstly, information technology has to become an integral part of schools from the very elementary levels. Secondly, the education and training of computers has to change face immediately. The present section will discuss these strategies separately, thus intending to provide a roadmap to design employment savvy education system.

IT in Education

The schools in India have computing as a subject from elementary levels, but the subject is taught in isolation of the dynamism of the field. Only the cash rich convent schools have an acceptable computer to student ratio. These too provide bare minimum practical training to the students. Most government aided schools, on the other hand, have an abysmally low ratio of computers to students. Many students may even pass out without ever having touched the mouse. This is matched with the fact that a very large segment of potential teleworkers for IT Enabled Services would come from these schools.

In order to transfer the benefits of IT to the students and increase their employability as teleworkers, technology has to be used as a tool, the effectiveness of which will depend not only it's accessibility, but on how it is implemented. The teachers can play a key role in integrating technology while educating the children. Lack of training for teachers in the use of IT is only encouraging avoidance of the use of the Web and computers in every day teaching. The main reason for this is that schools still look at it as a specific subject rather than a tool for learning.

Computer Education in Schools

The second strategy relates to changing the face of elementary computer education by changing the curriculum. Computers in most Indian convents are being introduced in the 2nd year of formal education. But the course contents are such that the children end up scoring grades in a subject rather than understanding its relevance in every day life. The fact that the students get hardly any exposure to the actual PC worsens the situation. There are even schools where the subject is not even introduced till the secondary level and if introduced, there is no exposure provided to computers.

The private sector in India is already doing relatively well in providing computer education to those youngsters who have obtained 8 to 12 years of general education. With over 35,000 certifications awarded since 1996, India is second only after the US in the number of Microsoft certified professionals. But all these efforts are only meant to complement the efforts that should essentially be made by the government of India.

Women Participation in Emergent Technologies

Presently, the Indian government is making many efforts to encourage participation of girls in the non-traditional and emergent technologies. Under centrally sponsored programmes, at +2 level vocational programmes with emphasis on entrepreneurship have been designed to cater to the needs of girls who drop out of schools. Special attention has also been given to the modernisation and establishment of women's Industrial Training institutes (ITIs) under the World Bank aided Vocational Training Project. Inspite of various efforts, gender disparities can be seen in programmes for skill development and training. There are many obstacles, such as unequal access to skill acquisition by women in many activities. Serious action on part of the government and civil societies is required, to alter the under-representión of women in high skill activities like information and communication technologies.

Women, Work and Flexibility

This section of the chapter deals with the class of women who are working at various levels in different organisations in India.

Working Women in India: Some trends

Before the statistics and strategies are discussed further, a few trends regarding working women may be quoted in order to familiarize the reader with various characteristics of working women in India. Later on this section will suggest various strategies in order to increase women's participation in the work force and enhance their contribution at the place of work.

- Going by the socialisation norms, parents do not use the earnings of their daughters. Therefore, either they do not want them to take up jobs or when they do, it is viewed as a short-term goal. This is because the traditional role expectations are such that the future parents-in-law and the husband would decide the future career options of the young women. Even if daughters start working, the reluctance to use daughter's income is quite common except among the very poor. Due to this, although higher education is socially accepted and taken for granted among the upper and middle strata in urban India, for a large majority it is not linked to careers.
- Career is definitely not the most important thing in a working woman's life. Women let their family take precedence any day (Nagaraj 2000).
- The notion of glass ceiling is more of a myth in India. A study by Rumjhum Chatterjee, who heads the task force on 'Women Managers in Indian

Organisations' at the Confederation of Indian Industry (CII) emphasises the sociological issues. Women from reputed institutes for professionals are absorbed in the work force as they pass out, which means that there are young woman executives out there. Yet there comes a sudden paucity at the mid manager level.

- Indian women at work are not too concerned about building friendly relationships in the office with either colleagues or bosses (Nagaraj 2000).
- There are more females who are getting attracted to IT than males. The underlying reason for this is not just the potential of the field, but also lesser mobility and greater flexibility attached to these jobs.

An analysis of the above mentioned trends takes us to the following conclusions about Indian working women:

Self development is slowly gaining priority in the lives of educated Indian women. To the greatest extent, Indian woman would like to balance career and family responsibilities. Instances of subordination of career aspirations to family demands are reducing at a fast rate. This means that either the participation of women in the work force has to be made smooth or it will lead to major distortions in the Indian society, the happiness of which still depends largely on women.

If technology can be practically used to blur the boundaries between office and home, the participation of women in the workforce can be increased because it will help working women manage home from office and vice versa. Instead of planning a trip to the market after office, groceries could now be ordered online, children's fee could be paid through the net and if the child is ill and requires regular attention, office work could be carried home in digital form. Moreover, with more and more online help, the strict division of a man and woman's domestic duty will also get blurred. Every family can thus have an arrangement convenient to both partners.

National Demand and Women Empowerment

This section reviews the state of local demand for IT and the government's efforts at e governance. It later analyses how e commerce and teleworking can help in the upliftment of the rural women who also constitute a large work force. Almost all of these women contribute to their family incomes through agriculture, mining, construction, art and craft and so on.

National Demand

> "It is doubtful if India's success in software exports would have been nearly as remarkable in the absence of economic reforms which removed the rigidities and controls that had stifled entrepreneurship in the past. Also the initial abundance of highly skilled manpower would not have lasted long in the absence of a concerted effort to augment its supply" (ILO 1998 : 128 – 129)

To date, Indian IT development strategies have focused mainly on attracting foreign investments into the local IT industry and exploring market opportunities in the western hemisphere. Today, more than 60 percent of India's software revenues are from exports. Even the increase in size of the domestic IT market is largely due to the booming demand for imported IT products. The national IT policy, released in 1998, highlights the importance of developing a policy framework and industrial strategy designed for making the Indian IT industry strong enough to meet the demands of a zero duty regime under the WTO-ITA by the year 2003 (GoI 1998). However, most of its major targets, such as achieving $50 billion software revenues by 2008, rely on exports. As a result of this emphasis on export-led strategies, the local IT market remains underdeveloped. Annual PC sales in India currently amount to no more than 1 million units, less than 1 percent of the global market. At 1.1 percent of GDP, the country's IT spending is also among the lowest in Asia (IDC India 1999; IDC Asia Pacific 1999). The lack of public initiatives to support the demand side has thus restricted the diffusion of benefits of the information revolution to boost local demand for IT products and services. The next section will highlight the domestic market opportunities that exist for local IT firms within India that will not only raise the global competitiveness of the local IT industry, but also spread the benefits of the IT revolution to all disadvantaged social groups in India.

Applications of IT in Government and Domestic Market

In this section, we highlight a wide range of business opportunities that exist for Indian IT firms in the educational, corporate, small scale, and government sectors. Besides helping the local IT industry tap into these opportunities, the Indian government can also act as a role model and catalyst to raise IT awareness in the society and encourage the adoption of IT in all segments of the state economy.

Governments in countries that are leading the IT revolution around the world also happen to be large consumers of IT products and services themselves. Their generous public IT expenditure, which has been increasing over the years, is a spur for their domestic IT industry, providing it with a regular revenue stream. The Indian government can embark on a similar comprehensive government computerization programme that aims to provide a wide range of services to its citizens. Taking small initial steps towards e governance, the government has set up websites that provide information services to citizens. However, these web sites offer only 'static' information. For instance, application forms provided on most web sites hosted by government departments cannot yet be filled up and submitted online. Government web sites with a two-way communication mechanism that will allow state departments to 'hear the voice of their citizens' will enable women to organise themselves better by taking care of various requirements without having to whirl around in the government offices. A further improvement in terms of less cases of default from citizens (owing to the complexities of bureaucratic procedures) will only strengthen overall governance.

Privatisation of Indian PSUs

India is in the process of privatising its Public sector undertakings. Once these Public Sector Units (PSUs) are privatised, they will need to increase their operational efficiency in order to compete globally. As we know, IT is the best enabler for business process re engineering. Indian IT firms should therefore be ready to satisfy the huge appetite for IT products and services that the 'navaratnas' will be developing in the coming years. These PSUs have a large proportion of women working at various levels. With the adoption of IT, these women will also be able to utilise the benefits of flexible working. Providing such benefits will become an imperative for the PSUs in light of the fact that their competitors - the private companies - have already started providing such benefits to their employees.

Taking Teleworking to Villages

Almost 60% of the Indian population resides in villages. Most rural women contribute to family income either by working in fields or mines or by making regional handicrafts which are sold by exporters from Urban India. IT can help give these women their due not only by giving them their rights through e governance, but also helping them earn enough and bring up their children to be educated citizens.

IT as an equalizer

In order to avoid a 'digital divide' within the society, the government can encourage the development of IT applications that benefit minorities and poor people in the state. For instance, IT can help hill and tribal women sell their handicraft product through the Internet. Export of Indian handicrafts generate a lot of revenue for the country, but it is being accumulated with the urban exporters rather than being distributed to artisans in the remote villages, where women spend afternoons and evenings creating classical pieces of handicrafts. Some non profit organisations and government agencies have already started setting up portals which exhibit and sell these handicrafts on the Net. Through such efforts, revenues are now reaching the lowest economic levels, thus giving indications towards a correction of the income disparities to a certain extent. The government can sustain these efforts by setting up web sites for handicraft products, targeted at both domestic and export markets. The same applies to readymade garments and other popular export products which employ a very large number of conventional labour force from the lowest socio economic levels.

Tele-education

In China, half the 92,000 students who graduate with degrees in engineering and technology each year are taught through distance learning provided by traditional universities (World Bank 1999). Similarly, the Indian government can reduce the expenses of education for the lower socio economic classes by providing tele education while they continue to live in their native places. This will encourage education among that segment of the rural or semi urban population which has been avoiding it for the following reasons:

Some villagers do not send their children to schools because they want them to be earning at an early age. Daily attendance at a school located at a distance would mean no time left to earn. Tele education can be taken simultaneously as the children continue to provide economic support to their families.

A large proportion of down-town residents do not go into higher education because it is not available in their own town, and living in other towns is unaffordable. Tele education can support life-long learning for them by setting up virtual universities to allow youngsters in small towns and housewives erverywhere to further their education at their own pace.

The lower socio economic stratum in India does not approve of teenaged girls interacting with males. This attitude prevents many girls from continuing education after they enter their teens. Tele education will make it possible for them to continue their education while conforming to the norms set by the society.

A non-formal approach to basic education has been advocated as an important tool by many educationists. It can play a complementary role in educating girls and women who are out of school. NGOs should remain essential partners in this process as they can carry out the programme in a non institutional environment based on a learner centered curriculum and flexible hours. It has been advocated that to increase the parental demand for girls' education the curriculum must be made relevant , linked with the every day life of girls and their future job requirements.

References

Bhattacharjee, D. (2000) 'India's 21st Century', in *Business World,* New Delhi.

Bhattacharyya, M. (1999) 'Gender Disparity and Poverty- Where We Stand', *Yojana* December.

Ghose,A. (1999) 'Current Issues of Employment Policy in India', in *Economic and Political Weekly*, Sept. 4, NewDelhi.

India, 1999, Publications Division, Ministry of Information & Broadcasting, Government of India.

'Indians are Among the World's Happiest' (2000) *Times of India*, New Delhi, Times of India.

International Labour Organisation (1998) 'Human Development Report 1998' 128 – 129.

Nagaraj, N. (2000) 'All about Attitude', *Urban Pulse*, Business Line, New Delhi.

'Spice Up Your Services' (1999) in *The Economist*, London, Economist Newspaper Ltd.

University Grants Commission (1995) *University Development in India*: Consolidated Data Statewise 1988-89 to 1993-94, New Delhi, Information and Statistics Bureau.

www.teleworkingindia.com